Creative Activities
for
Young Children

SECOND EDITION

To those who have taught us well . . .
Our children — Claire, Laura, Joey,
Mike, and Phil

Creative Activities for Young Children

SECOND EDITION

COPYRIGHT © 1980
BY DELMAR PUBLISHERS INC.

10 9 8 7 6 5

LIBRARY OF CONGRESS CATALOG CARD NUMBER: 78-52620
ISBN NUMBER 0-8273-1571-6

Printed in the United States of America
Published simultaneously in Canada
by Nelson Canada,
A Division of International Thomson Limited

MARY MAYESKY
DONALD NEUMAN
RAYMOND J. WLODKOWSKI

Mary Mayesky — Author, Part II

Jeanne Machado — Consulting Editor

DELMAR PUBLISHERS INC.
2 COMPUTER DRIVE, WEST — BOX 15-015
ALBANY, NEW YORK 12212

PREFACE

CREATIVE ACTIVITIES FOR YOUNG CHILDREN is designed for the person who is dedicated to helping young children reach their full potential. It is written for those people who want to know more about creativity, creative children, creative teachers, and creative activities.

Most people agree that creativity is natural to young children. However, creativity is a delicate skill that can easily be destroyed. Too few teachers receive instruction in the meaning of creativity or the ways in which creativity can be stimulated in children. This has been particularly true of teachers who work in early childhood education centers. Because these centers are rapidly increasing in number and size, the need for more trained teachers is especially great. Stimulation of children's creativity must be placed high on the list of priorities of all of these centers.

CREATIVE ACTIVITIES FOR YOUNG CHILDREN is written for anyone who is interested in children, but since it is written especially for busy persons who work with children in early childhood school-like settings, the following points are emphasized:

- The approach to creativity is a practical one. A wide variety of activities for children is included in each section. All activities have been successfully classroom tested with three- to seven-year-old children.

- Information on *why* activities should be carried out as well as on *how* to carry them out is presented. Theory is provided where it is needed.

- Student activities and skill builders are included, so readers can experience their own creativity.

- Each unit in Part I begins with carefully worded, easy-to-understand objectives, and ends with review questions.

To update and improve this revised edition, 16 completely new units have been added. These units (developed by Mary Mayesky) make up Part II of the text, and contain an extensive collection of early childhood teaching ideas and activities, based on the theory presented in Part I. Part II is organized into two sections: Section 9 (Seasons and Holidays), and Section 10 (Special Projects). The units in these sections provide creative experiences for young children in the following areas: art, music, games, finger plays, creative movement, environmental education, room organization, cultural education, poetry, cooking, exhibitions and displays, books for children, and reading readiness. Part II also contains a variety of diagrams giving step-by-step directions for making selected projects. Photographs of children's artwork provide further creative ideas to use with young children.

Each of the three authors has the educational background and personal experience in early childhood education essential to the production of **CREATIVE ACTIVITIES FOR YOUNG CHILDREN.** All are actively engaged in teaching, writing, and various professional organizations.

Mary Mayesky is a certified preschool and elementary teacher, a professor in the Education Department at Duke University, and principal of Mary E. Phillips Magnet School, Raleigh, North Carolina. Dr. Mayesky has worked in Head Start, Day Care, kindergarten, and Y.W.C.A. early childhood educational programs, and taught kindergarten through grade 4 in Detroit Public Schools. She is a member of the National Association for the Education of Young Children, and was recently named the Outstanding Young Educator of the Year by the Raleigh Jaycees.

Donald Neuman is both a certified elementary school teacher and college teacher who is currently chairman of the Curriculum and Instruction Department at the University of Wisconsin. Dr. Neuman specializes in the teaching of science to young children, and his vast experience includes service as an early childhood education teacher-aide, and authorship of another Delmar text, *Experiences in Science for Young Children.*

Raymond Wlodkowski is both a classroom teacher and school psychologist who has conducted research and published in the area of motivation and motivational strategies. He has just completed a year as the Human Relations Specialist for the Milwaukee Public Schools. Among his accomplishments, Dr. Wlodkowski has won an award as an outstanding teacher at the University of Wisconsin, where he is also an associate professor in the Department of Educational Psychology.

Other books in the Delmar Early Childhood Education Series include:
- Children in Your Life: A Guide to Child Care and Parenting - D. Radeloff and R. Zechman
- Early Childhood Experiences in Language Arts - Jeanne Machado
- Administration of Schools for Young Children - Phyllis Click
- Early Childhood: Development and Education - Jeanne Mack
- Home and Community Influences on Young Children - Karen VanderVen
- Understanding Child Development — For Adults Who Work With Young Children - R. Charlesworth
- Experiences in Math for Young Children - R. Charlesworth and D. Radeloff
- Experiences in Music for Young Children - M.C. Weller Pugmire
- A Practical Guide to Solving Preschool Behavior Problems - Eva Essa

A Current Catalog including prices of all Delmar educational publications is available upon request. Please write to:

Catalog Department
Delmar Publishers Inc.
2 Computer Drive — West
Box 15-015
Albany, New York 12212

CONTENTS

PART II

SECTION 9 SEASONS AND HOLIDAYS

SECTION 10 SPECIAL PROJECTS

PART I

Creativity and the Young Child

Unit 1 INTRODUCTION TO CREATIVITY

OBJECTIVES

After studying this unit, the student will be able to

- State a definition of creativity.
- List three ways in which children benefit and two ways teachers benefit from encouraging creativity in a classroom for three- to five-year-olds.
- Name five things a teacher can do to help children develop a willingness to express creativity.

Take a few minutes to watch a three- to five-year-old child in action. At one moment he is building a tower out of blocks. Suddenly he spots one of his friends playing with a homemade finger puppet. He wants to make one, too. A bit later he is playing with a guinea pig, stroking its fur and tickling its chin. Next, he is placing long, wide strokes of color on a piece of paper and getting spots of paint on everything in sight. He certainly knows how to spread those colors around!

What is this? Now he is at the sand table building a sand castle with a high sand tower that keeps falling over. He seems to have discovered something. It is easier to build a tower out of blocks than out of sand; so he is back building with wooden blocks. It looks as though he is back where he started except that the new block tower does not look anything like the one he started earlier.

It is exciting to really watch active young children studying the world around them. A couple of things become clear almost immediately. First of all, children are full of curiosity. They seem to enjoy investigating and finding out things. They seem quite capable of doing this successfully. They are very creative in finding answers to problems that arise from their curiosity. A child can figure out how to reach a needed block that somehow got thrown behind the piano. Another child selects interesting materials in order to make a finger puppet that is different from all the others.

Children in the three- to five-year age group seem to have a natural ability for coming up with creative answers, creative approaches, and creative uses of materials. Sometimes, adults do not appreciate the child's individuality or creative nature. Many adults

Fig. 1-1 Building a tower with blocks is one way a child shows creativity.

Fig. 1-2 Children explore many creative uses for materials, such as making their own finger puppets.

prefer to have all children act alike. They want the child to get into a pattern that is unnatural. Such adults may actually damage the child's good self-image.

People who are specially trained to work with three- to five-year-olds should know about creativity and have the skills to help children express their creative natures. They should realize the importance of creativity for children and for teachers. They should be able to identify creativity in children and be able to help them develop a willingness to express this creativity.

DEFINITION OF CREATIVITY

Perhaps the most important thing for the student to realize about creativity is that everyone possesses a certain amount of it. Some people are a little more creative, some a little less. No one is totally uncreative.

It should be recognized that young children tend to be highly open and creative. Unfortunately, many adults want children to conform. As outside pressures from adults grow, the children's environment closes in on them. They find it less and less rewarding to express interest in things, to be curious, to be creative in investigating their world.

One shudders to think about how many creative children have been "forced into line" by well-meaning adults. Even trained teachers

prefer children who are quiet; some even punish children who ask too many questions. It is important to know ways of encouraging a child's creativity in order to avoid these kinds of mistakes. To begin with, one should understand the meaning of the term creativity.

There are many meanings for this word. Few people can agree on a single definition. However, the following definition may help the student better understand the concept. *Creativity* is a way of thinking and acting or making something that is original for the individual and valued by that person or others. What this means is that any new way to solve a problem or to produce a new product, such as a song, a poem, or a new machine, is a creative act. A person does not have to be the first one in the world to produce something in order for it to be considered a creative act.

There are two kinds of thinking that produce solutions to problems. One of these types is called convergent thinking. The other type is called divergent thinking. *Convergent thinking* usually results in a single answer or solution to a question or problem. *Divergent thinking* opens things up and results in many answers to a single problem.

For example, if a child is asked to count the number of fish in an aquarium, there is only one correct answer. This is a question that leads children to convergent thinking. On the other hand, if a child is asked to tell as many things as possible about the aquarium, there are obviously many correct statements that can be made. Questions such as this encourage a child to do divergent rather than convergent thinking.

One of the problems in understanding the meaning of creativity is in recognizing the many kinds of creativity that exist. There is the kind of creativity that allows people to express themselves in a way that makes others listen and appreciate what they hear. There are creative abilities that enable human beings

Fig. 1-3 Asking a child, "How many things can you tell me about an aquarium?" encourages the child to do divergent thinking.

Fig. 1-4 Children enjoy activities in which they can participate freely and openly.

to discover meaning in nature — meaning that others had not understood before. In other words, creativity can be of many and varied types. It may result in the production of new inventions. It may lead to new or better designs. It may result in new ideas or new thinking. It may cause better plans to be developed. It may display itself in the production of new and attractive compositions.

Creativity begins in a person's mind. It usually results in some form of expression that can be seen, heard, smelled, tasted, or felt. A creative act is usually something novel — something not done before by the person doing it.

IMPORTANCE OF CREATIVITY

Encouraging or discouraging a child's creative nature makes a great deal of difference in the first experiences in a school setting. Children learn early and quickly that there is a reward for certain kinds of behavior. If the rewards they seek result from quiet, uncreative behavior, the children quickly learn to act in a quiet and uncreative way. It may take a teacher a long time to "shape up" the children. But in time, these "different" youngsters can be made to conform. In the process, however, the children's creative natures may be destroyed. One must therefore understand

the importance of encouraging a child's creativity.

Children want to express themselves openly. They want to bring out new ideas and have new experiences. They enjoy creativity and benefit from it in many ways, including:

- Learning to seek many answers to a problem.
- Developing their potential to think.
- Developing their individualities.
- Becoming encouraged to develop new skills.
- Learning to feel good about themselves.

Teachers also benefit from encouraging creativity, in such ways as:

- Being able to provide for more and greater variety in their program.
- Learning to recognize children for their unique skills.
- Being able to develop closer relationships with the children.
- Having fewer behavior problems.

IDENTIFYING CREATIVE CHILDREN

It is important to recognize four main things when identifying creativity in children.

- All children are creative to some degree.

- Some children are more creative than others.
- Some are more creative in one area than another.
- Creativity can be destroyed by a teacher who 'does not appreciate the act or the child who expresses the act.

With these points in mind, the student should consider these suggestions for identifying creativity in children.

Provide free periods when materials are available and children can do whatever they wish with the materials. During these periods, observe who gets tired quickly and goes from one thing to another. Identify those who become deeply involved with the materials. Also observe which children use materials in an unexpected way.

Question children in ways that permit them to freely express opinions and ideas. Some children have set opinions and are closed to new ideas. For them, questions usually have just one answer. Other children see many possible ways of answering a question and come up with unexpected ideas and solutions. They also look at problems in many ways.

Encourage children to share an experience. Then ask individual children to create a story about the experience or make a drawing. Some children just stick to the facts. Others are more imaginative in their stories or drawings. Unusual or unexpected relationships may be described by some children.

In other words, when children are being creative, they are flexible, original, confident, and adventuresome. They can redefine situations and are willing to work at things for a long time. They will work hard and can produce many possible answers to a single question.

This list of ways to identify creativity in children can be used as a starting point. Com-

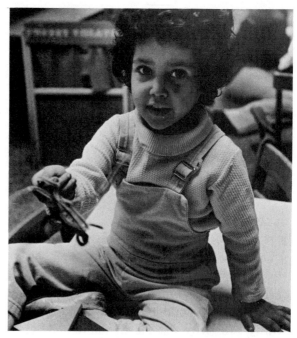

Fig. 1-5 During free periods, children may use materials in an unexpected way.

mon sense is also needed to help in this identification process. Regardless of the degree of creativity possessed, children should be encouraged to fully develop whatever creative potential they have.

HELPING CHILDREN EXPRESS CREATIVITY

There are at least eight things that can be done for children to help them express natural creative tendencies.

Help children accept change. A child who becomes overly worried or upset in new situations is unlikely to express creative potential.

Help children realize that some problems have no easy answers. This may help prevent children from becoming anxious when they cannot find an immediate answer to a question or problem.

Help children recognize that many problems have a number of possible answers. Encourage children to search for more than one answer.

Then they can evaluate all the different answers to see which ones best fit the situation.

Help children learn to judge and accept their own feelings. Children should not feel guilty for having feelings about things.

Reward children for being creative. Let children know that their creative ideas are valued. In fact, the more creative the idea or product, the greater the child should feel rewarded. It is also useful to help children realize that good work is sometimes its own reward.

Help children to feel joy in their creative productions, and in working through a problem. Children should find that doing things and finding answers for themselves is fun. The adult should establish the conditions that allow this to take place.

Help children appreciate themselves for being different. There is a tendency to reward children for conforming. This discourages creativity. Children should learn to like themselves because they are unique.

Help children develop perseverance — "stick-to-itiveness." Help children by encouraging them to follow through. Provide chances for them to stick with an activity even if everyone else has moved on to something different.

SUMMARY

Young children are naturally creative. This means they behave in ways and do things that are unique and valued by themselves or others. Creativity in preschool children is stimulated when they do divergent thinking. In many ways, both the child and teach-

Fig. 1-6 Children find that doing things for themselves is fun.

er benefit from activities that encourage creativity.

Children are being creative when they are solving problems, redefining situations, demonstrating flexibility, and being adventuresome. Adults can help children develop a willingness to express creativity in many ways, such as teaching them that change is natural in life and that many problems do not have easy answers. When children can go at their own pace and figure out their own way of doing things in a relaxed learning situation, they are likely to become more creative.

STUDENT ACTIVITIES

• **Changing the Known**

Although creative thinking can be hard thinking, that does not mean it cannot be fun. This activity is designed to prove it. Try it alone or with a few classmates. When the activity is completed, it may be enjoyable to compare lists with those of others.

A. Materials needed: paper, pencil, wristwatch (or clock).

B. Time allowed: two minutes.

C. Task: List as many uses as you can (not related to building or construction) for a standard brick. Do not worry if some of them may seem silly. The important thing is to think of using something in a new and different way.

D. It might be fun to try exercise C with a number of different objects: a nail, powder puff, paper clip, key, belt, cup, book, or other objects.

- **Just Suppose**

Creative thinking occurs when one imagines what might be. It is a way of "playing" with the mind. Here is an exercise that allows the student to experience this type of creative process. It can be done alone or with a few classmates.

A. Materials needed: paper, pencil.

B. Time allowed: unlimited.

C. Task: From the following six possibilities choose any number of tasks.

1. "Just suppose" that there is nothing made of wood in the room. What would change? What would things look like? What dangers might exist? What would one be unable to do?

2. "Just suppose" (try this with other people) you cannot use words, either written or spoken, for an hour. How can you communicate? What is frustrating about it? What is pleasing about it? What would it mean if it continued for days?

3. "Just suppose" you receive a million dollars and must spend it within two minutes. Make a list of ways to spend the money and compare it with others.

4. "Just suppose" you were the first person to meet a man from Mars and could ask him only three questions. What would they be? Compare your questions with those of others in the class.

5. "Just suppose" you were with Julius Caesar when he met Cleopatra for the first time. If you could say only one sentence, what would it be?

6. "Just suppose" you could be any person in the world for one hour. Who would it be? What would you do? Compare responses with classmates.

REVIEW

A. Discuss the following terms briefly.

1. Creativity

2. Convergent thinking

3. Divergent thinking

B. List five things a teacher can do to help children develop a willingness to express creativity.

C. List three ways in which children benefit from engaging in creative activities.

Unit 2 ACTIVITIES TO ENCOURAGE CREATIVITY

OBJECTIVES

After studying this unit, the student will be able to

- List three ways to foster a creative situation for children.
- Demonstrate four questioning strategies to encourage creative thinking in the young child.
- Describe ten approaches which help children to motivate themselves in creative activities.

Creative thinking is not a station one arrives at, but a means of traveling. It happens whenever a person comes up with a new answer to an old problem or when someone considers what might happen before it actually does happen.

Although it is a popular notion that creative thinkers are often geniuses, that is not so. The creative process can occur when one has a dream or makes up a fantasy about something. Children do it when they play house, listen to a fairy tale, or make a sand castle. Adults do it when they read a book, plan a trip, or just imagine what they are going to do with the savings in their bank account.

The creative process can also involve discovering and inventing. Whenever something is done or thought about in a new way, that is part of the creative process. It does not matter whether it is done when one is playing, cooking, gardening, or just rearranging furniture; it is still creative.

There is usually some degree of risk-taking when children are being creative. This does not mean the children are in danger of harming themselves. It does mean that they are probably doing something new and that they are uncertain about how it will turn out. Therefore, the children are taking a chance. At a time like this, they need freedom to explore

Fig. 2-1 **Playing house is one form of a child's creativity.**

and plenty of room for mistakes. Judgmental criticism or imposing adult standards of perfection will do them little good. At times like this, it is important for the teacher to show the children that their work is accepted and that they are "in charge" of where it goes.

Creative behavior in children has a much better chance of occurring when the child is open to more than one way of thinking or doing something. For example, there are many ways to draw a cat, many ways to make a house, and many ways to play tag. Children who are encouraged to try new ways of doing the same thing are more likely to be comfortable in creative situations.

Whenever a teacher is in the position of fostering a creative situation for children, these guidelines should be followed:

- Openly demonstrate to young children that there is value in their curiosity, exploration, and any signs of original behavior.

- Allow the children to go at their own pace when they are doing an activity that they are excited about and interested in.

- Let the children figure out their own ways of doing things if they prefer to do so.

- Keep the atmosphere relaxed.

- Encourage guessing, especially when the answers make good sense.

CREATIVE QUESTIONING FOR CHILDREN

The activities which follow deal mainly with ways of working creatively with children. They are specific ways of asking questions and beginning lessons or sessions which draw out the creative potential in young children. Activities which deal directly with specific arts, crafts, and media are found in later sections of this book.

Making Things Better with Your Imagination

One way to help children think more creatively is to get them to "make things better with their imagination." Asking children to change things to make them the way they would like them to be is a way of doing this. Here are some examples of questions of this type.

- What would taste better if it were sweeter?

- What would be nicer if it were smaller?

- What would be more fun if it were faster?

- What would be better if it were quieter?

- What would be more exciting if it went backwards?

- What would be happier if it were bigger?

Using Other Senses

Young children can have their creative talents stretched by asking them to use their senses in unusual ways. For example, children may be asked to close their eyes and guess what has been placed in their hands. (Use a piece of foam rubber, a small rock, telephone insulator, broken handle, etc.) Another approach is to have the children close their eyes and guess what they hear. (Use sounds like shuffling cards, jingling coins, rubbing sandpaper, or ripping paper.)

When doing this exercise, the children should be asked for reasons for their guesses. It is more fun to do so and a better learning experience for the children.

Fig. 2-2 One way to help "stretch" a child's creative talents is to have him close his eyes and hold his nose, and place a slice of orange in his hand. Can he tell you what is in his hand?

Divergent Thinking Questions

Any time the children are asked a question requiring a variety of answers, their creative thinking skills are aided. Here are some examples using the concept of water.

- What are some uses of water?
- What floats in water?
- How does water help us?
- Why is cold water cold?
- What are the different colors that water can be?
- What makes water rain?
- What always stays underwater?

Divergent thinking questions using concepts such as fire, sand, ice, smoke, cars, and similar topics are fun for children. They also encourage openness and flexibility of thinking.

What-Would-Happen-If Technique

The "What-would-happen-if?" technique has been used successfully by many teachers of young children to spark good thinking-and-doing sessions designed to ignite imaginations. Some of the following questions may be used.

- What would happen if all the trees in the world were blue?
- What would happen if all the cars were gone?
- What would happen if everybody wore the same clothes?
- What would happen if every vegetable tasted like chocolate?
- What would happen if there were no clocks or watches?
- What would happen if you could fly?

In How Many Different Ways

Another type of question which extends a child's creative thinking is one which begins with "In how many different ways. . .?" A few examples are given to add to one's own ideas.

- In how many different ways could a spoon be used?
- In how many different ways could a button be used?
- In how many different ways could a string be used?

All of these questioning strategies are intended to aid an adult's ability to encourage creativity in the young child. Often, the use of these strategies is enough to begin a long-running and positive creative experience for the child as well as the teacher. They are limited only by the user's imagination.

MOTIVATING SKILLS FOR TEACHERS

Some children need help in getting started. The fact that the activity is labeled "creative" does not necessarily make the child "ready to go." A child may be feeling restless, or tired, or may feel like doing something else. All teachers, even those with good ideas, face this problem. There are several ways to help children become motivated for the creative process.

Physical Needs. Make sure the child is rested and physically fit. Sleepy, hungry, or sick children cannot care about creativity. Their physical needs must be met before such learning can be appealing.

Interests. Try to find out, and then use, what naturally interests the child. Children not only want to do things they like to do, they want to be successful at them. Whenever children feel that they will succeed in a task, they are generally much more willing to get involved.

Friends. Permit children to work with their friends. This does not mean all the time, nor should it. However, some teachers avoid putting children who are friends together in working situations. They worry that these children will only "fool around" or disturb others. When this does happen, one should question the task at hand, since it is obviously not keeping the children's interest.

Activities for Fun. Allow the activity to be fun for the child. Notice the use of the word "allow." Children know how to have their own fun. They do not need anyone to make it for them. Teachers are giving children opportunities for fun if they honestly can answer "yes" to these questions.

- Is the activity exciting?
- Is the activity in a free setting?
- Can the children imagine in it?
- Can the children play at it?
- Is there a gamelike quality to it?
- Are judgments avoided?
- Is competition de-emphasized?
- Will there be something to laugh about?

Obviously, it takes a very perceptive teacher to provide opportunities for children to participate in activities which are fun.

Goals. Permit children to set and reach goals. Most of the excitement in achieving a goal is in reaching for it. Children should be given opportunities to plan projects. They should be allowed to get involved in activities which have something at the end for which they can strive. If the completion of an activity is not rewarding to a child, then the value of that activity is questionable.

Variety. Vary the content and style of what the children can do. This means that if the teacher changes the activity, it is wise to consider not only what will be next, but how it will be done, too. For example, the teacher has the children sit and watch a movie, then they sit and draw, and then they sit and listen to a story.

Fig. 2-3 **When provided with the proper materials, children know how to create their own fun.**

Fig. 2-4 **A teacher should question the activity at hand if children appear to be bored, or if their attention is wandering.**

These are three different activities, but in each of them, the children are sitting. The content of the activity has been changed, but not the style. This can, and does, become boring. Bored children are restless children. Restless children become behavior problems.

Fig. 2-5 The teacher who is continually in touch with a child's feelings shows this in a way that is open and caring.

Challenge. Challenge the children. This means letting them know that what they are about to do is something that they might not be able to do, but that it will be exciting to try. An example of this is letting the children know that their next activity may be tricky, adventuresome, or mysterious. It is the "bet you can't do this" approach with the odds in favor of the children.

Reinforcement. Reinforce the children. The basic need here is for something to come at the end of the activity that lets the children feel they would like to do it again. It could be the teacher's smile, a compliment, reaching the goal, or just finishing the activity. The main thing is that the children feel rewarded and/or satisfied for their efforts.

The Children's Feelings. Try to make certain the children feel good about what they are doing. Some teachers feel if a child is working

intensely or learning, that is enough. This may not be so. The most important question is not what the children are doing but how they feel about what they are doing. If children feel badly about themselves or an activity while doing it, this is a warning. If a child is made to continue the activity, it may be damaging as it tends to lower self-concept and/or security. It is a form of learning which is destructive and must be avoided. This means the teacher must be continually in touch with how the children are feeling. It is done when the teacher listens, watches, and is with the children in a manner which is open and caring.

SUMMARY

The creative process involves discovery and inventing. Risk-taking is a natural part of creative behavior. Teachers who allow children to go at their own pace, and be self-directed in a relaxed atmosphere, are fostering creative development.

Questioning strategies encourage creativity in young children. Even with creative activities, there may be motivational difficulties with some children. Appealing to natural interests, giving expectancies of success, reinforcing, and challenging are a few of the many ways to help children get started and keep going.

STUDENT ACTIVITIES

- **Invention Dice**

It has been said that the creative process involves discovery and inventing. Here is a game which provides experience in "making something up" for the first time. Try it with a few friends.

A. Materials needed: a single die, paper, pencil.

B. Time allowed: unlimited.

C. Task: players should sit facing each other or in a circle. A dice point list with directions is posted so that everyone can see it.

Dice Point List

1. Invent a story in which you experience a huge success.
2. Invent a story in which you experience a terrifying escape.
3. Invent a story in which you experience a moment of beauty.
4. Invent a story in which you experience tremendous fear.
5. Invent a story in which you experience great joy.
6. Invent a story in which you discover something important for the first time.

Each person takes at least two turns (more can be decided upon) throwing the die. If the cube comes up 2, for example, the person who has thrown the die "invents" a story in which the person makes a terrifying escape, perhaps from some disaster. (This game asks one to "pull out all of the stops." Surprise the listeners. Do not be afraid to exaggerate.)

D. After having tried some of these exercises, think about what was done. Notice how necessary it was to "let go" when one was being creative. How important was it to feel free and relaxed when doing the exercises? What do these exercises make one aware of when attempting to work creatively with children?

E. List three important things you learned as a result of doing these exercises.

F. List three personal experiences that were challenging to you. Consider each and get in touch with the feelings experienced on those occasions.

    1. Was there any chance of failure during these experiences?

    2. What was the motivation?

    3. How did it feel to succeed?

    4. What does this mean for working with young children?

    5. How does it relate to creativity?

    6. List some of your reactions.

REVIEW

A. List three ways to foster a creative situation for children.

B. Name four questioning strategies that encourage creative thinking in the young child.

C. State five approaches that help children to motivate themselves in creative activities.

Developing Aesthetics in Children

Unit 3 THE MEANING OF AESTHETICS

OBJECTIVES

After studying this unit, the student will be able to

- State a definition of aesthetics.
- List three things a teacher can do to help children to develop their aesthetic sensitivity.
- List five benefits of aesthetic sensitivity in children.

Aesthetics refers to a person's ability to sense and gain beauty and wonder from one's environment. It can be done with any or all of the five senses, as well as with imagination. It may be seeing beauty in a sunset, hearing rhythm in a rainfall, or loving the expression on a person's face. Each person has an individual and personal sense of what is or is not pleasing.

Aesthetic experiences emphasize doing things for the pure joy of it. Although there can be, there does not have to be any practical purpose or reason. Thus, one may take a ride in a car to feel its power and enjoy the scenery rather than to visit someone or perform an errand. A child may play with blocks to feel their shapes and see them tumble rather than to build something.

To develop an aesthetic sense in children means to help them be able to continuously find beauty and wonder in their world. This is any child's potential. In fact, it is the potential of every human being. To create, to invent, to be joyful, to sing, to dance, to love, and to be amazed are possible for everyone. However, since people learn to do this, it can be mislearned and unlearned. That is why the teacher is so important in this process.

Fig. 3-1 Although a child uses blocks to play with, aesthetically the child may like the blocks for their texture or the way they look.

The purpose of aesthetic experiences is to help develop a full and rich life for the child. It does not matter whether the activity is useful for anything else. There does not have to be a product or something that can be eaten or sold. That is the reason mud pies are still made and probably always will be made.

A child's reason for doing something should not always be to gain adult approval,

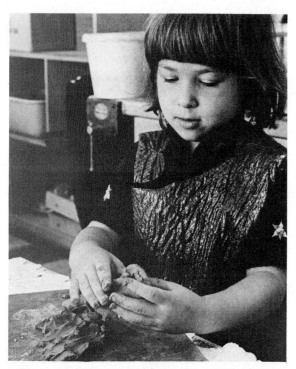

Fig. 3-2 **Molding clay with no other real purpose than to feel it in their hands gives children the motivation to continue the activity.**

Fig. 3-3 **Aesthetic development is taking place in children when they listen to music and let their bodies move to its rhythm.**

prizes, grades, or pay. At times, doing just for the sake of doing is a good enough reason. Teachers must be careful to allow for and encourage such motivation.

Children sometimes see and say things to please adults; teachers must realize this and the power it implies. Teachers who force children to see beauty as they, themselves, do are not developing good taste in children. They are developing uniformity and obedience. Only children who choose and evaluate for themselves can truly have their own aesthetic taste. The teacher's role is to provide opportunities and guidance, but not to set standards. Each child has a right to a personal choice of beauty, joy, and wonder. Each time a teacher says that something is pretty or makes some similar personal judgment, this influences the children. They must be able to feel that it is acceptable to differ with the teacher in such matters. "What you like is O.K., and what I like is O.K., too."

Children gain an aesthetic sense by doing. This means sensing, feeling, and responding to things. It can be rolling a ball, smelling a flower, petting an animal, or hearing a story. Aesthetic development takes place in secure settings which are free of competition and adult judgment. For example, children and their teachers can listen to music. They should all feel that they have a right to hear it for themselves and to create their own experience around it. For one person, it may mean happy memories; for another, it may mean an urge to dance; and for someone else, it may mean only the sound of music.

AESTHETICS AND THE QUALITY OF LEARNING

Children go to school for many reasons: to learn skills; to learn how to read and write; and to learn how to do arithmetic. Yet, this is only part of it. Skills help prepare people for a future job, but not for life, itself. What they can do is important. What they feel about what they can do is more important.

Aesthetic learning means joining what one thinks with what one feels. Having feelings about what one reads is what makes reading a human experience. Through art, ideas and feelings are expressed. People draw pictures and sculpt monuments to show their feelings about life. Art is important because it can deepen and enlarge understanding. All children cannot be great artists, but most children can develop an aesthetic sense for art.

Teachers can encourage the aesthetic sense in children in a variety of ways. Science activities lend themselves very well to beauty and artistic expression. Rocks, wood, leaves, and science exhibits can be placed in attractive displays. Reading readiness activities benefit from the imaginative use of color, shapes, and forms.

Children must have something about which to paint, sculpt, dance, and sing. This can be provided by reading stories to them, helping them explore the outdoors and their immediate neighborhood, and going on trips. Teachers must allow the children to evaluate and express these experiences. This means talking about what these experiences mean to the children and how they feel about them. It means allowing the children to express those feelings and meanings through paint, clay, collage, dance, or whatever medium each child chooses to use.

The arts should not be developed in separation from one another. After hearing a story, some children may want to act it out. Some may prefer to paint a picture about it. Others may wish to create a dance about it, and some may want to make the music for the dance. These activities can lead to others. There should be a constant exchange not only among all the art activities, but among all subjects. This prevents the children from creating a false separation between work and play, art and learning, and thought and feeling.

There is much hardware in preschool education today. Teaching machines, kits, and programmed learning materials are everywhere. Sometimes, use of such items is very rigidly structured. There may be no time for anything outside of the activity or material. Continuous conformity to this type of learning could dull a child's aesthetic sense.

Fig. 3-4 The imaginative use of color, shape, and form can help provide children with the reading readiness skills so necessary to later schooling.

Fig. 3-5 Although "hardware" such as teaching machines and kits are instructive to use at times, it is also desirable to have free periods when these materials are not used.

Because of this, it is important for the teacher to allow for "breaks" in the use of these materials. Also, if other subjects can be involved, use them. Sometimes "fooling around" with materials can lead to creative learning.

AESTHETICS AND CREATIVITY

When someone is creating something, there are usually two parts to that person's activity. The first part has to do with the discovery of an idea, plan, or answer. The second part has to do with working out, proving, and making certain that the idea or answer works or is possible. The first part, *discovering,* involves using the imagination, playing with ideas, and exploring. The second part, *proving,* involves using learned skills, evaluating, and testing. This is shown in the creative process model in figure 3-6.

The discovering part of the creative process is directly related to a child's aesthetic sense. The child's ability to "toy" with ideas, to "see into" things, and to "make up" more than what is there is needed for discovery. In fact, *more* is the key word. The truly creative person always sees more, feels more, and finds more than the less creative person. That is why the creative person discovers more.

An aesthetic sense does not mean "I see" or "I hear;" it means "I enjoy what I see" or "I like what I hear." It means that the child is using taste or preference. This must occur for discovery to take place. Children cannot be too concerned about results or the standards of others. They must choose what they feel is right in order to discover its meaning for themselves. This means that children must learn to work without self-consciousness, as a real artist does; children can be spontaneous and inventive. If they are trying to please the teacher and not themselves, they are denying their own aesthetic sense, and are stopping the discovery process.

Part I	Part II
Using the imagination	Evaluating ideas
Playing with ideas	Testing solutions
Exploring alternatives	Judging answers
Speculating with possibilities	Analyzing results
LEADS TO DISCOVERING	**LEADS TO PROVING**
Ideas	Acceptable ideas
Answers	Satisfactory answers
Solutions	Workable solutions

Fig. 3-6 Creative process model.

Fig. 3-7 Children enjoy exploring materials when they can discover new ways of doing things.

ENCOURAGING AESTHETIC SENSITIVITY

Teachers can encourage aesthetic sensitivity in children. This in turn encourages the discovery part of the creative process. Teachers can do this by supporting attentive play, avoiding giving answers (having children find their own answers), and by setting limits that do not pressure children to learn the one "best way." When answers are given by children in groups, teachers can ask the children to "think over" the response. Sometimes preschool children think the first right answer is the best answer. Teachers can encourage more guessing and trying out of hunches to avoid this.

In order to discover, children must "let go" their minds and their bodies. This is a natural tendency in preschool children. A teacher who stops this in children causes them to learn to not "let go;" a teacher who encourages this in children helps them learn to "let go." The choice and responsibility are with the teacher.

It has been said that aesthetic sensitivity is important for children because it improves the quality of learning and helps the creative process. Aesthetic sensibility in children has many other benefits, too.

- Children are more sensitive to problems because they have more insight into their world. This means they can be more helpful to other children and to adults.

- Children are more likely to be self-learners because they are more sensitive to gaps in their knowledge.

- Life is more exciting for children because they have the capacity to be puzzled and to be surprised.

- Children are more tolerant because they learn that there are many possible ways of doing things.

- Children are more independent because they are more open to their own thoughts.

They are good questioners for the same reason.

- Children can deal better with complexity because they do not expect to find one best answer.

For the teacher, the children become more exciting to be with, to learn from, and to teach.

SUMMARY

Aesthetics is the ability of people to sense and gain beauty and wonder from their environment. The purpose of aesthetic experiences for children is to help them develop a full and rich life. Children with improved aesthetic sensitivity have a greater chance to be creative and receive more enjoyment from learning. Teachers can help to develop the aesthetic sense of children by involving them in the arts, allowing them to explore their environment, and by avoiding single solutions to complex problems. Children benefit from their aesthetic sensitivity because it generates more excitement in their lives as well as more insight.

STUDENT ACTIVITIES

- **Being Aware**

    In order to use one's aesthetic sense, one must pay very close attention to that which is personally interesting. This means being very aware of oneself and one's surroundings.

    A. Try to find out if a new thought or discovery can be made by paying closer attention to yourself.

    B. Begin by going to a place that is quiet and relaxing. Sit down and take a minute to rest. Then say, "Now I am aware of . . ." and finish this statement with what you are in touch with at the moment. Notice whether this is something inside or outside of yourself.

    C. Make the statement again and see what happens.

    1. Has your awareness changed?
    2. Are fantasies, thoughts, or images part of your awareness?

D. Make the statement again, but this time think of a person.
   1. Who comes to mind?
   2. What does it mean?

E. Try the same sentence but change your awareness by thinking of different things such as a flower, a picture, someone from the past, a child, your favorite place, and so on.

F. Notice that when thinking of something outside, one cannot think of something inside at the same time.

G. What does this mean for working with children? Compare your answers with classmates, and find out how they feel about this activity.

- **Fruit**

This is an activity to find new discoveries by paying closer attention to everyday things.

A. Take three different types of fruit. Close your eyes and pick each one up. Feel them with your fingers from top to bottom.
   1. How are they different?
   2. How are they the same?

B. Place the fruits against your face.
   1. Do they feel differently?
   2. What about the temperature of the fruit?

C. Smell the fruits, being sure to keep your eyes closed.
   1. How different are the aromas?
   2. Which is your favorite?

D. Open your eyes and look at the fruits.
   1. Hold them up to the light.
   2. See if you can see anything new about each fruit.

E. What have you discovered from this activity? (Notice you did not taste or eat the fruit.)
   1. Could you still receive pleasure from the fruit without eating it?
   2. What does this mean for working with children?

F. Compare your answer with that of classmates, and find out how they felt about this activity.

REVIEW

A. Define aesthetics.

B. List three things a teacher can do to help children develop their aesthetic sensitivity.

C. List five benefits of aesthetic sensitivity in children.

Unit 4 AESTHETIC EXPERIENCES

OBJECTIVES

After studying this unit, the student will be able to

- Describe three types of sensing and feeling.
- Choose materials that have good aesthetic potential.
- List four guidelines to help children work with aesthetic materials.

People search their world for what is important to them. They look for what they need. They see what they want. This is as true for preschool children as it is for adults.

Imagine that a group of people are taken into a room and are asked to look at a table. On the table is some food, a glass of water, and a small amount of money. Those who are hungry are most likely to look at the food. Those who are thirsty will probably look at the water. Those who are in debt are apt to look at the money. And, those who need furniture probably take a closer look at the table.

Children also look for things they need and want. A child who is tired looks for a place to rest. A child who is lonely looks for a friend. The point here is that only when children are physically well, feel safe, and sense that they belong, can they be ready to learn in an aesthetic sense. Beauty is not seen when one is afraid. Children hide their feelings when they do not feel safe.

LOOKING AND SEEING

Children look in many different ways. Touching, patting, poking, picking, and even tasting are ways of looking for young children. As mentioned, children look for what they need, but they also see what they find to be stimulating. Something is stimulating to a child for many different reasons. It could be

because it is colorful, exciting, different, interesting, changing, moving, weird, and so on. The list of stimulating things is seemingly endless. However, there are some basic guidelines for preparing a stimulating activity or object.

Can the child experience it with more than one sense? Children enjoy what they can touch, see, and hear more than something they can only see or hear.

Fig. 4-1 Children "look" using more than the sense of sight. Even tasting is a way of "looking" for a child.

Can the child interact with it? Children tend to enjoy what they can participate in. For children, the picture of a guinea pig will never replace a live guinea pig.

Are the children interested in it? Children relate to what is familiar to them and part of their life. Talking about a television program that children have never seen cannot produce the kind of discussion that comes when they talk about their favorite program.

Is the activity well paced? Something that moves too fast or too slowly eventually becomes boring. When a game slows down, watch how many children drop out.

Is it colorful? Clowns, circuses, and cartoons are popular for this very reason.

Does it promise to be rewarding? Is the activity fun, adventurous, or exciting? Does it have something worthwhile at the end? If not, why should the child stick with it? Searching for a piece of a puzzle or looking for a hidden treasure is only fun if the children believe they can find it.

SENSING AND FEELING

There are basically three types of sensing and feeling. The first has to do with contact with the world outside of the person. This is the actual sensory contact with things and events. It is seeing, hearing, smelling, tasting, and touching. The second is what people actually feel within themselves. This includes what they experience under their skin. Itches, tensions, muscular movements, discomfort, and emotions are all a part of this type of sensing. The third type of sensing and feeling is the kind that goes beyond the present and reality. It is usually called fantasy, and includes dreams, memories, images, and guesses.

Fig. 4-2 A picture of a guinea pig could not replace the experience of holding the real thing for a child.

Fig. 4-3 Sensing and feeling can be done by children through fantasy, which can take place during dreams.

For a child, each of these types of sensing and feeling is very important. All three can take place during the same activity. Each can become more important than the other two, depending on what the child needs or wants at the moment. Most teachers are concerned about the child's sensory contact with the outside world. Children do many things that involve touching, seeing, and hearing; yet, what they feel inside and what they fantasize about are also important. The teacher must give attention to these two processes as well. They are part of aesthetic sensitivity. Attention can be given these by having two questions in mind each day when working with preschool children. Both should be answered, "Yes," followed by the question, "How?"

The first question has to do with the inside feelings of the children: "Have the children done something today that has helped them feel good about themselves?" The second has to do with the fantasies of the children: "Have the children done something today that has helped them to use their imagination in either the past, present, or future?"

Lesson plans, activities, and trips should be planned and evaluated with those two questions in mind. If teachers are sincere about the two questions, their teaching can relate to all the ways the children can sense and feel.

FINDING AND ORGANIZING AESTHETIC MATERIALS

Every teacher has many ideas about what materials are best for children. Sometimes the desired materials are too expensive or difficult to find. Schools have limited budgets, and even the ordinary can seem impossible to obtain. There are three resources that have great potential: 1) any kind of salvage material, commonly known as "junk," 2) the hardware store, and 3) things the children bring in.

Before describing the organization of these materials, it is helpful to have some guidelines for choosing materials that have good aesthetic potential.

- Choose materials that children can explore with their senses (touch, see, smell).
- Choose materials that children can manipulate (twist, bend, cut, color, mark).
- Choose materials that can be used in different ways (thrown, bounced, built with, fastened, shaped).

Children enjoy finding materials because it suggests exploration and discovery. The discovery of materials can be celebrated and shared in a "beauty corner" where newly found leaves, ribbons, and other treasures can be placed.[1] A small collection of colored cloths, a few blocks or boxes, and a table screen, pegboard, or tack board to fasten things on, all set in adequate light, can make a beauty corner. Children can develop aesthetic skills in sensing and exhibiting by helping to build such a place. They can learn to ask such questions as, "does it look better this way?" or "should we put more light on it?"

Usually, the finding of materials involves more than looking. Children need to play with the found materials to try them out for weight, texture, structure, and so on. After the materials have been tested and shared, they may go into the beauty corner or a classroom collection.

Sometimes the children's search can be focused on something, as in finding things for painting or building. As they find that their discovered materials make their day-to-day work more interesting, they become alert to new possibilities. For the teacher and the children, this can mean a constant supply of materials and new aesthetic experiences.

The experience of selecting, collecting, and using materials can be aided by classifying

---

[1]Chandler Montgomery, *Art for Teachers of Children* (Columbus, Ohio), p.197.

the materials according to their design possibilities. The number and names of classifications should be developed slowly with the children, as they bring in their findings. This may vary with age level and interest. The following classification has been found useful in some classrooms:[2]

Spots and Dots. Buttons, beads, bottle caps, flash bulbs, acorns, washers, marbles, pebbles.

Lines. Stiff lines: dowel sticks, bamboo reeds, umbrella ribs, rods, toothpicks, pipe cleaners. Free lines: strings, yarn, ribbons, tape.

Surfaces. Stiff surfaces: cardboard, coroboard, plywood, metal. Solid color surfaces: colored papers stored in separate folders for each family of colors, colored cloth stored in the same manner. Patterned surfaces: wallpaper sample books, gift wrappings, patterned cloth. Textured surfaces: corrugated materials, metals, sandpaper, shingles, rough cloth. See-through surfaces: screen, netting, cellophane, tissue, cheesecloth, film.

Textured Stuffs. Steel wool, cotton, shredded paper, raw fiber, sawdust (in glass jars or plastic envelopes).

Forms and Bases. Small cardboard boxes, wood cylinders, blocks, discs, yarn cones, spools, reels.

Children have many decisions to make as they sort and classify the materials they bring. For example, is an old movie film a line or a see-through surface? Such questioning is a useful step toward aesthetic sensitivity and creative thinking.

AESTHETIC USE OF MATERIALS

Uses for the materials collected by the teacher and children are unlimited.[3] Space,

time, and imagination may form some boundaries on what may be done. However, what is most important is that the materials and what is done with them become personal statements of the children and teacher. This is not done by what is made, but by how it is made — whether it is an art project, a building project, or another activity.

A common approach to collected materials is to turn them into representations of flowers, animals, dolls, or scenes. The value of these activities depends on the quality of individual discovery and the imagination of the child. Again, the important point is not what is made, but who planned it and how much of the child's thought and feeling went into it. Children must have the opportunity not only to find the materials but also to try them out. This means much experimenting with the materials to determine what the children feel they need. A question such as, "What would you like to say with these things?" might help both the children and the teacher to get started. Checking with the children's moods may be helpful too. Do they seem to feel happy, dreamy, sad, gentle, aggressive, or how? Such questioning can help the children reach their own purpose based on their experience and interests.

Fig. 4-4 Too many materials may confuse young children.

[2]Ibid., p. 198.
[3]Ibid., p. 201.

It is important to remember not to give the children too many materials too often. Too much to choose from can overwhelm a child. The qualities of one material can be lost in the midst of so many others. A child should have some experience in working with a main or theme material. Other materials can be brought in as a background, contrast, or small addition. An example of this would be to work with a certain color or a single material, such as buttons or paper. In this way, the children can learn more about making their own aesthetic choices, as well as mastering such skills as pasting and cutting.

Some guidance by the teacher in working with aesthetic materials is necessary. This guidance must be very gentle, supportive, and sensitive. If guidance is given in the selection or arrangement of materials, the child is pressured to produce "like everyone else" or like the models of older brothers and sisters. Children need to know they can take chances and be different. The teacher can give guidance in several ways:[4]

Ask questions aimed at helping the children reach out for and get the "payoff" they are seeking. A question that teachers can ask themselves which will help them ask the right question of the children is, "What can I ask the children that should help them better understand what they want?" When the children are working with paints, this question may be something about color. When they are working with paper, this may be something about form, such as "What shape would you like it to be?"

Avoid too many ready-made models or ways of doing things. When children learn over and over to do something in only one way, they may ruin their aesthetic sense. Repetition tells them to stop thinking. For example, why

Fig. 4-5 When children are painting, the teacher can help them find out what they want to do by asking them a question about color.

always start to draw in the middle of a piece of paper? Why not sometimes draw from the edges or bottom?

Help children to select the materials they prefer. This may mean asking the children which materials they plan to use first, which materials they may not use at all, and which materials they may possibly use.

Help children "hunt" for aesthetic qualities. This means helping children get in touch with what they feel about differences. For example, it means asking children to show what they like or think is better. It can mean asking what is brighter, darker, happier, sadder.

Help children to use other senses when only one sense seems necessary. Children can be asked to hear what they see in a drawing or to draw what they hear in music. Colors can be related to feelings, music, and body movements as well as to seeing.

Help children use art to deepen experiences. This means timing — for example, using painting, drawing, or sculpting to express a strong feeling rather than talking about it or, perhaps, talking about the feeling after the painting. It could mean playing music at an especially

[4]Ibid., p. 202.

happy time. In this case, the important question has more to do with when than how. When is a good time to paint, draw, or dance?

Often, children feel that "more" is better. To have more paint, more color, or more buttons, seems best to some children. They want the brightest colors, the most crayons, and the loudest music. When children learn to select based on the materials they like instead of choosing the amount, they can avoid the "more" complex. They must learn to take things out as well as to put them back. Teachers can reinforce children in "following through something" by sharing their interest, displaying their work, or just giving them sincere attention.

An important part of the teacher's role in developing children's aesthetic sensitivity is in showing their work. This means displaying and exhibiting to parents and others. A good rule of thumb is that if the children feel good about their work, let them show it. The work does not have to be complete. Parents should be helped to see what the child liked about it. All people have their own ideas of what art is. Parents are no exception. However, it is important that they understand and know what their children enjoy and feel is important. Parents may enjoy helping their children plan, choose, and evaluate their work. Having children take work home to get their parents' reactions, and then having the children work on it the next day, is a way of doing this. This may be followed by asking parents to help in finding useful materials.

Parents should be shown why some materials are used and others are not used by their children. Making gifts, exhibits, and posters are ways children can show parents their aesthetic sense. With artwork, the child is saying, "This is how it is with me." Parents want to know their children; children's artwork can help parents know more about their children.

SUMMARY

Children look for things they need and want. They are stimulated by things they find interesting, colorful, and rewarding.

There are three types of sensing and feeling. The first is anything contacted through the five basic senses; the second is what the person feels inside; and the third is fantasy.

Many materials with aesthetic potential can be found. Anything children can explore, manipulate, and use in different ways has aesthetic potential. What is most important is that these materials (and what is done with them) become personal statements of the children.

The teacher can give supportive and gentle guidance by asking helpful questions, avoiding too many ready-made models, and helping children "hunt" for aesthetic qualities. A good rule of thumb in displaying aesthetic work is if the children feel good about it, let them show it.

Fig. 4-6 A child who feels good about an aesthetic creation may want to display it.

STUDENT ACTIVITIES

- **Beautiful Things**

Each person has had some experience with beauty, and everyone has a special idea about what is beautiful. It can be a very interesting experience to examine this concept with each of the five senses.

A. Write down the three most beautiful things (living or nonliving) that you have ever experienced with each of your five senses.

B. As you write your list, try as much as possible to relive the sensations.

C. Answer the following questions.

    1. Were most of your answers living or nonliving?

    2. How many involved people?

    3. Did any of your answers surprise you?

    4. How often do you encounter beautiful things?

    5. Which sense seems to find the most beauty?

    6. How much does beauty in life depend on you?

    7. What does this mean for working with children?

D. Compare your responses with fellow students.

- **Amazing Journey**

A. Find a quiet place and relax. Close your eyes and think of something that amazes you or produces wonder in you.

B. Think of yourself as that something. (Take some time to get the feel of being it.)

C. Write a description of yourself as this something. (Use plenty of adjectives.)

D. As a result of this experience:

    1. What emotions do you feel?

    2. How are you like what really amazes you?

    3. How are you unlike it?

    4. Would you like to change in any way?

E. Compare your answers with classmates.

F. Do you think children would enjoy using their imaginations like this?

REVIEW

A. List three types of sensing and feeling.

B. Give three guidelines to use in choosing materials that have aesthetic potential.

C. List four suggestions to help children work with aesthetic materials.

Developmental Levels in Art

Unit 5 STAGES OF ART AND THE PRESCHOOL CHILD

OBJECTIVES

After studying this unit, the student will be able to

- Describe the scribble stage.
- Explain the basic forms stage.
- Discuss the development of first drawings.

As children grow older, they change in height and weight and gain new skills. They also develop different abilities in art. The artwork of a three-year-old is different from that of a four- or five-year-old. It is different in the way it looks, as well as in the way it is made.

One who works with young children must know the different stages children go through in the development of art abilities. These stages are called *developmental levels.* A developmental level is a guide to knowing what a child can do in art at different ages, but it is not a strict guideline. Some children may be ahead or behind the developmental level for their age. Developmental levels tell the teacher what came before and what is to come in the artwork of the preschool child.

There is no exact pattern for each age level. Not all three-year-olds behave alike, nor are they completely different from four-year-olds. But there is a gradual growth process that almost every child goes through. This growth process is called *development.* It begins in art with the first scribbles and goes through to drawing pictures. The following discussion of three stages in art development is a general guide to learning about the overall process of development.

An understanding of developmental levels means that the adult accepts each child at the child's present level, whatever it is. To understand development is to know that forced practice in art is unnecessary and useless.

Ability in art develops as the child grows and matures. As children's bodies and minds mature, so does their art ability. Children learn to paint, model, and build as they learn to walk — slowly, developing in their own way. They learn each new step in the process as they are ready for it. Preschool teachers must respect each child's own pace.

There are three developmental levels of concern to the preschool teacher: the scribble stage, the basic forms stage, and the first drawing stage. The basic forms and first drawing stages are of the most interest. The scribble stage gives an idea of how a child begins to draw.

THE SCRIBBLE STAGE

Most children begin scribbling at about one and one-half to two years of age. Children will scribble with anything at hand and on anything nearby. Their first marks are usually an aimless group of lines. Yet these first scribbles are related to later drawing and painting. They are related to art just as a baby's first babbling sounds are related to speech.

The crayon may be held upside down, or sideways, or even with the fist or between clenched fingers. Children may be pleased with this scribbling and get real enjoyment from it. However, they do not try to make any definite pictures with these marks. They simply enjoy the physical motions involved in scribbling. It is the act of doing — not the final product — that is important to the child.

Early Scribble Stage: Disordered Scribbling

During the early scribble stage the young child does not have control over hand movements and the marks on the page. The marks on the page can go in many directions. The direction of the marks depends on whether the child is drawing on the floor or on a low table. The way the crayon is held also makes the scribbles look different. But, the child is not able to make the crayon go in any one way

on purpose. There is neither the desire nor the ability to control the marks.

Later Scribble Stage: Controlled Scribbling

At some point, children find a connection between their motions and the marks on the page. This may be about six months after the child has started to scribble. This is a very important step. The child has now found it possible to control the marks. The adult cannot see any real difference in these drawings. They still look like scribbles — but they are different.

Gaining control over scribbling motion is a vital experience for the child. The child now is able to make them go in the direction desired. Most children scribble at this later stage with a great deal of enthusiasm, since coordination between seeing and doing is an important achievement.

Because children enjoy this newly found power, they are encouraged to try new motions. They now may scribble in lines, zigzags, or in circles. When the children repeat motions, it means they are gaining control over

Fig. 5-1 In the early scribble stage, a child may scribble with a crayon held clenched in a fist.

Fig. 5-2 In the later scribble stage, children can begin to control the scribbles, and make marks that go in a desired direction.

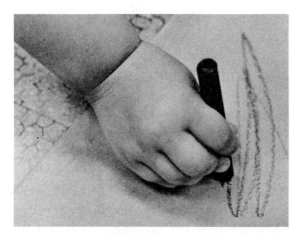

Fig. 5-3 The ability of children to repeat certain motions in drawing means they are beginning to develop better muscle control.

certain movements. Children can become very involved in this type of scribbling.

BASIC FORMS STAGE

Basic forms like rectangles, squares, or circles develop from scribbles. They develop as the child finds and recognizes simple shapes in the scribbles. More importantly, they develop as the child finds the muscle control and *hand-eye coordination* (use of both hand(s) and eyes at the same time) to repeat the shape.

At this point, the drawings look more organized. This is because the child is able to make basic forms by controlling the lines. A child in the age range of three to four years is usually in the basic forms stage.

It is important to note, again, that there may be an overlap between developmental levels in art. For example, one three-year-old child may be drawing basic forms and an occasional scribble. Another three-year-old may still be totally in the scribble stage. Developmental levels are meant merely as guidelines, not as set laws on age and ability levels.

Early Basic Forms Stage: Circle and Oval

Generally, the first basic form drawn is the oval or circle. It develops as children recognize the simple circle in their scribbles and

Fig. 5-4 There is some overlap in developmental stages in art; a child often draws basic forms and scribbles on the same piece of paper.

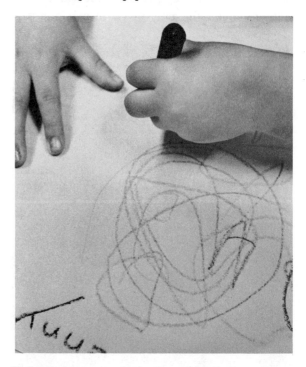

Fig. 5-5 At some point in the early basic forms stage, children may begin to recognize circles in their scribbles.

are able to repeat it. Both the oval and the circle develop from circular-type scribbles.

Another early basic form in this stage is the curved line or arc. The curved line or arc is made with the same swinging movement of the arm used in the early scribble stage. Now, however, it is in one direction only. This kind of line gradually becomes less curved, and from it come the horizontal or vertical lines.

Later Basic Forms: Rectangle and Square

As muscle control of three- to four-year-olds improves in this stage, more basic forms are made in their drawings. The rectangle and square forms are made when the child can draw separate lines of any length desired. The child joins the separate lines to form the rectangle or square.

The circle, oval, square, and rectangle are all forms made by the child's control of lines. These basic forms are needed in the next de-

Fig. 5-6 In the later basic forms stage, a child may decide he wants straight lines, and therefore will use some straight-edged object such as the end of a crayon box.

velopmental stage of art — the first drawings stage.

FIRST DRAWINGS STAGE

With the two earlier stages complete, the children now have the ability to draw the variety of marks that make up their first drawings. The first drawings stage is the next developmental level in art. Many four-year-olds and most five-year-olds are at this level.

First drawings are different from scribbling in that they are not made by chance. Instead, they are made by the child for a purpose. First drawings are what many people call *children's art*. The basic forms perfected in the preceding stage suggest images to the child which stand for ideas in the child's own mind. The children now begin to make certain figures. A new way of drawing begins. From the basic forms the child is able to draw, only particular ones are chosen. Miscellaneous scribbling is left out. In this way, children draw their first symbol. A *symbol* is a visual representation that stands for something important to the child; it may be a human figure, an animal, a tree, or similar figure.

The ability to draw symbols comes directly from the last stage. The basic forms gradually lose more and more of their connection to body motion only. Basic forms are now put together to make symbols. These symbols stand for real objects in the child's mind. In scribbling, the child was mainly involved in a physical activity. Now the child sees real meaning behind the drawings.

The human form is often the child's first symbol. A man is usually drawn with a circle for a head and two lines for legs or body. Other symbols include trees, houses, flowers, and animals.

Further attempts to make symbols grow directly from the basic forms the child can make. Flowers and trees are combinations of spiral scribbles or circles with attached straight

Fig. 5-7 To a child in the first drawings stage, a figure of a man can be made by drawing a circle for a head, and two lines for legs.

lines for stems or trunks. Houses, windows, doors, flags, and similar objects are simply made up of rectangles and straight lines.

Early First Drawings Stage

In the early period of the first drawings, a child works on making and perfecting one or many symbols. The child practices these symbols, covering sheets of paper with many examples of the same subject. For example, a child may draw windows and doors over and over in each drawing. Also at an early point in this stage, a child's picture may be a collection of unrelated figures and objects. This type of picture is a sampling of the child's many tries at making different symbols. At this point, pictures are done very quickly.

During this early first drawings stage, the child is searching for new ideas. Symbols change constantly. A picture of a man drawn one day differs from the one drawn the day before. In this stage, there is often the greatest variety of forms which stand for the same object. Early first drawings are very flexible in appearance. A man may be drawn differently in every picture.

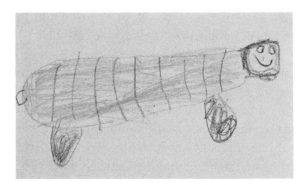

Fig. 5-8 An animal is another favorite symbol for the child of four or five to draw.

Fig. 5-9 Circles with lines leading down are usually a child's symbol for a tree.

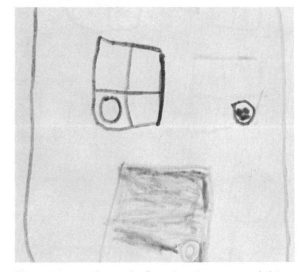

Fig. 5-10 In the early first drawings stage, children may practice symbols over and over. Many drawings are done of the same subject, such as a door and windows in a house.

Fig. 5-11 Seemingly unrelated figures and objects drawn together in one picture are common in early first drawings.

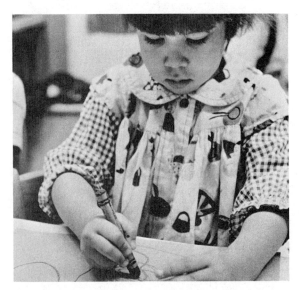

Fig. 5-12 A child aged four to five takes pride in making better and better symbols.

Later First Drawings Stage

Through much practice, a child can now draw symbols easily and more exactly. Many four-year-olds and most five-year-olds perfect to their own liking a series of many symbols. The child takes pride in these symbols.

A child at this later point often likes to see these symbols clearly and neatly set on the page. They are now drawn one at a time with few or no other marks on the page. The symbol is clear and well drawn. If children can draw the letters of their name on the page as well, they may feel this is all that belongs in the picture.

For awhile, children are content to make these finished yet isolated examples of their drawing skill, but it is not long before more complex drawings are made. Young children four to five years of age are able to use their symbols in drawings to tell a story or describe an event.

By five and one-half to six years of age, children generally are ready to make a picture of anything in their experience or imagination. Their drawings are made up of combinations of symbols they can draw. Children can also create new symbols.

Each child now has a special way of drawing the human form, houses, and other symbols. This individual way of drawing is called a *schema*. A schema, or individual pattern, often can be seen in drawings by the age of six. A schema comes after much practice with drawing symbols. Once the child has a schema, symbols become special marks. A schema is special for each child just as an adult has a unique signature.

Importance of Schema

The schema drawn by a child represents something that is important to the child. This is something that is part of the child's environment and experience. Things which are emotionally important to the child are included in the picture.

Children draw schema in the picture not in the size it should be, but in a size that shows the emotional importance of this object to them. For example, people and things important to a child might be drawn larger and

Fig. 5-13 People and other important figures in a child's life are often drawn larger than less important figures.

with more details. The people or things the child dislikes may be drawn smaller. If a tree is drawn, the limbs may be made larger because the tree is used for climbing. If it is an apple tree, the apples may be drawn very large.

Children express other responses to their environment in their drawings. A painting showing a child walking on wet grass may show the feet and toes large in size. This is to express how it feels to walk on wet grass.

Importance of First Drawings

At about the same time children develop their own schemas, they begin to name their drawings. To name a drawing is really an important step for children. It is a sign that their thinking has changed. They are connecting their drawings with the world around them. By naming drawings, children show that they are relating their thinking to things outside of themselves. This is the beginning of a new form of communication – communication with the environment.

Soon a five-year-old may think: "My daddy is a big man; he has a head and two big legs. My drawing has a head and two big legs. Therefore, my drawing is daddy." Through drawing, the child is making a clear relation-ship between father and the drawing. The symbol of a man now becomes daddy.

When using schemas, children express their own personalities. They express not only what is important to them during the process of creating, but also how aware they have become in thinking, feeling, and seeing. From early drawings to the most complex, children give expression to their life experiences.

SUMMARY

As children grow older and change in height and weight, they also develop different abilities in art. There are three developmental levels in art that are of concern to the preschool teacher. They are the scribble, basic forms, and first drawings stages.

The scribble stage ranges from about one and one-half to three years of age. It covers the time from the child's first marks to more controlled scribbles. The child enjoys the pure motion involved in scribbling.

The basic forms stage covers approximately ages three to four years. The child develops more muscle control and hand-eye coordination through scribbling. Basic forms come when children can see simple forms in their scribbles and are able to repeat them. The oval or circle is usually the first basic form, followed by the rectangle or square. Children now enjoy seeing forms emerge at their own will.

The first drawings stage generally covers ages four to six. Basic forms made in the prior stage are put together to make up symbols. The human form, birds, flowers, and animals are examples of some symbols. Naming drawings is an important part of first drawings. It means that children can now communicate outside themselves, and with their environment. A child's drawings are very individual and express the child's own personality.

STUDENT ACTIVITIES

- **Scribble Stage Experiences for the Student**

    A. Exercise 1. Goal: To experience some of the lack of motor control of a young child in the scribble stage.

    1. The student is to use the hand opposite the writing hand to "draw" a crayon picture. Using a large crayon in the hand that is not usually used for drawing, the student should experience difficulties like those of the young child.

    2. Consider and discuss the following:

        a. Clumsy feeling of the crayon in hand.

        b. Lack of good control over finger and hand movements.

        c. Inability to draw exactly what is desired.

        d. Difficulty in controlling crayon, paper, and hand movements all at once.

    B. Exercise 2. Goal: To experience the pure motor pleasure of scribbling.

    1. The student is to close both eyes and do a crayon scribbling.

    2. To experience feelings similar to the young child, consider and discuss the following.

        a. Difficulty of overcoming the adult need for seeing as well as doing.

        b. How it feels to move hand and fingers for movement's sake alone.

        c. What forms are seen in the scribbles.

        d. Feelings about how the drawing looks.

- **Recognizing and Evaluating the Three Art Stages**

    Obtain samples of drawings from children one and one-half to five years of age. Separate the examples into three groups (one for each stage). Give reasons for separating into groups, especially on the samples that are not clearly defined.

    A. Note and explain the differences in scribble stage examples:

    1. Early or later scribbling period.

    2. Type of scribbles (circular, jagged).

    3. Control of crayon.

    B. Note and explain the differences in basic forms examples:

    1. Type of basic forms used.

    2. How clear and exact the forms are.

3. Control of crayon.

4. Early or later basic forms period.

C. Note and explain the differences in first drawings examples:

1. Early or later period.

2. What basic forms are combined into symbols.

3. Observable symbols.

REVIEW

A. Describe a young child in the scribble stage in the following areas.

1. Age.

2. Degree of motor control.

3. Reason for scribbling.

B. List three basic forms that a child in the basic forms stage may be able to draw.

C. Describe a schema.

D. Give four examples of symbols.

E. Discuss the importance of children's naming their pictures.

Unit 6
EXPERIMENTS WITH TWO-DIMENSIONAL MEDIA

OBJECTIVES

After studying this unit, the student will be able to

- Discuss use of material by children in the scribble stage.
- Describe drawing techniques in the basic forms stage.
- Explain figures and detail in the first drawings stage.

The material presented here is a guide for observing developmental art theory in action. It is meant to be used in working with children. The student is to observe children making artwork to see how developmental levels really work. Written records of these observations should be kept. In observing children and their art, the student is to keep in mind the important points for each developmental level. Students may use the review chart shown in figure 6-1 to help guide their observations.

DEFINITION OF TWO-DIMENSIONAL MEDIA

The term *two-dimensional* refers to any art form that is flat. Art in two dimensions has only two sides, front and back. Examples of two-dimensional art processes are painting, drawing, collage, and scribbling.

THE SCRIBBLE STAGE AND TWO-DIMENSIONAL MEDIA

Children just beginning to scribble need tools that are safe and easy to hold and use. For a child between the ages of one and one-half to three years, large, nontoxic crayons are the best tool. Pencils are dangerous for the young child, and are also too hard to hold and use. Paint and brush also require more skill to use than the child has at this age. A good grade kindergarten-type crayon is the best tool. The crayon should be large and unwrapped. In this way, it can be used on both the sides and ends. Good crayons are strong enough to hold up for rough first scribbles. They also make bright, clear colors, which are pleasant for the child to use.

Since motion is the chief enjoyment in this stage, the child should have large blank paper (at least 18″ x 24″). This size allows enough room for wide arm movements and large scribbles in many directions. The paper should always be large enough to give the child a big open space for undirected, random scribbles.

The child should be provided with only one crayon color at a time. It is important that the child develop motor control in the early period of the scribbling stage. Seeing different colors of crayons may make the child stop scribbling to try these colors. This type of interruption breaks up arm movement as well as total physical involvement. The child should have a new crayon when a new drawing is started.

If possible, a child in the scribble stage should use large white paper. Crayon scribbles show up better on white paper. Therefore, the child can more easily see the results of the scribbling.

AGE RANGE	MOTOR CONTROL	PURPOSE OF ARTWORK	CHARACTERISTICS OF STAGE
SCRIBBLE STAGE: One and one-half to three years.	Lacks good motor control and hand-eye coordination.	Scribbles for pure physical sensation of movement.	1. Lacks direction or purpose for marks. 2. Does not mentally connect own movement to marks on page.
BASIC FORMS Three to four years.	Has more developed motor control and hand-eye coordination. Has control over direction and size of line.	Enjoys mastery over line.	1. Master basic forms: circle, oval, square, rectangle, lines. 2. Discovers connection between own movements and marks on page.
FIRST DRAWINGS Four to five years.	Has most advanced motor control and hand-eye coordination.	Communicates with outside world through drawing. Expresses personality and relationship to symbols drawn.	1. Combines basic forms to create first symbols. 2. Names drawings as a form of true communication.

Figure 6-1 Review chart: characteristics of three stages of art.

OBSERVATION POINTS FOR THE SCRIBBLE STAGE

The student observer of young children (ages one and one-half to three years) should be able to find the following points in observing scribbling. An observation sheet similar to the one shown in figure 6-2, page 39, should be used to record observations.

Age

Note the age of the child. Keep in mind the average range for the scribble stage (1 1/2 to 3 years). See how the child fits in the range. There may be an overlap between stages.

Motor Control

Note how the child holds the crayon. See if two fingers are used, or clenched fingers, or a fist. If the child uses a two-finger grip, this is the start of good motor control. The other methods of holding the crayon shows less control. See if the child can hold the crayon without dropping it during the entire drawing. This also shows good motor control. Note any other things that might show the child's degree of motor control.

Arm Movement

In scribbling, a child may use one type of arm movement, or a variety. Note if move-

Child	Age	Motor Control	Arm Movements	Type of Scribbles	Use of Paper	Early Period	Later Period
COMMENTS:							

Fig. 6-2 Observation sheet: scribble stage.

ments are wide, long, short, jabbing, or of other kinds. The type of arm movement used affects the basic forms the child will make in the future. For example, if circular scribbles are being made, later these scribbles become circles.

Type of Scribbles

Note the kind of scribbles the child is making. They may be controlled or uncontrolled, circular, lines, or others mentioned earlier.

Use of Paper

There are many ways of using paper for scribbling. Some are 1) moving across the paper from left to right, 2) moving across the paper from right to left, 3) scribbling only in one part of the page, or 4) moving the paper to make marks in the other direction. See if the child seems to know how to use the paper. Older scribblers often have more control over the paper.

Further Observations

- Provide the child with some soft colored chalk. See if this new tool causes any differences in the way the child scribbles.
- Change to a smaller-size paper. See if there are any differences in the child's

Fig. 6-3 A two-finger grip on the crayon is a sign of the start of good motor control.

arm movement, type of scribbles made, and use of paper.

- Place two extra colored crayons in the child's view. See if the child uses them. Then see if scribbles look different when they are made by the child using many colors. Compare an all-one-color drawing with a many-color drawing.

BASIC FORMS STAGE AND TWO-DIMENSIONAL MEDIA

Children in the basic forms stage have enough motor control and hand-eye coordination to use different tools. In addition to crayons, the child may now begin to work with tempera (poster) paint. Tempera paint is the best kind for children because it flows easily from the brush onto the page. Large lead pencils are good for children in the later period of this stage. There is less danger of injury with these older children. (A complete list of proper materials is included in a later unit on selecting materials.)

Felt-tip pens are an excellent tool for this stage. They make clear, quick and nice-looking marks. In the basic forms stage when the child really enjoys seeing the marks come out as desired, these pens are best. Felt-tip pens should be nontoxic and water soluble. In this way, spots can be washed out of the child's clothes.

The largest paper size is not as necessary in this stage as in the scribble stage. Because the child now has better motor control, it is easier to keep marks on a small space. Room for wide, uncontrolled movements is not necessary. Yet, paper of many sizes should be available.

Different colors of paper and pens should be available to the child. Children in this stage like to make basic forms in many colors. It is an exercise of their skill in making basic forms.

Student observers should realize that the child of this age likes to repeat forms. An observer should not try to force a child to "make something else." It is important that children practice making their own basic forms. The

Fig. 6-4 Basic form drawings may look simple, but they represent a great motor achievement for the child.

forms may look simple, but each drawing stands for a great motor achievement for the child. The children may rightly be quite proud of their basic form drawings.

OBSERVATION POINTS FOR THE BASIC FORMS STAGE

The student observer of young children in the basic forms stage should be able to find the following points when observing the children. The points should be recorded on an observation sheet like the one in figure 6-5.

Age

Note the age of the child. Check the review chart for the average age range for the basic forms stage. See how the child fits in the range. See if there is an overlap between stages.

Motor Control

See how the child holds the crayon. Note if the crayon is held very tightly or if the child can draw with sureness and ease. Also note if the child draws with a lot of arm movemnt, or uses just the hand to draw. The child who uses more hand movement and less arm movement is showing good motor control. In the basic forms stage, children use fewer unnecessary arm movements.

Types of Basic Forms

Write down the number and type of basic forms mentioned earlier which the child can draw. See if the shapes are well drawn or look rough and unclear. Rough, less clear forms are made in the early stage. A child in the later basic forms stage draws clear, easy-to-recognize shapes.

In drawings with a variety of forms, see if one form is clearer than another. Clearer forms are the ones that the child first began

Child	Age	Motor Control	Arm Movements	Type of Basic Forms	Use of Paper	Early Period	Later Period
COMMENTS:							

Fig. 6-5 Observation sheet: basic forms stage.

to draw. The less clear forms are in the practice stage and should soon become clearer.

Use of Paper

Use the same checkpoints for the ways of using paper that were used in the scribble stage section. In addition, see if the child fills the page with one or many basic forms. If the same shape is made over and over, it means the child is practicing a new basic form. Practice like this occurs at an early point in the stage.

Further Observations

- Give the child pieces of cardboard in square, circular, and rectangular shapes. Show how to trace lines around the forms. After the child has traced the forms for awhile, see if freehand basic forms improve. Discuss the need for such practice. Consider if it is possible to speed up the development of basic forms by tracing. Base your answers on the information given in unit 5, where basic art stages were described.

Fig. 6-6 Good motor control is shown by the child who uses more hand movement than arm movement.

- Arrange poster paint and brushes so the children can paint. Mark down the ages of the children who are best able to handle these tools. Are the older children

Fig. 6-7 **The child who draws the same shape many times on a piece of paper may be practicing a new basic form.**

always the best at painting? See if the children who can draw good basic forms are able to do the same with paint. In general, a child who shows good motor control with crayons should be able to paint as well.

FIRST DRAWINGS STAGE AND TWO-DIMENSIONAL MEDIA

Children in the first drawings stage have the best motor control of all the young children in this age group. Their drawings have the most variety of forms and figures.

A wide variety of materials for drawing and painting should be given to the children in this stage. Children ages five and six in this stage can use crayons, paint and brush, pencils and pens, and other similar tools. Paper of many types and sizes should be supplied. Interesting textures, colors, and sizes of paper

all help the child make pictures in many different styles. The fun of making these pictures is open to the child who has a wide variety of materials.

OBSERVATION POINTS FOR THE FIRST DRAWINGS STAGE

The student should find different points when observing children in the first drawings stage. This is because of the more complex and varied type of drawings made by children in this stage. The following points apply to this stage. Observations should be written on a form similar to the one shown in figure 6-8.

Age

Write down the age of the child. Check to see what the average age range is for the first drawings stage. See how the child fits in this range. There may be an overlap between stages. For example, the student may see figures as well as simple basic forms in one drawing.

Combination of Basic Forms

See how the child puts basic forms together to make figures. Very simple combinations mean the child is at an early point in the stage. An example of this early point is a flower made up of a single circle and one-line stem. On the other hand, a flower of many circles with oval petals and a stem of many leaves is a more complex combination of basic forms. This more complex example shows that the child is at a later point in the stage.

Size of Figures

A child in both the early and later periods of this stage may use size to show importance. The larger size figure means that the figure is important to the child. Note, for example, if children draw themselves or other figures such as their mother, in a very large size. Extra

Child	Age	Combination of Basic Forms	Size of Figures	Number of Figures	Details	Use of Figures	Naming Pictures	Early Period	Later Period
COMMENTS:									

Fig. 6-8   Observation sheet: first drawings stage.

Fig. 6-9   Notice how the child puts basic forms together in a drawing.

Fig. 6-10   A large size figure usually means it is something that is important to the child.

large heads on a small body are found mainly in the early period of this stage.

Notice the relative size of certain things in the picture. For a child who likes animals, the size of a dog may be far larger than the size of a human form. Here, too, size indicates that the object is important to the child.

Fig. 6-11 The relative size of objects to each other in a drawing also indicates what is more important to the child.

Fig. 6-12 A child in the early period of the first drawings stage still uses stick figures and only a few details in a picture.

Number of Figures

Mark down the number of figures in each drawing. A drawing with few figures or a single figure means that the child is at an early point in the stage. The child making this type of drawing is working on developing a symbol.

At a later point, the child can draw many types of symbols and figures in one drawing. Also, drawings at a later point look as if they tell a story with the figures.

Detail

Note the type of details and the number of these details a child uses in a drawing. The type and number of details are signs that the child is at a particular point in the stage.

Figures with only a few details are made in the early first drawings stage. For example, a circle-shaped head, round body, and stick arms and legs make up an early human form. A picture of a man with details such as full arms, hands, and fingers is a sign that the child is in a later period of the first drawings stage.

See if certain objects are drawn in greater detail than others. A child's experience with certain objects can cause this increase in detail. As an example, tree limbs may be unusually large in the drawings of children who love to climb trees. Special sense experiences can also cause increase in detail. For example, a child may draw large raindrops in a drawing after a walk in the rain.

Use of Figures

Note how the child uses figures. See if the paper is filled with many unrelated figures. See if the figures just fill space and look like practice forms. If there is no real connection between figures, it can mean the child is at an early point in the stage. This means the child is practicing drawing a symbol and is not yet ready to tell a story with it.

If there seems to be a connection between figures, this means the child is at a later point. This type of drawing is a narrative drawing, one that tells a story. It is a visual form of communication for the child.

Naming Drawings

Be sure to listen to the child who wants to talk about a drawing. See if the child names certain things, figures, or the whole thing.

Never force the child to tell you "what it is." Naming must come only through the child's own idea. This is an important step in the children's ability to communicate with their environment. It can only be worthwhile when the child sees the meaning in the work and wants to name it.

Further Observations

- Read a story about animals to the children before art period. Do not tell the children what to draw. See how many children draw animals. Do this with other types of stories and discuss the results with classmates.

- Display prints of famous artworks. (Examples: Mondrian's "Composition with Red, Blue, and Yellow," Pollock's "Detail of One (#31, 1950)," and Van Gogh's "Cypress Trees.") See if these examples affect the children's choice of colors, type of figures made, and amount of details in their pictures.

- Play a record during part of the art period. Compare the drawings made with music to those done without music.

SUMMARY

Two-dimensional refers to any art form that is flat. Painting, scribbling, drawing, and collage are examples of two-dimensional media.

Wide, good quality crayons are the best tools for the scribble stage. Large-sized paper should be given to the child to allow room for wide arm movements. Age, motor control, use of paper, and type of scribbles are all points to find in scribble stage observations.

A wider variety of art materials can be used with children in the basic forms stage. Age, motor control, use of paper, and basic forms used are all points to find in observations of the basic forms stage.

In the first drawings stage, children make the most varied and complex drawings. Points to find in observing this stage are the age of the child, and figures and details in the drawings.

STUDENT ACTIVITIES

- Discuss the following points based on information from your observations of children in various age groups, stages, and media.

    A. Amount of overlap between stages.

    B. Importance of the right materials to each stage.

REVIEW

A. Define the term two-dimensional media and give an example of a two-dimensional art process.

B. List the materials that are right for children in the scribble stage and basic forms stage.

    1. For the scribble stage, what are the best (a) crayon size and type; (b) paper size and type; (c) number of colors at one time?

    2. For the basic forms stage, what are the best (a) tools for drawing; (b) paper size and type; (c) number of colors at one time?

C. Choose the answer that best completes these statements about the basic forms stage.

    1. The child with good motor control

        a. drops the crayon often.

    b. uses a clenched grip.

    c. uses more hand than arm movement.

2. An early type of basic form is

    a. well drawn.

    b. a less clear form.

    c. combined to make a symbol.

3. In the later period of basic forms, a child

    a. cannot draw good basic forms.

    b. easily draws clear forms.

    c. fills the page with practice forms.

D. Complete the following for the first drawings stage.

1. Give an example of an early and a later combination of basic forms.

2. Draw two examples of an early and a later combination of basic forms.

3. In the following, decide which period best shows each listed characteristic.

Period	Characteristics of Drawing
(A) Early Period of First Drawings Stage	a. Few, unrelated figures
	b. Greater degree and amount of detail
(B) Later Period of First Drawings Stage	c. Narrative or story drawings
	d. Greater size to show importance
	e. Larger head size for figures

Unit 7
EXPERIMENTS WITH THREE-DIMENSIONAL MEDIA

OBJECTIVES

After studying this unit, the student will be able to

- Describe how a child aged one and one-half to three works with clay.
- Discuss how a child aged three to four works with clay.
- Explain how a child aged four to five works with clay.

The term *three-dimensional art* means any art form that has at least three sides. Three-dimensional art is in the round, which means that one can look at it from many sides. Modeling with clay, working with play dough, making plaster molds, and creating other sculpture forms are examples of three-dimensional art activities.

Just as in drawing, there are three basic stages of art development in work with three-dimensional material. The basics of development for three-dimensional media are the same as for two-dimensional media. Therefore, this unit is a short summary of facts already presented — as they apply to three-dimensional media. The names of the stages in two-dimensional art, however, do not apply to three-dimensional work. A child does not "scribble" with clay; but the age range for each stage is the same. The basic ideas are also the same.

Development of work with three-dimensional material is noted here by age range. The age range is only approximate for each stage. Each child has a somewhat different pace for growth. Clay modeling is used here as the main example of use of three-dimensional material. Yet, the same ideas given for clay can be used for all other three-dimensional art materials.

THREE-DIMENSIONAL MATERIAL AND THE CHILD ONE AND ONE-HALF TO THREE YEARS OF AGE

When children aged one and one-half to three learn to use a three-dimensional material like clay, they go through the same process of growth as in the scribble stage. At first clay is squeezed through the fingers in a very uncontrolled way. This is comparable to the early scribble stage. With both clay and crayons, the child in this age range has little control over hand movements. The feel of the clay in hand while squeezing it is what the child enjoys about the clay.

Just as children make early scribbles in many directions, they also make early clay forms in many ways. A child of this age (1 1/2 to 3) beats and pounds clay for no special purpose, just like scribbling in all directions. The child does not try to make anything definite with the clay. What is made depends on whether the child pounds, flattens, or squeezes the clay.

Real clay is a very good three-dimensional material for the child of this age. It is easy to use because it is soft and elastic. It can be bought in either dry or moist form. Plasticene, a plastic-type clay, is more expensive and is

Fig. 7-1 A child's first work with clay is just like early uncontrolled scribbling. Both the scribbling and the first clay forms show that the child does not have the muscle (motor) control to make definite objects yet.

(a)

(b)

(c)

harder for the young child to use because it is not as soft and elastic as real clay. A child is likely to use an easy-to-use material more often. The more the child uses it, the more it helps muscle control grow.

When children's muscle control gets better, they begin to pat and roll the clay. This matches the controlled scribbling stage. In both scribbling and clay work, the children now enjoy seeing the effects of their movements. They find that they can use their hand movements to make the clay go in desired ways. At this point, a child may roll the clay into thin lengths (ropes), pound it, or shape it into balls.

Children make these ropes and balls with clay at about the same time they control scribbles in drawing. At this point, children enjoy seeing their control over the material. Lines drawn with crayon, and rope lines made of clay are both proof of the child's growing muscle (motor) control.

Fig. 7-2 As their muscle control improves, children begin to work the clay into desired forms, making short, fat shapes (a and b), and long, thin lengths (c).

THREE-DIMENSIONAL MATERIAL AND THE CHILD THREE TO FOUR YEARS OF AGE

A child of three or four who can draw basic forms can also make clay into similar forms. Rolling clay to make balls is an example of a basic form (circle) in clay. Boxes made of clay are examples of basic forms (rectangles) in a three-dimensional material.

In drawing and in clay, the circle is one of the first basic forms made. In both two- and three-dimensional media, the child is able to make this form by controlling the material.

The rectangular form usually comes after that of the circle. Just as in scribbling, the rectangle is made with clay when the child can shape it into whatever length desired.

Methods of Working With Clay

There are two ways of making basic forms with clay: the synthetic way and the analytic way. In the *synthetic way,* the child makes things out of clay by putting together separate pieces to make a whole. For example, a clay box made in the synthetic way is made by putting together separate pieces of clay. The child makes separate pieces for the bottom and the sides and then joins them into a box.

In the *analytic way,* the child shapes the object from the whole piece of clay. The child does not use separate pieces and then join them together. In the analytic method, a clay box is made by shaping the box from one whole piece of clay.

By the synthetic method, a child puts parts together to make an object. In the analytic method a child shapes the whole piece of clay, always using it whole and not putting parts together. Both methods are shown in chart form, figure 7-5, page 50.

Children practice their own ways of making basic forms with clay. Just as in drawing, they make the same form over and over again until they can make it as desired. In this way,

Fig. 7-3 This is an example of a clay box made in the synthetic way. The pieces for the bottom and sides were each made separately and then joined to form the box.

Fig. 7-4 In the analytic method, a clay box is made by shaping a whole piece of clay to make the object, not by putting separate parts together.

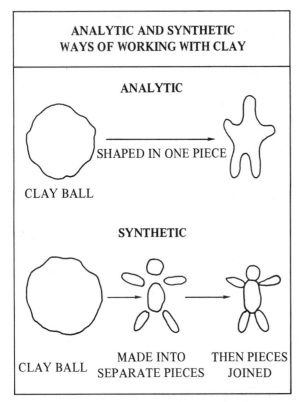

Fig. 7-5 Analytic and synthetic ways of working with clay.

Fig. 7-6 A detailed clay figure such as this can be compared to a child's later first drawings.

they improve muscle control even more. They also perfect the forms that are used in the next stage of three-dimensional media.

THREE-DIMENSIONAL MEDIA AND THE CHILD FOUR TO FIVE YEARS OF AGE

A child aged four to five can put together basic clay forms to make up figures. This is the same as the first drawings stage in two-dimensional media.

Most children in this age range (4 to 5 years) like to make definite things with clay. They combine basic forms to build objects that are like figures in drawing. They begin by making simple things out of basic forms. The child working with clay puts together a round clay ball (circle) for a head and a clay stick-type line or lump for a body. This is an early combination of basic forms in clay. It is a lot like the stick figure made in early first drawings.

Later in working with clay, children put these forms together in more complex ways. They may make a person with legs, arms, fingers, and feet. This is like the later first drawings stage when a child draws more details.

Children of this age do not make the same forms over and over again for practice as in the stage before. This is because a child of four or five has the muscle (motor) control and hand-eye coordination to easily make any form desired.

The clay is now used to make a definite object, a symbol which stands for something important to the child. The children make human figures, animals, houses, pies, and many other things with clay. The forms are made in the child's own special way, just as in drawing.

This special way (schema) of working with clay is the same for two- and three-dimensional media. It comes from much practice in making symbols and is the child's own special way of making these symbols.

Just as in drawing, children may make things that are more important to them (symbols) bigger than things that are less important. They may use more details for an important clay figure, too. At this stage, these details may be made by putting other pieces on the clay like buttons for eyes, straws for legs, and cotton for hair.

NAMING OBJECTS

Children start to name their clay objects at about the same time they start to name their drawings. This is just as important with clay as with drawing. In both cases, it means the children are expressing their ideas in art. The children now can tell other people just what these ideas are by naming their work.

THE VALUE OF CLAY

At all ages, work with clay gives the child many chances for creative experiences. Most children like the damp feeling of clay. They like to pound it, roll it, poke holes in it, pull it apart. Just as in drawing, it is the fun of working with the clay that counts. The end product is not as important as using it; a child becomes really involved in the "using" process.

Most children like to do messy things with their hands, and clay gives them a chance for this experience. Working with clay can be a

Fig. 7-7 Children are often more involved in the process of using the clay than in the finished product.

social experience, too. Sitting around a table in small groups, children enjoy trading and sharing lumps of clay.

PROCEDURES FOR WORKING WITH CLAY

Since clay is messy, it should be used carefully with young children. However, working with clay is no fun for the children when the teacher always has to remind them about the right use. Proper setup will make this unnecessary. Some tips for clay setup are listed.

- The tables used for working with clay should be placed away from wheel and climbing toys. The tables should be covered with linoleum or formica to make cleaning easier.

- The number of children at a table at one time should be limited.

- Each child should be given a lump of clay about the size of a large apple. The clay may be worked with in any way the child wants. However, the clay should not be thrown on the ground, and no child should interfere with another child's work.

- The teacher may sit at the table and mold the clay, too. This adds to the social feeling. But the teacher should not make objects for the child to copy. This discourages the child's creative use of the clay.

- When the children are done, the clay is put away. It is best to make it into balls, each about the size of an apple. A hole filled with water in each ball helps keep the clay just right for use the next time. Clay should be kept in a container with a wet cloth or sponge over the top of the clay. The container should be covered with a tight-fitting lid. Clay becomes moldy if it is too wet. It is hard to handle when it becomes very dry.

SUMMARY

Three-dimensional art refers to any art that has at least three sides. It is "in the round," which means one can look at it from many sides. Examples of three-dimensional art are modeling with clay and play dough and other forms of sculpture.

Just as children have different drawing abilities at each age, they work with clay in a different way at each age. A child aged one and one-half to three uses clay just as a child uses crayons in the scribble stage. In work with both crayons and clay, children at this age have little control over their hands or the material. The child enjoys the feel of the clay, but does not have good control in working with it.

A child aged three to four who can draw basic forms like circles or rectangles can also make clay into similar forms. Clay balls and boxes are examples of basic forms in clay. Children's muscle (motor) control helps them make these forms.

A child aged four to five can put together basic forms in clay to make up figures. This is the same as making figures in the first drawing stage of two-dimensional media.

Children name their clay objects at about the same time that they name their drawings. Naming is an important form of communication in both two- and three-dimensional media.

A teacher must set up the room for good use of clay for young children. Proper tables, number of children, and care of clay are all points to keep in mind when planning for clay work.

STUDENT ACTIVITIES

- **Exercise 1**. Goal: To experience how a child aged one and one-half to three years works with clay, try the following activity.

    A. Use your hand opposite your writing hand.

    B. Use a piece of real clay about the size of a large **apple**.

    C. Squeeze the clay in one hand only.

    D. Keep these points in mind:

        1. How it feels to lack good muscle (motor) control.

        2. How hard it is to make an exact object.

        3. How the clay feels in the hand.

- **Exercise 2**. Goal: To feel the differences in clay, try the following activity.

    A. Prepare large-sized balls of real clay, plasticene (oil-based) clay, and play dough.

    B. Use the hand opposite the writing hand to squeeze and feel each of the three clay balls. (This should help the student experience the child's lack of muscle control and different materials, too.)

    C. Consider the following points while working with each of the three balls of clay:

        1. Which is the easiest to squeeze?

    2. Which feels the best?

    3. Which was the most fun to use?

    4. Was the type most fun to use also the easiest to use?

D. Try the above activity with children aged one and one-half to three years. Ask them the above questions. Compare answers.

- **Exercise 3**. Goal: To practice analytic and synthetic ways of working with clay, try the following activity.

A. Use two balls of clay.

B. Make two clay boxes — one in the analytic way, and one in the synthetic way.

C. Ask other students to identify which box is the analytic example, and which is the synthetic example.

D. The two sample boxes should look different. Discuss how each box is different in the way it looks because of how it is made.

E. Variation: Draw a figure of a man in the analytic and in the synthetic way. Use the same procedure as above for discussion.

F. Obtain some samples of children's (aged 3 to 4 years) clay objects. See which are synthetic examples and which are analytic examples. Discuss how they look.

G. Observe children as they work with clay. See how they make their objects. Note if they work in the synthetic or analytic way.

H. Obtain samples of children's clay objects. Look for these points:

    1. Which basic forms are made.

    2. Which forms are made the most.

    3. Whether there are practice forms or definite objects.

- **Exercise 4**. Goal: To help you understand how children feel when they are given a model to copy, try the following activity.

A. Obtain and display small glass or porcelain figures. These could be decorative birds, glass dolls, or any other finished figure from the dime store or other source.

B. Provide all the students with small balls of clay. Have each student try to copy the model.

C. Look at and discuss the finished objects.

    1. How did it feel to copy such a difficult model?

    2. Was it a pleasant or frustrating experience?

    3. Did this copying exercise make you feel happy about working with clay? Did it make you like to copy?

4. How do you think children feel about trying to copy models the teacher sets up?

5. Why is it undesirable for a teacher to have children copy a model?

- **Exercise 5.** Goal: Obtain some pictures of modern sculpture. (Henry Moore's is a good example.)

A. Show the pictures to the children before they work with clay.

B. See if there are any effects on their work in relation to:

  1. Kinds of objects made.

  2. New shapes made.

  3. More or less clay work done.

  4. Change in the way objects are made.

  5. Change in the way child works with clay.

- **Exercise 6.** Goal: Read an exciting story to the children before they work with clay. For example, **try M.** Sendak's *Where the Wild Things Are* or Suess, *To Think it Happened on Mulberry Street.*

A. Do not tell the children what to make.

B. See if their work with clay shows any influence from the story, regarding:

  1. Type of figures made.

  2. Size of figures made.

  3. Details of figures made.

REVIEW

A. Define three-dimensional art and give one example.

B. Choose the answer that best completes the following statements about the child one and one-half to three years old.

  1. Children aged one and one-half to three years

    a. make basic forms with clay.

    b. combine basic forms to make objects.

    c. squeeze the clay in an uncontrolled way.

  2. Children aged one and one-half to three years work with clay similar to the way they draw in the

    a. scribble stage.

    b. basic forms stage.

    c. first drawings stage.

3. For children aged one and one-half to three years, the most important thing about working with clay is

   a. what they can make with it.

   b. how it feels.

   c. how they can control it.

4. The best kind of clay for children one and one-half to three years is

   a. real clay.

   b. oil-based plastic clay.

   c. ceramic, nonelastic clay.

C. Define the two ways of working with clay.

D. Decide which answer best completes each statement about the child three to four years old.

   1. A child aged three to four who draws basic forms

      a. cannot make similar forms in clay.

      b. can make clay into similar forms.

      c. combines these forms to make clay objects.

   2. Rolling clay to make balls is an example of

      a. lack of motor control.

      b. uncontrolled movement like scribbling.

      c. a basic form (circle) in clay.

   3. Children aged three to four can make basic forms in clay because they

      a. can name their clay objects.

      b. now have better muscle (motor) control.

      c. do not have enough muscle (motor) control.

   4. Some simple basic forms the three- to four-year-old can make in clay are

      a. balls, boxes, and coils.

      b. flowers, houses, and animals.

      c. triangles, hexagons, and pyramids.

E. Choose the answer that best completes each statement about the child four to five years old.

   1. Most children aged four to five like to make

      a. nothing particular with clay.

      b. just balls and boxes with clay.

      c. definite things with clay.

2. When working with clay, a child aged four to five can

    a. combine basic forms to make a definite object.

    b. make only basic forms in clay.

    c. make only uncontrolled hand movements with clay.

3. A simple combination of basic forms in a clay object is a

    a. house with four floors of clay and a four-part chimney.

    b. clay box.

    c. man made of a round ball head and a stick-type body.

4. When children aged four to five name their drawings, they

    a. have no muscle control.

    b. also name their clay objects.

    c. are not yet ready to name their clay objects.

5. When children name clay objects, it means they are in the related two-dimensional stage called the

    a. scribble stage.

    b. basic forms stage.

    c. first drawings stage.

6. A more complex combination of basic forms in clay is a

    a. man made of a round ball head and a stick-type body.

    b. clay man with feet, fingers, hands, and arms.

    c. clay ball.

7. When a child aged four to five makes a clay figure with many more details than another figure, it means

    a. nothing of any particular importance.

    b. that it is an important figure for the child.

    c. that it is a simple combination of basic forms.

8. When a clay object is made large, it means the object

    a. is a basic form.

    b. is not very important.

    c. stands for something important.

F. Describe the right room setup for clay work, in regard to

    1. Table type

    2. Location of clay tables

    3. Number of children at table

    4. Amount of clay for each child

    5. Kind of storage container for clay

Relationship of Art to Total Development

Unit 8 ART AND SOCIAL-EMOTIONAL GROWTH

OBJECTIVES

After studying this unit, the student will be able to

- Define the term self-acceptance.
- Describe how the art program can add to the child's feeling of self-acceptance.
- Discuss how the art program helps the child in child-child relationships, adult-child relationships, and group-child relationships.

The term social-emotional growth refers to two kinds of growth. Emotional growth is the growth of a child's feelings within, and social growth is the child's growth as a member of a group, or society. This unit covers both the social and emotional growth of the child as it happens in the preschool art program.

Social-emotional growth occurs at the same time as physical-mental growth. To make it easier for the student, however, the two are covered in separate units in this text.

SELF-ACCEPTANCE

All children like to feel good about themselves. This good feeling about one's self is called *self-acceptance*. Children who feel that they are good people who can do things well have a good sense of self-acceptance.

Children who accept themselves know what they can and cannot do, and can live with this knowledge. Children must have this good feeling about themselves before they can ever learn to accept others. A good preschool art program can help children develop and improve self-acceptance.

Children learn to accept themselves from birth all the way throughout life. They learn

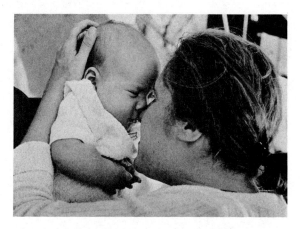

Fig. 8-1 A baby feels accepted when held closely and with tenderness.

about themselves by the way they are treated by others. The way a mother holds her baby makes the baby feel accepted. A baby who is being held closely with tenderness learns to feel loved and good. The only way babies understand this is by physical touch, since they do not yet understand words.

As babies grow into young children, they keep learning to accept themselves. When toddlers are encouraged and praised for messy, but serious attempts to feed themselves, they learn to accept themselves and feel good about what they do. If children are accepted as they

57

are, they learn to accept themselves. This is the only way they learn to feel accepted.

In the preschool art class, children must continue to learn to accept and feel good about themselves. The art program can be of special help in developing children's good feelings about themselves. When children feel they can do things well in art, they grow both in self-confidence and self-acceptance.

A preschool teacher should plan the art program so that it gives each child a chance to grow in self-acceptance. The art program should be *child-centered,* which means that it is planned for the age and ability levels of the children in it. The art program should never be adult-centered, or planned to suit only adult ideas of what children should do. The adult-centered program does not consider the age and ability of the children in the group.

A teacher must know about developmental levels in planning the art program. Knowledge of the way children develop helps the teacher plan a good setting for the level of the children in the program.

WAYS TO ENCOURAGE SELF-ACCEPTANCE IN THE ART PROGRAM

To plan an art program which gives each child the chance to have a good experience with art, a teacher should keep in mind the following points.

Children must be accepted at their present level. If the adult accepts the child in a positive way, the child feels this acceptance. This does not mean that the child should not be challenged. Art activities can be planned that are a slight challenge for the child's present level. But, they must not be so hard that they frustrate the child. By feeling successful in art activities, children learn to feel more sure about themselves and their skills.

The art room should be a comfortable place for the age level of the group. This means that the room is planned so that it is a place where preschool children can feel at home. The room should have tables and chairs the right size for young children. There should be covering on the floor and work areas so that the children can work freely without worry about spills. It is hard for children to feel good about themselves and their work when they are always being told they are "too messy." If sponges and towels are within reach, children can clean up their own mess. A little thing like this is fun for them, as well as a good way to help them de-

Fig. 8-2 The child's developmental level must be considered when planning the setup for a preschool art program.

Fig. 8-3 Children feel more at home in an art room that is comfortable for them, including tables and chairs of the right size, space to work, and materials that are appropriate for their ages.

velop independence and confidence. By being in charge of keeping their own room clean, children learn to feel good about how they can take care of themselves. This strengthens children's self-acceptance, and helps them feel pride in themselves.

Materials should be planned for the age group of the art program. By giving children tools they can work with at their age, the teacher helps the children have more success in art projects. Being given quality materials helps children make a nicer looking finished product. Success helps children grow with pride and confidence, and know that they can do things well.

Activities should be planned for the age and ability levels of the group. Projects should be fun at the child's age, ability, and interest level.

Children get a good feeling about themselves when they are able to do art projects all by themselves. Activities that are right for the child's age, ability, and interest levels help children become more self-assured and confident about their art ability.

Guides to Help Children Develop Self-Confidence and Self-Acceptance

Some basic guides that help develop children's self-confidence and self-acceptance are listed.

- A child should be encouraged to try again after mistakes.

- A child should be complimented on things that are done well.

- A child's parents should be told of the child's success with activities or materials.

CHILD-TO-CHILD RELATIONSHIPS

It is only after a child has developed self-acceptance that it is possible to accept other children. In the preschool art program, there are many chances for a child to be with other children of the same age. Children who have had good art experiences are the ones who can honestly accept their own abilities and those of other children.

The art program is a good place for child-to-child relationships. It is a good time for children to work, talk, and be together. If the art activities are right for the group, the art period is a relaxed time for exploring, trying new tools, or using familiar ones again. Art time should be a comfortable time when children have a chance to interact with each other in many ways.

The freedom of art itself should encourage children to talk about their own work or the work of other children. Working with colors, paint, paper, and paste can give children an endless supply of things to talk about. Art time is a social time for children.

Fig. 8-4 The art program is a good place for children to learn to work with others of the same age.

Sharing Ideas

Art time is a good time for a child to learn how other children feel about things. For example, a three-year-old boy may hear for the first time how another child his own age feels about his painting. At home, this child hears mostly adult comments; now in the school art program, he can experience the ideas and feelings of another child his own age.

Although this sharing can be a new and exciting thing for a child, it can also be hard for some children to accept at first. If children have good feelings about themselves and their work in art, however, they can accept these ideas about their work from others.

The chance to share ideas and talk about one's own work or the work of others is the beginning of a new type of relationship. It is a sharing relationship between children. The child begins to see that other children have different ideas and feelings. This type of sharing makes the child see that people can have different feelings and ideas and still be friends. A child can learn that everyone does not have to agree all the time. Artwork gives the child a chance to share ideas and opinions.

Cooperation and Sharing

Working together with other children in an art program gives a child the chance to learn

Fig. 8-5 In art, there are many opportunities for children to work together and share ideas, such as joining efforts to draw a mural.

about being with others. Being with others teaches a child the value of sharing and cooperation.

Working with limited amounts of crayons, paint, and paper means that a child has to share. The child soon learns that sharing is a part of being in a group. One can of red paint for two young painters is a real life lesson in sharing.

Cooperation between children is another part of the art program. A child learns the meaning of cooperation while helping another child glue seeds on a paper, clean a brush, or button a painting shirt. This is truly learning by doing.

Getting Along With Others

Getting along with other children in the art program helps a child feel good. It gives a child a good feeling of belonging and being accepted by others.

By working with other children, a child learns to enjoy people other than those in one's own family. This is an important step toward growing up. Being in the art program is often the first time the child is away from home. This is why it is so important for the child to have a successful experience. A child's feelings about these first school experiences affect all the other school days to come.

ADULT-TO-CHILD RELATIONSHIPS

The teacher in the preschool art program is a very important person in the child's eyes. Children look up to teachers and take their presence very seriously.

The teacher is often the first adult the child works closely with outside the home. For this reason, it is important that the teacher do all that is possible to encourage the child's social and emotional growth.

Adult Acceptance of Child's Ideas

To help a child's social and emotional growth, a teacher must help the child feel ac-

Fig. 8-6 **Using paints with others teaches a child cooperation.**

cepted. This means accepting the child in many ways.

Developmental Level. One way of accepting the child is to accept the child's developmental level. This helps children feel accepted and secure at their present physical level. For example, a three-year-old does not have to feel ashamed if unable to cut very well with scissors; the teacher still accepts the child warmly. The art teacher who accepts every child, whatever their ability, helps each child find self-acceptance.

Children's Ideas. Another way of helping the child toward self-acceptance is to allow free and honest self-expression. When the child expresses ideas this way, the adult must respect the feelings expressed.

By letting children honestly express ideas in art, the teacher is encouraging the children to be themselves. And when the teacher respects the ideas expressed, it tells the child that it is all right to be one's self. In other words, when the child's work seems to say, "This is me and the way I feel," and the work is respected, the teacher is saying to the child, "I accept you and your feelings in your work." In this way, a child learns that it is good to be one's self, which is what self-acceptance is all about.

Fig. 8-7 **The teacher in a preschool art program is a very important person to the children.**

Children Accepting the Ideas of Others

The only way a child can accept others is by first experiencing self-acceptance. The child who feels accepted in the art program is more likely to be able to accept others.

When the teacher accepts and respects each child's physical and artistic abilities, it is then possible for the children to accept each other. By accepting each other, children learn about ideas, opinions, and feelings different from their own. These new ideas make the art program more rich and exciting for the children.

The art teacher must always keep in mind that children act as they are treated. Only the child who is treated with respect can treat others with respect. The teacher who respects each child's ideas and abilities is teaching

Fig. 8-8 When allowed to express themselves freely in art, children learn to accept their own feelings and ideas.

each child how to respect the abilities and ideas of others.

Enriching the Adult-Child Relationship

The teacher can make art a time when the children share ideas and experience new ones. By bringing ideas to the program, a teacher can enrich the lives of the children in the art group.

For example, a teacher can encourage a child who often draws animals to develop new ideas by bringing in toy models or pictures of many different animals. Giving the child a chance to see the other animals can be very stimulating. It may encourage the child to draw more detailed animals or to think of more ideas.

As another example, a teacher can plan field trips to give the children new ideas. The children may use these new ideas in their paintings and drawings. For example, animals seen on a trip to the circus may be made up as hand puppets, drawn in a mural, or painted in tempera colors. Although children have a large

supply of their own ideas, the teacher can be a source of many new ones.

Teacher-Child Relationship

A child learns new ways to be with an adult in the art program. The teacher is an adult, but not the child's parent; therefore, a new type of relationship opens up. This is the teacher-to-child relationship. Of course, it is different in ways from the adult-child relationship the child has at home.

The school setting is unlike the home situation. Children learn how to be and act in a place other than the home. They learn how it is to be in a larger group than the family and how to share an adult's attention with many more children.

The children learn about art as well as about themselves from the teacher. The teacher helps the children feel that it is safe to be themselves, and to express ideas in their own way in art.

The sensitive teacher lets the child know that the fun of making the project is more important than what the finished artwork looks like. A teacher opens up many new art skills and feelings for the child. Thus, it is not unusual for the teacher to be a very important person in the eyes of the child.

The teacher may be the first real adult friend for the child. It is therefore important that a good teacher-child relationship develops during the art program. A happy feeling between teacher and child affects the child's school days to come. A child who has a satisfying first experience with a teacher goes on to kindergarten expecting more good things. Of course, this attitude makes each new experience easier and more fun for both child and teacher.

Some Ways to Build a Warm Relationship

Building a warm and friendly feeling between teacher and child is not always easy;

it may not happen quickly. The best learning and teaching take place, however, when the child and teacher have this feeling for each other.

Listed are some ways to help build a warm teacher-child friendship.

- Welcome each child into the room. Make the child feel wanted and special. Have a special place to put each child's clothes.

- When speaking to children, use their names.

- Help the children find their places and a toy to play with when they first arrive.

- Remember that small children enjoy being held, even though they may not want to be held very long.

- Understand that children like to feel proud of themselves.

- Talk and listen to every child as much as possible.

GROUP RELATIONSHIPS

When taking part in the art program, a child learns to be in a group. Being in a group at school is not the same as being in a family. In school, the child is a student as well as a member of the group.

As a member of a group, the child learns many things. In the art program group, a child learns how to follow. Learning to use a paintbrush so it will not drip is an example of learning to follow directions.

When making a mural with a group of children, a child learns to follow and work with group ideas in planning the project. Learning to follow rules about cleanup is another way a child learns to follow in a group.

A child learns how to lead in a group, too. Being in charge of a group painting is one way a child learns to lead. Children who can go ahead with ideas on their own are learning the qualities of a leader. In art projects, children have many chances to learn that sometimes they can be leaders and sometimes they must be followers.

Being a member of a group is a social learning experience. A group of children in the art program is a little social group for the child. In society, or a group, or an art program, children learn how to share and cooperate. They learn that being in a social group has advantages such as being with other children their own age, working, sharing ideas, and having fun with them. Children also learn that it is sometimes a disadvantage having to work with the group's rules and that it is not always easy to take turns or to play with others each day in school.

A child learns to respect the rights and ideas of others by being a member of a social group like the art program. Learning to respect others is also a part of the child's life outside the school. The things children learn about being members of a group in school help them be members of social groups outside the school.

SUMMARY

Social-emotional growth refers to growth of a child's feelings (emotional) and growth as a member of a group (social). A well planned art program helps children develop good feelings about themselves (self-acceptance) and their abilities. In the art program, a child learns to be with other children (child-to-child relationship), to be with adults (adult-to-child relationship), and to be in a group (group relationship).

STUDENT ACTIVITIES

The following activities can be used with classmates or with children in laboratory situations. Remember them for real-life classroom use.

- **Looking in the Mirror**

    A. Materials: A large, full-length mirror or small individual hand mirrors.

    B. Purpose: To admire and feel good about one's self.

    To learn about one's self.

    To learn the names for body parts.

    C. Procedure: Let the children look in the mirror and tell you what they see.

    1. Have them name parts of their body.

    2. As they look, ask them such questions as

    a. "Why do people look in mirrors?"

    b. "Why do people like to look at themselves?"

    D. Try gluing or taping a small mirror to the back of each child's "cubbyhole" (storage space) for the child's personal use and enjoyment.

- **Making a Photo Album**

    A. Purpose: To see one's self and others.

    To learn to admire one's self and others.

    B. Procedure: Have each child bring in a photo of himself.

    1. Use large pieces of colored paper. Punch holes in the side of each sheet of paper. Tie yarn through the holes to hold the pages together.

    2. Paste each child's photo on a page. Print the child's name under the photo.

    C. Leave the photo album out so the children can look at and enjoy the pictures.

- **Field Trips**

    A. Purpose: To help enrich the child's preschool experience.

    B. Procedure: Take the children on a field trip.
    1. Talk about what they are going to see before they go. Use books, records, or toys to familiarize them with the subject in advance.

2. After each trip, use follow-up materials. Take pictures for re-call or use a scrapbook. If the visit is to a zoo, have the children paste or draw pictures of what they saw and did. Make a book out of their pictures.

C. Some suggested field trips:

grocery store	classmate's home
fire and police stations	office building
library	ride on a city bus
television studio	pumpkin farm
neighborhood park	dairy farm
zoo	any farm
circus	train station
airport	department store

- **Activity for Self-Awareness, Self-Acceptance, and Cooperation:**

Body Shapes

A. Purpose: To encourage children's positive feelings about themselves and their bodies. To encourage cooperation among children.

B. Materials: Large pieces of brown paper, crayons, and paints.

C. Procedure: Have a child lie down flat on a piece of paper. Another child uses a crayon to trace the other child's body outline on the paper. Then the first child paints or colors in his own body shape outlined on the paper.

D. Encourage the children's self-awareness by having them notice what they are wearing and the colors before they paint their outline.

- **Activity to Encourage Group Feelings:**

Patty-Cake (for three-year olds)

A. Purpose: To learn to use body parts.

  To learn other children's names.

B. Procedure: Teacher begins by singing and clapping

  "Patty-cake, Patty-cake, Baker's Man,
  Bake me a cake as fast as you can,
  Roll it and pat it, mark it with (Use a child's initial)
  Put it in the oven for (Use a child's name) and me."

1. Use all the children's names in the song. (Or each child can have a turn to sing the song and name another child in the group in the song.)

2. Repeat it often so that children learn each other's names.

- **Getting Acquainted Song/Poem**

    A. Purpose: To participate in a group activity.

    To learn each other's name.

    B. Procedure: The teacher or child says the poem pointing to another child, who then answers by saying his own name in the poem. Try it with a whole group.

    Song/Poem

    My name is (Mary, Mary, Mary)
    My name is (Mary)
    Who are you?

- **Activity for Child-Child and Child-Group Relationships: Making Mural**

    A. Make up a mural after a field trip. It can be made by all of the children working together on one large piece of paper, or it can be made by pasting separate paintings together on a large piece of paper.

    B. Variations: Decorate some windows in the school.

    Plan and give a puppet show.

    Have two children make one puppet.

    Have two children make one mask.

REVIEW

    A. Define the term "self-acceptance." Describe a child with a good sense of self-acceptance.

    B. Decide whether each of the following statements helps develop self-acceptance, does not help develop self-acceptance, or whether it does not apply to the situation.

    1. Holding a baby closely with tenderness.
    2. Giving a baby enough vitamin C each day.
    3. Encouraging a baby who tries to feed himself.
    4. Teaching a child to feed himself when the parent wants the child to do it.
    5. Leaving an infant alone as much as possible since too much touching spoils him.
    6. Having early dental care.
    7. Praising a child who dresses himself.
    8. Discouraging the child's messy eating habits.
    9. Getting yearly eye examinations.
    10. Making a child ashamed of an inability to walk well.

C. Describe what each of the following means.

    1. Child-centered program.

    2. Adult-centered program.

D. Choose the answer which best completes each of the following statements about an art program and a child's self-acceptance.

    1. An art program should be planned so that it is

        a. adult-centered.

        b. child-centered.

        c. year round.

    2. With each child in the program, a teacher must

        a. encourage the child to do more advanced work.

        b. praise only successful work.

        c. accept the child's present level.

    3. To challenge children, the teacher must provide activities that are

        a. a bit beyond their present level.

        b. two or three years advanced.

        c. for some children only.

    4. A well-planned art room

        a. is best on the north side of the building.

        b. has child-sized chairs and tables.

        c. has mostly large chairs and tables.

    5. A teacher should choose art materials on the basis of the

        a. age group using them.

        b. price of materials.

        c. type of distributor.

    6. A good reason for buying high-quality material is

        a. the low cost of the art materials.

        b. children prefer quality materials.

        c. the good results children get with quality art materials.

    7. In planning art activities, a teacher must consider each child's

        a. ethnic origin and sex.

        b. age.

        c. age, ability, and interest level.

    8. Success in art projects

        a. depends on having high-quality materials only.

      b. helps the child's pride and self-confidence.

      c. depends on the teacher's daily attitude.

9. One good guide to help children's self-confidence is to tell children

      a. what they are doing right.

      b. to improve their drawing.

      c. to copy other children's work.

10. Another good guide to help children's self-confidence is to

      a. tell them what they are doing wrong.

      b. guide their hands to help improve their drawing.

      c. encourage them to try again after mistakes.

E. Complete the statement in column I about child-to-child relationships by selecting the letter of the best choice from column II.

Column I

1. A child can accept other children
2. Sharing ideas helps children
3. Helping another child clean a brush
4. Getting along with other children
5. A good preschool experience

Column II

A. See that not all people have the same ideas.
B. Affects all the other school days to come.
C. Makes the child feel good about himself.
D. Has no effect on a child.
E. Is an example of learning to cooperate.
F. Only after he accepts himself.
G. Is an example of selfishness.

F. Discuss the reasons why the teacher is so important in the preschool art program or any preschool program.

G. List two ways a teacher can help a child feel accepted.

H. List three things children learn by being part of a group.

I. List some advantages for the child in a group.

J. List some disadvantages for the child in a group.

Unit 9 ART AND PHYSICAL-MENTAL GROWTH

OBJECTIVES

After studying this unit, the student will be able to

- Explain how art helps a child's physical (motor) development.
- Describe how art helps a child's mental (concept) development.
- Discuss the place of art in the total preschool program.

This unit presents the ways in which art relates to physical and mental growth. Physical, mental, social, and emotional growth all occur together in a child. Physical and mental growth are discussed separately to help clarify basic ideas about them for the student.

ART AND PHYSICAL (MOTOR) DEVELOPMENT

The term *motor development* is another way of saying physical growth. Both terms (motor development and physical growth) refer to growth in the ability of children to use their bodies.

In the preschool art program, things like drawing, painting, pasting, and all other activities that exercise muscles help a child's motor development. Exercising muscles in art activities helps the child's muscles grow stronger. As these muscles develop, the child's motor development increases. Different muscles are exercised in various art activities.

Small Muscle Development

Small muscles are the muscles in the fingers, hands, wrists, and arms. These small muscles are used in art activities such as painting, cutting, and pasting, which are called *small motor activities*. Any other activity that requires the use of small muscles is also called a small motor activity. The more work children do in art, the better their small muscles become.

A teacher of young children must know that small muscle skills are different for a child at different ages. For example, many three-year-olds do not have good small muscle development. So, the muscles in their fingers and hands are not quite strong enough to enable them to use scissors very well.

Through practice in using blunt scissors in art activities, the three-year-old's small muscles grow stronger. The better the small muscle development, the easier it is to cut with scissors.

Small muscles can grow stronger only by practice and exercise. A teacher can encourage a child to exercise these small muscles in small motor-type artwork. A few examples of small motor-type artwork that help exercise a child's small muscles are cutting, pasting, working with clay, making and playing with puppets, and finger painting.

A teacher encourages a child to exercise small muscles by providing the right small motor tools. Tools for small muscles are pencils, scissors, felt-tip pens, paintbrushes, and small-sized paper.

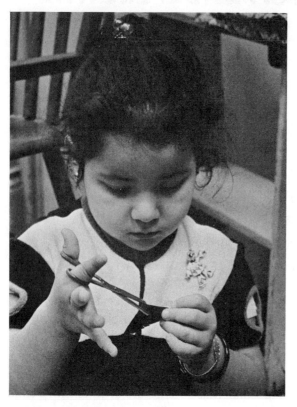

Fig. 9-1 A child's small muscles are exercised by using blunt scissors in art activities.

Fig. 9-2   As children become more experienced in small-motor type artwork, cutting with blunt scissors becomes easier.

Small muscles are often better developed in four- and five-year-olds. Small motor activities are still, however, necessary to help the child's small muscles keep growing. Drawing with pencils, crushing paper into shapes, modeling figures with clay, and making mobiles are examples of more advanced small motor activities.

In the art program, it is important to plan small muscle activities for older children, too. Older children soon enter school programs in which they learn to write or print. Working with small muscles in small motor-type art activities helps make learning to write much easier for the child.

The control over hand and finger movements used for finger painting and clay modeling is the same control the child needs to be able to write. Preschool art activities give the child a chance to practice and develop the small motor skills needed in schoolwork to come.

Large Muscle Development

Large muscles in the arms, legs, head, and trunk develop first. This is because all physical growth follows the pattern of large to small. In this pattern, large muscles develop first and small muscles develop later. The chart in figure 9-3, page 71, shows this pattern of growth.

By the time children reach the preschool art program, they are able to use large muscles quite well. They can walk, run, sit, and stand at will. They can use their arms and hands quite easily in large movements like clapping, climbing, and holding.

Just as with small muscles, the use of large muscles depends on the age of each child. Often, younger children are more involved in large motor play activities. Most three-year-olds and many four-year-olds are actively using their large muscles in running, wiggling, and jumping. This is the age group that is not yet

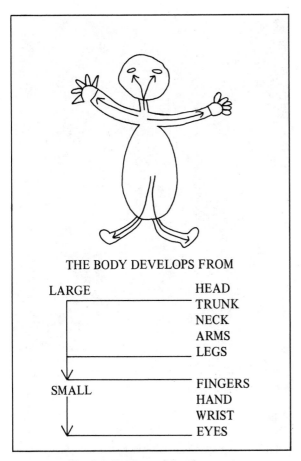

THE BODY DEVELOPS FROM

LARGE   HEAD
                      TRUNK
                      NECK
                      ARMS
                      LEGS

SMALL   FINGERS
                      HAND
                      WRIST
                      EYES

Fig. 9-3 Pattern of development.

Fig. 9-4 Easel painting provides good practice in using large muscles, which are exercised during wide arm movements.

Large and Small Motor Activities

as developed in small motor skills (like cutting) as five-year-olds.

The preschool art program gives the child a chance to practice large motor skills in many ways other than just in active games. Painting with a brush on a large piece of paper is good practice for wide arm movements. It is only by first developing these large motor skills that a child can develop small motor skills.

The art program should provide for practice with these large muscles. Some art activities for exercising large muscles are group murals, tracing body shapes, easel painting, clay pounding, crayon rubbings, and woodwork. Tools suitable for large muscle activities are large-sized paper, kindergarten crayons, wide brushes, and large amounts of modeling clay.

The preschool art program should have a good amount of both small and large motor tools and activities. A child needs to develop both large and small muscles, and artwork provides this chance. A small motor activity like cutting is fun as well as serious work for the child. Just as much fun and equally as important to the child's growth is painting large brush strokes at an easel. Painting combines both large and small motor skills. Small muscles are used to hold the brush, and large muscles are used for the wide arm movements.

The art teacher must respect each child's need to develop both large and small muscles at any age. This means a teacher must have the right equipment, but more important, the right attitude, for the level of each child. The right attitude is one that lets the child know it is all right to try many large and small motor-type activities at any age.

Fig. 9-5 The teacher should allow children to experiment with art materials, such as using two brushes at the same time to create a painting. This also helps large and small muscle coordination.

Fig. 9-6 One activity in which hand-eye coordination is used is finger painting.

In this type of art program, not all four-year-olds are expected to cut well, or even at all. Five-year-olds, as well as younger children, can enjoy pounding clay for no other purpose than the fun of pounding. In an art program with this type of freedom, a child naturally uses artwork in a way that helps large and small muscles grow.

Hand-Eye Coordination

In the art program, as children exercise their small and large muscles, they also improve their hand-eye coordination. *Hand-eye coordination* refers to the ability to use hand(s) and eyes at the same time. Painting is an example of hand-eye coordination. When children are painting, they are using their eyes to choose the colors, and their hands to hold and use the brush.

Hand-eye coordination is also used for clay modeling, making a mobile, pasting, and

finger painting. In all of these art activities, the child is receiving practice in *coordinating* (using together) the hands and eyes.

Hand-Eye Coordination and Reading

Hand-eye coordination is important for future schoolwork. Many reading experts feel that good hand-eye coordination helps a child learn to read. They feel that the ability to use hands and eyes together in things like painting or playing ball helps a child learn the motor skills needed in reading. Holding a book in two hands and using the eyes to read from left to right is simple hand-eye coordination. Hands and eyes are used at the same time.

Reading experts feel that the growth pattern of large-to-small muscles affects reading ability. In other words, reading experts feel that a child must have a chance to develop large muscles before being able to use small muscles — such as the eyes in the right-to-left movements of reading.

In artwork, a child gets the chance to exercise both large and small muscles. In this sense, art activities are important for future reading. Exercising hand-eye coordination and the two kinds of muscles in artwork helps prepare the child physically for reading.

Development of Motor Control

All of the above facts about muscle growth and hand-eye coordination are part of the growth of total motor control. Muscle growth and hand-eye coordination are parts of basic motor control — the control of the body.

When children grow in small and large muscle skills and in hand-eye coordination, they are growing in total motor control. The process of growing in motor control is seen as the child works in art.

Early scribbling is the beginning of motor control. The child holds the crayon and scribbles with very little motor control. As children grow in motor control, they can control the direction of their scribbles, then control lines to make basic forms, and finally draw pictures.

Therefore, a teacher can know about children's general control over their bodies by knowing the children's artwork. In this way, the teacher knows what the children can physically do in art as well as in other areas. For example, the teacher who knows that a certain five-year-old cannot yet cut with scissors knows how to reply to parents who ask if this child is ready for piano lessons. On the other hand, a teacher would know that a child is ready for more advanced puzzles by the way the child puts together and pastes objects on paper in a collage. Thus, knowing about each child's motor control in artwork helps the teacher know each child's motor control in other school areas.

ART AND MENTAL DEVELOPMENT

As children grow physically, they also grow mentally. This is because a young child learns by doing. The physical part and the mental part of growth go together. Learning by doing is what child psychologists call *sensorimotor learning.* Most children up to the age of about six or seven learn this way.

The word *sensorimotor* refers to the two words *sensory* and *motor.* Sensory refers to using the five body senses and motor refers to the physical act of doing. Sensorimotor learning involves the body and its senses (sensori) as they are used in doing (motor) an activity.

Sensorimotor Learning in Art

An example of sensorimotor learning in art is modeling with clay. In using clay (the motor activity), children use their senses (sensory), such as feel and smell, to learn about clay and how to use it. A teacher can tell the children how clay feels and how to use it; but children really learn about clay by physically using it themselves. A child must have this sensorimotor experience of learning by doing to truly learn mentally about clay, or any other art materials.

In the art program, children learn many things in this sensorimotor way — learning through doing. Many ideas, or concepts, are learned from different art activities. Just as children exercise different muscles in art activities, they also learn new concepts in many kinds of art activities.

Concepts Learned Through the Sense of Touch

Art activities that use the sense of touch teach children many important concepts. For example, working with clay helps children learn the concepts of hard and soft. The children feel the softness of clay in their hands through the sense of touch as they work with it. When the clay is old and needs water, the children feel how hard the clay has become. In using clay this way, children learn not only that clay is soft, but that clay can be hard, too.

Concepts like big and small can be learned by making or using clay balls in different sizes. Painting on different sizes of paper can be a learning experience about big and small.

Vocabulary and Art

A child's vocabulary (use of words) can grow through working with different materials. For example, in making a collage, a child can learn many new words to describe the feel of familiar things.

The teacher introduces words like soft and smooth to describe the feel of velvet material scraps. Scraps of burlap are called rough, bumpy, or scratchy. Even the word *texture* is one that can be used with young children. As they feel the different kinds of cloth, the different "feels" can easily be called "textures." Children then put together in their minds the feel of the velvet with the words soft, smooth, and texture. This is sensorimotor learning – learning through sensing as well as by association.

Improving the Sense of Touch in Art

In art activities, a child's sense of touch can be improved. For example, in the same

Fig. 9-7 In sensorimotor learning, children associate the feel of a spray of water with the word "wet."

collage activity, children learn to match scrap materials that have the same feel or texture. They match the ones that are soft and smooth (velvet and corduroy), the ones that are rough (burlap and wool), and the ones that are fuzzy (fur and cotton balls).

Making a collage can be an art activity as well as a touching game. This activity helps sharpen a child's sense of touch. A teacher can use this and many other art activities to help improve the sense of touch.

Art Activities Help Future Learning Experiences

Learning to notice the different way things feel – soft and hard, for example – teaches a child about concepts that are opposite. The concepts of opposite, or different, are used in subjects like math and science.

The difference between hard and soft is like the idea of adding and subtracting in math; both ideas are opposites. A child learns in art that soft is not the same as hard. In math, a child learns that adding is different from, or the opposite of, subtracting.

Mastering opposite concepts used in doing artwork helps the child learn the mental concepts needed in other school subjects. Learning basic ideas about opposites helps mentally prepare a child for school subjects in the future.

Concepts Learned Through Sense of Sight

Art activities involve the sense of sight as well as feel. A child sees and feels the art material being used. The sense of sight in artwork helps the child learn many important concepts.

Color Concepts. Concepts about colors are learned in the art program. While painting and drawing, children learn the names of colors, how to mix colors, and how to make colors lighter or darker. They "learn by doing" (sensorimotor learning) that colors are not set things, but things that the children, themselves, can change. This is an important thing for the child to know. It is a concept about change that can be used in many other subjects and situations.

Concept of Change. By using color, mixing colors, and making color lighter or darker, the child learns that things can go through the process of change. Clay can change from hard to soft. Plaster can change from liquid to solid.

"Learning by doing" in art helps a child grow mentally. The child learns to think of some things in the process of change and not as permanent things. The ability to think this way is called *reverse thinking.* This type of thinking is shown in chart form in figure 9-8.

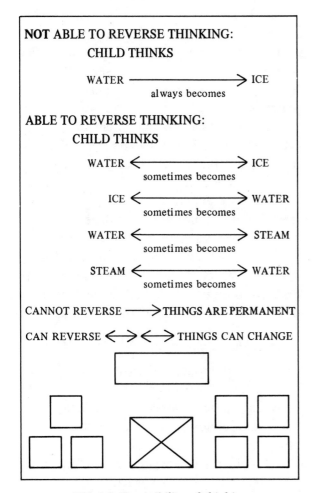

Fig. 9-8 Reversibility of thinking.

Being able to reverse and change their thinking helps children become mentally prepared for school. Math, spelling, and science all use this type of thinking — thinking that accepts change (reverse thinking). In science, a lesson on ice is about the changes water goes through in the process of becoming ice. Division problems are examples of how numbers change. How single words become plural is an example of change found in spelling.

Other Concepts Learned Through Sense of Sight

Just as with the sense of touch, many important concepts are learned through the sense of sight. The child sees the sameness and the difference in size, color, shape, and texture when working with different materials. Children learn concepts like big-small and wide-thin by using many types of art materials. A child sees that different sizes of crayons make different sizes of lines. Wide brushes make paint strokes that look different from strokes made with a thin brush. The child learns that a figure drawn with a felt-tip pen looks different than the same figure made with paint and a brush.

Ideas about basic shapes are learned in cutting with scissors, working with clay, painting, and drawing. A child also finds many basic shapes in the scrap materials used for a collage.

In artwork, the child sees how things can look alike but feel different. Sand and cornmeal may look alike, but they feel different to the child as they are glued onto paper. In this way, a child learns that the sense of sight alone is not enough to really learn about a material.

Improving the Sense of Sight in Art

The sense of sight can be improved in art activities just as with the sense of touch. Learning to see things as clearly as possible is part of mental growth.

Fig. 9-9 While making a collage, a child learns about basic shapes by looking at and handling various scrap materials.

The teacher who encourages children to really look around them for art ideas helps the children sharpen their sense of sight. Encouraging children to tell about what they see as they look out the window on a familiar scene is one way to improve looking.

The teacher may ask children to tell about all they see outside the window. This way, the teacher encourages the children to really look hard at the everyday scene and not miss a detail. This close-looking exercise teaches children to really see their surroundings — not just to glance at the familiar things.

Seeing the differences between colors is another way in which art helps sharpen mental growth through the sense of sight. Making different shades of red by adding a little bit more of white each time is one way to train the eye to become sharper in seeing the fine differences between colors. Picking out and matching colors of paper from a pile of mixed colors is another way that artwork trains the eyes to see better.

Being able to see small and large differences is an important part of physical and mental growth. Good observation skills help in science, reading, and math at a later time.

Hearing, Tasting, and Smelling in Art

Art activities help a child grow mentally by improving the child's sense of hearing. Hearing and listening well are important to a child's good physical and mental growth. Being able to hear and follow directions in art activities is good exercise for hearing sense. Learning to listen well in art makes learning in other subjects easier. Really hearing an explanation of how to mix up play dough makes it easier for the children to make the play dough by themselves. Later in school, a child uses this same good hearing sense that was learned in art to really hear and listen to a math lesson on adding.

Smelling and tasting often are part of artwork, especially for the younger child, who learns about things by tasting and smelling as well as by the other senses. It is an important sensorimotor experience for children. They learn mental concepts about differences between hard and soft by tasting with their tongues as well as by feeling with their hands. To learn mental concepts about things that are different or opposite, a child can use the sense of smell as well as the senses of sight and touch.

Art and Mental Attitude

The art program must be a place where children are free to explore ideas with both body and mind. Doing artwork in this way helps the child develop a creative mental attitude.

Children have creative mental attitudes when they are open to new and different ideas and are eager to experiment and try new things.

Fig. 9-10 A child may learn the mental concept for "frank-furter" by using more than one sense — such as touch, smell, taste, and sight. Mental concepts that are attached to these senses are also part of artwork.

This creative mental attitude can grow only in a program that allows children the freedom, time, and place to experiment.

Children must have the feeling that the "doing" is more important than whether they succeed or fail. In the art program, one of the most important goals should be for the child to develop a creative mental attitude. This creative mental attitude helps the child work well and enjoy art as well as all other curriculum areas.

ART AND THE TOTAL PROGRAM

The preschool art program helps a young child grow in social, emotional, physical, and mental ways. The art program gives children a chance to be themselves and grow at their own individual paces.

Art should not be the only part of the preschool program where this growth can occur, however. Freedom for growing at the child's own pace should be part of the whole preschool program. The exploring, creating, and relaxing parts of artwork should be part of all the other preschool activities.

Art helps a child grow through creative ways of thinking and feeling, not only about art but about all other things. The confidence and good feelings about themselves and their work that children get in art also apply to other things in and out of school.

Seen in this way, art cannot be thought of as a separate part of the program. It is and always must be a unit inseparable from all the rest.

SUMMARY

Young children learn mentally as they do things physically. In the art program, a child learns many important concepts or ideas that are used later in other learning experiences. Art activities give the child a chance to learn through the use of the body, senses, and mind.

The child learns important concepts like hard-soft and same-different by doing artwork. Artwork helps in developing a child's mental abilities: learning to think in terms of change (reversibility), being able to see fine differences, and being able to hear and listen well. Finally, art helps the child develop a creative mental attitude which will be applied to all school subjects. Art is an attitude that cannot and should not be separate from the total preschool program.

STUDENT ACTIVITIES

The following activities are designed to help the child exercise both small and large muscle skills and develop hand-eye coordination. Students should try the activities themselves, with classmates, and with children.

- **Small Motor Activities**

    A. String Pictures[1]

    1. Dip yarn or string in a mixture of paint and white glue.

    2. Then make designs on colored paper.

    B. Printing[2]

    1. Provide several pie tins of different colored easel paints.

    2. Let children "print" by dipping a variety of objects into the paint and making impressions on absorbent paper. For printing, use such objects as vegetables, hair curlers, nuts, bolts, kitchen utensils, and plastic table toys.

    3. Very young children tend to make a painting or scribbling experience out of this. Kitchen tools with handles, such as mashers and cooky cutters, are good for beginners.

    C. Sticky Paper Art

    1. Cut up colored sticky tape into many sizes and shapes. (The children can help in cutting the tape.)

    2. The children glue the sticky tape pieces in a design on colored paper. (Colored paper could be cut into a heart for Valentine's Day, a shamrock for St. Patrick's Day, a pine tree for Christmas.)

    D. Crayon Scratching

    1. The children make small crayon drawings (about 4 inches by 6 inches). They then color their whole drawing with a heavy coat of black crayon.

    2. When they scratch a design in the black crayon layer with a pen tip, paper clip, or pin, the colors underneath will come through in the design.

[1] Doreen J. Croft and Robert D. Hess, *An Activities Handbook for Teachers of Young Children* (Boston, 1972), p. 89.
[2] Ibid.

E. Carbon Paper and Pencils

  1. Obtain pieces of carbon paper (new or used) and a supply of large pencils or ballpoint pens.

  2. Children draw and make "copies" as they draw.

- **Large Motor Activities**

A. Roll Painting[3]

  1. Fill empty roll-on deodorant bottles with slightly thickened tempera.

  2. Let children use at the art table for making designs on paper.

B. Crayon Rubbings

  1. Provide large pieces of newsprint and large crayons. Show the children interesting textures such as wood and cement around the room.

  2. When they put the paper over the surface and rub with the side of the crayon, the texture comes out as a design on the paper.

C. Mixing Soap

  1. Children enjoy mixing up a solution of soap and water with egg beaters to make it sudsy.

  2. The water can be colored with food coloring for variety.

D. Sand Painting (Individuals or Group)

  1. Spread glue on a large piece of paper.

  2. Children drop sand onto the glue. (Shake the extra sand off.)

  3. The children may make a mural, working together on one large piece of paper.

E. Clay Cookies and Cakes

  1. Have a clay party.

  2. The children pound cooky shapes, dish shapes, cake shapes, and similar items.

- **Hand-Eye Coordination Activities**

A. Water Pouring

  1. Set up a pan filled with water.

  2. Provide different-sized plastic containers, squeeze bottles, funnels, and strainers.

  3. The children enjoy pouring water from one container to another.

[3] Ibid.

B. Beanbag Toss

   1. Make a large circle on the floor with a rope.

   2. Children aim and toss a beanbag into it.

C. Block Bowling

   1. Set up a long unit block on the floor.

   2. The children sit in a circle around it.

   3. Each child has a chance to knock it down by rolling the ball at it.

D. Music and Painting

   1. Play music while the children paint.

   2. Suggest that they make their strokes go with the music's rhythm.

E. Ball Rolling

   1. Play catch with the children who are able, or roll the ball to the children who cannot catch yet.

   2. Notice which ones can catch and return the ball.

   3. Compare this ability with their motor control in art.

F. Painting with Water (Outside Activity)

   1. Fill a bucket with water and let the children "paint" the building or sidewalk with water.

   2. The children should use large "real" paintbrushes (1 1/2 inches — 2 inches wide) and buckets of water small enough to be carried around.

- **Activities for Checking Motor Control**

   A. Artwork Samples

      1. Collect examples of artwork from children aged two — six years.

      2. Divide up the examples into the degree of children's motor control as seen in the examples.

   B. Obstacle Course

      1. Make an obstacle course of chairs, tables, or blocks to climb under, over, or around.

      2. Notice how easy or difficult it is for children aged three, four, and five.

      3. Compare the abilities of three-, four-, and five-year-olds.

   C. Action Songs

      1. Sing an action song, such as, "If you're happy and you know it," using different directions: "clap your hands," "clap your

hands and tap your head," "clap your hands and shake your head."

2. Notice which children can do the combined actions and which can do the single actions.

3. Note their ages.

D. Rope Games

1. Put a long rope on the floor in a zigzag pattern and have the children walk on it. Note how many of the children can do this and how well they can do it.

or

2. Put the rope in a straight line and pretend it is a tightrope. The children "walk the tightrope" with a real or pretend umbrella in their hands for balance. Note the balancing ability of each child.

or

3. Two children take turns holding the rope very high at first and then gradually lower and lower. The rest of the children go under the rope without touching it.

or

4. Place the rope straight out on the floor. The children walk across it, hop on one foot across it, hop on two feet across it, crawl across it, jump across it, and cross it any other way they can think of. Note each child's physical control.

- **Activities for the Senses**

The following activities are designed to exercise the senses. Students should try the activities themselves, with classmates, and with children.

Seeing Activities

A. Game With a Magnifying Glass

1. Provide the children with a magnifying glass and a tray full of different objects — stamps, coins, leaves, and so on.

2. Use the magnifying glass to look at your fingernail and a child's fingernail, a bug, and the other things in the tray.

3. Ask the children to look carefully and to tell what they see. Use the magnifying glass outside on a nature walk. Encourage the children to talk about what they see. This helps them to express ideas and learn new words.

B. Paper Towel Telescope and Binoculars

1. Use rolls from paper towels for making telescopes.

    2. The children look through the rolls out a door or window.

    3. Ask them to tell all about what they can see. Two bathroom tissue rolls can be taped together for binoculars and used in the same way as the telescope.

C. Classifying Objects by Their Properties[4]

Problem: In what ways are things alike and different?

Materials: three cigar boxes
contact paper
assortment of buttons; large variety of objects of different shapes and materials, such as marbles, dice, erasers, bolts, bottle caps, coins, spools, plastic objects, pieces of cloth, paper clips, etc.

Procedure: 1. Cover cigar boxes with contact paper.

    2. Draw buttons on the lid of one box and fill with buttons.

    3. Draw pictures of objects with round, square, triangular, and rectangular shapes on another box.

    4. Draw pictures of objects made of different kinds of materials on the last box.

    5. Fill each box with appropriate objects for sorting.

    6. Have children sort according to size, shape, color, texture, and materials from which each is made (metal, plastic, wood, cloth).

Conclusion: Things are alike and different because of their color, shape, size, the way they feel, and the things they are made from.

D. Examining Objects in Different Colors[5]

    1. Use different colored pieces of transparent plastic or colored cellophane.

    2. The children look at the things around them through transparent, colored material. They can see how the brown table looks through "yellow" or how the blue sky looks through "red," for example.

    3. When the children seem to understand how the color of different objects changes when seen through another color and have been satisfied using just a single color, they may look through two colors at once (superimpose red over blue) and see still another change.

[4]Ibid., p. 67.

[5]Iris M. Silverblatt, *Creative Activities* (Cincinnati, 1964), p. 16.

E. Mixing Paints[6]

1. Six saucers, six teaspoons, and paint (red, blue, yellow, as a start) are needed.
    Each child may experiment with mixing paints while painting a picture.

2. A small amount of each color of paint may be placed in each of three saucers — a dish of red, one of blue, and one of yellow. Put a spoon in each and let the child mix the various colors in the three empty saucers.

3. A styrofoam egg carton may be used for mixing the colors. Prepare three separate juice cans of color (one red, one blue, and one yellow). Put an eyedropper in each can. The child drops the colors into each of the separate cups in the egg carton and mixes them with a tongue depressor or wooden stick. The egg carton can be rinsed out for another child's use.

F. Prism[7]

1. Hang a prism in an area where it will be in the direct rays of the sun.

2. Call attention to the different colors seen in the prism itself and to those reflected on the wall.

3. Relate these colors to the colors seen in a rainbow.

4. Be on the lookout for a real rainbow and/or provide pictures of rainbows.

G. What are some things you can tell with your eyes[8]?

Materials: Objects which feel the same but look different, such as different colored apples, crayons, or cups; paper with and without pictures or printing, etc.

Procedure: 1. Have children close their eyes.

2. Let each child hold an object and determine what it is.

3. Have the child describe all the properties of the object without looking.

4. Ask questions about each object such as:
    Is it rough or smooth?
    Is it hard or soft?
    Is it round or flat?

[6] Ibid.
[7] Ibid., p. 17.
[8] Croft and Hess, p. 66.

What color is it?

Is there a design on it?

Conclusions: 1. One's eyes can tell a person about the color of things.

2. One's eyes can tell if things have designs or printing or pictures on them.

Feeling Activities

A.   Different Objects to Feel — A feeling game

1.   Encourage the children to feel cotton first and then a piece of sponge against their skin.

2.   Talk about the hardness and softness of each.

3.   Ask them to feel a rock and then a chair.

4.   Talk about the hardness of each.

5.   Then have them touch the cotton and sponge again.

6.   Encourage them to talk about how these objects feel.

B.   Paper Bag With Objects

1.   Fill a paper bag with common objects, such as a pencil, ball, comb, key, wallet, coins.

2.   Each of the children puts one of their hands in the bag (with eyes closed) and feels one object.

3.   The child must decide what the object is and describe it. (Add more and different items to make the game harder.)

C.   Touching Game With Textures

1.   Fill a box with two pieces each of sandpaper, glass, rock, plastic, wood, cotton, corduroy, or velvet.

2.   Take out a piece of sandpaper. Tell the children what it is and how it feels. (Rough)

3.   Let each of them feel it.

4.   Ask a child to find the other piece of sandpaper in the box.

5.   Repeat for all the other items. Everyone has a turn to match up the textures.

6.   Vary this activity by walking around the room to find things that are hard, soft, smooth, rough. This variation may be done outside, also.

Hearing Activities

A.   Sound Experiments

1.   The children may close their eyes and name the different sounds they hear in the room.

2. Make up noises and sounds (birds singing, blocks dropping, sawing wood, bells, drums and other instruments, tearing paper, water splashing, for example). Have the children guess what they are.

3. A child may close both eyes while another child speaks. The first child tries to guess who is speaking.

B. Recognizing Sounds[9]

Purpose: Recognizing sounds

Materials: Bag or box with lid
Noisemaking objects, such as a bell, rattle, whistle, paper (to tear), pieces of sandpaper (to rub together), cricket, horn

Procedure: 1. Say:
"We are going to play a listening game.
When we are listening what do we hear? Noises.
Every day we hear lots of noises.
What do we hear the noises with? Ears.
Take your hand and wiggle your earlobes, like this. I have a box with some things in it that make noises. I am going to make a sound and then ask who can tell me what is used to make that sound. Cover your eyes with your hands."

2. Make a sound with one of the objects and ask who knows what object made the sound.

3. Go through the entire selection of objects, trying to call on each child.

4. When the children become more skillful at identifying the sounds, have them cover their eyes while you make two sounds. Ask if the sounds were the same.

5. After this first introduction, the children can play this in a group by taking turns being the one who chooses the noisemakers.

C. Hearing and Repeating Sound Sequences[10]

Purpose: Hearing and repeating sound sequences

Materials: Noisemaking objects: bell, rattle, sandpaper, paper (to tear), wooden blocks (to hit together).

[9]Ibid., p. 15.
[10]Ibid., p. 16.

Procedure: 1. Start with three objects on the table.

2. Hold up one object and ask if anyone knows what it is called and what it does.

3. Pass it around and let each child use it. Do the same with the other two objects.

4. Say:
"I am going to make three noises. First I will shake this rattle, then I will ring the bell, and last I will tear the paper. What noise did you hear first? What noise did you hear next? What noise did you hear last?"

5. Give another example.

6. Ask the children to cover their eyes with their hands.

7. Have them listen carefully to more noises and then have them make the same noise.

8. Add new objects and increase the number used.

9. Introduce sounds they can make (clapping, stamping, tongue clicking).

Smelling and Tasting Activities

A. Tasting Activity

1. Place small pieces of cheese, apple, carrot, and banana on a tray. Show the tray to the children. Ask them to identify the foods on the tray and tell where they come from.

2. Give each child a turn to taste each of the foods with both eyes shut. Ask the children to identify each food they eat.

3. Try the activity again, tasting different drinks, such as milk, water, soda, and orange juice.

B. Smell-o-gram[11]

1. Collect items for a smelling game with a group of children. Use a variety of things: perfume, bacon, clay, paint, wood shavings, flowers, chocolate, soap, onions, and spices.

2. The children close their eyes and try to identify familiar odors of objects held in front of them.

3. Encourage sensitivity to different kinds of odors, for example, outdoor odors after a spring rain, food cooking, and so forth.

C. How Do Different Things Taste?[12]

Problem: How do different things taste?

[11]Silverblatt, p. 22.

[12] Croft and Hess, p. 66.

Materials: Variety of common foods, such as apples, popcorn, bread, dry cereal, peanut butter, etc.

Procedure: 1. Have children close their eyes.

2. Put a small amount of food in each child's mouth.

3. Have the children guess what they are tasting.

4. Have the children hold their noses as well as close their eyes.

5. Place food in their mouths and have them guess what they are tasting.

Conclusions: 1. Different things taste different.

2. Smelling something helps to tell how it tastes.

D. Community Fruit Salad

1. To further experiment with how things taste, the children may help make a community fruit salad. Each child brings a different fruit: apples, peaches, pears, seedless grapes, tangerines.

2. The children help peel bananas and oranges, wash grapes, and cut the fruit with blunt or serrated knives.

3. The children should taste each fruit separately as they are preparing the salad. Then they should taste how the fruits taste together.

4. Talk about how each fruit tastes, looks, and smells different from the others.

REVIEW

I. Physical Development

A. Define motor development.

B. List three examples of locations of small muscles.

C. Define small motor activities and give three examples.

D. Define large motor activities and give three examples.

E. List three examples of locations of large muscles.

F. Tell whether each of the following activities helps a child develop a small or a large motor skill.

1. Tracing body forms	5. Finger puppets
2. Using scissors	6. Painting with a brush
3. Pounding clay	7. Pounding nails
4. Finger painting	8. Clay modeling

G. Choose the answer which best completes each statement describing a child's motor development in art.

1. Most three-year-olds
   a. have good small muscle development.
   b. do not have good small muscle development.
   c. have good small and large muscle development.

2. One way to check small motor skill is by having a child
   a. pound on clay.
   b. walk a balance board.
   c. cut paper with blunt scissors.

3. Good tools for large muscle activities are
   a. large-sized paper and wide brushes.
   b. small-sized paper and thin brushes.
   c. any size paper and any width brushes.

4. Development of the body goes from
   a. small muscles to large muscles.
   b. large muscles to small muscles.
   c. arms to legs.

5. In order to be able to use small muscles, a child must first be able to use
   a. finger muscles.
   b. large muscles.
   c. eye muscles.

6. By the time children are in preschool, they can use
   a. small muscles quite well.
   b. both large and small muscles quite well.
   c. large muscles quite well.

7. An art activity that exercises large motor skills is
   a. painting on large-sized paper with a wide brush.
   b. cutting paper with scissors.
   c. finger painting.

8. In planning the art program, a teacher should include
   a. mostly large motor activities for four-year-olds.
   b. mostly small motor activities for three-year-olds.
   c. both large and small motor activities for all ages.

9. The age group that uses mostly large muscle activity is the
   a. three-year-old.
   b. four-year-old.
   c. five-year-old.

10. A teacher in the art program should let children know that they are free to

    a. use only small motor activity.
    b. try all types of activities.
    c. try only large motor activity.

H. Define hand-eye coordination and give two examples of it.

I. Discuss what reading experts say about the importance of hand-eye coordination.

J. Describe how one can see motor control develop in a child's artwork.

II. Mental Development

A. Define sensorimotor learning and give one example of it.

B. Which of the following mental concepts does a child learn in art by the sense of touch?

a. New words	f. Names of colors
b. Hard-soft	g. Feel of clay
c. True-false	h. Difference in shades of color
d. Large-small	i. Feel of play dough
e. Smooth-rough	j. Sweet-sour

C. Choose the answer which best completes each of the following statements about how art helps mental development.

1. Concepts are

    a. phrases.
    b. songs.
    c. ideas.

2. The mental concept of opposites learned in art is also used in

    a. math.
    b. finger plays.
    c. cooking.

3. Introducing new words in art activity

    a. often confuses the children.
    b. helps improve the child's vocabulary.
    c. has little effect on young children.

4. An example of an activity that improves the sense of touch is

    a. a piano lesson.
    b. work on a collage.
    c. a seeing game.

5. Some concepts of color a child learns in art are

    a. how to erase color errors, to paint over, and to choose colors.

    b. how to choose colors, mix colors, and color over.

    c. names of colors, how to mix colors, and how to make colors lighter or darker.

6. An important new way of thinking that a child learns in art is

    a. reversibility.

    b. irreversibility.

    c. permanent thinking.

7. Seeing and learning that clay can have many shapes and textures helps the child develop

    a. irreversibility of thought.

    b. permanent thinking.

    c. reversibility of thought.

8. In artwork, very young children often use the senses of

    a. touch and sight only.

    b. smell, taste, touch, sight, and hearing.

    c. touch and smell only.

D. Discuss development of a creative mental attitude as a goal in the art program for young children.

E. Discuss what other aspects of the preschool program should be like the art program.

F. Should art be considered a separate part of the preschool program? Explain your answer.

The Arts and Crafts Program

Unit 10 BASICS OF ARTS AND CRAFTS

OBJECTIVES

After studying this unit, the student will be able to

- Discuss the importance of arts and crafts in the preschool program.
- List the basic equipment required for the arts and crafts program.
- Describe the basic objectives and techniques required for the teacher of arts and crafts.

The arts and crafts program is a part of the preschool curriculum in which young children have the chance to work with many kinds of materials and use many techniques to make an original end product. The things a child makes in the arts and crafts program are as varied as the ways to make them. For example, an original end product in arts and crafts may be a collage, a puppet, or a crayon drawing.

THE IMPORTANCE OF THE ARTS AND CRAFTS PROGRAM

The arts and crafts program gives the child a time and place to put together thoughts, ideas, feelings, actions, and abilities into a product. The goal in arts and crafts is not how this product looks, but the process of making it. It is in the process of making a product that the child expresses experience and feelings. The expression of feelings is what is important here, not what the object looks like.

Children take paints, bits of cloth, clay, wood, and/or stone, and put them together into products which express their own ideas. In the arts and crafts program, the emphasis must be on continued satisfying experiences with many kinds of materials and a continued

Fig. 10-1 Creative works in the arts and crafts program are often an expression of each child's individual experiences and feelings.

involvement in the process of making. Success in arts and crafts helps children feel self-confident about themselves and their abilities.

ARTS AND CRAFTS AT DIFFERENT AGES

Children at different ages have varying abilities in work with arts and crafts. This is because of the difference in muscle control and coordination at each age level.

The Three-Year-Old

Three-year-olds are developing good motor (muscle) control mainly with large muscles.

Fig. 10-2 Three-year-olds often have trouble buttoning their own clothes because their small muscles are not yet well developed.

They are sure on their feet and good with arm and leg movements. The small muscles in their fingers, hands, and wrists are not yet well developed. Dressing is difficult because they lack good small motor control. Buttoning and unbuttoning is a small motor task often too hard for the three-year-old's small muscles to handle.

In arts and crafts, this means an activity like cutting with scissors is not easy, or sometimes is not even possible for many three-year-olds. The small muscles in the fingers, hands, and wrists are not yet developed enough to handle cutting or any similar activity very well.

The arts and crafts program gives the three-year-olds a chance for self-expression, and a time to use small and large muscles. Using scissors, pasting, and drawing are examples of activities that help the child develop small muscles through practice.

The Four-Year-Old

Four-year-old children have good large muscle control. They are also beginning to have better control over small muscles. Because they have more muscle control, they can usually dress themselves. Cutting is not as difficult at this age level. The four-year-old can try a number of art materials that the three-year-old could not. Using plaster molds, making puppets, and printing are some activities in which the four-year-old may practice control over small muscles, as well as self-expression in art.

The Five-Year-Old

By the time children are five years old, they usually have good control over both large and small muscles. At this age level, the arts and crafts program should provide the greatest variety of materials for exercise of muscle control, as well as for self-expression.

Because the five-year-old has the physical ability to do many kinds of things, the arts and crafts program must provide a variety of tools and techniques. Choosing materials for this age is a matter of knowing what is most creative and interesting for the five-year-old. Since the child can handle most kinds of material by this age, the arts and crafts program must now be supplied with equipment to keep up the child's interest. New uses for familiar media, new techniques, and new materials help to encourage the child's continued interest in arts and crafts, which is vital for growth and self-expression.

OBJECTIVES OF THE PROGRAM

The most basic objective of the arts and crafts program is to meet the needs of the children in it. This means that it must be designed to meet their level in age, ability, and interest. Thus, a program for three-year-olds is set up to have the right material and activities for a group which has a limited span of interest and limited motor control. It has material and activities that interest them, and that they can use without a lot of adult help. The same applies to arts and crafts for four- and five-year-olds. In a mixed age group, the program must be set up so that a variety of materials and activities are available for all children in the group.

Another important objective of the arts and crafts program is to give each child the

Fig. 10-3 **One important objective of the arts and crafts program is to give each child the opportunity to experiment with materials and work independently.**

chance to think originally and to learn to work independently. In work with art, a child has the chance to use and explore all kinds of materials. This encourages original thought. Also, giving children material that they can control at their physical level encourages independent work. These two things (originality and ability to work on their own) are basic to children's creativity.

Another goal in an arts and crafts program is that children learn to be creative thinkers. Creative children work freely and flexibly. They attack each problem without the fear of failure. Children in an arts and crafts program that is right for their level are able to work creatively, freely, and flexibly. They can handle the material in this setting, which helps them feel more sure of themselves.

Finally, the arts and crafts program must allow children to grow at their own speed. Activities may be planned to stimulate children,

Fig. 10-4 **If the arts and crafts program is geared to the children's developmental levels, it enables the children to work more creatively, freely, and flexibly.**

but true growth comes only at their own pace. Just as children learn to walk on their own, they learn to paint by painting in their own way.

Respecting each child's rate of growth helps children feel good about themselves. Children who feel good about themselves can be successful in the arts and crafts program and in other learning situations, too.

BASIC EQUIPMENT FOR THE PROGRAM

In setting up a room for arts and crafts, the age of the group must be kept in mind. As each age group has varying abilities, some different equipment is necessary for each.

Some basic materials are the same for all ages. The following is a general list of materials needed in the arts and crafts program. In choosing from the list, the teacher must keep in mind the motor control and coordination of the children in the group.

- Crayoning Materials
    1. Sturdy sheets of paper (manila or newsprint, eight by twelve inches or twelve by eighteen inches). Spread the paper on a table or on the floor, or pin it to a wall or easel.
    2. A basket of jumbo crayons about three-quarters of an inch in width. These are a good size for the muscle control of small fingers. Unwrap the crayons so they can be used on both the sides and the ends.
- Chalking Materials
    1. A blackboard and eraser, and/or a stack of wet or dry (or both) paper.
    2. A container full of colored and white chalk.
- Brush Painting Materials
    1. Two easels (at least) with two blunt-tipped nails sticking out near each

upper corner to attach the paper. (Or paper can be held on the board with spring-type clothespins.) Easels must be at the right height so that a child can paint without stretching or stooping.
    2. Sheets of paper (eighteen by twenty-four-inch plain newsprint), white or in assorted colors.
    3. Three or four jars of tempera (poster) paint.
    4. Paint containers. These must have flat bottoms so they will not tip over easily. Quart size milk cartons (cut down) are good as they can be thrown away after using.
    5. Large, long-handled brushes in each jar. Those with twelve-inch handles and three-quarter-inch bristle length are easy for young children to use.
    6. Smocks. An old shirt with the sleeves cut to the child's arm length makes a practical smock. Oilcloth or plastic aprons are also good.
    7. A place to dry finished paintings.
- Finger Painting Materials
    1. Paper that has a shiny surface. This can be butcher paper, shelf paper, or special finger paint paper.
    2. A water supply to make the paper damp. A damp sponge or rag works best.
    3. Finger paint. This can be special finger painting paint or dry tempera paint mixed with liquid starch or liquid detergent to make a thick mixture.
    4. Racks to dry the finished work. Cake-cooling racks work well for this.

Fig. 10-5 A smock keeps a finger painter's clothes clean while experimenting with the paints.

    5. A smock for each painter.

    6. A nearby sink and running water for washing hands and cleaning up.

- Pasting Materials

    1. Small jars of school paste. (Or give each child a square of waxed paper with a spoonful of paste on it. This prevents waste.) A wooden tongue depressor is a good tool for spreading the paste, or paste can be spread with the fingers.

    2. Sheets of plain or colored manila or construction paper in many sizes.

    3. Collage materials. Some of these can be paper shapes in different colors, scraps of cloth, feathers, yarn, tinfoil, string, beans, sawdust, and any other things that look interesting.

    4. Blunt scissors, for both left- and right-handed children.

Fig. 10-6 Collage materials can be anything from scraps of cloth to beans, as long as they are interesting to the children.

- Puppet Materials

    1. Paper bags in any size.

    2. Scissors, colored papers, paste, paints and/or crayons, tape, and stapler.

    3. Sticks for stick puppets. Some kinds are yardsticks, twigs, wood scrap sticks, and tongue depressors.

    4. Cardboard rolls for tube puppets.

    5. Socks or mittens for sock and mitten puppets.

    6. Styrofoam balls for heads.

    7. Miscellaneous material to make faces: buttons, pins, old jewelry, and yarn.

- Scrap Art Materials

    1. Paste, glue, tape, and stapler.

    2. Colored tissue paper.

    3. Colored sticky tape, gummed circles, stars, and/or designs.

    4. Tempera paint, chalk, crayons, and felt-tipped pens.

    5. Odds and ends of scrap material — egg cartons, styrofoam pieces, plastic containers and lids, pine cones, feathers, and buttons.

Fig. 10-7 A puppet is easy to make out of everyday items such as a paper bag, some bits of cloth, yarn, ribbons, and buttons.

- Clay Work Materials

    1. Real clay kept in an airtight container.

    2. Clay table. Use a table with a formica top or any table that is easy to clean. (Or use large pieces of plastic spread out on the table, or cut one for each child's use.)

    3. Tools for clay work like toy rolling pins, cooky cutters, spoons, and blunt plastic knives.

- Papier Maché Materials

    1. Newspaper.

    2. Water.

    3. Wheat paste, wallpaper paste, or laundry starch.

    4. Mixing bowl.

    5. Tempera (poster) paint.

    6. Recipe for papier maché.

Fig. 10-8 Although children can be supplied with rolling pins and cookie cutters to use with clay, sometimes all they need is the clay and their own imaginations.

- Woodwork Materials

    1. A bin of soft lumber pieces (leftover scraps of lumber).

    2. Supply of nails with large heads.

    3. Wooden spools, corks, and twigs.

    4. Wooden buttons, string, ribbons to be nailed to wood or tied to heads of nails already hammered into the wood.

    5. Bottle caps.

    6. Small-sized real tools. Hammer and nails are best to start with. Saws, screwdrivers, a vise, and a drill may be added later.

    7. Workbench.

    8. Sandpaper.

BASIC TECHNIQUES FOR THE PROGRAM

After choosing the right materials for the arts and crafts program, a teacher must know how to use the materials with the children.

- Tear newspaper into 1/2-inch strips or shred paper into small pieces.
- Soak paper in water for 24 hours.
- Squeeze out excess water and add flour paste, wallpaper paste, or laundry starch.
- Let the children help mix.
- Paper strips can be molded alone or over a balloon or wire figure.

Fig. 10-9 Papier mache´ recipe.

Some points to keep in mind to help in proper use of the materials are listed.

- When dealing with children who have had little or no contact with the art material, a teacher must be aware that children will be exploring and experimenting with the materials most of the time. In such cases, it is important to begin with just the basics: crayons or one or two colors of paint with plain paper; clay or play dough; one type of object to use with paste and paper.
- Activities should be simple and free from too much extra material, which may distract the children.
- When the children are ready, the teacher may gradually provide more complex materials. Variety can be added later, after the children have had enough time to really explore and experiment with the basics.
- Avoid making models for children to copy.
- Avoid asking the children what they are making. They are expressing themselves. The process is more important than the product.
- Avoid comparing one child's work with another's and judging the work.
- Let the children explore and experiment with the materials in their own way, with the least possible amount of adult direction.

Fig. 10-10 For children who are not very familiar with the use of art material, it is important to begin with the most basic equipment, such as crayons and paper.

- Set up the activity in an area where the children can be free to create.
- Give the children plain paper to use. This encourages creativity.

SPECIFIC TECHNIQUES

To keep the materials and activities in the arts and crafts program running in good order and with the least amount of trouble, the teacher should know specific techniques for each activity. In any arts and crafts activity that is messy, the teacher should be prepared for the situation.

Painting

An activity like painting should be done in a part of the room near running water. Floors, tables, or anything that must be kept paint-free should be covered before starting any messy activity. Each child should wear a smock to prevent soiling clothes. Painting should be done in an area away from large-motor games, toys, or activities like blocks, rocking boats, and climbing toys.

At the easel, it may help children to see that if they wipe the brush on the side of the jar the paint does not drip or run. An adult can show the children that keeping each brush in its own paint jar keeps the color clear. Children can be shown that color can be mixed on paper by brushing one color over another.

For finger painting, prepared finger paints may be used, or the children may help mix the recipe given in figure 10-11. If the recipe is used, the mixture may be separated into three or four parts and coloring added — either food color or the powdered paint used for easel painting. Children like to add their own color; they may use salt shakers containing powered paint and mix in the color with their fingers. Adding soap flakes (not detergents) to the paint mixture increases variety.

Finger Painting Procedure. For finger painting activity, the tables should be covered with linoleum, formica, or plastic, and children should wear aprons. The work area should be placed nearby. Plenty of paper towels and clean rags should be provided. Smooth-surfaced paper is used. It must be dipped in a pan of water and spread flat on a table.

A large tablespoonful of each color is placed on the paper for each child. The children may choose the colors they want. They must be allowed to experiment as they wish with the paint, using their fingers, the palms of the hands or wrists.

Note: Another method for finger painting is to cover a table with white oilcloth and let the children work on the oilcloth. The mixture can later be washed off with a hose, or under a faucet. This activity is good for all ages.

- Mix dry tempera paint with about one-half cup liquid starch or liquid dishwashing detergent.
- Add the liquid starch gradually until desired thickness is reached.
- Paint extender can also be added to dry tempera paint.

Fig. 10-11 Finger paint recipe.

The children must be shown where to put their paintings and where to get a cloth to wipe up. If necessary, the children should be reminded to wash their hands before taking off their smocks.

Easel Painting Procedure. Easel painting requires running water, a work shelf area, and paint supply shelves at child height. In some centers, a stool or steps are needed so children can reach an adult-height sink.

Each jar of blue tempera (poster) paint should be labeled with a strip of blue paper clearly printed blue. (Use the same label idea for each color.) Brushes should be thoroughly washed and in good condition. This makes the need for their care and washing more obvious to the children. Children must be shown how to mix the dry paint into a liquid. The teacher must also show them the kind of wiping up and washing needed in cleanup.

At the end of each day, all paintbrushes are washed thoroughly in running water and dried before being put away. Easels and aprons are washed with a wet cloth and soap if necessary. Paint containers are washed and put away. Leftover paint must be covered with a tight lid or aluminum foil. Aprons and smocks are hung up.

Pasting

Pasting should be done away from climbing toys, building blocks, and similar large motor activities. All the materials for pasting should be on a shelf at child level.

Fig. 10-12 In easel painting, the easel must be at child height, to allow easy access to paints and painting.

Pasting Procedure. Paste should be kept in small plastic containers or jars. To help the children learn to keep lids on jars, the bottom and top of each jar is marked with a number for that jar, or a colored X is used. The children are shown how to match up the jar with its lid by matching colored X's or numbers. In this way, children learn to keep the lids on the jars, and how to recognize numbers and colors.

Children should be shown how to rinse out paste brushes and where to return all pasting material. A place to put finished work to dry should be set up. The teacher must be sure that all young children have only blunt scissors. The children should learn about safety rules for using scissors early in the year.

Puppets and Scrap Art

For puppets and scrap art activities, it is necessary that materials be in good order. This is because both activities require a large supply of materials. A special place is needed for all supplies within the child's reach and eye level.

Scraps of cloth may be kept in one box with scrap pieces glued on the outside to show the child at a glance what is in the box. Buttons may be kept in a muffin tin, feathers in a plastic bag, and old bits of jewelry for puppets in a plastic shoe box. The point is to keep each material in a specific place so that it is ready for planned or spontaneous projects.

Organizing material in this simple and easy-to-find way helps children learn to work on their own. Having glue, scissors, paper, and all other materials on shelves at the child's height also encourages independent work. Cleanup time is much easier, too, when the children can see "what goes where" and can reach the places where materials are supposed to go.

When painting puppets or scrap artwork, the suggestions in the painting section can be used. The important thing to keep in mind is preparing the room and the child for a messy activity. This preparation makes painting more fun and relaxing because neither the teacher nor the child has to be so concerned about the mess.

Clay, Play Dough, and Papier Maché

Working with clay, play dough, and papier maché requires a place away from wheel and climbing toys. The tables should be covered with formica or oilcloth to make cleaning easier.

For clay and play dough, the points to keep in mind were discussed earlier in unit 7. A recipe for play dough is given in figure 10-14. Papier maché work needs a good place for drying finished objects. Since papier maché takes a few days to dry, this place must be away from frequently used areas. The basement, coatroom, windowsill, or a special rack are all good places for drying.

Before starting papier maché projects, the teacher must be aware of the children's interest span. This is because papier maché

Fig. 10-13 A formica-topped table makes cleaning easier for such activities as clay work.

- Mix 3 cups flour with 1/4 cup salt.
- Add 1 cup water with coloring and 1 tablespoon oil gradually.
- Add more water if too stiff; add more flour if too sticky.
- Let the children help with the mixing and measuring.
- Keep dough stored in plastic bags or a covered container.

Fig. 10-14 Play dough recipe.

projects take longer than any other type of arts and crafts work. Some children lose interest and never finish what they start.

The teacher must consider the time needed for preparing the material, making the objects, drying them, and painting them. Then it must be decided if the children's interest is strong enough to last through the time needed for the whole project. It is an unpleasant experience for both teacher and children when a project must be "pushed" to completion. This takes the joy out of the work.

Woodwork

Carpentry should be done in a special area away from other activities. Children should be provided with plenty of good wood and satisfactory tools. A sturdy workbench of the right height is helpful.

Nails should be of various sizes to fit the thickness of the wood. Children should use lightweight adult-size hammers. Toy hammers do not prove to be successful.

Cabinet shops are a good source for scrap lumber. Only smooth lumber should be used. Pieces of various lengths and sizes provide interest. The greater the variety of wood, the greater the challenge for building.

Woodwork needs careful adult supervision, since children can easily hurt themselves or each other with a hammer and saw. General guides for adult supervision include the following:

- Stay very close to the woodwork activity. Be within the reach of each child.
- There should be no more than three or four children for one adult to supervise. Only one child at a time should use a saw.
- Show the children how to saw away from their own fingers and from other children. Show them how to avoid hitting their fingers with the hammer.
- Hand out nails a few at a time.
- Never turn your back on the activity for even a few seconds.

SUMMARY

The arts and crafts program is a part of the preschool curriculum in which young children have the chance to work with many kinds of materials and techniques to make an original end product. It provides a time and place for children to put together their thoughts, ideas, feelings, actions, and abilities into their own creations.

Children of different ages have different abilities in arts and crafts because of varying degrees of muscle control and coordination. The objectives of the arts and crafts program are aimed at the interest, age, and ability level of the children. The arts and crafts program also has as one of its goals the growth of a child's creativity and ability to work independently. But above all, the main goal is to let the children grow at their own individual paces.

Teachers play a large part in the success of an arts and crafts program. They must be able to choose the right material as well as know the right way to set up and use the material for each activity.

STUDENT ACTIVITIES

- Visit one or possibly several preschool programs and observe the arts and crafts activities. Keep in mind these points in observing:

    1. Are the equipment and activities right for the age, ability, and interest levels of the children?
    2. Is the area well-planned for each activity?
    3. Are the children free to make what they want with the material?

- Set up a classroom, real or imagined, for one or more of the following activities:

    Finger painting

    Collage

    Making puppets

    Making egg carton animals

    Making papier maché masks

Consider the following in setting up the activity:

    Location of water source

    Preparation of area

    Preparation of materials

    Preparation of children

    Teacher preparation

    Activity itself

    Cleanup

    Drying and/or storage space for work in progress or finished

- Draw up a plan of a room setup for arts and crafts for three-, four-, and five-year-olds.

    A. Include the following areas:

        Brush and finger painting

        Clay

        Puppetry

        Papier maché work

        Crayon and chalk work

        Woodwork

        Scrap art

    B. Show on the plan where the following areas would be found:

Storage space

Child-level shelves

Drying areas

Water source(s)

Light source(s)

- Ask young children what they think is the hardest part about cleaning up. Record their answers. See if there is one thing that is mentioned more than others. Check on the problem to see if it is caused by room setup, supply setup, water source, or something else.

- Go on an odds-and-ends hunt.

    A. See how many different kinds of things can be found for use in art projects. Things to look for are spools, styrofoam, feathers, buttons, and foil, for example.

    B. Sort the material and store it in the best way possible. Label each container so that children will know what is inside.

REVIEW

    A. Is the product or the process more important in the arts and crafts program? Explain your answer.

    B. Choose the statements that describe an important purpose of arts and crafts in the preschool program.

        1. Arts and crafts give the child a chance to try new materials and techniques.

        2. Arts and crafts help the child make perfect artwork.

        3. The child has a chance to express experiences and feelings.

        4. The emphasis in arts and crafts is on continued good experiences with many kinds of materials.

        5. In arts and crafts, the child learns how to copy models.

        6. Learning to judge one's own work and other children's work is very important in arts and crafts.

        7. Being successful in arts and crafts helps develop a child's self-confidence.

    C. Select the items that should be included on a list of equipment for each activity.

        1. Crayoning

            a. Newsprint or manila paper, 8″ x 12″, or 12″ x 18″

            b. Lined white paper

       c. Colored tissue paper, 18″ x 24″

       d. Felt-tip pens in many colors

       e. Jumbo crayons, unwrapped

       f. Jumbo crayons, all wrapped

2. Chalk work

       a. Colored chalks, white chalks

       b. Colored tissue paper

       c. Paper, wet and dry

       d. Blackboard

       e. Eraser

       f. Pencils

3. Brush painting

       a. Easels

       b. Lined 9″ x 12″ paper

       c. Newsprint, 18″ x 24″, plain or pastel

       d. Construction paper

       e. Tempera paint

       f. Finger paint

       g. Glue

       h. Brushes, long (12″) handles and 3/4″ bristles

       i. Smocks

       j. A place to dry finished paintings

4. Finger painting

       a. Dull, porous paper

       b. Shiny-surfaced paper

       c. Water supply

       d. Crayons

       e. Finger paint

       f. Colored tissue paper

       g. Smocks

       h. Racks to dry finished work

5. Pasting

       a. Glue in small jars

       b. Paste in small jars

       c. Lined 9″ x 12″ paper

      d. Colored tissue paper

      e. Plain or manila construction paper

      f. Scissors, blunt, left and right types

      g. Collage materials

      h. Stapler and staples

6. Puppets and scrap art

      a. Paper bags

      b. Boxes

      c. Scissors, paper, paste, paints

      d. Sticks

      e. Play dough

      f. Colored sticky tape

      g. Cardboard rolls

      h. Odds and ends

      i. Airtight container

      j. Socks and mittens

7. Clay and play dough

      a. Plasticene

      b. Real clay

      c. Open containers

      d. Airtight containers

      e. Formica-topped tables

      f. Oilcloths

      g. Paint

      h. Scissors

      i. Tools for clay work

      j. Play dough, purchased

      k. Play dough, made with help from the children

8. Woodwork

      a. Paint

      b. Workbench

      c. Supply of soft lumber pieces

      d. Bottle caps

      e. Sandpaper

      f. Wooden spools, corks, twigs

g. Clay

h. Supply of nails

D. Choose the answer which best completes each of the following statements describing the basic objectives of the arts and crafts program.

1. The most basic objective of the arts and crafts program is to

   a. produce the best artists possible.

   b. meet the age, ability, and interest level of the children.

   c. fit into the total preschool program.

2. Learning to be a creative thinker is

   a. more important in the elementary grades than for younger children.

   b. not an objective in arts and crafts.

   c. an important objective in arts and crafts.

3. The arts and crafts program must allow children the freedom to

   a. grow at their own individual paces.

   b. do anything they please.

   c. go against safety rules.

4. A program for three-year-olds is set up for children with

   a. limited small motor control.

   b. good large and small motor control.

   c. good small motor control.

E. Choose the answer which best completes each of the following statements describing techniques for using material in arts and crafts.

1. With very young children, it is best to begin with

   a. a great variety of materials.

   b. the basic essentials.

   c. only small motor-type activities.

2. A teacher must avoid

   a. making models for the children to copy.

   b. helping the children with the material.

   c. giving suggestions at cleanup time.

3. Painting work should be done

   a. in an area near the quiet activities.

   b. in an area away from climbing toys.

   c. only if sunlight is available.

4. Finger painting works best with

    a. dull, porous, dry paper on wood tables.

    b. shiny paper on the floor.

    c. shiny paper on a table covered with formica or oilcloth.

5. It is best to keep pasting supplies

    a. out of the child's reach.

    b. on a shelf at child level.

    c. in a locked cabinet.

6. Puppets and scrap art activities require

    a. a good deal of organization of supplies.

    b. no special order in supplies.

    c. a small amount of supplies.

7. Woodwork is an activity that

    a. needs very little supervision.

    b. needs careful adult supervision.

    c. is too dangerous for young children.

8. In woodwork and all arts and crafts, it is important to encourage children to

    a. copy the teacher's models.

    b. copy the ideas of the other children.

    c. do what they want with the materials.

Unit 11 ARTS AND CRAFTS
FOR THE THREE-YEAR-OLD CHILD

OBJECTIVES

After studying this unit, the student will be able to

- Discuss the skills and abilities of the three-year-old.

- Describe some arts and crafts activities with two-dimensional media for three-year-olds.

- Discuss some arts and crafts activities with three-dimensional media for three-year-olds.

To plan an arts and crafts program for a group with some or all three-year-olds in it, a teacher must know what the right materials and activities are for the group. This means knowing not only the ages of the children, but also the ability and interest level of the group.

AGE AND ABILITY LEVEL

Not all three-year-olds are alike, but there are some general facts that apply to most of them. Three-year-olds often have better large muscle development than small muscle development. This means they can run, walk, and jump well and are quite sure of themselves with all types of foot and arm movements. However, the small muscles in the fingers, hands, and wrists are not as well developed as the large muscles in the legs and arms. This is why buttoning, using scissors, and similar activities that require the use of these small muscles are not usually easy for three-year-olds.

Control over small muscles comes only through a child's normal physical growth and through practice. In arts and crafts, a three-year-old has the chance to use small muscles in many ways. For example, holding crayons and paintbrushes helps the small muscles develop. A child learns how to control small muscles by holding and using a tool with two fingers. This

Fig. 11-1 Small muscles are exercised when children hold and use paintbrushes.

is necessary later when the child is learning how to write.

Arts and crafts for children with this limited motor control should include materials that the child can handle and which help in the development of small and large muscles. Some of the right tools for three-year-olds are blunt scissors, large blank sheets of paper, large unwrapped crayons, finger puppets, wide brushes with long handles, real clay, play dough, and finger paint. The teacher may add to or take away from the list when children can handle the tools.

Fig. 11-2 Although children have a relatively short interest span at three years of age, certain activities may keep a child's attention for longer amounts of time.

INTEREST LEVEL

Most three-year-olds have a short span of interest and attention. Many activities, even the most interesting, only hold their interest for ten to fifteen minutes. Less time is, in fact, more usual. It should be remembered that each child is different and interest spans may be shorter or longer for each individual.

The point is that the teacher must plan activities that, first of all, appeal to the interests of the children. Simple, basic arts and crafts activities are of most interest to the child of three. Secondly, the teacher must be prepared to accept the fact that the activity may hold the child's interest for only a short time. It helps to remember that a period of time that seems short to an adult may be quite long to the three-year-old. Finally, alternative and extra activities should be available for those

children who may not be interested in the first activity planned.

With this young group, it is usually best to use only the basic materials at first. This helps keep the arts and crafts program from being too confusing for the child of three. Using only a few crayons or paints, or pasting one or two kinds of things at first is a good idea. It encourages children to experiment with each new tool and medium. Children learn to use the basic tools and materials first. When the children have acquired the basic skills, more colors and variety can be added.

TWO-DIMENSIONAL ARTS AND CRAFTS

Painting, pasting, and working with crayons are suitable activities for this group. The possibilities are many and varied. Some ideas are presented here; the student may wish to add others.

Collage

Making a collage is a good activity for three-year-olds. It helps them grow physically in their ability to use small muscles as they cut, tear, and paste. It also helps them grow mentally as they learn to choose items to use in the collage, and to arrange them into a design. When children paste together a collage, they learn about the feel, shape, and color of many things and develop the ability to use things in unusual ways.

At times, it may seem as if the three-year-old is focusing more on the paste than on the items being pasted, but that is part of the fun. The teacher must be sure that the objects available are suitable for the child of three who is using them. For example, it is good to keep tiny, nonedible objects away from children who still put things in their mouth.

Three-year-olds who are new to this activity should begin with just one thing to paste. A good idea is for them to make a

Fig. 11-3 Sometimes, when working on a collage, a child concentrates more on the pasting part of the activity than on the materials to be pasted. This, however, is all part of a child's enjoyment.

tear-and-paste collage. To do this, they are given pieces of newspaper, colored tissue, or any colored scrap paper that tears easily. The teacher shows them, if necessary, how to tear large and small pieces. Then they paste these torn bits of paper into a design on colored construction paper. This is a good activity for three-year-olds who do not want to, or who are not yet able to, use scissors. Some scissors should be available for children who want to try cutting the pieces to paste on the collage. Children should not be forced to practice cutting, however.

As the children master the basic technique of pasting, more objects can be added to the collage. Some good things to add are large buttons; bits of cloth and paper in different colors, textures, and shapes; and bottle caps. Care must be taken to be sure the materials are not sharp, not painted with lead-type paint, and not small enough to swallow.

For a change of pace, different materials may be used for the backing of the collage. The children may use styrofoam meat trays to paste things on, or shoe box lids, or even pieces of burlap. The teacher and children use

their imaginations to come up with new ideas for the arts and crafts materials.

Paints

Children grow in coordination and small and large muscle control when using paint – at the easel, in finger painting, and in printing.

At the Easel. Three-year-old children get much satisfaction in working with paint at the easel. They like to experiment with color and form, making designs, and later simple pictures. They also like to paint one color on top of another and enjoy the effect.

Bright colors of paint help the child develop the ability to see differences in color, shape, and size. Mixing powder paint helps a child learn the reaction of various substances with water. Holding and using a brush helps children develop small muscle control. Painting also helps a child discover new forms of self-expression.

Plain newsprint paper in white or pastel colors should be used for the child of three. Plain paper shows the brush strokes more clearly. Painting on lines or printed newsprint makes a picture too confusing for the three-year-old to see well.

Finger Painting. Using finger paints gives three-year-olds a chance to use their bodies freely and to arrange the paint at will. In work with finger paint, a three-year-old feels a sense of relaxation which often leads to communication with others. A child communicates best when relaxed.

Finger paint is an especially good media for this age group, as it can be arranged over and over again. In this way, the process is stressed, not the product. This is very important for three-year-olds who, at this age, are learning the basic ways to use paint.

This age group enjoys the feel of the paint and gets a good deal of small motor practice as they use their fingers. Large arm movements are also used by young children as they finger paint. Sometimes they even use their upper arms and elbows to help in their designs.

To save on the cost of finger paint paper and to try something new, adults can sometimes let the children finger paint on a formica table top, an enamel-topped table, a sheet of smooth formica, or even linoleum. When this is done, a print can be made from the child's finger painting by laying a piece of newsprint paper on the finger painting and gently rubbing it with one hand. The painting is transferred in this way from the table top to the paper. More finger paint activities are suggested later in this unit.

There may be some three-year-olds who do not like the feel of finger paint. If this is so, the child should never be forced to use it. Instead, another art activity can be found that the child will enjoy.

Printing. Printing with objects is an arts and crafts activity that is right for the age, ability, and interest levels of three-year-olds. In a basic printing activity, the child learns that an object dipped in or brushed with paint makes its own mark, or print, on paper. Children use small muscles in the hand and wrist as they hold the

Fig. 11-4 When they are deeply involved in finger painting, children often use more than just their fingers to create their artwork.

object, dip it in paint, and print with it on paper. They learn that each object has its own unique quality as each thing makes its own imprint.

For the child of three, stick prints are best to start with. In this type of printing, children dip small pieces of wood of various sizes and shapes into a thick tempera paint and press them onto a piece of paper. Twigs, wooden spools, wood clothespins, and bottle caps are objects suitable for three-year-olds to use in printing.

After stick printing is mastered, printing with vegetables is good with this age group. Green peppers, carrots, turnips, and potatoes are some vegetables to try. The vegetables are sliced in half, making two smooth surfaces for printing. A good way for three-year-olds to begin printing is to "walk" the inked vegetable across the paper in even "steps." When it gets to the other side, they walk it back again. By making three or four lines, or walks, the child has made a pattern.

After one color is used, the vegetable can be wiped clean and another color used. Three-year-olds like to try many colors with the same printing object. They may even print over their first prints in a different color. More printing activities for three-year-olds are found later in this unit.

Crayons

Crayons are the most basic of the arts and crafts tools for this age group. They are also the most familiar and the easiest to use. Large crayons are easy to hold and they can be used to make attractive colored marks on paper.

Drawing with large crayons helps the three-year-old develop small muscle control and also discover new forms of expression.

Crayon Drawings. Most preschools have crayons, but often drawings on paper are the only use made of them. There are other ways

Fig. 11-5 Children make vegetables "walk" across the paper when doing vegetable prints.

to use crayons that the teacher might try to make the program more varied.

Crayons can be used to draw on many surfaces. Cardboard in any form (including corrugated cardboard, paper gift boxes, and food trays) is a good surface for crayon drawings. Crayons can also be used on styrofoam. Crayon drawings on sandpaper have an interesting effect.

Crayon Rubbings. Drawing pictures with crayons is only one of the uses for crayons. Crayon rubbing is a technique that three-year-olds can easily master. To make a crayon rubbing, the child puts a piece of paper over a textured surface, and rubs the sides of a peeled crayon over the paper.

The crayon picks up the texture on the paper in a design. Some surfaces that can be used are bumpy food trays, bark, leaves, the sidewalk, bricks, and corrugated cardboard. This is a good activity for developing both small and large muscles.

Crayon Resist. Another way to use crayons is in crayon resist drawings. To make a resist drawing, the child first draws a picture on paper with crayons, pressing hard. The child then paints over and around the crayon drawing with thin paint (tempera paint diluted with water).

Fig. 11-6 Crayon resist drawing.

A dark-colored paint works best. The dark color fills in all the areas that the crayon has not covered. In the areas covered with crayon, the crayon "resists," or is not covered by, the paint. Crayon resist gives the feeling of a night picture. It is a thrilling experience for the child to see the changes that come when the paint crosses the paper.

THREE-DIMENSIONAL ARTS AND CRAFTS

Three-year-olds may express themselves and gain muscle control at the same time through various three-dimensional art activities. Several materials are discussed here; the possibilities are almost limitless.

Clay and Play Dough

Soft, easy-to-use clay and play dough are excellent materials for three-year-olds. They help improve small muscle control, as well as encourage self-expression. Simply pounding or squeezing clay and play dough is good exercise for children.

A child develops a sense of control when using a flexible material. Many three-year-olds release their feelings by manipulating clay.

In working with three-year-olds, a teacher must realize that not many children of this age are interested in making definite objects.

Fig. 11-7 Children at the age of three usually enjoy rolling clay into long snakes, or forming it into small, round balls.

They like the feel of clay and enjoy using it for its feel alone. Some may make snakes or balls. What matters is the experience of holding, feeling, forming, and pounding it.

Three-year-olds sometimes enjoy using tools with clay and play dough. Blunt knives, forks, rolling pins, cookie cutters, spatulas, and potato mashers are among the objects that can be used.

Allowing the children to help mix the play dough is a good learning experience for them. As they learn how to make play dough for arts and crafts, they learn many other things. They learn how to measure, mix, and color the play dough. Children truly enjoy using a material that they have made.

Puppets

Puppets for three-year-olds must be simple. The child should be able to make a

Fig. 11-8 A stick puppet is a fun arts and crafts activity for a three-year-old.

puppet without too much adult help. Making puppets is a good arts and crafts activity as well as an aid to communication for the child of three. A puppet can say things for the children that the children often will not say themselves. Listening and watching a child's performance with a puppet can give the teacher a good idea of the child's own ideas and feelings.

Stick Puppets. Stick puppets are fun and easy for a three-year-old to make. The teacher can gather some sticks from the lumber yard, large twigs, or wood popsicle sticks. With this type of puppet, the child puts a bag or piece of cloth over the stick and stuffs the bag or cloth with wads of newspaper or cotton. The child then ties the top of the bag to the stick, making a head. A rubber band may be used instead of string to form a head.

The child can then paint the head or make a face with crayons or colored paper and paste. Scrap yarn, wood shavings, and buttons are also good materials for the puppet's face.

A body can be made by adding a dress cut out of paper and stapled to the stick. Scrap pieces of fabric can be used to "dress" the puppet; wallpaper samples are an inexpensive material for puppets' clothes.

Bag Puppets. The common paper bag in any size makes a good puppet for a three-year-old. The bags are stuffed with wads of newspaper and stapled or glued shut. A body is made with a second bag stapled to the first, leaving room for the child's hand to slip in and work the puppet.

A face can be made with paint, crayons, or colored paper and paste. Odds and ends are fun to use for the face, too. Buttons make eyes; crumpled tissue, a nose; yarn, hair. The search for the right odds and ends to make the puppet is as much fun as using the finished puppet later.

Finger and Hand Puppets. For those children just beginning in arts and crafts, finger and hand puppets are good to try. The child can use a felt-tip pen to paint a face on one finger, to turn it into a puppet. A button on the fingertip could be the puppet's hat.

A child's hand can be a puppet, too. Making a face on the palm turns a hand into a puppet. These simple starts in puppetry give the three-year-old an idea of what the activity is all about. The fun of discovery involved in puppetry with other materials is the next step.

Object Sculpture

A good supply of scrap wood, styrofoam, boxes, wire, pipe cleaners, and various other items to use in creating provides fun for three-year-olds.

Scrap wood pieces may be glued together with white (Elmer's) glue to make a sculpture object. Spools, toothpicks, corks, and popsicle sticks can be glued to larger wood scraps to create many unique objects.

Three-year-olds' imaginations find many uses for boxes, too. A supply of empty cereal boxes, cake mix boxes, pudding boxes, toothpaste boxes, and jewelry boxes are fun for young children. Boxes can be glued together for paper sculpture. Miniature cities, buildings, and free-form art can be created by three-year-olds using only empty boxes and glue.

Plastic-covered wire and pipe cleaners can be bent in many interesting ways. Clay or play dough can be used as a base. The pipe cleaner is stuck in the clay and can be bent in many shapes — to a child's delight!

SUMMARY

Arts and crafts must be planned to suit the age, ability, and interest levels of the group. Some good two-dimensional arts and crafts for children of three are easel painting, finger painting, printing, collage, and crayoning. Three-dimensional arts and crafts activities suitable for three-year-olds are clay and play dough, puppets, and object sculpture.

STUDENT ACTIVITIES

Since a teacher of young children should not introduce an unfamiliar activity to children, try the following projects with classmates first. Then use them with children. Remember these activities when you are working in early childhood education.

- **Crumpled Paper Designs**
    1. Bits of different colored tissue or newspaper can be crumpled up by the children.
    2. The paper wads can then be dipped in school paste and pasted onto colored construction paper to make a design.

3. Paper shapes can be filled in with crumpled paper for Christmas ornaments, Valentine hearts, and Thanksgiving turkeys.

4. A group of children can work together to make a cooperative collage for the room. Choose a theme like toys, holidays, friends, seasons, or likes and dislikes.

- **Using Finger Painted Pictures**

Save the children's finger painted pictures. These may be sprayed with a plastic coating and used for covering books, wrapping gifts, or making wastebaskets. A round ice cream carton or coffee can may be covered with finger painting to make a wastebasket for the room.

- **Rubber Cement Painting**

1. Drip or smear rubber cement on paper, avoiding making large globs of glue. Set the paper aside to dry. (It dries fast.)

2. Paint over the dried rubber cement.

3. After the paint has dried, the rubber cement can be rubbed off, leaving an interesting design.

- **Painting With Soft Objects**

1. Dip a cotton ball in a shallow dish of wet paint. Smear it or squish it on paper or another surface.

2. Dip a cotton ball into dry powdered paint. Rub it across dry paper to create an interesting soft effect.

- **Screen and Toothbrush Painting**

1. Hold a piece of screen above a sheet of paper.

2. Dip a toothbrush into paint and brush it across the screen.

3. If desired, leaves, twigs, or different shapes of paper may be placed on paper, paint spattered over them, and the objects removed. (A design is made this way.)

- **Sponge Painting**

1. Cut sponges into different shapes.

2. Dip each shape in paint. Then dab, press, or rub it on paper.

- **Paper Towel Painting**

1. Wad a paper towel into a ball.

2. Dip it in paint. Then dab, press, or rub it on paper.

- **Crayons**

  A. Surfaces for crayon drawings

  Children may draw with crayons on these surfaces for variety:

fabric	paper towel rolls	sticks and stones
egg cartons	wood scraps	spools and clothespins

  B. Crayon Shavings Designs

  1. Make shavings by scraping the side of a crayon with the blade of blunt scissors. Sprinkle shavings between sheets of waxed paper (folded in half).

  2. An adult can then press the paper with a warm iron, protecting the iron with an old cloth. The shavings melt and the sheets of paper stick together.

  3. For variety, bits of tissue paper, colored cellophane, or fall leaves can be put between the pieces of waxed paper.

  C. Candle Stub Resists

  1. For paint resist, instead of using crayons, use a candle stub to draw a picture.

  2. Paint over the design with thin paint.

- **Printing**

  A. Toy Prints

  1. Dip the wheels of an old toy car, truck, or other toy in paint.

  2. Make tracks on the paper.

  B. Plastic Alphabet Letters and Numbers

  1. Dip plastic alphabet letters and numbers in paint.

  2. Then print them on paper.

  C. Paper Cup Printing

  1. Dip the rim of a paper cup into paint.

  2. Press the rim on paper to make a design.

  D. Comb Printing

  1. Dip the teeth of a comb into paint.

  2. Print with it by drawing it along the paper.

  E. Printing With Modeling Clay (Plasticene)

  1. Children pound the clay into small flat cakes about an inch thick.

  2. Then, they carve a design on the flat surface with a bobby pin or popsicle stick.

  3. The design is either brushed with paint or dipped in paint and pressed onto paper to print the design.

- **Puppets**
  A. Paper Plate Puppets
      1. A plain paper plate can be made into a face with crayons, paint, or glued-on colored paper pieces.
      2. A popsicle stick is then stapled to the bottom of the plate to make a handle.
      3. The plate can be moved along a table edge as a puppet, or used as a mask.
      4. A hole can be made for a mouth, through which the child uses one finger as a tongue to make the puppet "talk."
  B. Cylinder Puppets
      1. Roll a piece of 9″ x 12″ or 12″ x 18″ drawing or construction paper into a cylinder. Staple or glue it together. This is the head of the puppet.
      2. Using paper, scissors, and paste, make a face on the tube.
      3. Hats of paper, yarn hair, and scrap ribbon bows are some ways to decorate the puppet.
      4. The puppet is slipped over the child's finger. If desired, a body, skirt, or suit can be cut out and pasted or stapled to the tube.
  C. Food Puppets
      1. Fruits and vegetables make good heads for puppets. A potato or an apple may be used, with a clothespin inserted to hold it by.
      2. Buttons, pins, or old jewelry pieces can be used to make a face.
      3. Yarn can be used for hair.
      4. Bits of cloth or an old sock may be used as a dress or suit.

REVIEW

A. Choose the answer which best completes each of the following statements describing the skills and abilities of the three-year-old.
    1. The three-year-old often has
        a. better small than large muscle development.
        b. better large than small muscle development.
        c. good large and small muscle development.
    2. For a three-year-old, activities like buttoning and using scissors are generally
        a. quite easy.

b. impossible.

c. quite difficult.

3. The interest span for a three-year-old is usually quite

a. long, more than twenty minutes.

b. short, not more than one minute.

c. short, between ten and fifteen minutes.

4. In lesson plans for three-year-olds, the teacher plans

a. only one main activity for the whole group.

b. alternative activities for those who have different interests.

c. only difficult activities to stimulate interest.

5. Some good art tools for three-year-olds are

a. blunt scissors, wide brushes, and large crayons.

b. narrow brushes, ballpoint pens, and clay.

c. Plasticene, play dough, and felt-tip pens.

B. List two activities with paint and two with crayons for three-year-olds.

C. Choose one of the activities you listed for question B, and discuss the following points.

1. Importance of activity for muscle development.

2. Proper material for the activity.

D. List three activities for three-year-olds using three-dimensional media.

E. Choose one of the activities you listed in question D, and describe the following.

1. Importance of activity to child's development.

2. Proper equipment for the activity.

Unit 12 ARTS AND CRAFTS FOR FOUR-AND FIVE-YEAR-OLD CHILDREN

OBJECTIVES

After studying this unit, the student will be able to

- Discuss the skills and abilities of the four- to five-year-old child.
- Describe some arts and crafts activities with two-dimensional media for four- to five-year-old children.
- Discuss some arts and crafts activities with three-dimensional media for four- to five-year-old children.

Just as in the case of the three-year-old, there are preferred and suitable materials and activities for children four and five years old. Although there may be considerable overlap, children in this age group generally differ significantly from the three-year-old child.

ABILITY AND INTEREST LEVELS

There are some general traits that apply to most children in the four- to five-year-old age group. Small-muscle development in the fingers, hands, and wrists is much improved. Whereas three-year-old children may have great difficulty buttoning their clothing or using scissors, most in this older group do not. Use of crayons, magic markers, and, in some cases, pencils and pens is quite possible. With their vocabulary now expanded to over two thousand words, they are quite capable of speaking in sentences of four and five words. Their ability to converse, coupled with their increased attention span (fifteen to thirty minutes), now allows for some small group activities in the arts and crafts program.

Since these children are very interested in life beyond home and school, art activities including outside environments (television characters, for example) can be stimulating. Youngsters of this age paint and draw with more purpose. Designs and pictures are within their abilities. These will probably be somewhat simple, but nonetheless fun and exciting for the children to do.

Four- to five-year-old children usually are very interested in music. They enjoy dancing and performing to musical accompaniments. Arts and crafts activities with musical stimulation should be successful.

The child of this age is able to listen for longer periods to stories with wider content. Thus, making art activities relate to story presentations is a good tool to help motivate such children.

It is also quite possible for children of this age group to build elaborate block structures. They are not only capable of naming these creations but also can tell interesting stories about them. Block building can be a cooperative activity for several children working together. Very often, pictures of these block creations occur in the paintings and drawings of children of this age.

Whereas younger children should use only the basic materials, four- and five-year-olds can explore with more materials. They need not be restricted to a few crayons or paints. Generally, in familiar activities such drawing, painting, and pasting, a wide variety of resources can and should be used.

Fig. 12-1 Four- and five-year-old children can explore a wider variety of materials than three-year-olds.

ARTS AND CRAFTS

As in the previous unit, each activity discussed here is intended to provide enjoyment, skill building, and developmental progress for the child. These activities are not intended to replace those mentioned earlier, but rather to build upon them. In all activities, the process is always much more important than the product.

Watercolor Painting

Children of any age can lose interest or lose confidence when attempting to create something. This often occurs when children cannot produce what they want to produce. Sometimes their skills to create are not adequate to allow them to create what their awareness tells them they should create. Children enjoy watercolors, yet often have real difficulty creating the designs and pictures they prefer. If this is the case, "accidental watercolor" may be a good activity to try.

Each child is given a large sheet of paper. The children are instructed to apply water to the entire sheet with a brush. Then the teacher announces that the children may try watercolor experiments which fit their mood or fantasies. Music can be used to create or influence the children's moods.

The first mood might be a happy one. The children are asked to decide which colors are "happy" and to moisten each of them in their watercolors. When the chosen colors are wet, the children are asked to pick one with their brushes and to put it on their paper any way they want. They are then asked to choose another color and to apply it, being very careful not to cover one color with another. The children should continue in this way until the entire paper is covered with colors that should combine in unusual ways to create a variety of brilliant "accidents."

Different moods can be attempted while the previously painted pictures are drying. The children must not pick up the paintings while they are still wet, or all the colors will mix into a drab gray. When the paintings have dried, children may talk about them and the mood or fantasy they express.

After the original paintings have dried, black watercolor or India ink can be used to outline the brilliant colors. This adds a dramatic touch to the work.

This same method can be used with tempera paints. They are very rich and are even better for overpainting. When watercolors and tempera paint are both available, they may be used together. This provides another variety and form of expression.

Mosaics

Mosaics are surface decorations made of small pieces of colored glass, stone, or other inlaid materials. The young child can make a very simple mosaic using torn or cut colored paper. This can be a very exciting project because it combines the elements of drawing, cutting, pasting, and putting a puzzle together. It may be used as a group project.

Fig. 12-2 A cat is a good subject for a mosaic.

The children begin by cutting colored paper into half-inch square pieces. They keep the colors separate by placing the pieces in different small boxes or containers. When enough pieces have been cut, the group can try a mosaic picture. An art book with illustrations of mosaics which can be shown gives children a better idea of the meaning of this project.

Pictures of animals, flowers, and many other things are possible. The main idea is to keep the project simple. A cat, a car, and a tree are just a few of the many possibilities.

After the children have decided what they want to do, they select the colors that satisfy the idea they have in mind. They should apply the bits of paper by starting with the central figure or object and working toward the edges. Mosaics are more attractive if they are pasted on a background of colored paper or cardboard. Interesting variations can be made from books of wallpaper samples which are often discarded by wallpaper stores.

Some of the children may be able to make slightly more complex mosaics by combining a variety of materials. Gravel, pebbles, seeds, pods, and various types of grains make unique mosaics when combined in imaginative ways. However, these materials require a type of glue that has greater strength than library paste. There are several milk-white liquid glues that are satisfactory for this kind of activity. They are completely safe and nontoxic for children of any age.

Printing

Paper Stencils. The four- to five-year-old child can begin to use stencils in a most creative manner. Paper stencils are good because they do not require many materials.

Each child may be given four or five pieces of drawing paper about four inches square. With scissors, the child cuts holes of various sizes and shapes in the center of each piece. It is a good idea to cut more than one hole per piece. When the holes have been cut, each child is given a cleansing tissue, small piece of cotton, or patch of cloth. This is rubbed on a piece of colored chalk to pick up enough dust to stencil. Then the child selects a shape and places it on the paper on which the design is to go. The child rubs the tissue across the hole, making strokes from the stencil paper toward the center of the opening. This is continued around the edge of the opening until the paper under the stencil has a clear print. The same shape can be continued across paper, or other shapes and colors may be added according to the child's preference. Visual rhythms and themes can be printed without boring repetition.

A child can choose the shapes and combinations desired. Holiday cards, programs, and classroom decorations may be made in this manner. The same stencil technique can be used with wax crayons instead of the chalk. The crayons are rubbed directly on the stencil. If unbleached muslin or cotton material is used to print on, attractive door and wall hangings can be produced.

The Spatter Technique. Simple spatter or spray printing is both fascinating and fun for the young child. It also has the advantage of allowing for a wide variety of patterns and shapes. Children can work individually or with partners on this project.

Several of the children can bring in old toothbrushes. Besides the toothbrush, only a small amount of water paint and paper is

Fig. 12-3 A stencil such as this one would make a good classroom decoration or cover for a holiday greeting card.

needed. The method used is to "spray" the paint with a toothbrush. This is done by dipping the brush in paint and gently pulling a straightedged object (ruler, emery board, or tongue depressor), across the ends of the bristles. This causes the bristles to snap forward throwing small particles of paint onto the paper.

The children create designs by placing small, flat objects on the paper. When the bristles snap the small particles of paint forward, the object prevents the spray from striking the paper directly under the object. This leaves the shapes free of paint spray while the rest of the paper is covered with small flecks of paint.

This technique has endless possibilities. Not only can a variety of shapes be used, but colors can also be superimposed on one another. Natural forms such as twigs, leaves, and grass are excellent for this activity. Several forms can be combined, leading to interesting arrangements with unlimited variety. A field trip to a vacant lot is a way to find new print forms and shapes. Thus, children are encouraged to find and learn about beauty in their own environment. Another strength of this project is that it avoids stereo-

Fig. 12-4 Spatter technique.

- Combine one cup table salt with one-half cup cornstarch and three-quarters cup of cold water in a double boiler placed over medium heat.
- The mixture is stirred constantly, and in about two to three minutes it should become so thick that it follows the spoon in mixing it.
- When the consistency is similar to bread dough, it is placed on a piece of wax paper or aluminum foil to cool.
- After cooling to a point where it can be handled, it should be kneaded for several minutes.
- It is then ready to use.
- If wrapped in wax paper or placed in plastic bags, it can be stored for several days.

Fig. 12-5 Salt dough recipe.

typed designs and ready-cut patterns. The children create beauty for themselves.

Three-Dimensional Arts and Crafts

Salt Ceramics. Salt dough is an excellent substitute for clay. It can be made in the kitchen by parents as well as by teachers. (See the recipe in figure 12-5.)

It hardens to a stonelike material and is excellent for painting with any type of paint. Salt dough has several advantages over clay.

Fig. 12-6 Salt dough is more durable than clay, and children enjoy its flexibility and texture.

It does not shrink when drying. It is much more durable than clay. It is clean. It does not powder and shed dust as clay does.

Young children may use salt dough to make ceramic-type objects and shapes. Animals and other forms of wildlife are popular. The children should be allowed to make their own choices. Films, trips, slides, and tapes can be used to stimulate their thinking and imagination.

Box Building. Cardboard boxes can be found in stores, basements, garages, closets — everywhere. Young children like to build with them as though the boxes were huge blocks of stone. They go inside of the boxes and imagine new or old worlds. The children think of their boxes as houses, trains, airplanes, buses, cars, stagecoaches, and spaceships.

Children should have as many boxes as seem necessary or possible. The teacher may stimulate, suggest, and demonstrate, but should let the children choose what they want to make.

The children may choose a road scene where they imagine their boxes to be trucks, cars, or buses. Using tempera paints and large brushes, they paint and design their vehicles. What comes next is up to the teacher and the children.

Waxed cardboard containers (quart, half-gallon, and gallon sizes) are also useful in a variety of ways. They can be cut into different shapes and used as tables, vehicles, people, or animals. Brass fasteners and a stapler are useful for this kind of construction.

SUMMARY

Four- and five-year-olds have more advanced small and large muscle coordination than younger children. This means they can use smaller paintbrushes, magic markers, and crayons with greater skill. They are also much better at cutting and pasting than three-year-old children. They often have vocabularies of more than two thousand words and can participate in simple small-group activities.

Watercolor painting, mosaics, stencil printing and spatter printing are good two-dimensional arts and crafts activities for the four- to five-year-old child. Creative three-dimensional activities include salt ceramics and box building.

STUDENT ACTIVITIES

The activities described should be tried alone or with classmates before being used with children. Enjoy being creative!

- **Plaster of Paris Molds**

Plaster of Paris can be bought at hardware stores or hobby shops. Follow directions on the package for adding water.

   A. Free Form Sculpture

      1. Mix plaster and mold it rapidly; it dries quickly.

      2. When it is dry, it can be painted.

   B. Hand or Foot Prints

      1. Pour wet plaster into a mold, such as a food tray, or try pouring it into a plastic bag or rubber glove.

      2. Place a hand or foot in the wet plaster; leave it until the plaster begins to harden. The impression may be painted when dry.

   C. Nature Design

      1. Gather together assorted objects from nature, such as shells, weeds, stones, and sticks.

      2. Pour plaster in the bottom of the food tray. Quickly, before the plaster hardens, arrange the objects in the plaster.

      3. This design may be painted when dry.

- **Tie-Dyeing**

      1. Tie-dyeing techniques can be used to decorate a piece of old sheet.

      2. Wrap rubber bands or string around bunches of the fabric, or gather up a section of the fabric around a few stones and then tie it.

      3. Put the fabric into a dye solution. (The brands which require hot water, but not boiling water, are safer.)

      4. When the fabric is the color desired, remove it from the solution and take off the string or rubber bands.

- **Masks: Scrap Art**

Face masks made from paper bags usually inspire make-believe activities. Children love them and can do all the decorating once an adult has cut out the holes for the eyes, nose, and mouth.

      1. Mark the spots for the features while the bag is on the child's head so that the holes are in the right places.

      2. Remove the bag, cut the holes, and let the child decorate it. Some children enjoy pasting on yarn for hair, or fringing paper and pasting it on.

REVIEW

A. List five skills, interests, and abilities which the four- to five-year-old child usually possesses.

B. List three two-dimensional arts and crafts activities for four- to five-year-old children.

C. Give three reasons why salt dough is an excellent substitute for clay.

Unit 13 THEORIES OF PLAY

OBJECTIVES

After studying this unit, the student will be able to

- Name four kinds of human growth that are influenced by play.
- Describe two differences in the way three-, four-, and five-year-old children play.
- List five characteristics that determine the usefulness of play equipment.

Some children are busily involved in activities in a school for three- to five-year-olds. One group of three-year-olds is removing the wheels from the steel trucks in the room. Now they are having races by pushing the wheelless trucks along the floor. One child notes the scraping sounds being made, while another discovers that the trucks without wheels make marks on the floor. One four-year-old child is preparing a tea party for three friends. The child has baked an imaginary cake and has just finished putting on icing. Now the table is being set and the chairs arranged. A group of five-year-olds is carefully observing several small furry animals on the other side of the room. While petting one of the animals, a child noticed an unusual bump on the animal's back. Several more children join this group to see why everyone seems so excited.

Are these children working? Are they playing? Is there a difference between work and play for a young child? Must children be involved in games in order to be playing? Must toys be involved? Is play natural or can children be taught to play?

The answers to these questions are important. They help clear up the meaning of the word "play." The answers lead to an understanding of how children benefit from play. They give direction for the purchase and placement of materials that guide children's play. They help adults plan activities that help children grow through play.

WHAT IS PLAY?

For adults, play is what they do when they have finished their work. Play is a form of relaxation. For young children, play is what they do all day. Playing is living, and living is playing.

For older children and teenagers, learning may be a chore. When they complete their chore, they can play. For young children, everything they do is play. Growth of their minds results from their play. Growth of their ability to deal with the problems of life results from play. Growth of their imaginations results from play. Growth of muscles results from play.

Play is an activity. It does not necessarily result in a product. Play may involve one child, or groups of children. Play may be built around toys and tools or may involve nothing more than the child's imagination. A play period may last a few minutes or it may go on for days.

Most people who have studied play agree on one thing about its meaning. No single definition or statement can describe the true meaning of this term. Therefore, the best way to define play is not to define it at all, but to look at its characteristics.

A natural part of a child's life. Adults do not have to tell children how to play.

Fig. 13-1 For young children, play is an activity that may involve toys and equipment, or just the power of their imaginations.

Self-directed. Adults should not interfere because play is determined by the personality of the player, not the desires of adults.

An activity, not a production. Adults should not concern themselves with what the children might produce during play. The outcomes are never certain.

A total activity. Children become completely involved as they participate in games. Thus, play may last a long time or it may end quite suddenly.

A sensitive thing for children. Play may sound noisy, and children may seem deeply involved, yet it can be easily destroyed by interference from other children or suggestions from adults. There is no blueprint for play — no right way or wrong way to play. Play is a highly creative and highly individualized activity.

There are two main types of play: free play and organized play. In either type, children may work alone or in a group. Each type may involve materials and equipment, or it may not. Basically, *free play*, as its name suggests, is flexible. It is unplanned by adults. It is an open exercise. *Organized play* may also be open and flexible. However, some structure

Fig. 13-2 Free play often involves equipment, such as structures to climb on in a playground.

is provided in terms of materials and equipment or directions given by teachers. Play may be further subdivided.

Dramatic play. Children act out the parts of one or more characters who may be real or imaginary.

Play involving materials and equipment. Children may use materials alone or in groups. Sometimes equipment is used in dramatic play.

Games. Games can be invented by the children on the spot, or they can be existing games known to most children or adults. Only somewhat older children can engage in games that are played according to rules.

IMPORTANCE OF PLAY

Play activities influence children's growth. The opportunities children have to play

Fig. 13-3 Placing one block on top of another block adds to a child's hand-eye coordination and muscle development.

influence them in terms of their physical, mental, emotional, and social growth.

Physical Growth

Play contributes to muscle development in many ways. Throwing a ball or lifting objects helps children's muscles to develop. Placing an object on top of another and grasping tools also add to a child's muscle and hand-eye development. Another type of physical growth involves developing the senses through play activities. Play forms that require children to look at objects, feel textures, smell various odors, hear sounds, and taste substances help them develop their senses.

Mental Growth

Play helps children develop important concepts. Through play activities, a child learns the meaning of up and down, hard and soft, and big and small. Play experiences contribute to a child's knowledge of building things and arranging things in sets. Children learn to sort, and to probe for answers.

Fig. 13-4 In creative play activities, children learn how to arrange a set of blocks to their own liking, to build a block tower.

Emotional Growth

One of the keys to the quality of children's emotional health is their feelings about themselves. Creative play activities help a child develop a good self-concept. In play activities, there are no right answers or wrong answers. Children are not faced with the threat of failure. They almost always are successful to one degree or another. They learn to see themselves as capable performers. Even when things do not go well, there is little pressure built into play. Thus, young children learn to view themselves as successful and worthwhile human beings through play. This is an important first step in developing a healthy outlook on life.

Social Growth

When children play together they learn to be together. The development of common interests and goals takes place among children during play. Children must learn to "give a little" as well as "take a little" when involved in play activities. Whether two small children

Fig. 13-5 Social growth takes place when children can play together on a slide, and learn to wait their turn.

are arguing over the possession of a toy, or a group of children are playing together on a jungle gym, play helps children grow socially.

Psychologists feel that three- to five-year-olds need to do things together and to talk about what they are doing. Children in this age group seem to see the world from only their own point of view. They must learn to realize that other people see the world differently and that these other people can be correct in their views. Children can begin learning this for themselves through the experiences they have with other children. Play activities provide the needed experiences by drawing children together and providing them with chances to listen to each other's ideas.

PLAY AT DIFFERENT AGES

It seems clear that play serves a number of useful functions in a child's life. Play is

- A source of enjoyment and learning.
- A way of developing friendships and feelings for other children.

Fig. 13-6 Children like to "pretend" in their play activities, whether they are taking care of dolls, or pretending to be a favorite television character.

- A means of learning to control or channel one's feelings.

However, the kinds of play activities enjoyed by three-year-olds are different from those enjoyed by four-year-olds. In a similar way, five-year-olds act differently and play differently from three- and four-year-olds.

The Play of Three-Year-Olds

Three-year-old children enjoy dramatic play. They often pretend to be another member of their own immediate family when they are involved in this kind of play. Children may act out the part of their mothers or fathers, by cooking, cleaning, caring for others (dolls), driving an imaginary car to the store, or mowing the lawn. Three-year-olds also like to pretend they are some television character. They find it difficult to separate real people from "pretend" people when they are playing. Therefore, children often become convinced that they really are some imaginary person. They may even become angry when an adult uses their real name rather than their imaginary one. However, children of this age shift their roles very quickly, often from moment to moment. They may be a horse one minute and a jet pilot the next.

Three-year-olds collect anything that is attractive to them or to others in their group. They like to collect things such as books, puzzles, and toys. The child of three repeats games or play activities over and over, never seeming to tire of repetition.

The Play of Four-Year-Olds

Four-year-old children are generally more imaginative than three-year-olds. Their play often reflects more aggressive activity. Playing monster or ghost characters is one of their favorites. Dramatic play involving aggressive television characters is also common. There is a tendency for children to act out male or female roles to an extreme. They like to wear costumes that show the strength of the character.

Four-year-olds are better coordinated in using tools and equipment than three-year-olds. An interesting trait at this time is that of hiding things. Toys, tools, and blocks are often buried in the sandbox. The children delight in playing hide-and-seek.

Four-year-olds differ most from three-year-olds in their ability to distinguish the real from the imaginary. They are beginning to know the difference between playing a character and actually being the character.

The Play of Five-Year-Olds

Five-year-old children begin to play games which have rules. They start to understand the need for rules. They also understand the meaning of games that have certain objectives.

Children of this age play out their fears and sometimes relieve their aggressions through dramatic play. Rather than to hit another child, a five-year-old pretends to be a ghost who frightens that child. Dramatic play be-

comes more complicated in terms of roles children play and characters they become. Some characters are taken from their everyday life (a fire fighter or nurse), and some are made-up characters (a spaceadventurer or queen).

Five-year-olds become interested in their bodies and sometimes play "doctor" with children of the opposite sex. They also show some interest in romance by playing bride-and-groom games.

Improved coordination enables these children to play with more complicated toys. Some are able to ride two-wheeled bicycles. Muscle development helps them handle smaller tools. They can hold a paintbrush so that the brush begins to respond to their wishes. The five-year-old can build tall block towers and interesting block castles.

SELECTION AND CARE OF PLAY EQUIPMENT

The kinds of equipment available to young children can help or hinder their play activities. If equipment is to improve the quality of play, that equipment should have certain characteristics.

Simple in design. Too much detail destroys the children's freedom to express themselves. Crayons, blocks, clay, sand, paints, and even empty cardboard boxes are examples of simple, but useful, equipment for young children.

Versatile. Equipment should be usable by both boys and girls for many kinds of activities.

Stimulating. The equipment should be the kind that allows children to do things, and motivates them. If adults must supervise children every minute that they are using the equipment, this may hinder creativity. Long explanations on how to use the equipment should not be necessary.

Large and easy to use. Because of the growth of muscles during this time, very small

Fig. 13-7 Play equipment for very young children should be simple in design and easy to use.

Fig. 13-8 Large, durable equipment is good for play activities for children aged three to five.

equipment can cause young children to become anxious. Big trucks and wagons are just right. Large, hollow blocks are better than small, solid ones.

Durable. Breakable equipment soon is broken by three- to five-year-olds. Equipment made of a hard wood such as maple is less likely to splinter than equipment made of soft woods such as pine. Rubber-wheeled riding toys are preferred to those with wooden wheels.

In proper working order. Nothing angers children more than a bicycle with wheels that do not turn or a cabinet with drawers that do not open. Sometimes hinges have to be oiled in order to make equipment operate properly. Other times, care must be taken in the selection of materials. The equipment that costs the least may not be the least expensive in the long run.

Available in proper amounts. Too many toys or too much equipment can decrease the effectiveness of those materials. In order to carry out creative play, a child needs room. Of course, it is important to have enough blocks, too, so that a child can finish a building. On the other hand, if there are too many blocks, the child may never start to build.

Designed to encourage children to play together. Many pieces of equipment are designed for one child to use alone. This is not considered bad. However, children need to work together and find out what the others are thinking and doing. Therefore, equipment designed to get children together should also be provided. Housekeeping equipment from a grocery store or kitchen often draws children together for play.

MAINTAINING EQUIPMENT

After selecting proper equipment for play, it is important to maintain that equipment properly. Wooden materials may sometimes need resanding and refinishing. Wheels may need replacing.

Proper storage is another important factor in handling equipment. Equipment should be organized so that children know where to find things and where to return them. Storage

Fig. 13-9 Play equipment, whether it consists of some old tires or a set of playground equipment, must be free from any hazards that may injure children, and must be the type that children want to use.

cabinets should be easy to open. Shelves should be low enough for children to reach things without having to climb on furniture or risk hurting themselves. Equipment that is not weatherproof should be kept indoors or under a covering out-of-doors. Bicycles and wagons should be protected from harsh weather when they are not in use.

All equipment should be checked for hazards. Sharp metal ends, splinters, loose wheels, a loose head on a hammer, and cracked or chipped blocks are some of the items which cause serious injury to children. Equipment checks should be made on a regular basis.

SUMMARY

For young children, playing is a central part of life, not something they do when they finish working. Play may be organized, or it may be free. It may involve dramatics. It may require equipment.

Play helps children grow physically, mentally, emotionally, and socially. Play is quite different for three-year-olds than it is for five-year-olds. Three-year-old children often cannot separate the real from the pretend. They prefer to be characters about whom they know something. Four-year-olds tend to be aggressive and choose to play characters which enable them to display their aggressive feelings. Five-year-olds can separate the real world from the world of their imaginations. They are better able to control their emotions.

In helping children play, it is important to select proper equipment. The best kinds of play equipment are (1) simple in design, (2) versatile, (3) easy to use, (4) large, (5) durable, (6) working properly, (7) available in needed amounts, and (8) designed for group play. It is also important that play equipment be stored properly so that children can reach it easily. Play equipment should be maintained in good shape and function properly so that children are not injured.

STUDENT ACTIVITIES

- Observe children of various ages at play. Without letting them know you are watching, observe one or more children from each of the age groups at play for periods of at least ten minutes for each group. How are the play activities similar? How are they different?

- Obtain a toy and equipment catalog or go to a toy store. Make a list of materials that would be useful for children's play. Imagine that you have $1,250 to spend on equipment. Make a list of items you would purchase. Assume you may not go over the $1,250 amount.

- Make a list of ten games or play activities that help children play together in groups. List five activities that would help children develop better muscle control.

REVIEW

A. List the four kinds of growth that can be helped by play and related activities.

B. Name five characteristics that are helpful in selecting proper equipment for three- to five-year-old children.

Unit 14
PLAY ACTIVITIES TO ENCOURAGE CREATIVITY

OBJECTIVES

After studying this unit, the student will be able to

- List eight activities that help children develop large muscle skills.
- State five activities that help children develop small muscle skills.
- Describe three kinds of play activities done in groups.

Play is central to the lives of small children. For them, playing means learning, living, and enjoying. Therefore, if children are to live full and creative lives, they must be given a chance to play. It may be free play, or organized play. It may be free play in a group or free play alone. It may be play organized by an adult for a special purpose, or it may be organized by the children just for the fun of it. It may be play that involves a great deal of equipment, or it may be play that springs from a child's imagination. Whatever the case, children need to play. Adults who

Fig. 14-1 The child's ability to pretend and imagine is often enough to keep an activity going.

care for children need to know how to plan for and carry out many kinds of play activities.

CREATIVE PLAY USING LARGE MUSCLES

Children are able to do things with their large muscles before they are able to control their small muscles. The large muscles are those of the upper and lower arms, upper and lower legs, and those that control head, shoulder, and hip movements. A child develops control over these muscles only by using them. Large muscles which are not used remain small, weak, and of little use. On the other hand, when these muscles are used, they become large and strong. Children with well-developed muscles are better coordinated and more confident about their ability to deal with life's demands.

Some activities that help children develop large muscle skills are listed.

- Lifting hollow blocks, cartons, or other large materials, such as boards or bags of objects.
- Piling large blocks or cartons in stacks.
- Climbing trees, a rope ladder, or a jungle gym.
- Swinging on a swing or on parallel bars and hanging from a horizontal ladder.
- Riding a tricycle, pushing a coaster or a tricycle, or pulling a sled.

Fig. 14-2 Climbing on playground equipment is a very good way for children to exercise the muscles in their arms and legs.

Fig. 14-3 Using a shovel to put sand in a pail is also a good activity for large muscle development.

- Digging with a shovel, raking leaves, sweeping with a broom, and sponging with a mop.

- Pounding nails and sawing wood.

- Balancing on a low board.

- Bouncing on a trampoline.

- Running on sand or grass (sometimes in shoes, other times barefoot).

- Jumping over low objects and from low objects.

- Throwing large rubber balls; tossing beanbags.

- Making creative movements to music; dancing; and doing other rhythm activities.

- Working with finger paints.

Certain activities are suitable for three-year-olds while others work better with children who are four and five years old. For instance, skipping is a fun activity for five-year-olds, but some younger ones find it very difficult. Four-year-olds can throw a ball either underhand or overhand, but with poor aim. Three-year-olds find it hard to throw a ball overhand. Five-year-olds have better direction when throwing a ball.

The following are some creative play activities that require the use of large muscles and help in the development of those muscles.

Follow the leader. The leader child moves about freely. The leader may imitate animals — a rabbit hopping or a fish swimming. The others must follow the leader.

Guess what I am. Without saying a word, a child tries to act out the movements of some object. This may be an airplane making a landing, a rooster strutting around the barnyard, a

Fig. 14-4 In "follow the leader," the players follow the motions of the leader.

cement truck dumping its load, a clock telling the time of day. The child may think up things to do, or the teacher may whisper suggestions.

Water play. A water table or a large tub is used. Children make suds and create shapes from the suds. They use water and a large paintbrush to "paint" a fence or the school building. A variety of objects can be put together to make a boat that floats. (Aluminum foil works well for this.) Creative cleanup can be developed by children as they find how water, tools, and materials can help them clean up messes.

Playing with a hose. A child enjoys playing with a hose connected to an outlet with the water on strong. The children learn about what happens when they put their thumbs over the nozzle. They discover the push effect as water leaves the hose. They make rain by sprinkling water into the air. They create a rainbow. They hear different sounds as the water strikes different materials.

Building with sand, mud, and clay. Children use large muscles to build sand mounds with moats around them. Sand pies and sand forts can be built in a sandbox, on a sand table, or at the seashore. Children use mud to make large structures. Clay is also used to create structures and shapes.

Creative play with blocks. Large, hollow blocks can be used to build a city, grocery store, beauty parlor, bridge, tall tower, and many other structures.

Using empty cartons. For their birthday, many children receive toys that come in large cartons. After a short time, many of these children put aside the fancy toys and play with the empty cartons. In view of this, it makes sense to provide such boxes for children to play with. The boxes can be used in many creative ways — they can be arranged into trains, they can serve as houses and stores; they can be used as a cave or a hideaway. Children can paint the outsides and insides.

CREATIVE PLAY USING SMALL MUSCLES

Small muscle skills develop after large muscle skills. Small muscles control finger and toe movements, hand movements, and other similar movements. As with large muscles, the small muscles develop only if they are used. Some activities that develop small muscle skills in children are listed.

- Dressing and undressing themselves, buttoning coats, lacing and tying shoes, pulling on boots, and hanging coats on hooks.

- Dressing and undressing dolls.

- Eating with forks and spoons, and pouring juice from a pitcher into a glass.

- Putting jigsaw puzzles together.

- Playing with small toys and blocks.

- Cutting out figures and painting with a small paintbrush, crayon, or felt-tip pen.

- Working with small tools.

- Using finger puppets and other finger play, such as making shadow designs on a screen.

In creative play, it cannot be predicted that all children will behave in a certain way at the age of three, or four, or five. But in most cases, activities requiring fine muscle skills

Fig. 14-5 Placing small, round sticks into small holes in a piece of wood helps children develop small muscle skills.

should be saved for somewhat older children. Four- and five-year-olds are better able to use their fingers than are three-year-olds. They can make smaller motions with their arms and have better muscle control than the younger children.

Many of the following activities may be used more effectively with older children in the three- to five-year age range.

Creative homemaking. Play activities which involve baking, general cooking, simple repair work, knitting, and sewing are included here. Playing house can lead into these activities.

What can you make? Given some nails, wood, a small saw, and a hammer, a child can create a new toy or a game. The child can create

Fig. 14-6 Creative homemaking activities help five-year-olds develop fine muscle skills.

Fig. 14-7 Older children can create their own games given some nails, a hammer, some wood, a small saw, and some string.

something that serves a special purpose, such as a toothbrush holder or a stand to support a broom.

Using sand and water. Building a city out of sand using different cookie shapes is a creative way to play. Lakes and roads can be added around and in the city, using waxed paper or aluminum foil. Children can then try to draw a picture of their city, using crayons or felt-tip pens.

GROUP PLAY

Some play activities are best carried out by one child working alone. Other activities work best when they are done in a group. This section discusses some group play activities.

Group Games

Certain factors should be considered when planning and carrying out group games. The teacher should know the abilities of the children who are expected to play the games. Games and equipment must be free from safety hazards. Outdoor games should match weather conditions, such as fast moving games for cool weather. Care should be taken that enough space and all needed equipment are available. Leaders should know the game rules. It is wise to select games in which the feelings of children who lose will not be hurt. Children should not be forced to play a game. The size of groups should be kept small so that each child gets a chance to play. If the game involves choosing a child to be "it," favoritism must not be shown in picking that child. Some games that work well with groups of young children are listed.

Stop and go. Children walk around doing whatever they want with their arms and bodies. When the teacher says "stop," the children must freeze and hold that position until the teacher says "go." Children who lose their balance while the game is stopped must sit

Fig. 14-8 In group games, the size of the group should be kept small so that each child gets a turn to be "it."

down. Children move creatively and assume interesting positions.

Jump over the river. Teams can be selected for this game. Two long sticks can serve as the banks of the river. Children must jump from one bank to the other. The sticks should be moved further apart at times to make a wider river. Children must find ways to get their team from one side of the river to the other.

Call and roll. Children sit in a circle. Two large rubber balls are used. The balls are handed to two children on opposite sides of the circle. Each child with a ball must call out the name of another child in the circle and roll the ball to that child.

Creative Dramatics

One of the best ways children have to express themselves is through creative dramatic play. Here, they feel free to express their inner feelings. Often, teachers find out how children feel about themselves and others by listening to the children as they carry out dramatic play. Many times, creative dramatics begins with one child, and others soon join in.

Playing store with a storekeeper and a number of customers is a form of creative

Fig. 14-9 Children enjoy many different types of activities in creative dramatics, one of which is the use of hand puppets to put on a show.

play. Speaking on a toy telephone to a friend is another form of creative play. Puppet shows in which children use finger puppets and make up a story as they go along is still another form. By pretending that a coaster is a car, or a train, or an airplane, children can take an imaginary trip. They can make up and act out stories for other children as part of creative dramatics. Children can listen to music and tell what they see in their mind as they hear the music. They can even make up a story about the music. Then each child, in turn, can add to the story.

Play Kits

Teachers of young children can help build children's imaginations by providing kits containing "props" for them to use. Children can select the props and use them in groups to play roles or create games. Materials for the kits can be kept together in shoe boxes or other containers. Some examples of these kits are listed.

- A supermarket kit containing cash register, play money, paper and pencil, empty food cartons or play canned goods, and empty paper bags.

- A beauty parlor kit that has combs, brushes, scarves, wigs, fingernail polish (use water colored with food coloring), cash register, and play money.

- Doctor and nurse kit including stethoscope, tongue depressors, plastic syringe (without a needle), cotton balls, plastic bottles of water, white coat, nurse cap.

- House painter kit with paint cans full of water, brushes, drop cloth, painter's hat.

- Fire fighter kit which provides hat, hose, badge, red coaster wagon, small ladder, boots.

HELPING CHILDREN PLAY

Adults can help children play, or they can get in the way. A teacher can help children in a number of ways without getting in their way. Some of these ways are listed.

Setting up. The classroom and outside areas can be set up so that many materials are easily available to children. Materials should be placed at a height that children can reach. Materials should be interesting and attractive to the children. There should be choices of activities and materials. However, too many choices are just as bad as too few. There should be variety in the choices. Some should lead children to quiet play while others help them use their energy.

Helping a child get started. When suggesting an activity, an adult must consider how the child feels. If children are tired or angry, a quiet game helps them relax. If the children are bored, the adult should try to interest them in some activity that is exciting. Children sometimes need help in gathering materials for games or other play activities. If children lack needed materials, it is helpful if an adult shows them what is missing.

Keeping a child's interest alive. Once a child is involved in a play activity, a few words of encouragement may be all that is needed to keep the child interested. It is wise to avoid judging a child's work. One can encourage without passing judgment. It is useful to watch for children who are having problems. A little help may be needed to solve a small problem. Children need enough time to finish a game. A good teacher makes sure children are not stopped just when they are beginning to have fun. Successful play can be planned and encouraged by well-informed adults. Time is provided. Materials are gathered. Children are given enough freedom to do things. Adults supervise, but do not oversupervise, the children.

SUMMARY

The needs of children are met through play. Children learn about the world around them and develop many skills. Play helps children acquire large muscle coordination. Activities that contribute to this are playing with blocks, climbing, running, swinging, riding on wheeled toys, throwing, pounding, dancing, and similar creative movements. Children's small motor coordination also develops through play. Such activities as drawing and painting, dressing and tying shoes, building puzzles, and using tools help a child's coordination.

Children play well together in groups. Group games, group dramatics, and play kits help children in these group activities. Finally, adults can help children play. They can also hinder play. If adults properly prepare for the activity, help the children get started, and keep the children's interest alive, play becomes a successful part of programs for young children.

STUDENT ACTIVITIES

- Observe a group of children at play. Record evidence of each of the following situations.
  A. A child discovers something about nature as a result of play.
  B. A child seems to overcome a fear as a result of play.
  C. A child discovers what other children are like as a result of play.
- A game you should try is called the Animal Cracker game. It is an example of a game that children enjoy and one that helps the student develop a better understanding of the creative possibilities of games.
  A. Obtain a box of animal crackers. Stand before a full-length mirror and without looking, take one of the crackers from the box. Look at and then eat the cracker. With that action, you "become" the selected animal for two minutes. Observe your behavior as that animal. Do this a number of times.
  B. Answer the following questions about this activity.
    1. How did you feel about doing this?
    2. How is creativity different from silliness?
    3. How do games help people develop creativity or become more creative?
- There are things that teachers do that help create a good climate for play in their classes. There are other things that teachers do that keep children from playing.

A. Make a list of five do's and five don'ts for play in the classroom.

B. If possible, compare your list with lists made by other people.

- Make up a play kit of "props" children might use in one of the listed activities.

A. Playing mail carrier.

B. Playing dentist.

C. Playing airline pilot.

D. Playing waitress.

REVIEW

A. List six activities that help children develop large muscle skills.

B. List four points that teachers should remember when planning and carrying out group games.

Creative Activities in Other Preschool Curriculum Areas

Unit 15 CREATIVE MOVEMENT AND DRAMATICS

OBJECTIVES

After studying this unit, the student will be able to

- Give the objectives of creative movement.

- Describe an acceptable approach to working with young children in creative movement.

- List the items needed to assemble at least five dramatic play kits.

Imagine a child who is unaware that anyone is watching him. He is outdoors, walking along, pulling on tree leaves and bushes. Suddenly, he hears some music from a distant marching band. He throws up his arms and begins to step with his knees rising high and fast. His arm is making motions as though he were twirling a baton. His arms raise up and his eyes veer skyward. The baton is in the air. His arms snap back and his knees tuck in. He has caught it! On he goes, twirling and marching.

CREATIVE MOVEMENT

There is usually no planning or forethought on the part of children in creative movement. They forget about themselves and let the music's rhythm or an idea carry their bodies away. There is no pattern of movements to be practiced or perfected. Young children are free to move about in any mood which the music or rhythm suggests to them.

In creative movement, children are allowed to develop and express their own personalities in their own style. They do not have an example to follow or an adult to imitate. Creative movement can occur in any situation where children feel free and want to move their bodies. It can be done to poetry, music, rhythm, or even silence. By feeling a pulse, beat, idea, or emotion, children's bodies become instruments of expression. They are musical notes running along a keyboard or wheat waving in the wind. They are anything they want to be. Their movement is an expression of that being.

If creative movement is a regular part of the young child's curriculum, a number of objectives may be reached:

- Relaxation and freedom in the use of the body.

- Experience in expressing space, time, and weight.

- Increased awareness of the world.

- Experience in creatively expressing feelings and ideas.

- Improvement of coordination and rhythmic interpretation.

- Increasing sensitivity in aesthetic judgment.

In order to provide the music or rhythm for creative movement, only a few items may be necessary. A phonograph and some records along with a drum, sticks, and bells may be more than enough. Depending on the circumstances, hand clapping can be a rhythmic addition or a last resort.

Some basic concepts for the teacher to remember when working in this area are listed.

- The teacher should make it clear that anything the children want to do is all right, as long as it does not harm themselves or others.

- The children should understand that they do not have to do anything anyone else does. They can do anything the music or idea "tells" them to do.

- The child should be allowed to "copy" someone for a start if desired.

- The children should understand that each child is different and all people move in different ways.

- Dancing is a healthy form of exercise for everyone; it takes no special talent or skill to be fun.

- The children should have help in realizing the experiences of freedom of movement, the relationship of movement to space, and the relationship of movement to others.

With Music

Listening to music is a natural way to introduce creative movement. Distinctive types of music or rhythm should be chosen for initial movement experiences. (The following suggestion is only one way to approach creative movement. There are many more ways and numerous books that can give teachers more ideas on this topic.)

The teacher may begin the experience by playing music on a phonograph. A record should be chosen that has a strong and easily recognized beat or rhythm. The children should not be told what to listen for. They should not be told the name of the selection or see the album cover. The teacher should let

Fig. 15-1 Dancing is a healthy and fun form of creative movement for young children.

them listen and then ask them to think what the music is saying to them.

While the children are listening, the teacher may turn the music down a bit lower, and ask them to form a circle facing inward. The teacher should talk about what the music is saying with each child. Some of the children probably are already moving to the music by this time, and the teacher may join in. It should be suggested that the children may go anywhere in the room and do anything that the music "tells" them to do. For this exercise, clapping, stomping, and even shouting are all possible and helpful. When appropriate, a quieter piece of music may be played to allow the children to rest and to give them a sense of contrast.

This general approach can be adapted to movement with dolls and puppets; movement of specific parts of the body, such as hands, feet, or toes; and movement in different kinds of space or group. The imaginations of the children and the teacher are the only limits.

Fig. 15-2 When listening to music, children often start moving to the music before the teacher begins to talk about the activity.

Fig. 15-3 A creative movement exercise can begin with the teacher reading a poem to the children, and then the children act out the characters that were of most interest to them.

With Poetry and Prose

For creative movement, poetry has rhythm as well as the power of language. It is not necessary to use rhyming verses at all times. In the beginning, poems that rhyme may be helpful to start a feeling of pulse and rhythm. Poems should be chosen that fit the young child's level of appreciation. By adult standards, they may be quite simple. They are usually short, vivid, and lively descriptions of animals or motion. However, children should not be limited to these, as there are many books and collections available with a wider variety. The local library is the best resource for this.

A suggested beginning (again, many books and articles have additional ideas) may be to ask the children to listen to the reading of a poem. After they have heard it, they may pick out their favorite characters in it. The teacher should encourage some discussion about who those characters are and what they do. The poem should be read a second time; teachers can suggest that the children act out their characters as they listen to the poem. Anything goes — the children may hop like bunnies, fly like planes, or do whatever they feel.

As the readings continue, more complex poems can be selected. These poems may contain a series of movements or simple plots. The same general idea can also be carried through with prose.

As children become more comfortable in acting out poetry read aloud, they may become more sensitive to the less obvious actions or emotions described by the poetry. When stories or poems that have several characters and more complex interaction are read, the entire selection should first be read for listening only. Then, it can be discussed to get some idea of the children's understanding and appreciation. If the children are interested, several readings may be necessary.

The procedure of reading-listening, picking roles, and acting out what is read, can be used over and over. Children may ask to "play the story" whenever they enjoy something that is read to them. Costumes and scenery may be added. Notice how much the wearing of hats can stimulate imagination and involvement.

CREATIVE DRAMATICS

A disturbing sight in some early childhood settings is a small group of children tensely acting out a play. The lines are memorized and said in a stilted, artificial manner. The children feel and look out of place in the costumes they are wearing. They may be excited, but many are also frightened — afraid of tripping or spoiling the show. Adults can be found looking on and making remarks such as "isn't that cute?" Adult anxiety for the children is hidden by nervous laughter. This is not creative dramatics; it is a mistake. The error is made because the play is meant to please adults rather than to relate to children. It is a "show-off" when it should be a "happening."

Drama is an excellent means for developing the creativity and imagination of young children. The children have instinctive ways of dealing with reality. They need no written lines to memorize or structured behavior patterns to imitate to fantasize their world. What they do need is an interesting environment and freedom to experiment and be themselves.

As stated earlier, creative movement can be started by the use of carefully chosen music, poetry, and prose. After the children have had satisfying experiences with creative movement, they can be introduced to drama. The use of simple props, costumes, and puppets is all that is needed. Although an audience can heighten children's enjoyment of drama, the emphasis has to be on their personal creativity. Urging children to conform to adult aesthetic standards is not acceptable.

Dramatic Play

Dramatic play occurs daily in the lives of young children. It is one of the ways that children naturally learn. Children constantly imi-

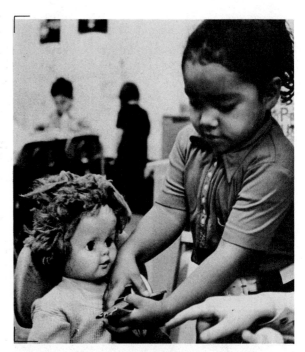

Fig. 15-4 For creative dramatic play, children do not need very elaborate equipment to enjoy themselves. A child's imagination can turn a doll into a baby that must be cared for, or a customer in a beauty parlor.

tate the people, animals, and machines in their world. They begin to put on their parents' slippers at twenty months of age. They enjoy recreating the exciting experiences of their lives. Dramatic play is their way of understanding and dealing with the world. One of the best ways to stimulate this spontaneous kind of drama is to provide young children with some simple props and the freedom to experiment.

By assembling a variety of available, everyday items into groups which have a common use or theme, *dramatic play kits* are created. Just letting the children know what the use of these kits may be is often enough to get them started. Some common types are suggested.

Supermarket. Old cash register, play money, paper pads, pencils or crayons, punchers, paper sacks, empty food cartons, wax food, grocery boxes, cans with smooth edges.

Post Office. Index card file, stamp pads, stampers, crayons, pencils, old Christmas seals, old envelopes.

Beauty Parlor. Plastic brushes, combs, makeup, cotton balls, scarves, clip-on rollers, colored water in nail polish bottles, empty hair spray cans, wigs.

Cooking. Pots, pans, eggbeaters, spoons, pitchers, salt and flour shakers, medicine bottles with colored water, tablecloth, aprons.

Cleaning. Small brooms, mops, cake of soap, sponges, toweling, plastic spray bottle, plastic basin, clothesline, clothespins, doll clothes to wash.

Doctor. Tongue depressors, old stethoscope, satchel, Bandaids, cotton balls, uniforms, discarded plastic hypo syringes without needles (available from clinics and should be boiled).

Mail Carrier. Hats, badges, envelopes, mail satchel.

Fire Fighter. Hats, raincoats, boots, short lengths of garden hose.

Farmer. Shovel, rake, hoe, seeds.

Plumber. Wrench, plastic pipes, tool kit.

Gas Station Attendant. Shirt, hat, tire pump, boxes for cars.

Many more dramatic play kits can be added to this list. It is important to encourage both boys and girls to assume a variety of roles. Imagination can also be used to transform regular classroom items into "new materials." Chairs can become trains, cars, boats, or a house. A table covered with a blanket or bedspread becomes a cave or special hiding place. Large cardboard cartons which children can decorate can become houses, forts, and fire stations.

Fig. 15-5 **In dramatic play activity, boys and girls both play a variety of roles.**

Role Playing

Pictures can be excellent starting points for experiments with role playing. A picture showing the action or conversation between two or more people should be chosen. It is helpful if one of them is a child.

The chosen picture may be of a doctor talking with a young child. While showing the picture, the teacher asks questions to create a thinking atmosphere. Some questions might be: "What are the people? (doctor, patient) Where are they? What are they doing? What is the child saying? How does the child feel? What is the doctor saying? What do you think happens next?"

The teacher may choose volunteers to be the doctor and the child. The children take the places of the people in the picture. They almost "step into the picture" as they begin to speak and act the roles of the doctor and the child. When these volunteers have finished, other children can demonstrate their views of the same scene. Some children may think the child in the picture is sick. Some may see the doctor as the child's father. Some may think the doctor is telling the child about a brother or sister. All interpretations are new creative opportunities.

The teacher can change the pictures used to create more role-playing situations, although a picture is not always needed for role-playing. The reading of a story can be stopped midway and the children can act out its finish. Children can role-play their dreams. Television programs and movies are other good stimulators.

Role-playing is also a way to help children see the viewpoints of other people. When feelings and emotions come out, sensitive and open discussions after the role-playing can offer new insights and learnings. This is a good way to help young children explore their feelings and find ways to handle their emotions and their relationships with others.

Puppets

Puppets can be used for almost any of the dramatic experiences that have been described here. They offer the child two ways to express creativity: (1) the artistic experience of making the puppet and (2) causing the puppet to come to life. Many kinds of puppets are suitable for use by young children. Some of these are finger puppets, hand puppets, stick puppets, poster puppets, and marionettes. Their construction and use were discussed earlier.

SUMMARY

In creative movement, the children are allowed to develop and express their personalities in their own ways. Creative movement

Fig. 15-6 Making finger puppets "come to life" is one kind of dramatic play activity that helps children express their creativity.

can occur with music, rhythm, poetry, prose, and even silence. It can develop relaxation, freedom, and increased awareness and sensitivity in young children.

Drama is another excellent means for developing creativity and imagination in young children when it is related to the child's personal sense of reality without imposed adult standards. Dramatic play kits are easy to make and help develop opportunities for creative play. Role-playing helps children explore their feelings. The use of puppets provides opportunities for creative movement and dramatics.

STUDENT ACTIVITIES

- Create two dramatic play kits not listed or suggested in this unit.
    A. Try to make one that no one else might think of making.
    B. Compare with those of classmates.
- Often, teachers ask children to do something they have never experienced. This can be a mistake for obvious reasons.
    A. Have some fun. Each class member is to bring in a picture of two people (in any situation). Put all the pictures in a common pile.
    B. By random selection, have class members in sets of two select a picture and role-play it for five minutes.

REVIEW

A. List six objectives of creative movement.

B. What are four important concepts to remember when working with young children in the area of creative movement?

C. List three things to avoid in creative dramatics with young children.

Unit 16 SCIENCING–DEVELOPING THE SENSES

OBJECTIVES

After studying this unit, the student will be able to

- State the meaning of sciencing.
- List three reasons why sciencing activities are important to the development of young children.
- Name and describe three general kinds of sciencing.

When considering creative activities, it is not possible to skip the area of science. This is because true science is a highly creative activity. There is a purpose in using the word "true" with the term science. Most of the science learning that takes place in schools is not true science. Instead, it is the learning of science history — learning about facts that others have discovered in the past. Learning facts is not very creative, but learning science is.

THE MEANING OF SCIENCE

There are twenty young children in a classroom. Each has just been given a small box that is wrapped in brightly colored gift paper. There is a big ribbon around each box. There are some objects inside each box. Each child is trying to find out what is in a box without taking off the ribbon and paper.

Some children are shaking their gift boxes. Some are holding them up to their ears and listening very carefully. Others are squeezing them. A few are punching the boxes. The children are interested in finding out what is in their own wrapped-up box.

Is this a game? It may seem so, but it is not. It is a way in which children make creative discoveries. In many ways, it is also the way that scientists make creative discoveries. The little gift box is somewhat like the world in which the children live. The children study their own little "worlds" by shaking the box,

Fig. 16-1 **In one sciencing activity, children are asked to find out what is inside a wrapped gift box without opening it up.**

smelling it, squeezing it, and looking at it. Each child makes some discoveries but cannot find out everything because the box cannot be unwrapped. The children may be able to make some good guesses after studying the boxes, however. Some things are open to the children's discovery. Some things are not. Scientists are faced with the same problems. They, too, study the world. They, too, can observe some things and can only guess about others.

There are two things, then, that both the child and the scientist do. They *investigate*

Fig. 16-2 A child who is not familiar with musical instruments may enjoy the opportunity to investigate this new equipment.

(carefully study the world around them) to discover *knowledge* (find answers to questions or problems about that world). Science consists of two phases, or parts, which cannot be separated: investigation and knowledge.

WHAT IS SCIENCING?

If science is investigating in order to gain knowledge, then what is sciencing? In dealing with young children, it has been found that investigating is much more important than the knowledge that comes from investigating. To help people understand that exploring is more important for children than the information turned up, the term *sciencing* is used. Science is a noun — a thing. Sciencing is a verb — an action. Young children need a lot of action, not a lot of knowledge about the thing. This does not mean that understanding the world is put aside completely for young children. It just means that learning how to find answers is considered more important than the answers themselves. If the words "investigation" and

"knowledge" were written according to their importance for preschool children, they would look like this:

> **INVESTIGATION**
> **Knowledge**

However, investigation and knowledge are a team. They cannot be completely separated from one another. To provide the experiences children need to develop scientific creativity, teachers must understand the meaning of sciencing. They must help children investigate in order to find answers to questions about the world. How can a teacher do this?

There are three types of activities that help a teacher provide the kinds of experiences children need. These activities are called formal sciencing, informal sciencing, and incidental sciencing. Each of these terms will be explained in detail later. In general, however, *formal sciencing* is a teacher-organized, skill-building activity. *Informal sciencing* is nondirected, free investigation by the child. *Incidental sciencing* is a happening. (That is, incidental sciencing takes place when something happens to one or more children that is of interest to the group. It is usually unplanned and often is unexpected.)

IMPORTANCE OF SCIENCING

Sciencing is important to young children in a number of ways. First, it is well known that some children are very able thinkers but are not good at talking about their thoughts. Those children who express themselves well are almost always noticed by teachers and other adults. They are usually rewarded for their ability. Nonverbal children (those who do not speak very well or very often) are usually considered to be less able thinkers. Somehow this information is passed on to the nonverbal children. They start to believe that they are less able. They act the part they think that "dumb" children ought to act. Their actions then confirm the suspicions of teachers and other adults.

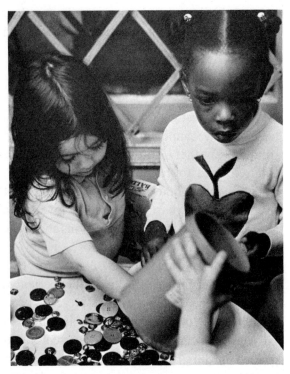

Fig. 16-3 Children who are investigating are learning by doing, and do not have to talk about it.

Fig. 16-4 A sciencing skill, such as identifying the taste of a particular food, is important since this knowledge can be transferred to other areas.

This is a tragic chain of events that takes place too often. What is most tragic is that many of these children are good thinkers. They merely have trouble expressing their thoughts. If only they could be given a chance to show their skill without having to talk about it! Sciencing is a way of doing this. When children investigate, they learn by doing, not by speaking or listening. Moreover, a teacher can see what the child is doing. The children do not have to speak about results — unless they want to. Thus, the teacher may be able to discover bright but nonverbal children by watching them during sciencing activities. Somehow, the teacher will let these children know they have been discovered.

Second, sciencing activities are designed to help children develop skills in using their senses. Uses of these skills are not limited to sciencing. These skills can be used every day. They can be used throughout a person's lifetime.

Educators use the term *transfer of learning* to describe knowledge and skills that are gained in one area and used in many other areas. Sciencing skills are particularly important because they are so highly transferable. Skills in seeing, feeling, and tasting are not limited to sciencing even though they do represent the basic skills that are taught.

Third, children with creative potential must be given a chance to show off their creativity. Activities that give a child this chance are needed in the curriculum. Sciencing is designed to let children show off their skills. Activities are also needed that help creative children further develop their skills. They need a chance to "play" with ideas and materials. They need openness — the freedom to do things without fear of being "out-of-line." Sciencing is designed for this.

SCIENCING ACTIVITIES

In order to carry out sciencing in the classroom, the teacher must know about the three phases of sciencing: formal, informal, and incidental. The chart in figure 16-5 is designed to explain each phase.

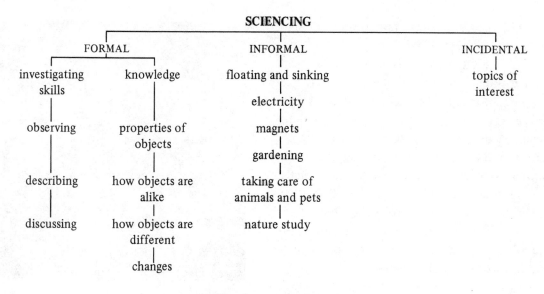

SCIENCING

FORMAL — INFORMAL — INCIDENTAL

FORMAL:
- investigating skills
  - observing
  - describing
  - discussing
- knowledge
  - properties of objects
  - how objects are alike
  - how objects are different
  - changes

INFORMAL:
- floating and sinking
- electricity
- magnets
- gardening
- taking care of animals and pets
- nature study

INCIDENTAL:
- topics of interest

Fig. 16-5 The three phases of sciencing.

Formal Sciencing

Only this phase of sciencing is planned by the teacher. Activities are planned that develop children's observation skills. Other activities are planned that give children a chance to use these skills. Children then apply the skills to some basic areas of knowledge.

Thus, children first learn how do be better observers. Then they apply their observing skills to observing properties, observing similarities and differences, and observing changes. Children can learn words that help them describe their observations. They then describe properties, similarities and differences among objects, and changes that take place.

Informal Sciencing

Unlike formal sciencing, the informal phase calls for little or no teacher involvement. Children work on their own, at their own rate, and only when they feel like it. They select the kinds of activities that interest them. They spend as much or as little time working at a given activity as they desire. It is when this sort of openness is available to children that creative potential begins to show up. A certain need to explore and a willingness to deal in the unknown are signs of a creative child.

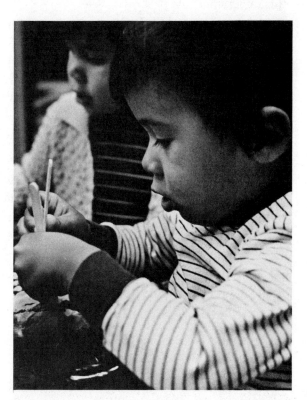

Fig. 16-6 In the formal phase of sciencing, activities are planned that exercise a child's observational skills.

The ability to keep at a task is another sign that a child is creative.

When a child shows signs of interest and creative skill, the informal sciencing activities become important. Materials provided for children can encourage them to continue their quests of discovering. Materials and equipment should be available in large enough numbers that several children can investigate at the same time. Care must be taken that dangerous materials and broken equipment are kept away from children. If materials are available, the only other thing that a child may need is a word of encouragement.

Incidental Sciencing

Incidental sciencing cannot be planned, even by a clever teacher. Incidental sciencing sometimes does not take place once a week or even once a month. It does not always appeal to every child in a class. Just what is incidental sciencing?

A city or town may be struck by a violent windstorm. Limbs of trees are knocked down. Whole trees are uprooted. Great sheets of rain fall and streets become flooded. Children are scared by the great noise and wild lightning as the storm passes. Finally the storm is over.

Is this the time for an incidental sciencing experience? Of course it is! This is the time for those children who are interested to learn many things. They can study the roots of trees; they may have the chance to observe growth rings. They are able to examine tree bark. They can observe what happens to water as it drains from a flooded street. Some might want to talk about their feelings as the

Fig. 16-7 An incidental sciencing session can result from a storm, when a teacher takes the children outside to see what changes took place because of the storm.

lightning flashed and the thunder crashed. Some may wish to create a painting about this experience.

A teacher cannot plan such an experience. A good teacher can, however, take advantage of such an experience by letting children explore and seek answers to questions. A teacher can encourage children to be more inquisitive and creative.

SUMMARY

Sciencing is an activity in which children gain knowledge about the world around them by investigating that world. In sciencing, the emphasis is on investigating. The knowledge gained is less important for the child. Sciencing is important for children because it gives them all an opportunity to succeed.

STUDENT ACTIVITIES

- **Making Some Observations**

The ability to make many accurate observations is an important skill for both children and adults. The following activity is designed to test one's ability to make observations and use all of one's senses (hearing, smelling, tasting, touching, and seeing).

A. Materials: one package of peppermint Life Savers, one ruler, one book of matches, one small nail, one sheet of sandpaper, a glass of water, waxed paper.

B. How many observations can be made about a package of peppermint Life Savers? Can as many as forty observations be made? Try doing this with one or two partners, if possible. Do it for each of the items listed in part (A).

C. List all the observations and write down the sense or senses that were used to make each observation (seeing, hearing, etc.).

- **Describing Similarities and Differences**

It is fun to see how many ways three objects can be compared. How are they alike? How are they different from one another? This activity is designed to provide the student with the chance to do this.

Fig. 16-8 Observing similarities and differences in shapes and sizes of objects can help children learn the many ways things can be compared to each other.

A. Materials:

Set 1: Dolls. Three dolls, each different from the others.

Set 2: Toy cars. Three Hot Wheels cars or similar toy cars.

Set 3: Fruit. A banana, an orange, and an apple.

Set 4: Animals. Pictures of a bird, a lion or tiger, and a snake.

B. In how many ways are the sets of materials alike? In how many ways are they different?

C. Make a list of all the ways that the objects in a set are alike. Then make a list of how they are different. Check each item in each list to see which senses were used in deciding about similarities and differences.

- **Exploring Magnetism**

This activity is an example of an informal sciencing experience. The student should investigate the materials to find out some information about magnetism.

Fig. 16-9 One informal sciencing experience involves the use of magnets with several objects that are magnetic, and several objects that are not magnetic. Children experiment with each of the objects to discover which types are attracted by the magnet.

A. Materials: one small bar magnet, iron filings, newspaper, a glass of water, thin pieces of wood, a thin piece of iron or steel, nails, glass, marbles, coins, and sawdust.

B. What can be learned about magnetism from the materials listed?

C. Explore the materials to find out at least one thing about magnetism. Write down what was found out. Compare results with those of other students. Try out the various statements made by others to see if they work. (This is called verifying the findings of others.)

REVIEW

A. Name the five senses on which observations are based.

B. 1. What are the two phases of formal sciencing? 2. Which phase is more important for young children?

C. List three ways in which children benefit from sciencing.

D. Choose the answer that best completes each statement about sciencing.

1. The teacher is most involved in planning for

    a. formal sciencing.

    b. informal sciencing.

    c. incidental sciencing.

2. The teacher cannot plan for

    a. formal sciencing.

    b. informal sciencing.

    c. incidental sciencing.

3. Observing skills are taught to children in

    a. formal sciencing.

    b. informal sciencing.

    c. incidental sciencing.

4. Free investigation is used most often in

    a. formal sciencing.

    b. informal sciencing.

    c. incidental sciencing.

Unit 17 SCIENCING-SOME CREATIVE ACTIVITIES

OBJECTIVES

After studying this unit, the student will be able to

- Describe at least one activity that can be used for creative formal sciencing.

- Discuss at least one informal sciencing activity by listing materials needed and describing the role of the teacher in carrying out the activity.

- Name six sources of materials for sciencing.

In the preceding unit, three kinds of sciencing were described:

Formal Sciencing. Teacher-planned activities carried out by children. Children learn the skills needed to study the world around them and to apply those skills in three simple knowledge areas (properties, comparisons, and changes).

Informal Sciencing. Free discovery by children with little or no teacher guidance. Children feel free to use science materials to see what they can discover. No special period is set aside for informal sciencing. Children work with the material at their own pace, when they feel like it.

Incidental Sciencing. Unplanned activities that take place at times when children find things of interest. An incidental sciencing session may begin any time a group of children ask questions, find an interesting object, or respond to something in their environment. A session may last for two minutes or may go on for a much longer time.

This unit is designed to provide ideas for carrying out formal and informal sciencing. A few creative activities and a list of materials are suggested. The list is not complete; creative teachers can think of many more activities which help children to be creative.

FORMAL SCIENCING ACTIVITIES

These activities have been tested with young children. They work well if a few simple suggestions are followed.

- All equipment and materials needed for an activity should be on hand and ready to go. Nothing kills an activity faster than for the child to have to stop in the middle because one key item is missing.

- Children should be free to learn for themselves if possible. Teachers who talk too much destroy the creative desire of children in the process.

- All of the children should not be expected to carry out all of the activities at the same time. Children need freedom to move around in order to be creative. This means that they need freedom to move ideas around. They need to try out hunches when they are working with sciencing materials. Directions that leave no room for individual discovery destroy rather than help creativity.

- It helps children get started if they can work at tables or on the floor. They need plenty of room to move and spread out their equipment. A room with running water is desirable.

Fig. 17-1 Some of the most creative discoveries take place when a child works alone.

- Children may want to work with a partner at times. However, the most creative discoveries take place when children work alone. It has been found that arguments are avoided if children have similar equipment when starting an activity. Additional things can be provided on an individual basis.

- Some formal sciencing sessions may hold a child's interest for only a few minutes. There are other times when children wish to work with materials for as long as thirty or forty minutes. Children should not be forced to work on an activity if they are not interested.

- Above all, children should never be made to feel that they have failed in a sciencing activity. All of the children should feel that they have done something right and have learned something of value in sciencing. If children feel they have failed, something is being done wrong by the teacher.

- Classrooms become noisy. This is to be expected when children are busy at work.

Process Skill Building Activities

The following are two examples of the many activities that can be used to help children learn to investigate.

Observing color changes. In this activity, children mix paint and food coloring to see how many new colors they can create.

- Objectives: At the end of this activity, children should be able to

  a. Mix red and blue to get purple; mix blue and yellow to get green; mix red and yellow to get orange.

  b. Identify and name the colors red, orange, yellow, green, blue, and purple.

- Materials: Each child receives

  a. Eight small plastic pill bottles, each of them half-filled with water.

  b. Red, blue, and yellow tempera paint.

  c. Red, blue, and yellow food coloring.

  d. Three eyedroppers.

  e. Eight wooden stirrers.

  f. Waxed paper and newspaper.

- Procedure:

  a. Distribute all the materials to the children.

  b. Make sure that the newspaper is spread out on the child's table or on the floor.

  c. Let children mix colors as they wish at first.

  d. Later, ask children if they can make the colors green, orange, and purple from any of the colors they have been mixing.

  e. An interesting follow-up is to let children mix a variety of colors in larger containers. They can use plastic cups

Fig. 17-2 Children enjoy watching food coloring and paint mix in water; they also learn how two colors mix to form a third color.

Fig. 17-3 Children learn how to describe objects and their placement on a cork board by playing this activity with a blindfolded teacher.

or gallon containers, and food coloring for this. Many colors can be created in this way.

The "Blind" Teacher. In this activity, children discover ways to describe objects and their positions to a "blind" teacher (teacher is blindfolded).

- Objectives: At the end of this activity, children should be able to

  a. Describe three characteristics of some common objects.

  b. Describe the position or location of those objects.

- Materials:

  1. One master set consisting of

     a. Construction paper circles: two red, two green, two blue, two yellow, two orange.

     b. Construction paper squares: two

brown, two black, two purple, two white.

  c. Photographs of each child in the class mounted on a large piece of tag board.

  d. Cork board or felt board for mounting circles and squares.

  e. Blindfold for the teacher.

  2. One set for each two children with

     a. Ten construction paper rectangles: two red, two green, two blue, two yellow, two orange.

     b. Ten paper triangles in four colors: brown, black, purple, white.

     c. Felt board or other surface for placing colored shapes.

     d. Blindfold for child.

- Procedure: Demonstrate the need to communicate information in a very careful way.

a. Explain to the children that their teacher cannot see.

b. Put on the blindfold.

c. Someone is asked to place the various shapes on a cork board or on a felt board.

d. The blind teacher does not know where the shapes are. A "helper" is selected.

e. The "helper" must direct the blind teacher to the location of the colored shape — up, down, this way or that way, until all the shapes have been removed from the board.

f. Repeat the activity using a blind folded child, another helper, and photographs of children in the class mounted on a tag board.

g. Volunteers name children and the helper directs the "blind" child.

h. Children can then receive their own sets of equipment and play the game in pairs.

i. They can try to create their own game using the materials.

j. Children then try to communicate the rules of their game to the teacher or another group of children.

Content Activities

The following activity is presented as one example of the many content activities that can be used in formal sciencing.

- Objectives: At the end of this activity, children should be able to

  a. Identify materials that are liquids.

  b. State that some liquids mix and some do not.

- Materials: Each child receives

  a. A set of five pill bottles with screw-on caps. Each set contains the following

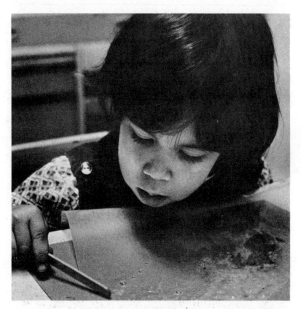

Fig. 17-4 In this activity, children can learn about the properties of liquids by dropping beads of water, baby oil, etc., on a piece of wax paper, and using a stirrer to investigate the liquids (for example, to see if they mix).

  liquids: water, baby oil, liquid hand cream, liquid starch, dishwashing detergent.

  b. Five eyedroppers

  c. Plastic wrap

  d. Wooden stirrers

  e. Newspapers

  f. Three or four plastic mixing cups (5 ounce)

- Procedure:

  a. Distribute materials to each child.

  b. Cover tables or other work areas with newspaper. It might be wise to have children wear smocks.

  c. Ask children to mix and match liquids to see what happens to the combinations.

  d. Help children identify the liquid materials in their sets.

  e. Talk with individuals about which liquids mix and which ones do not.

Process	Activities	Materials Suggested
Observing	Using the senses of sight, smell, hearing, tasting, and feeling to improve observations.	Paints, crayons, color chips (paint chips), seeds, rocks, leaves, cloth of various textures, sandpaper
	Observing smells to identify objects.	Perfumes, room fresheners, flowers
	Increasing the accuracy of observations by using more than one sense.	Tape recorder, bells, musical instruments, sound effects
	Increasing awareness of sounds and smells in the environment.	
Communicating, Describing	Building child's ability to describe objects in terms of one observable property.	Colors: felt material, paint chips
		Textures: swatches of material of various textures, sandpaper of many grades
	Developing skill in describing objects in terms of more than a single property (such as soft and red).	Shapes: 3D wooden shapes
		Size: large and small corks, cups, cutout figures, shells, stones
	Developing a child's vocabulary related to describing words:	Odors: room fresheners, perfumes, colognes, vanilla, almond extract, coffee
	colors, textures (roughness/smoothness), size (large/small), odors (sweet/foul), sounds (high/low pitch, loud/soft), shapes, shininess	Sounds: musical instruments, pop bottles filled with water, noisemakers
		Shininess: foils, papers, paint samples, coins

Fig. 17-5 Investigative processes.

Other Formal Sciencing Activities

Figures 17-5 and 17-6 list some activities that can be used in formal sciencing. Lesson plans are not provided. However, it is expected that such plans would follow a format similar to the three lessons outlined earlier.

INFORMAL SCIENCING ACTIVITIES

Informal sciencing activities are designed to be carried out by individual children. Little or no information is to be provided by the teacher. Experience has shown that informal sciencing works best when these suggestions are followed.

- A section of the classroom should be provided for the storage of materials. The materials should be easy for the children to reach. Materials are best stored in color-coded boxes such as shoe boxes. It is easy for a child to take the equipment needed from a green box and return it to a green box. If possible, a work area should be provided for informal sciencing.

- Open moments should be provided during the school day when children can feel free to play with sciencing materials. If possible, children should be encouraged to try things out.

- A teacher should not hover over the children. The teacher should watch those who are working, however, to make

Content Area	Activities	Materials Suggested
Properties	Reviewing words that name properties.	Use many of the same materials used in building communicating skills.
	Sorting objects on the basis of one property.	Sets of buttons, shells, rocks, leaves, seeds, toys, dolls, pictures of animals, dowels.
	Finding objects that have a particular property.	Sets of materials which may all be related such as a set of crayons. Sets of materials that are not related in some obvious way.
Comparing	Using all the senses to observe how some objects are alike.	Sets of objects with similar properties, such as color, shape, size, texture.
	Using all the senses to observe how some objects are different.	Sets of objects with some similar properties but one obvious difference, such as: a set of buttons of the same size and shape but all of different color; a set of buttons of same size and color but with a different number of holes.
	Counting the number of objects that are alike in a set; counting the number that are different.	Set of objects: half float in water, half sink; set of shapes: some are triangles and some are circles, or some are red and some are green.
Changes	Observing common objects change in shape.	Salt or sugar dissolving in water; ice cubes melting; sawing a square into 2 triangles or 2 rectangles; building blocks; cutting material (patterns).
		Pouring sand from one container into another.
	Observing changes in properties and states of matter (gas to liquid, liquid to solid).	Melting sugar; dissolving materials such as salt; melting ice; ice to hot water to steam.

Fig. 17-6 Content activities.

sure that children are not hurting themselves or others.

- A wide variety of attractive materials should be available for the children.

- If children become upset when working with materials, they can be given small clues to help them move along. The adult should not do the work for the children. A good approach is to give clues by saying "I wonder what would happen if . . . ?"

Informal Sciencing Materials

The following materials can be used to help children develop their creativity in sciencing. Materials that are carefully selected and organized help children make discoveries.

- Floating and sinking

  a. Plastic containers: one-gallon aquariums, shoe boxes, large freezer containers.

Fig. 17-7 Children should be provided with the desired materials and "open moments" in the school day when these materials can be used for informal sciencing activities.

Fig. 17-9 A battery, a light, some wire, and some switches are several informal sciencing materials that give children the chance to learn about electricity.

Fig. 17-8 A child can discover a great deal about fish, plants, and other living things by observing the happenings in an aquarium.

    b. Various objects that float and sink: paper clips, aluminum foil, corks, rocks, screws.

    c. Oil-base clay that can be formed into boat shapes.

    d. Baby food jars, capped and filled with different amounts of sand.

    e. Salt water versus tap water.

- Small animals and fish in the classroom

    a. Terrariums that contain woodland plants and animals, or desert plants and animals.

    b. Aquariums with goldfish, guppies, tropical fish, various plants.

    c. Small animals in cages: guinea pigs, rabbits, mice. (Children can handle some animals. They can observe the living and eating habits of others.)

- Magnets

    a. Magnets of various sizes and shapes.

    b. Iron filings and paper.

    c. Variety of magnetic and nonmagnetic objects.

d. Various materials through which magnetic force passes.

- Simple electricity

    a. Energy sources such as D-cell battery or dry cell.

    b. Wires, lights, and sockets.

    c. Small DC motors.

    d. Switches.

    e. Clips for connecting wires at terminals. (Children can connect one light to a cell using two wires. Using additional wires, they can add a switch. Then they can add more lights, a motor, and more switches.)

- Indoor gardening

    a. Small wooden flats filled with soil.

    b. Variety of seeds.

    c. Gro Lux light (if available).

    d. Absorbent paper (toweling). (Children can watch seeds germinate and discover conditions that make plants grow. Seeds can sprout on moist paper toweling. These activities work best in the fall or spring of the year when the heat is not on in the classroom.)

- Outdoor activities

    (A later unit deals with children exploring their environment.)

Finding Sciencing Materials

The keys to children's success in sciencing are the amount and kind of materials available. There must be enough materials to provide them with a creative challenge. Much of the equipment needed is simple and can be homemade. Materials which cannot be made at home may be obtained from other sources. Several suggestions are included here to help a teacher increase the number and variety of

Fig. 17-10 Children can explore their environment through sciencing activities on the school grounds.

materials in the classroom. Basically, if less is paid for materials, more can be obtained for a given sum of money.

- All of the needed materials often can be obtained in junk shops, resale shops, backyard sales, rummage sales, and barn sales.

- Often, material that is discarded by local industrial plants is just the kind of equipment that is needed for sciencing.

- Scrap bins in lumber yards are a source of inexpensive wood products.

- Hospitals, nursing homes, and drugstores may be contacted for pill bottles and other discarded material that can be useful.

- Materials may be bought from discount stores when they have sales. Remnants are available at department stores. Store catalog sales offer a means of saving money on equipment.

Fig. 17-11 **In sciencing activities, children can often investigate the materials on their own, making discoveries for themselves.**

- Donations from children's parents and friends provide many needed materials.

- As a last resort, needed equipment may be purchased from a science supply catalog. This is, however, the most expensive way to obtain materials.

SUMMARY

Formal sciencing activities are divided into two general categories. First, there are activities designed to help children become better investigators. These are called process skill-building activities. The second category is represented by the kind of science content that helps a child apply the process skills.

Informal sciencing is made up of a number of open activities that children may choose to use or to ignore. Informal sciencing is less structured than formal sciencing. Creativity is therefore better served by informal than by formal sciencing.

There are two keys to a child's success in sciencing: (1) the willingness of a teacher to let children investigate and (2) the availability of equipment. Equipment is available from many sources. Some is free or inexpensive, while other equipment is more expensive. It is important for a teacher to know about and use every source of material that is available.

STUDENT ACTIVITIES

- **Finding Objects For Making Observations**

  A. Find ten objects that could be used for making observations. Each object should provide opportunities for an observer to use all five senses. For instance, an ice cube can be one of the objects used for this purpose.

  B. After finding the ten objects, try the following:

    1. Decide what other materials would help in making observations of this thing. A ruler or magnifying glass may be needed. Make a list of these materials.

    2. Collect all materials needed for observing each item and place them in small packages or boxes.

    3. Choose a partner. Make observations of three of the partner's objects using materials provided by the partner. Then let the partner try out your objects and materials.

- **Describing Shapes**

  A. Draw three shapes on a piece of paper. The shapes should not be something everyone recognizes.

B. Choose a partner. Try to describe each of the objects in such a way that the partner can draw pictures of them without seeing them. This is a difficult task.

- **Making an Electromagnet**

  A. Materials:

  D-cell battery and battery holder or a dry cell

  Four feet of thin wire

  One iron nail

  Thirty or forty tacks or paper clips

  B. The student should try all of the activities listed.

     1. Make an electromagnet with the materials.

        Note: This approach has been proven successful with children. Time and patience are needed for discovery learning to take place.

     2. Find out how these materials can be put together to make a stronger electromagnet (one that will pick up more tacks or paper clips).

     3. Find other things that can be picked up by the electromagnet. Find uses for an electromagnet.

     4. Try this investigation with a four- or five-year-old child. See how the child goes about these tasks. Compare the child's investigating methods with the way adults try to solve these problems.

- **Finding Materials**

  A. Visit rummage sales, farm auctions, store sales, and secondhand stores. Look for materials that could be used by children in sciencing.

  B. Make a list of things that can be bought, how much they cost, and where they can be purchased. Compare lists with two or more other students.

  C. Prepare a master list of these materials.

REVIEW

  A. Describe three topics around which content is built in formal sciencing.

  B. List the three processes used in formal sciencing.

  C. Name six informal sciencing topics that can be used with three- to five-year-olds.

  D. Name seven sources of sciencing materials.

Unit 18 ENVIRONMENTAL EDUCATION

OBJECTIVES

After studying this unit, the student will be able to

- Describe three creative activities that can be carried out in the school environment.

- Discuss three creative activities that can be carried out in the school grounds environment.

- Describe three creative activities that can be carried out in the environment of the school neighborhood.

It has been said many times that if children are to grow up in a world fit for human survival, the environment must be protected. Children should learn about nature from their earliest years on. Nature is not the only part of a child's environment, however. Home, school, and neighborhood are all parts of the child's environment. In fact, everything that contributes to children's experiences — good or bad — is part of their environment. Can a child learn creativity by learning about the environment? Can a child learn to improve the environment? The answer to both questions is "yes." Most of all, learning about these things can and must begin when a child is young.

Fig. 18-1 The time to begin environmental education is when children are young.

THE MEANING OF ENVIRONMENT

Their environment is one of the most important influences in the lives of children. They need an environment full of love. They need an environment that provides for their other basic needs: water, food, clean air. Children need an environment that provides for their safety. They need an environment that helps them grow intellectually. They need an environment that they can understand and control.

In other words, children need to learn about their environment because their lives depend on that environment. This learning can be done in a very creative way. Activities that help children understand their environment can also help them become more creative thinkers.

For the purposes of this unit, the term *environment* means two things. It refers to both man-made and natural things that children meet in their surroundings. Streets, houses, and schools are examples of man-made things in the environment. Trees, grass, and birds are parts of nature. Street lights, cars, and buildings are man-made. Animals, clouds, and snow are natural things. Noise, light, and smells may be man-made or a part of nature.

Children have many environments in which they live. Home is one. It may be a pleasant part of a child's life, or an unpleasant one. School is another environment that influences a child's life, and it, too, may be an enjoyable experience or an unpleasant one. The neighborhood environment which influences a child may be friendly and safe, or it may be hostile and dangerous. There are many people who are part of a child's environment: parents and neighbors, grocers and police officers, teachers and doctors. The people who make up the communities in which children live may make the children feel very good about their lives, or these people may make the children feel unhappy.

In these environments, there are also natural things and natural happenings: grass, trees, and flowers; rain, wind, and earthquakes; cats, rats, and beetles. All of these things are parts of a child's environment. They all affect

Fig. 18-2 The neighborhood in which a child lives and plays is one environment that influences the child's life.

one another. Nature influences people; people influence nature.

IMPORTANCE OF ENVIRONMENT TO CHILDREN

Because children's environment influences their lives so completely, it is important that children learn about it. Children must develop basic understandings about the world around them. They must develop attitudes and build skills that will help them deal with their environment.

What Can Children Understand About Their Environment?

Children can understand many things about their environment. Several of these are listed.

- Children can learn to pay attention to the things around them that make them feel better and those that make them feel uneasy. They can pay attention to how factor A influences factor B, how B influences C, and how they all influence each other.

- Children can begin to realize that they are part of their environment. They can make things better, or they can make things worse for themselves and others.

- Children can learn about pollution and the way it can ruin their lives and the earth. They can also learn about beauty and how it can add to life.

What Attitudes and Skills Can Children Learn By Exploring Their Environment?

By investigating their environment, children learn many skills and attitudes.

- Children can learn to respect each creature of nature — whether it is an ant or a human being.

- They can begin to respect the rights and privileges of others in their environment. They can gradually develop the awareness that nature belongs to everyone.

- Above all, young children can learn to observe the world around them with skill and accuracy. They can become skillful in protecting nature.

Early experiences with the environment are thus important to a child's growth and development. Moreover, activities that help children learn about their environment also help them become more creative. The following activities are designed to build an understanding of the environment and to develop creativity in young children.

ACTIVITIES IN THE SCHOOL

The activities described in this section are examples of those that are appropriate to use with three- to five-year-olds.

What would happen if . . . ? This activity is designed to help children understand how cleanliness and order add to the pleasantness of their environment.

- What would happen if no one cleaned up the schoolroom or picked up the toys?

Fig. 18-3 What would happen if . . . no one cleaned up the schoolroom or picked up the toys?

The children may at first think this is a good idea — that toys should be allowed to lie about. They soon realize that toys cannot be found and games cannot be played. It may take several days for the full meaning of this activity to become clear to the children, but they will see the need for order in their environment.

- What would happen if no one gave directions? For a period of time, no one in the class can suggest activities or provide leadership. The children are allowed to do what they want (except for hurting themselves or others). Without some order in the environment, children soon become tense.

- What would happen if no one could work, speak, or play together? Children quickly discover how important it is for people to interact. If the environment is to be a pleasant one, things that live together in that environment must be able to work together. As an extra challenge, the teacher should ask children to solve problems that usually require the efforts of several people. However, each child must work alone. They cannot speak to anyone.

Growing Things

Children can observe both plants and animals in the school. They can observe the effect of different environments on the growth patterns of plants and animals.

Indoor gardens. What environmental factors influence the growth of plants? Is watering a factor? Is amount of water a factor? Is the type of soil a factor? Can seeds grow in sawdust? If seeds are planted in pint milk cartons, what happens if two seeds are planted? Four seeds? Sixteen seeds? Is sunlight a factor? (Bean seeds are good to use since they are hardy. They sprout quickly, usually in one day.)

Fig. 18-4 In the school environment, a child can help to care for a guinea pig, while observing the animal's living conditions, the things it eats, how it moves, and what its moods seem to be.

Note: This activity is best carried out in the autumn or spring when classrooms are moist. During winter months or in cold climates, the dry, indoor air does not permit good growth to take place.

Small animals. Mice, gerbils, guinea pigs, frogs, turtles, snakes, salamanders, ants, bees, and meal worms can be kept alive in a classroom. Children can observe them and find answers to such questions as: What and how do these living things eat? Do they seem happy or unhappy? How can their environment be changed to make them happier? How do they move? What makes them move?

Aquariums. Fish tanks are a source of beauty and learning for a young child. The tanks can be made in a simple way or can be very fancy. Care must be taken that an aquarium does not become too crowded with fish and plants. If it does become overcrowded many fish and

Fig. 18-5 An aquarium is a good source of beauty and learning for a young child.

plants may die. The easiest types of fish to keep in an aquarium are guppies or goldfish. Either type is hardy and is inexpensive to buy. Children can study the eating habits of fish. They can see how fish move and how they are affected by other fish. Children can look for changes in fish over a period of time. They can also see what happens if the water gets too cold, if too much food is added to the aquarium, or if new fish are added to the tank.

Terrariums. A terrarium is a glass-enclosed tank without water. Usually dirt or sand is placed on the bottom of the terrarium and plants are added. A terrarium can be made to look like the desert when sand, cactus-type plants, and desert-type lizards are used. This kind of terrarium is placed in a warm part of the room and given plenty of sun. A terrarium can be made to look like a forest. It can be made to look like a grassy area. Insects, small snakes, frogs, and small lizards may be added.

To help children learn about the terrarium environment in a creative way, two things should be done. First, the children should help build the terrarium. They should choose the plants and animals and know what types and how many they start with. Second, the children should watch for changes in plants and animals. Are they growing? What are they eating? Which one eats first? Are they disappearing? What changes should be made?

ACTIVITIES ON THE SCHOOL GROUNDS

Many activities work well inside the school. Others are more suited to the area around the school building. The following are suggestions for activities for the outside grounds of the school.

Gardening. Common vegetables or flowers can be used. Seeds from fruits can be used. Seedlings can be transplanted, also. In order for children to be creative gardeners, they should be given some choices: Where is the best place to plant seeds? What seeds should be planted? How far apart should they be planted? How much water do they need? When is the best time of the year to plant seeds? How much plant food or fertilizer is needed? In some way — perhaps by tape recording — the children's decisions about these things should be kept. The children should be allowed to dig up plants to see what is happening as growth takes place. They should compare the growth of their plants with the growth of other children's plants. Is there a difference? If there is, why?

Bird feeders. Children can try to design bird feeders and build them in some way; or they can design the feeders and their parents can help them build the structures. Professionally built bird feeders can also be used for this.

Children can try to discover what kinds of food attract various kinds of birds. Where is the best place to put a bird feeder? When is the best time of year to watch for birds? What time of day is best for bird-watching at a feeder?

Cloud and sky watching. On a mild, partly sunny or cloudy day, children can learn much about their environment. They can lie on the ground and look up at the sky. They may see clouds of many shapes. Clouds may join together. The sun may disappear. It may get cool very suddenly. Birds may fly past. An airplane with a long trail of vapor may go by.

The children may have many different feelings as they lie still and watch the sky. Questions may arise. How do clouds seem to move? What do they look like? Are there many colors in the clouds? What do clouds look like just before a storm? Ask the children if they can make up a story about the clouds.

Fig. 18-6 On the school grounds, a child and teacher can make up sciencing activities, such as looking for natural things that can be found outside, and making observations about them.

The sounds of nature. Walking in the woods or along a busy street can be made exciting by listening to the sounds. In the area next to a school, there are many sounds, too. When most of the children are indoors, one or two supervised children may want to go outside and just listen. They can take a cassette tape recorder along and record sounds, too.

How many different sounds can they hear? Can they hear sounds made by birds? By animals? What do the leaves in the trees sound like? How do trees without leaves sound? What other sounds can be heard? How do noises made by cars differ from noises made by trucks? How does a person feel if there is too much noise?

What happens to rain water? After a rainstorm, children can try to follow the paths taken by the water. Does all of the water flow into a sewer? Does some of it go into the ground? What happens in paved areas compared to grassy areas? What happens in dirt areas compared to grassy areas?

Smells around the school. Children can search for different smells around the school. Some are good smells. What things give off good smells? What things have an unpleasant smell? Can any cause for bad smells be found? Can any reasons be found to explain why some things smell good and others do not? Does everyone agree on what smells good and what does not?

It is stimulating for children to compare their feelings with those of others. Are leaves changing colors in the fall beautiful? Are flowers beautiful? What about weeds? Can a cloud formation be beautiful? What about a rainbow? Is there beauty in a swing set or a slide? Can a bicycle be thought of as beautiful? How many words can the children think of that make them feel or see beauty?

Animal hiding places. There may be a small hole in the ground or a sand hill in a crack on the playground. Thick grass or bushes serve as hiding places for an animal. Under a large rock or near the foundation of the school, there may be places for living things to hide.

Children seek answers to many questions about animals. Why do animals need hiding places? Can a child create a place where an animal will choose to hide? How many natural hiding places can be found? Can children create hiding places for themselves? How do they feel when they are in their hiding places?

If creativity is to be a part of activities such as these, decisions must be left to the children. Help from the teacher should not become orders on what to do and what not to do. Advice is good. Orders or carefully worded "cookbook" directions are not good.

ENVIRONMENTAL ACTIVITIES IN OTHER AREAS

There are places other than the school building where children can learn about their

Fig. 18-7 Children can learn a great deal about the environment from a trip to the zoo.

environment. There are places outdoors where learning about the environment can take place besides on the playground. It is important for adults to know about these other places and to think about how they can be used with children.

A trip to the zoo. Creative learning at a zoo is very possible if some care is taken in advance. Children should be given something definite to look for. They might be encouraged to watch and see how animals pace back and forth in their cages or what the large animals eat. Do the animals seem happy? Do they play together? Why are animals different colors?

A trip to a nature study area. Often, a nature study site has a naturalist to take groups around. Young children need to participate in activities; they do not need a long-winded guide. A nature area is a good place to go to listen to natural sounds. How many sounds can be heard? What might the sounds mean? What is making the sounds? Where are they coming from? A nature area is also ideal for looking for beauty. Natural beauty can be seen everywhere. The children can be asked to find a beautiful thing in the nature area. They can be asked to describe it — to tell why they like it. Many nature sites have shallow rivers flowing through them. It is a new experience for most children to wade in the river. They can take off their shoes and socks and roll up their pants. They can then explore under rocks, and feel the flow of the water and mud oozing between their toes.

What can the children find out about river life? What things live in a river? How do they live? Where do they find food? Are there animals that live both on the land and in the river?

Neighborhood polluters. A walking trip in the area around a school can be interesting.

Fig. 18-8 While at a nature study area, children can look for things of beauty that exist in nature.

Children can use their senses to find people or places that make life unpleasant. Noise is one form of pollution children can observe. How or what is making the noise? How can the noise level be reduced?

Dirt, ugliness, and a run-down appearance are other forms of pollution. Foul smells are another way that the environment is polluted. Children can observe these, find who or what is causing them, and suggest solutions.

It is in the solving of problems that a young child can show creativity. It might even be possible that simple cleanup campaigns can be started by children. At least, the children can suggest ways that neighborhoods can be cleaned up.

Safety to make life better. In many neighborhoods, hazards to the health and safety of children can be seen. Children know about them but do not realize the full danger. Old houses about to be torn down attract young children who are curious. Abandoned refrigerators are another safety hazard in many areas. The exhaust from cars that have been left on in the street, broken glass, and leaded paints are other sources of danger. Exposed electrical wires and hungry animals roaming the streets are still other dangers. When learning about the environment, children begin to think about ways to make life better.

SUMMARY

Children should begin to understand that all forces in the environment affect one another. Animals influence other animals. Plants affect animals. The climate has an effect on the environment. People can make the environment pleasant or very unpleasant.

Children should have experiences with both the natural and the man-made environment. These experiences take place in the school building and in the play area around the school. They also take place in the community in which the children live. While children are exploring the environment, they can also express their creativity.

STUDENT ACTIVITIES

- Spend three hours of one day with a group of fellow students, but do not speak to any of them. They may not speak either. Try to do something with two or more people without communicating in any way: no words, no hand signs, no head nodding.

- Find an area around the school or the neighborhood that needs cleaning up. Organize a cleanup committee. Take pictures before, during, and after the cleanup.

- Do the following pollution experiments.

  A. In a team of four to six people, prepare four wide-mouth gallon-jar aquariums. (Mayonnaise jars can be used.) Water for the aquariums should be aged, which means the water should be kept in large containers for at least three days before being used in the aquariums. Tap water contains a chemical called chlorine. Chlorine takes the place of oxygen which, of course, is needed by animals. During the "aging" process, chlorine leaves the water, and oxygen takes its place.

  B. In the jars, place clean, washed sand. Place a small number of water plants such as elodea or eel grass in the jar. Anchor the roots of the plants in the sand. Fill the jar with aged water. Add one or two small fish. (Goldfish or guppies are good for this.) A live snail will help keep the aquarium clean.

  C. The four jars should be placed in indirect light and kept warm, but not hot. A very small amount of fish food may be used at first. Before long, the plants should be able to provide some of the food for the fish. The water should be clean.

  D. After two or three weeks, compare all of the aquariums. They should all look about the same. At this point, pollute three of them. Oil, garbage, soapsuds, and other things may be used. If oil is used, only one jar should be polluted with the oil. Enough oil to form a thin, oily layer on the surface of the water should be used. Pollute one other jar-aquarium with dish soap. Pollute a third jar with some other "junk." Keep one jar unpolluted.

E. Observe changes in the aquariums and discuss the following questions with the group.

1. Do all living things die at the same time?

2. Which pollutants kill living things most quickly?

3. What happens to the water after the living things die?

4. What does all this mean for human beings?

5. How does this activity help children learn about the environment?

- It is possible to find polluters in every town and city.

A. Try to find at least two places where pollution is taking place. A factory may be dumping wastes into a river or lake. A house may be falling apart. Someone or something may be causing noise pollution.

B. Make a list of polluters.

C. Discuss with other students the following questions.

1. Why is pollution bad for human beings?

2. What can be done about this?

3. How can an activity like this be used with three- to five-year-olds?

- An area in the community should be found where nature can be studied. Try any or all of the following activities.

A. In a fifteen-minute period of time, how many birds can be seen? How many different kinds of birds are observed?

B. In an area three feet by three feet and six inches deep, how many living things can be found?

C. How many living things can be found under a small rock?

D. In a five-minute period of time, how many different sounds can be heard?

E. How many different kinds of plants can be found in an area fifty by one hundred feet?

REVIEW

A. Name two facts a child can learn in order to understand more about the environment.

B. Describe one attitude a child should develop about the environment.

C. List three environmental activities that can be done on school grounds.

D. List three environmental activities that can be done in areas other than the school grounds.

Unit 19 FOODS: A CREATIVE APPROACH

OBJECTIVES

After studying this unit, the student will be able to

- State five ways in which food activities help three- to five-year-old children learn.
- Name seven rules that help make food activities more creative.
- Describe two creative group activities and one creative individual activity involving foods.

Activities involving foods are included in most programs for three- to five-year-old children. However, many of the food-type activities are under the complete direction of the teacher. The children sit and watch the teacher do the work. Sometimes the children are given spoons and told to stir a mixture, or are allowed to pour liquids from one container to another. Sometimes they are given the job of listening for a timer to "ding." Rarely is the child allowed to decide what foods to use, how to use them, in what order to mix them, or for how long to stir things. Food activities that do not include more of the children's input are not very creative.

The use of foods in a classroom can be one of the most creative parts of the program. Foods are a part of each child's experience. Foods and cooking are interesting to children. All of their senses are used in activities involving foods. They see the foods. They smell them, touch them, and taste them. The children can even hear many kinds of foods boiling, popping, or frying. Other learning is helped by food activities, too. Art, sciencing, and aesthetics are all related to cooking in some way.

IMPORTANCE OF FOODS TO THE TOTAL PROGRAM

Foods are well known to all children. They are a part of every child's basic needs. Children come into contact with foods many times each day. They experience foods in the school, at home, and in stores. Foods are highly interesting for children. Therefore, activities involving foods can be used in many ways: (1) to help children learn new information, (2) to help them gain new skills, and (3) to help them develop positive attitudes about themselves and about learning.

Building Information

There are at least five ways in which food activities help children understand new concepts.

Fig. 19-1 Children enjoy activities that involve cooking in the classroom.

Children learn to describe things. Children experience many shapes, sizes, and colors. They see that some things start out in a round shape and become long and flat during the cooking process. Many foods change in size when they are heated. Foods come in many colors, and the colors sometimes change with mixing, or heating or cooling. The child thus learns to name shapes, compare sizes, and describe colors.

Children learn about tastes. Children find out how heating or mixing changes taste. They learn that some things, such as salt or sugar, can change the taste of foods. They discover that some foods taste good when they are mixed together and that others do not. Children also learn that a change in the outward appearance of some foods does not mean that the foods taste any different. Apple juice has the same flavor as a whole apple. The carrots in a carrot cake can be tasted.

Children observe changes. As they did in sciencing, children observe that foods change from liquids to solids and from solids to

Fig. 19-2 A child learns that forming a candy mixture into different shapes does not change the flavor of the candy.

liquids. The children also see steam (a gas) rising from liquids that are heated. In addition, they sense odors — some good and some bad — as foods change from solids to liquids to gases.

Children learn to express themselves. Language develops as a result of food experiences. Words like bitter, sour, sweet, and salty have real meaning. Hot, cold, warm, and cool, are part of the food vocabulary. Children may learn the words delicious and tasty. They learn a more complete meaning of terms like liquid and solid, freezing and boiling, smelly and odorless. When the words relate to direct experiences, the child's vocabulary grows.

Children think more logically. Growth in a more logical view of the world takes place in children who have creative food experiences. In order for logical thinking to develop, children need to know certain things, such as the following:

- Some processes can be *reversed*. When milk is poured from container A into container B, the procedure can be reversed; that is, the milk can be poured back into container A. If two pears are taken from a can and placed in a dish, they can also be returned to the can.

- A change in place does not mean a change in *identity*. If ice cream is scooped from a large container and placed on a cone, it is still ice cream. Moreover, the ice cream on the cone is the same ice cream that was in the scoop. It is also the same ice cream that was in the larger container. Young children need many experiences before they realize this fact.

- Foods can be classified in many ways. A section of grapefruit can be sweet or sour. If it is sweet, the grapefruit is then sorted with other sweet things such as oranges. If it is sour, it is grouped with a section

Fig. 19-3 Slices of grapefruit can be used in a sciencing experience to help children with their classifying skills.

of lemon. In addition, the grapefruit may be warm or cold. Learning to identify more than one way to classify an object is a big step forward in logical thinking.

- Pouring a liquid from a glass of one shape into a glass of another shape confuses many children. When orange juice is poured from a short, fat glass into a tall, skinny glass, many children misjudge amounts. They somehow think that there is more juice in the tall, skinny glass because it is tall. They forget that it is skinny.

Experiences such as these in which foods are poured back and forth, identified, sorted, and changed in shape, help children to think. They learn to think more clearly and more logically.

Building Skills

There are a number of skills that children can learn from working with foods. These skills can be developed during other parts of

Fig. 19-4 A child's small muscles and coordination develop when experimenting with foods.

the program, also, but working with food-related activities is one of the best ways to build these skills.

Small muscle coordination. Mixing foods and pouring liquids from one glass to another are ways in which children develop coordination. The small muscles in the hands develop so that a child can hold a large spoon. Children's eyes coordinate with their hands in order to pour the juice from a pitcher into a small glass.

Simple measuring abilities. By using cups and spoons that have marks showing amounts, a child begins to understand measurements. A three- to five-year-old is not expected to read a recipe. The child is not expected to measure exactly one cup or one tablespoon. The child is, however, able to observe that a tablespoon is larger than a teaspoon, and to tell that a cup is more than a tablespoon.

The child can also begin to realize that by using too much flour, water, or salt, foods can be ruined. The understanding begins to develop that the amount of each ingredient used makes a difference in the final product. This realization leads the child to look for ways to figure out amounts. This is the time when measuring tools are discovered.

Social abilities. Many young children work best by themselves. At times, they also play with one or more other children. When they do, it is usually because they choose to do so. Rarely do they feel it is necessary or important to socialize with others.

A child may turn to others and work with them in order to reach a goal. In the process of working toward a goal with others, children learn social skills. They learn to give and take. They learn to talk to others. They learn cooperation.

In cooking, a child may need help in holding a pan steady while pouring something into it. A child may need help in carrying ingredients or finding certain foods. A child may need some new ideas for a special frosting. One child may need an "expert" opinion on how much sugar to add to a drink. These things call for some working together. As children work together, they learn social skills.

Developing Attitudes

In addition to gaining information and skills, a child also acquires attitudes from working with foods. These attitudes are very important to the child in several ways.

A feeling of being successful. Human beings like to feel good about themselves. They must see themselves as capable performers. They must have an inner feeling of being able to succeed. In order to develop this feeling, people must have life experiences in which they do well. If they fail all the time, they see themselves as failures.

Children, especially, must have experiences that lead them to feel good about themselves. They must know they can succeed. Playing with foods to see what develops is a way of helping children succeed. When things do not turn out as desired, the children can try again. They are not told that they are stupid. They are not told that they are guilty of wasting good food. They are encouraged to try again. In this way, children see themselves as successful.

Fig. 19-5 **During food activities, children often learn social skills, such as cooperation.**

Fig. 19-6 **In creative food experiences, children learn while having fun.**

A feeling of having fun. Children often learn information by mistake. That is, they learn while they think they are doing something else. When children are having fun, they are encouraged to continue what they are doing. Thus, if children learn while having fun, they want to continue learning. Working with foods is fun.

A desire to stick to a job. One of the most important attitudes creative people have is that of sticking to a job. They can work at a job for hours. They work at a problem until they solve it. They also work at things that are interesting to them. Creative people work best at things that allow them to be active in a search for answers.

When children are given a chance to search for answers in an active way, they will do it. In the process of doing this, they develop the ability to stick to a problem. Although three- to five-year-olds are not able to work for hours or days at a problem, most of them can work at solving a problem for a much longer time than most adults think. If there is an answer to a problem and the materials needed to solve it are available, the children will work. And while working, they learn the attitude of "stick-to-itiveness." When this attitude is developed, the children are more likely to solve problems in a creative way.

Food activities can help children develop this attitude when the activities are viewed as problems that need to be solved. Food activities have final products that work or do not work, that taste good or do not taste good. Children tend to stick with an interesting activity until the end product is created. They develop the attitude of stick-to-itiveness while working with foods.

FOOD ACTIVITIES THAT HELP CHILDREN'S CREATIVITY

If food activities are to help children be-

Fig. 19-7 A teacher should allow the children to be open and creative in their food activities.

come more creative, there are seven main rules that should be followed.

1. **Activities should be open.** If all children must follow the same directions at the same time, they will not become creative. In fact, just the opposite will happen. The children will be conformers and do only what the teacher tells them to do.

   To some adults, this may sound like a good thing. It is — if the only concern of a teacher is a quiet, orderly class. Teachers who want to help children to be creative must help them to be open. The teacher must let the children create their own directions and work at their own pace.

2. **Activities should be challenging, but not too difficult for the children.** If food activities are too hard, children will give up and quit. If they are too easy, the children will not be challenged. It is important to start with easy things. It is also important to increase the possibilities, so children will do harder things as they go on.

3. **Activities should be varied.** Children get bored if they do the same thing day after day. Variety is needed. Children should work with foods they know. They should also work with new foods — things they have not seen or tasted before. Some

activities should be very short. Others should take a long time to finish. In some activities, children should use just one type of food. In other activities, they may mix in several ingredients.

4. **The end product is not all important.** Emphasis should not be placed on what the children create, but on how they have done it. If only the final product is considered, then many children will fail. Things do not always taste good — especially when children create new recipes. But if children are rewarded for the way they create, then what they have created does not seem so important.

5. **Inexpensive materials and small amounts should be used.** No child should feel heartbroken if a recipe does not work. If, however, a great deal of money is spent on foods, it is hard to justify wasting the food. If ingredients are inexpensive, there is less chance that children will be made to feel guilty because something they made did not taste very good.

6. **Dangerous foods must be kept away from children.** Only those things that are safe for people to eat are used. Make certain that available foods are safe when mixed together. Some foods are safe when eaten by themselves, but can produce illness when mixed with other foods. The teacher controls this by being careful about the foods made available to the children.

7. **Activities should be carried out in a variety of places.** Food activities do not have to be limited to the indoors. They can also be done outside the classroom. They work well on the school grounds or in a nearby woods.

   Note: An important restriction for outdoor cooking is that the teacher sees and inspects all food before it is used. Poison

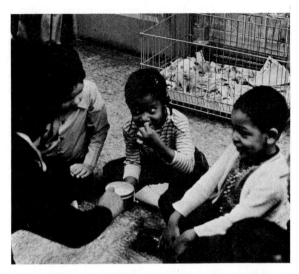

Fig. 19-8 Food activities can also be carried on outside of the school grounds, such as in a nearby park.

mushrooms and berries are sometimes gathered by children. These foods must be avoided.

WAYS OF GETTING STARTED

If children are to be creative in working with foods, the teacher cannot get them started by saying, "Now do this!" A few suggestions are given that should help.

- Set out all the foods that are needed.

- Warn children of dangers, if any exist.

- Help children when what they are doing is dangerous.

- Start by asking questions such as:
  "What if . . . ?"
  "Do you want to try . . . ?"
  "Has anyone ever . . . ?"
  "I wonder whether . . . "

- Increase the children's options as time goes on. The first times children work with foods, more teacher direction may be needed. The teacher should not, however, become a crutch on which the children lean, if they are to be creative. Thus, after a short while, teachers must help children think and work for themselves.

ACTIVITIES TO TRY

Creative food activities may be done in groups or by a single child. Suggestions for each are given.

Group Activities

Two or more children make a group. Some activities work best with a larger group. Some work best with small groups. If step-by-step recipes are needed for any of the activities, a good cookbook may be used.

Community fruit salad. Each child may select one fruit to add to the salad. A large bowl is needed. Children decide the way they add their fruit to the salad (crushing, slicing, whole). Sugar water may be added for flavor if a syrup is desired.

Topless popcorn. Children sit around a popcorn popper. Popcorn is added to preheated oil, but the top of the popper is left off. Interesting results follow.

Making ice cream. A hand-operated ice cream maker is needed. Children can turn the crank in relays. Flavorings can be the creation of the children involved. Coffee beans or vanilla beans are interesting to use. Syrups of other flavors can also be created. Directions for making ice cream usually come with the maker. Children can suggest creative uses of materials that go into the cream container.

Creative gelatin or pudding. Using clear gelatin and a variety of other foods for flavoring, children can be creative. They can select a variety of flavorings to add. They can whip gelatin into sponges and puddings. They can make or select their own molds. In cold climates, gelatin or pudding sets in a short time on a window ledge as children watch. Bavarian cream-types, fruit-flavored gelatins, or puddings can be created by children as they experiment.

Fig. 19-9   Two children can create a good-tasting pudding together and watch the mold set.

Note: As a precaution, an adult must provide the boiling hot water (heat and pour). The children direct this part of the activity, but must never be permitted to do it themselves.

Creative use of a blender. An activity that is both fun and valuable for creative learning is making a cocktail juice. The children can select the vegetables for their own drink. A variety of flavors results when certain vegetables are added to or omitted from the juice. Soups can be started in a blender. Peanut butter can also be created, using about two tablespoons of vegetable oil per cup of peanuts. Other nuts, such as almonds or walnuts, might make an interesting butter.

Making fancy bread. Beginning with a prepared bread dough, children can add other foods to make creative bread. Nuts, fruits, cinnamon, and a variety of other foods can be used. Baked breads can be topped with creative frostings or other toppings. Various containers can be used to bake the bread in unusual shapes. Tasks such as placing breads in and removing them from an oven should be done by adults – never by the children.

Individual Activities

Some of the activities suggested for groups can also be done by one child. Likewise, some of the individual activities mentioned here may also be carried out in groups, if desired.

Collecting and using seeds. Seeds that are edible as well as those that are not can be used. Children may be provided with a variety of seeds, or they may be asked to find the seeds. Pumpkin, watermelon, orange, cherry, and green pepper seeds are usually available. Many creative uses for seeds can be found. Edible seeds can be baked or cooked in a variety of ways. Lima beans can be planted as well as cooked.

Creative decorating. Creating an "ideal" frosting or cookie topping is a good activity for children. Cupcakes or cookies can be baked in advance. Materials for making frosting or decorating can be provided. Children should be encouraged to try out foods. When they have created their "ideal" topping, they can frost their own cupcakes or decorate their own cookies.

Creative snack time. In place of a teacher-planned snack for the entire group, the children each create their own snack. Materials from which to choose are provided by the teacher. Choices are left up to individuals. A homemade soup, a special milk shake, or a peanut butter sandwich (homemade peanut butter) might be selected. A special fruit juice may be created.

Flavored butter. Whipping cream, interesting flavors, and a chilled bowl and beater are needed. Placing the butter in a creative container is an added touch. (This makes a nice gift for children to take home.) Lemon, orange, or honey are just a few flavors that can be added to the butter. It is best for the chil-

Fig. 19-10 One of the rewards of participating in creative snack time is sampling the creation.

dren to make the butter, then warm it and add the flavorings.

Creating rock candy and lollipops. When sugar is added to water, it dissolves in the water. When enough sugar is added, a point is reached where the sugar no longer dissolves. The water is said to be *saturated* with sugar. Children begin with a saturated sugar-water solution. Given a few hints about bringing the solution to a boil and putting a string into the solution, the children can observe the sugar forming crystals of rock candy. (The process takes about one week.)

Lollipops can be made, too. A sugar-water solution is combined with corn syrup, a small amount of butter, and oil-base flavoring (oil of oranges or cherry), and then brought to a boil. A mold is made, into which the heated mixture is placed. A lollipop stick or cord is also placed in the mold. Food coloring should be added to give the lollipop some color.

Note: These activities require much teacher involvement and might best be done as a group demonstration. Individual children can prepare their own molds. They can also select the flavoring and the color of their candy.

SUMMARY

Foods can be used in activities that help children become more creative. Food activities help children learn new information. They develop knowledge about (1) names of shapes and colors; (2) tastes; (3) changes in shape, size, color, and taste; (4) new words; and (5) a logical view of the world. Food activities also help children develop skills in (1) hand-eye, small-muscle coordination; (2) simple measuring; and (3) socialization. Finally, food activities help children develop good attitudes about themselves and learn how to deal with problems while having fun.

In order to help children become more creative, food activities must meet certain standards. They must (1) be open-ended, not like a cookbook; (2) be challenging, but not too hard for three- to five-year-olds; (3) be varied, giving children choices; (4) emphasize the doing, not the end-product;

Fig. 19-11 It is important that children have the freedom to make decisions and choices for themselves in food activities.

(5) involve inexpensive materials; and (6) not be dangerous to children.

Food activities can be done in groups or by children working alone. It is important that children are allowed to make decisions for themselves about what foods to use and how to use them.

STUDENT ACTIVITIES

- Try testing the sense of taste of some fellow students by making "creative cocktail juice."

    A. Materials and ingredients:

    Blender

    Common vegetables: cucumber, carrots, tomatoes, cabbage, celery, green pepper, and parsley root

    Salt

    Sugar

    Lemon juice

    B. Begin with any two vegetables. Add one-half cup of cold water or crushed ice and blend. A pinch of salt and sugar and a small amount of lemon juice will improve the flavor. Taste a small amount. (It may not taste good.)

    C. Add a third vegetable to the mixture. Taste. Keep track of the vegetables and amounts used. Continue to add vegetables, one at a time. Try to make

        1. A tasty vegetable juice.

2. A juice whose vegetables no one can identify.

3. A mystery juice.

4. A bad-tasting juice. Then try to improve the taste using ingredients suggested above.

- Observe a group of children experiencing a type of food for the first time — perhaps eggplant, squash, or beef tongue.

    A. What kinds of expressions do they make when they taste the food?

    B. How do they react when they find out what the food was that they tasted?

    C. What can be said to make a child more willing to taste new foods?

- Experiment with the taste sense of adults and children.

    A. Each person who tastes a food in this experiment must be blindfolded.

    B. Use small slices of baking apples or potatoes and a freshly sliced onion or garlic.

    C. Hold the onion under the blindfolded person's nose. Slip a small piece of apple or potato into the person's mouth. Have the person chew up the food and tell what it was.

    D. Try this holding other strong-smelling foods under the nose of the blindfolded person.

        1. Are children or adults better at discovering what it really is they are chewing?

        2. Try telling adults that they are chewing onion. Hold garlic under their noses, and place pieces of potato into their mouths.

        3. Ask children and adults what this experiment tells them about the sense of taste.

REVIEW

A. Name five ways in which food activities help children learn information.

B. Name three skills that develop from activities with foods.

C. Name three attitudes that develop from activities with foods.

D. Decide which of the following statements are true.

    1. Teachers should give detailed directions to children during food activities.

    2. Children should work at their own pace.

    3. Food activities must be very easy so that no child feels challenged.

    4. Food activities should be varied.

5. Children should work with new kinds of foods — things they have never tasted before.

6. The end product is all that counts in food activities.

7. Foods used in food activities should be inexpensive, if possible.

8. Children must be warned never to throw foods away.

9. Food activities should always be done in a kitchen.

10. Food activities can sometimes be done in groups.

Unit 20 USING MEDIA TO BUILD CREATIVITY

OBJECTIVES

After studying this unit, the student will be able to

- State the meaning of the following terms: media, software, and hardware.
- Name nine types of media that can be used to help build a child's creativity.
- List four reasons why media should be used with young children.

The word media may be a new one for some students. *Media* are materials — things that are used to help improve a school's program. Media are the machines used to see movies or hear records. Media also are the things that go into the machines — the films and the record discs. Because most machines are made of metal, they are called *hardware*, figure 20-1. Films, tapes, papers, and most of the other things that are used in the

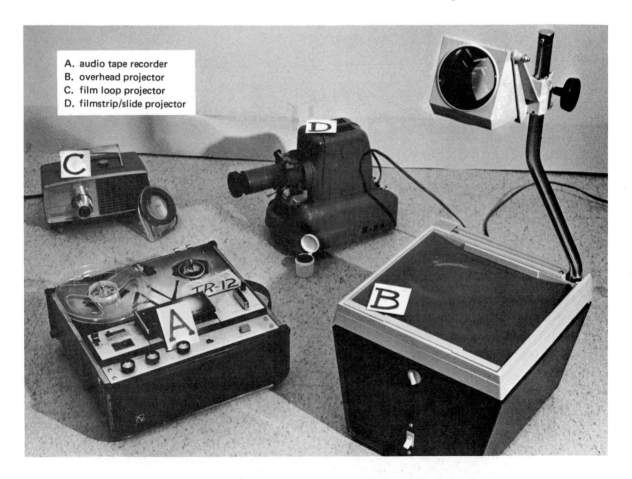

A. audio tape recorder
B. overhead projector
C. film loop projector
D. filmstrip/slide projector

Fig. 20-1 Several types of hardware that may be used in a school.

	Hardware	Software

• **Projectors and Cameras**	Motion picture cameras
	  8 millimeter
	  Super 8 millimeter
	  16 millimeter
	
	35 millimeter still camera (makes slides
	  or photographs)
	Other cameras – instamatics, box cameras
	
	Motion picture projectors
	  8 millimeter
	  Super 8 millimeter
	  16 millimeter
	Film loop projectors
	  8 millimeter
	  Super 8 millimeter
	Slide projectors
	  Hand operated
	  Semiautomatic
	  Full-automatic
	Filmstrip projectors
		8 millimeter film
		Super 8 millimeter film
		16 millimeter film – color or black and
		  white
		35 millimeter film – color or black and
		  white
		Various sizes of film in color or black and
		  white
		Motion pictures – silent or sound
		
		Motion pictures in plastic cartridges
		
		2x2 slides
		plastic containers
		
		Film connected in long strips

• **Video (television) equipment**	Videotape recorder:
	  Television camera
	  Recording and playback deck
	  Microphones
	  Television viewer
	  (television set with plugs that connect
	  the viewer to the playback deck)
		Videotape to fit the recording/playback
		  deck

• **Sound tape recording**	Reel-to-reel tape recorder Cassette tape recorder Microphones	Reel-to-reel tape Cassette tape
• **Overhead projections**	Overhead projector Screen Copier	Projection transparencies Other clear plastic materials
• **Opaque projections**	Opaque projector Screen	Any printed or drawn materials
• **Viewing boards**	Chalkboard Magnetic board Felt boards Cork boards	Chalk, erasers Materials with magnetized backing or magnetic materials Materials with felt backing Paper; tagboard, thumbtacks
• **Hand-held or table top viewers**	Slide viewer Filmstrip viewer View-master	2x2 slides, filmstrips, color reels
• **Phonograph recording**	Phonograph	Record discs
• **Printed materials**	Not necessary	Books, pictures, charts

Fig. 20-2 Hardware and software to use in a program for young children.

hardware are soft or flexible and are called *software.* Hardware is of no use to a school without the proper software. In the same way, most software cannot be used without the proper hardware. Thus, if media are to be used in a school, the school must have both the proper hardware and software.

TYPES OF MEDIA

There are at least nine different kinds of media that can be used in a program for young children. With one exception, each type has its special hardware, and each type of hardware has its special software. See figure 20-2, page 187, for a listing of the materials. Activities for using the materials effectively to help children grow creatively are described later in this unit.

LIMITATIONS IN THE USE OF MEDIA

Media add a great deal of fun and excitement to a program for young children. However, there are some practical limits to the use of many media.

Cost. The high cost of the hardware keeps many schools from buying large numbers of materials. Even more expensive than the original cost of hardware is the cost of software. Many cameras are quite inexpensive to buy. It is the cost and processing of the film that makes these cameras costly to use. An additional problem is the cost of upkeep; repairs can be very expensive. A large supply of phonograph records is a real help in a preschool program. But, if the phonograph is broken, the records are of no use.

Availability. In some areas, hardware is not available. In other areas, the hardware can be found, but the necessary software is not available. Unless both the hardware and the software can be obtained with ease, the media are useless. In addition, some way of making

equipment available to all personnel within a school must be worked out. Three teachers cannot show three different filmstrips on one projector at the same time.

Ability to use equipment. Some teachers are afraid to use equipment. They worry about breaking things. They are afraid things will not run right. They feel it is easier not to use the "fancy gadgets."

Someone in each school must learn how to use all the equipment. This person is the media specialist, who sets up all the equipment and makes simple repairs, such as changing a bulb in a projector. If no one in a school is willing to do this, the use of the media is limited. It is helpful for the media expert to teach others how to use the hardware and how to prepare software.

IMPORTANCE OF USING MEDIA

Even though there are some limitations, it is very important that teachers use media in their programs. Media serve a number of purposes.

They provide variety in the program. Some children learn best when they view a film or hear a record. The total preschool program must meet the needs of a variety of children. Therefore, the program must have a variety of activities for each child. Using media is one more means of meeting the needs of children.

They provide children with highly interesting learning experiences. Media help children learn facts, learn to enjoy the school setting, and develop skills — particularly creative skills.

They get children involved in the creation of materials. Some of the software can be made by one child working alone or by a group of children working together. This gives the children a chance to handle the materials and to create useful things for their class. "Hands-on" activities are very important for young children. The creation of media software is a hands-on activity.

They build on and reinforce other preschool activities. It is important that young children learn and relearn. After learning some information, the child can relearn it through the media. Thus, learning through the use of media can reinforce concepts a child learned earlier.

ACTIVITIES TO DEVELOP CREATIVITY

Media serve a number of purposes in a school program. As just mentioned, media provide variety, interest, involvement, and reinforcement. One of the most important things media provide is a chance for a child to develop creativity. The creativity comes when a child designs and puts together software for the machines. The activities suggested in this section involve the creation of software by children.

Motion pictures. It is possible for children to plan and produce movies of class activities. They can take movies of dramatic activities and dancing. Movies can be created during a field trip or an outdoor activity around the school.

There are several problems that may be encountered in film making. It is very expensive to buy film and have it printed. It is easy to ruin film. It is not easy to take good movies. A camera is easily broken if it is dropped.

A more practical use of motion pictures is to obtain professionally made movies by renting them or on a free loan basis. These movies can then be used to introduce creative activities. The films can help teach children a creative skill such as jewelry or pottery making, or drawing. The children then can be given a chance to create jewelry or pottery of their own design. Creative dramatics can begin with a movie. The movie can introduce a story and some characters. At the proper time, the movie can be turned off, and children take the parts of the characters. The children can then create their own ending to the story.

A new type of film projector is now available for 8-millimeter film. It is called a film-

Fig. 20-3 Learning to use a simple camera can be an exciting experience for a child.

loop (or single concept) projector. Film is placed in a special plastic case. The case fits into the projector and the film is ready to be shown. It is easy enough for a child to use. The projector is lightweight. This type of projector is especially good for creative use by children.

Filmstrips, slides, and snapshots. Using an inexpensive camera, children can take slides of many activities. Children can create a slide show for parents or other children. Creative dance or drama can be the subjects of the show. A children's art show can be the theme of a slide show. Sound can be added by making a tape recording. A click or other signal may be used to tell the person showing the slides to move to the next picture.

Slides can also be used for demonstrating a skill. Creative cooking can begin with a slide show on how to get started. Creative baseball hitting can be demonstrated using slides. Slides are used to build interest and to entertain. Slides of a trip (for example, to Disneyland or to Mount Rushmore), can lead children to new creative interests.

Filmstrips are a series of slides made in a strip of film rather than cut up and placed in mountings. A film processor will send 35-millimeter film back in a strip of film; it is necessary to request this when turning in the film for developing.

Children can take their own slides, though many times they do not hold the camera steady, and their pictures tend to be blurred. The teacher may take pictures of scenes chosen by children and avoid this problem. If sound is desired, it is more creative for children to plan the words and record them in their own voices.

A storybook could be created using snapshots made by children. Snapshots from home may be used for this, or picture books that tell stories about school experiences can be created. Pictures can be printed in duplicate so that more than one child may create a story using the same pictures. The same snapshots can be used in them in many different ways. A story library of pictures taken by children can be built. Books in which pictures are taken by one child and the story created by another can be made.

In all of these examples, creativity is helped if children plan and carry out the activities. If the teacher does everything, little creative gain is made by the child.

Video. Today, there is fairly inexpensive television equipment available to schools. It is lightweight, easily moved, and easy to use. This equipment is also easily broken if it is dropped; otherwise it is portable and useful.

Television can do all the things that movies and slides do. In addition, television is less expensive to use. Videotape can be reused. Mistakes may be erased. Children see the results of their work right away. Video can be used with theatre-arts type activities; a play can be videotaped; a children's art show can be recorded. Some children enjoy doing "man-on-the-street" interviews. Playtime games can be created and taped.

Many portable units can be taken on field trips. Tapes made on field trips can be used to

Fig. 20-4 Young children enjoy recording their own voices on a cassette tape, and take pride in being able to play back the tape all by themselves.

spark creative story telling and the creation of new games.

When children get tired of a tape, it can be erased and reused. Thus, although the cost of hardware is high, the cost of software can be relatively low.

Cassette tape recording and radio. Small tape recorders that are inexpensive and easy to use are available to all schools. They are called cassette tape recorders. The cassettes are the small plastic cases into which recording tape is placed. The cassette is dropped into the recorder and is ready to use. Young children use these recorders with few problems, recording their own voices — just for the fun of it. They can also record common sounds, creative plays, and man-on-the-street interviews. Older-style reel-type recorders are often heavier and much harder to use. They are more expensive, but give better sound reproduction.

Radio programs have been available for many years as a classroom activity. Several educational stations present programs that are especially designed to build creativity.

Overhead projectors. These are lightweight machines that project pictures and words on a screen. Light must pass through the film or plastic being projected. The projectors rest on a tabletop and project onto a screen.

Overhead projectors can be used to help children develop creativity in many ways. The machines can be used to project silhouettes (shadows) on a screen. This is a creative way for children to learn names of shapes. The children can create their own shapes and project them on the screen. Another way to encourage creativity in children is to have them make their own transparencies, or pictures and drawings on pieces of clear plastic. The transparencies are made by drawing on a piece of clear plastic with a grease pencil or by using a special copy machine. Pencil line drawings, some pictures, and words are easily copied onto the plastic transparency.

The transparency is placed on the overhead stage and projected on a screen. Creative sketches can be shown to groups or can be enlarged in this way. Creative stories are built from pictures shown on the overhead screen. Sketches made by a child may be used for this purpose.

Opaque projectors. With this device, book pages, photographs, and paintings can be shown directly on a screen. The things to be projected must be quite thin and must lie flat. They are then placed on a stage in the projector and brought into focus on a screen. Small pictures are made to look large. A page of a book can be enlarged on a screen.

Opaque projectors can be used in several ways. Drawings made by individuals can be shown to the whole group. A picture from a book can be used to start children on creative storytelling experiences. Snapshots may be

Fig. 20-5 Children like to see the pictures they draw enlarged on a screen through the use of an opaque projector.

used to begin a creative art experience. Pictures and shapes from a book can be traced onto paper or a chalkboard. The shapes or parts of the pictures can be used to start a creative art or story experience.

Viewing boards. There are several types of boards that can be used to help children be creative. Children truly enjoy writing on chalkboards (sometimes called blackboards). Chalk is available in many colors and is inexpensive to use. As an art experience, a large chalkboard gives a child the chance to "stretch out" the size of a work. The child's imagination may also stretch out in this way.

Pictures and drawings can be displayed on felt boards. Small pieces of felt material are glued onto the backs of the pictures to be displayed. Rubbing the palm of the hand across the paper makes the paper stick to the felt board.

Metal (iron or steel, only) objects stick to magnetic boards. Letters and words, colored

Fig. 20-6 A child can find many creative uses for materials on a pegboard using some string, a few pegs, and a little imagination.

pieces, shapes, and other things are produced with magnetic backs. These can be moved about on the board by children to help them learn words, letters, and numerals. Shapes can be taken apart or put together to form new shapes. Colored pieces may be arranged to make creative designs.

Cork boards are useful for display purposes. Using thumbtacks, both adults and children can place creative drawings and designs on the cork board. Group drawings can be arranged in a creative way on these boards. Pegboards also have many uses.

Viewers. There are several small viewers that can be used by one child or a small group of children. They are usually inexpensive, lightweight, and easy to use.

Color slides can be placed in a slide viewer. The use of slides often gives children ideas for art projects or stories. They can learn facts from the slides. When children see their own projects on film, they are encouraged to create more projects. Filmstrip viewers are used in the same way that slide viewers are used, although they are a bit harder to use. Viewers

and the films to use in them can be bought at many stores. The films help children experience many kinds of things.

- Common stories for children are available on small films that fit into these viewers.
- Children "travel" to the Grand Canyon on film. They see Niagara Falls or the Empire State Building.
- Some films show children how to do a specific thing. They can see how to hold a baseball bat or how to mold clay. Knowing how to begin a skill activity helps a child become more creative in that activity.

Phonographs and records. Phonographs are so common that many people have one or more of them in their homes. Many children have a phonograph of their own. Record discs are available in stores and through material catalogs. Using records helps children develop creativity in many ways.

- Recorded music helps children express and develop creative movement.
- Music helps develop creative imaginations in children. Classical music is very good for this.
- Music that builds feeling in children leads to many creative art experiences. The music sets the mood. Then the children create.
- Records that tell stories or parts of stories can help children become creative. The stories build a mood as well as tell a story.

Printed Materials. Many people do not consider a book or a chart to be media. However, books and charts do help children become creative. Printed materials are software. No hardware is needed to use them. Several common forms of printed materials are available in almost every school.

- Books. A story read from a book can help a child build creative images. A story read by a teacher can lead a child to create a story.

- Charts and pictures. Creative experiences often begin with an interesting picture. A drawing of a stick figure can lead a child to tell a creative story. A chart may lead a child to make a creative drawing.
- Magazines. Advertisements in magazines are often useful in developing a child's creative interests. Interesting pictures can also help lead to creative experiences. Travel and geographical-type magazines are very good for this.

SUMMARY

The full meaning of media involves two main things: hardware and software. The hardware includes the machines and instruments — usually made of metal or a hard plastic. Hardware is used to show pictures or reproduce sounds. The software includes the materials that are shown or heard when the machines work. Software can be most useful in developing a child's creativity.

Media help the total preschool program because (1) they provide variety in the program, (2) they lead to interesting learning experiences, (3) they lead children to create materials or develop new ideas, and (4) they build on other things children have experienced in the preschool program.

Nine types of media that can be used are (1) projectors and cameras, (2) video materials, (3) sound tape recordings, (4) overhead projectors, (5) opaque projectors, (6) viewing boards, (7) slide viewers, (8) phonographs and records, and (9) printed materials.

STUDENT ACTIVITIES

- Taking Creative Slides

  A. Obtain an inexpensive camera that takes slide pictures. Shoot a roll of color slide film trying to make each picture creative.
  B. Try to get pictures of
     1. a beautiful sunset
     2. an ugly, broken-down house
     3. a beautiful building
     4. interesting-looking people
     5. a flower in bloom
     6. an animal
     7. a brightly colored bird
  C. Use the slide pictures to tell a creative story about some experience. The story may or may not be true.

- Using Hardware

  Learn how to use each of the following kinds of hardware.
     1. a motion picture projector
     2. a slide projector
     3. a filmstrip projector
     4. an overhead projector
     5. an opaque projector

- Using a tape recorder, make tape recordings of interesting sounds. Try to get fellow classmates to recognize the sounds. Try any or all of the following sounds.
    1. a typewriter
    2. a door closing
    3. a car starting
    4. a jet plane taking off
    5. voices
    6. music
    7. popcorn popping

- Make a list of software materials that could be made by children. The cost of raw materials for the software should be determined. How much money would be needed for a good supply of materials?
    A.   Find catalogs that list prices of film, blank tape, and other materials.
    B.   Contact film processors to figure the cost of developing and printing the film.
    C.   Decide how materials should be stored and taken care of.

- Make a list of hardware needed for a program involving media. Figure out costs of hardware by checking school supply catalogs, camera stores, and discount department stores. How much money would be needed?

REVIEW

A.   Define the term hardware.

B.   Name three limitations in using media.

C.   List four reasons why using media is important to preschool programs.

D.   Name nine kinds of media that are appropriate for use with young children.

E.   Choose the answer that best completes each statement about media.
    1. A single concept projector shows
        a. slides.
        b. filmstrips.
        c. movies in a plastic case.
    2. Video is good to use because
        a. videotape can be reused.
        b. the hardware is inexpensive.
        c. the equipment is durable.
    3. Opaque projectors can
        a. show slides on a screen.
        b. project a page of a book on a screen.
        c. record children's voices.

F.   Name four kinds of viewing boards.

G.   What kind of hardware is needed for children to use printed material?

Planning, Presenting, and Supervising Creative Activities

Unit 21 PLANNING AND PRESENTING ACTIVITIES TO ENCOURAGE CREATIVITY

OBJECTIVES

After studying this unit, the student will be able to

- Ask a series of diagnostic questions in order to better know and work with young children.

- List and describe interest centers which stimulate children's creative behavior.

- Describe a proper physical environment for creative activities with young children.

Planning always begins with the child. What this means is that each child is unique. Children each have their own way of being. Each has a way of responding to the world. The teacher must try to know what each child is like. A teacher should be aware of the child's level of development, strengths, abilities, and special personality. With this knowledge, teachers can relate their own personality and unique skills to the young child. Thus, an atmosphere is created in which both adult and child remain themselves in order to help and respect each other.

Watching a child at play helps an adult understand this young person. A teacher is able to see how the child uses materials and relates to other children. Answers to the questions listed here can help adults better understand and work with a young child.

- What is special about the child?

- What are the child's interests?

- What are the child's strengths?

- What abilities and skills are already developed?

- What is the child's home life like?

- How does the child relate to adults?

Fig. 21-1 Watching a child at play can give a teacher a better understanding of the child.

- How does the child respond to other children?
- What are the motor skills (large and small muscle) of the child?
- How is self-expression shown by the child?
- How does the child speak?
- What beliefs have developed?
- How are problems solved by the child?
- With what materials does the child enjoy working?
- How does the child learn?
- What is the child ready to learn?
- How does the teacher feel about the child?

The last question is most important. Helping children in creative activities is done through the relationship between adult and child. To think one knows a young child without realizing one's own feelings toward the child is a mistake. How the teacher feels toward a child affects how the teacher acts toward the child. An honest understanding of how one feels toward a child must be combined with knowledge of the child if the teacher is really to help the child to be creative.

PLANNING FOR CREATIVE ACTIVITIES

Creative activities are generally designed to foster and increase a child's aesthetic sense, divergent thinking, self-evaluation, and personal talents. Several qualifications are necessary. One is that planning for creative activities includes ideas for building general skills and abilities in young children. Developing large and small motor skill, increasing vocabulary, fostering self-help skills, and reinforcing sharing experiences are just a few of the many ways that children benefit from creative activities.

The other qualification is about planning itself. Children often are capable of starting,

enjoying, and learning from activities that they initiate themselves. *Interest centers* (areas set apart for activities which have common or similar goals and require the same materials) provide a place where children can choose their own activities. Teachers must have some idea of what the young children are experiencing and learning. This does not mean, however, that they must also guide and direct each child's every moment. A balance is necessary. One way is to have knowledge of what children can learn with certain materials. This means trusting the children to learn and grow from contact with certain items, such as clay, blocks, and paint. Asking children what they want, need, or like, and responding through planning, is a way of giving young children opportunities to choose. What the children must not learn is to be dependent on adults to give them things to do. Children learn to create their own life experiences and learning.

Determining Activities and Materials

One approach to determining activities and materials is to create interest centers and identify activities or materials for each, based

Fig. 21-2 Children can learn and grow through their own experimenting and talking during block play.

on the children in the class. For the young child, most educators and experts recommend the following interest centers.

Art Area. A place for painting, collage-making, cutting, pasting, chalking; should be located near water and light.

Housekeeping Center. A place for acting out familiar home scenes with pots, pans, and dishes.

Block-building Area. A place where children can create with both large and small blocks, tinker toys, logs.

Manipulative Area. A place to enhance motor skills, eye-hand coordination, and mental, language, and social skills through the use of play materials such as toys, climbing structures, and games.

Science Center. A place to learn about nature. Here, children can display what they find at home or on nature walks, for example. It is a place to explore and ask questions.

Music Center. A place for listening to records, singing, creating dance, and playing musical instruments.

Books and Quiet Area. A place to be alone, quiet in one's thoughts, and to explore the world in books.

A teacher can certainly add other interest centers to this list. The sample room arrangement in figure 21-4 shows how interest centers can be designed. Again, it is a suggestion, to be fitted to the needs of the children and the teacher.

The following factors are important to the selection of proper creative activities when structured planning is desired. The things to consider include:

Children's needs and interests. Children want to do things that relate to their feelings and desires.

Children's levels of development. The limit of a child's ability depends on the child's level

Fig. 21-3 One interest center is the block-building area, where children can experiment with large blocks.

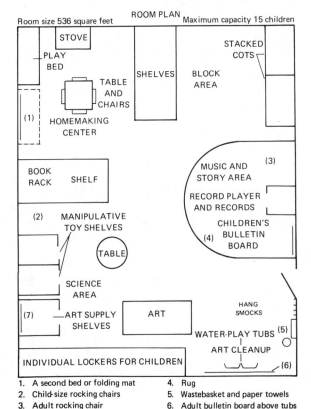

Fig. 21-4 Sample arrangement of interest centers in a classroom.

of development. If a teacher understands this, then failure, frustration, and waste can be avoided.

Available materials and resources. Teachers are limited to materials they have and those they know how to acquire.

The teacher's own needs and interests. Teachers who are excited about their work encourage the enthusiasm of the children.

The teacher's skills and knowledge. Teachers who are aware of their own abilities and knowledge will choose reachable goals and know which new areas to learn and expand.

Planning for the Day and Week

A broad range of creative activities should be included each week. This gives children a variety of choices to suit their many interests. Not only should each of the previously mentioned interest centers be highlighted, but certain types of behavior must also be considered. Dramatic play, creative movement, singing, outdoor activities, and small group projects should all take place within each week.

Do not move too fast when presenting new ideas or activities for young children. They need time to create and explore with new materials. For the younger child, even more time may be needed. An activity may be repeated if the children learn a new way of approaching the material, or if they expand their understanding by the repetition.

Proper sequencing should be given close attention. Activities should build upon each other. For example, some children may want to taste, feel, and smell an apple before they draw or paint one.

The number of adults necessary to supervise an activity must be considered when planning for it. Planning must always be flexible. Cues from the children should be followed and plans modified accordingly.

At the end of the day, the teacher should evaluate the day. Ideas for the next day can be

Fig. 21-5 **A child is continually learning new ways to approach materials. It is therefore necessary to provide enough time for children to explore new materials, and to repeat desired activities.**

revised or created based on what then appears best. What were the successes of the day? How interested were the children in what they were doing? What did their conversation and play indicate? What does the teacher feel like doing? The key words are question, think, feel, decide. A person who works with young children must always be open to new information and feedback.

PRESENTATION OF CREATIVE ACTIVITIES

The success of any creative activity is influenced by how it is presented. How it is presented is affected by how prepared the teacher is for guiding the children in the activity. In planning for each activity, the teacher should

- Identify goals for the activity.

- Identify possible learnings from the activity.

- List the materials which are necessary for the activity.

- Determine how to set up the activity.

- Decide how to stimulate the children.

- Anticipate questions the children might ask.

- Plan for ways to evaluate the activity.

- Consider follow-up activities.

- Consider cleanup time and requirements.

Environment for Creative Activities

The setting in which a creative activity takes place is very important. Young children are very perceptive to mood and environment. A dark room or tight space can have much more effect on them than a rainy day. Some suggestions for providing a positive physical environment for creative behavior are listed.

- The room should be large enough for children to work together cooperatively and freely. Approximately 40 to 60 square feet per child is recommended.

- The shape of the room is a point to consider. A rectangular room seems to lend itself more readily to activities than a square one. L-shaped rooms are difficult to supervise with young children.

- Satisfactory acoustics help communication. Therefore, draperies and carpets should be used to help eliminate noise, as well as add beauty and comfort.

- Wall colors should be selected that add to the light available in the room. Yellow and other light colors are good. It is best if walls are washable at least as high as children can reach.

- Floors should be sanitary, easily cleaned, suited to hard wear, comfortable for children to sit on, and should deaden sound. Some suitable floor coverings include linoleum, carpets, and rubber or plastic tiles. A carpeted section of the floor makes possible a comfortable arrangement for group activities without the need for chairs.

- Proper heat, light, and ventilation are important.

- Time should be available for rest and relaxation periods for young children. Cots, pads, mats, small rugs, and blankets make the rest periods more relaxing and comfortable.

- Running water and sinks are a must for preparing and cleaning up after some creative activities. They should be near the area where they are needed.

- Easy-to-reach storage space for equipment that is in daily use should be provided so that children learn to put their things away.

- Chairs should be light enough for the children to handle and move without too much noise. Since the chairs are used at tables for creative activities, the kind without arms should be used.

- There should be some tables that accommodate from four to six children for group activities. Rectangular tables are better for art activities involving large

Fig. 21-6. In order to allow more children to take part in a particular creative activity or demonstration, it is desirable to have several tables in the room which can accommodate a group of children.

sheets of paper. Some small tables designed to be used singly or in combinations are quite versatile. Tables with washable surfaces such as formica are best.

- Shelves should be low and open so that children have a chance to see, touch, and choose materials independently. Sliding doors are preferred for shelves which have to be closed. Shelves that are sturdy, but easy to move, are more flexible in room arrangement and help to create interest centers. Bulletin board or pegboard backing provides display areas for creative products.

FINISHING A CREATIVE ACTIVITY

The importance of evaluation has already been mentioned. Before the teacher has time to evaluate, however, some other things may be required.

Finishing an activity involves cleanup. Young children can be very helpful with this. It is important to remember that they learn this behavior. They acquire good habits if the teacher takes time to teach them and serves as a model to them. Reinforcement of the right habits is necessary. Young children usually want to help out and enjoy feeling needed.

A place to start is to encourage the children to be as tidy as possible. This can be done by having napkins handy for spills and always keeping cleaning materials nearby.

It should be made as easy as possible for the children to be neat and orderly. For example, if they are to take care of their own possessions such as paints, smocks, and paste, then hooks and shelves must be located near where they work. Materials can be put away when children clearly understand where the materials belong.

The teacher may ask different children to be responsible for taking care of items such as the wastebasket and art supplies. This is done on a rotating basis to guarantee fairness. Children think of this as a privilege if the teacher responds with enthusiasm and gratitude for the help. Some confusion is to be expected and must be accepted until a routine is established.

Completing an activity is important to young children. They finish something with a sense of accomplishment. The teacher has to allow time for individual differences in finishing creative activities. All children cannot be expected to work at the same rate. Sometimes it is fun to leave something purposely undone until the next day. The children are usually excited to return and finish their efforts.

SUMMARY

Planning has to begin with an awareness of the young child. There are many questions to ask about the child, the child's environment, and the teacher's own feelings about the child, in order to plan properly. A balance between teacher planning and children's self-direction is necessary. Interest centers help children in making their own choices.

Fig. 21-7 **Children often experience a sense of accomplishment when they are able to follow through and complete a creative activity.**

Planning for the day or week means proper sequencing of creative activities within a broad range of choices. For each activity, a series of items such as goals, materials, setup, cleanup, and follow-up must be considered. To ensure the proper environment for creative behavior in young children, careful attention must be given to space, light, sound, and furniture. Ending an activity includes not only some form of evaluation, but also the practical side of cleaning up. Young children can learn this and be very helpful.

STUDENT ACTIVITIES

- Make up an interest center not found in this unit. Describe it in detail. List the items and activities it would include.

- Draw an ideal room plan for creative activities. Imagine you have all the money, materials, and space necessary. Be creative. After drawing it, list what you feel is important in it, starting with the most important feature. Share this list with classmates and discuss it.

REVIEW

A. List ten important questions that should be asked in order to better know and work with young children.

B. List five interest centers which early childhood experts recommend.

C. List ten items to consider in creating a positive physical environment for young children.

Unit 22 SUPERVISING CREATIVE ACTIVITIES

OBJECTIVES

After studying this unit, the student will be able to

- Define the term, facilitate.
- List the necessary steps to prepare for a creative activity.
- Explain the difference between having feelings and expressing feelings.

In many educational experiences, and especially in creative activities, the teacher's role is incidental to the creative process. This does not mean that the teacher is unimportant; the teacher is, instead, a facilitator. *Facilitate* means to help along, to guide, to provide opportunities, and to be sensitive and caring without interfering. The meaning as used here is that the teacher allows the young child to deal directly with the materials, with the teacher acting as an aide rather than a leader or judge. The teacher's superior knowledge and skills are tools that help children to do better. These qualities are not standards that children must meet or suffer failure.

Since there is divergent thinking and no single right answer in creative activities, judging is not necessary. Yet, guidance and feedback are helpful. Because creative activities are open-ended situations, there are no simple standards for evaluating them. The teacher's role, then, is one of encouraging, questioning, and experimenting. The teacher also tries to help young children to be more comfortable about not being sure of themselves and what they are doing. Young children may have difficulty handling a brush or crayon in art activities. A child may add a color to a picture which changes the picture in a way not intended. Another child may use too much glue or too little glue. These

and similar difficulties can cause discomfort for the child. The teacher's own patience, calmness, sense of humor, and support help greatly in these frustrating circumstances.

HOW A TEACHER'S ATTITUDE AFFECTS CHILD'S CREATIVITY

The basic agent for helping the teacher in the role of facilitator in creative activities with young children is attitude. Attitude tells a teacher what to do. Change a teacher's attitude, and the whole teacher is changed. Some teacher attitudes and ideas that help in facilitating creative behavior in young children are listed.

Toleration for small mistakes. When children do not have to worry about being perfect, they have more energy to be creative.

Avoid telling the child the best way to do things. To tell the child the best way means, first, that the teacher knows it; second, it means the teacher assumes the child does not know it; and third, it means the child has to ask the teacher in order to know the next time.

Concern about children doing — not about the final product. In creative activities, young children are in a process — playing, drawing, painting, building. Although they are interested in mastering tasks and producing

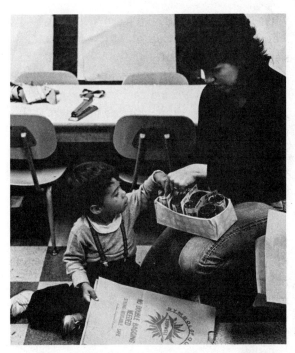

Fig. 22-1 Teachers can encourage creativity in a young child by letting the child "discover" the best way to do something, without telling him.

Fig. 22-2 A teacher who takes the children on a field trip is being a companion and friend to them, and shows them that the activity is worthwhile.

things of which they are proud, they are not like adults. The final product may not be as important as experimenting, as using their minds and senses while doing it. That is why young children often build a complex structure with blocks and then take great joy in knocking it over. They want to see what happens!

Resist the temptation to always have quiet and order. Silence may not be the spirit of joy. Cleanliness may not be the companion of discovery. Timing and flexibility are all important in these matters. Only one rule is necessary: "When learning stops and respect for the other person is lost, then order and direction must come."

Get involved. The teacher who is painting, drawing, and working beside the children, or accompanying them on a field trip or a walk, is a companion and friend. To the children, the activity must be worth doing

if the teacher is doing it too. This helps motivation and is a legitimate entry into the children's world. Besides, it's fun!

PREPARING FOR A CREATIVE ACTIVITY

Often, teachers attempt a creative activity that they have not experienced before. They may have read about it in a book, heard about it from a friend, or seen it at a workshop. They try it because they feel it should work and the children should gain something from it. Most often it does succeed, but sometimes it does not. The unfortunate part is that when it does not, the teacher may not know whether it was because of the activity itself, or the way it was prepared for and offered. For any activity, especially for a first time experience, the following suggestions may be helpful.

- "Walk through" the activity before giving it to the children. (In other words, "try it, you might not like it.") Do this physically, if possible, or else mentally.

Sometimes things sound better than they really are. The children should do the experimenting, not be the ones to be experimented on.

- Make sure all necessary physical equipment is present. Toys without batteries, paints without brushes, and paper without paste can cause a great deal of frustration.

- Read the directions completely. Any creative activity should have the full chance to succeed. Ignorance about how to do something lessens the opportunity for success.

- Modify the activity, if necessary, to meet the particular needs of the children. Few activities are right for all cultures, all situations, or every type of child. All teachers must be sensitive to this.

- Arrange the parts of the activity for easy distribution. When getting started is more effort than the activity itself, motivation suffers.

- In as little time as possible, explain the activity so that the children know how to begin and proceed. For this part, rules are not necessary, but understanding is.

- After the children have started, circulate among them offering suggestions where helpful, and answering questions as needed. Try to let the children answer their own questions as well as solve their own problems. The teacher's role remains that of a facilitator.

COMPETITION

Young children naturally compare their work to others and seek their teacher's approval. However, they do not naturally try to be better than one another, make fun of another child's work, or try to be the best at what they do. This is learned. It may be learned from their parents, their brothers and sisters, or other adults and children. It is not to be learned from their teacher.

At such a young age, creative growth is not helped in a competitive atmosphere. This is because to win or gain approval, a child must learn to meet another person's standards. At this age, the children are beginning to learn about themselves. It is harmful for a four- to five-year-old to try to please others in activities meant for exploring and wonderment. It stops self-growth. It puts pressure where pleasure should exist. Instead of complete involvement in the materials and task, it means manipulating the task to gain something outside of it. Discovery is sacrificed for recognition; and insight, for approval. This is too great a cost for a young child.

When confronted with competitive striving in a young child, the teacher is to respect this. Not only is it learned behavior, but it may be a chosen value of the child's parents. Teachers do not have the right to change parents' values in children without the parents' permission. But teachers do have a right to their own values. They do not have to reinforce competition in young children. They can ask the children for their own judgments as well as refer them back to their parents for approval. Children at this age can also grasp the idea that they, and their creative works, are unique, and therefore it is not fair to compare with others without some qualification.

EXPRESSING EMOTIONS

Creative activities are usually unstructured, allowing for individual freedom and expression. Deep feelings or strong emotions often occur when young children are involved. The important job that the teacher has at such times is neither to stop nor encourage the child's feelings, but to help the

Fig. 22-3 When children are involved in creative activities, they may express strong feelings or emotions.

child find acceptable ways to express these feelings. The flexibility and broad range of available creative activities should facilitate this.

If given the chance, free from outside judgment, children usually let the materials and their fantasies take care of the emotions they are feeling. They may pound clay, throw a puppet, or crumple paper to vent anger. Or, they may kiss a puppet, stroke the clay figure, or gently paint on paper to show affection. In this way, the children can let go the feeling when it occurs. They can then go on to create and involve themselves in other productive activities.

If one child interferes with other children when expressing emotions, the other children's responses may be enough to help the child stop and adjust. If the child still cannot stop or adjust, then the teacher may have to help out. The teacher should respect the child's feelings, but show that there are limits to what the child can do. In no way

does this mean punishment. It means helping a child to know limits (setting them when necessary), and then, helping the child to channel emotions in a more positive direction. For example, a child angrily knocks over some clay figures he just made and in the process, also knocks over some that belong to other children. The children are a bit frightened and back away. The child is still pounding the clay figures. The other children are just standing around.

The teacher may have to come into this situation and do one or more of several things — depending on the circumstances.

- Ask the child if he notices what he has done to the other children's clay figures.
- Ask the child if he wishes to continue his current behavior.
- Ask the child to help the other children pick up their clay figures.

This list is by no means complete. There is no one best way to handle behavior. Problems demand creative responses from the teacher. A discipline situation is usually one that requires divergent thinking on the part of the adult.

It is important that young children learn that there is nothing wrong with having personal feelings. It is the expression of these feelings that may cause problems. If children think that feelings are bad or wrong and must not be felt, they are likely to hurt themselves emotionally. They may develop defenses which stop them from feeling good about themselves, being open to others, and trusting themselves or others. A young child should learn that the expression of some feelings can hurt others. The child must understand that it is the means of expression and not the feeling itself that may be harmful. Thus, children learn they have freedom to feel and accept those feelings as part of themselves. They also learn that they do not have

Fig. 22-4 **Working with other children, a child learns to respect the feelings of others.**

freedom to express feelings in any manner without regard for others.

RELATING TO CREATIVE STYLES

Children, as well as adults, have a right to their own styles of working, learning, and creating. Therefore, it is very difficult to decide when to attempt to influence or modify a child's behavior. Individual differences are to be accepted. Sometimes a teacher notices behavior in a child which may be harmful or prevent the child from being successful or happy in an activity. At such times, a safe approach is to suggest other ways to the child which may increase the choices and give new behaviors from which to select. Some creative styles which may limit children are listed. For each there are also some suggestions that may expand their choices and create alternatives.

The highly active-impulsive style. These children choose too quickly. They appear to do things without thinking or exploring. They tend to jump from one thing to another. They are in the paint, then in the clay, then in the paste. Without punishing them, place the children away from distracting materials for a start. Encourage them whenever possible to stick to activities. Ask them to stay with an activity for a period of time rather than as long as it interests them.

Fig. 22-5 **Sometimes children work with materials in an impulsive manner, and do not follow through with an activity. It may be helpful to encourage these children to stay with the activity, so that they can see the results of their efforts.**

Give reinforcement for doing so. Help children see the value of finishing things by displaying their work or honestly complimenting it. Make remarks that help them see the next step toward a goal.

The rigid-inhibited style. These children must have things one way. They have difficulty with flexibility and change. They may have difficulty sharing or working with other children. They are often unhappy about trying new things. The children need structure and security so that they do not have to change unreasonably. They must not be forced to try new things. No one must make fun of a child for sticking with one activity. Trust is the most important thing here. Gentle acceptance and time are needed. If something new is to be started, it should be as simple as possible. Perhaps the teacher can work along with these children until they are comfortable. The better they know what to expect the greater their chances of getting involved.

The acceptance-anxious style. For these children, adult approval is very necessary. They must have their work checked often. They constantly ask for the teacher's attention. The slightest disapproval can bring tears, and withdrawal from the activity. It is usually helpful to put these children on a time schedule for looking at their work. If they know the teacher is coming every so many minutes, they can get into their work without worrying about whether the teacher is paying attention or not. Asking the children to finish a certain amount of work before requesting teacher attention is another choice. Letting the children know the teacher likes what they like could be helpful. The teacher may encourage the child to experiment and make "way-out" ideas. Perfection is not stressed in this situation.

In all creative activities, the teacher has two basic questions to ask in helping young children. The first is, "How is the child being creative?" The second is, "How does the child feel about it?" Sensitive answers to these questions can tell the teacher what to do. The goal is to never stop asking them.

SUMMARY

In creative activities, the teacher's role is to facilitate creative behavior. This generally means having a sensitive and caring attitude toward the children and helping them interact with their materials. It means guidance without interference or judgment. Some of the ways teachers can prepare for new creative

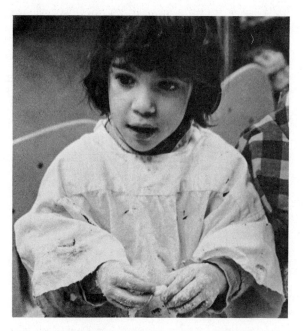

Fig. 22-6 In creative activities, it is important for a teacher to find the answers to two basic questions: "How is the child being creative?" and "How does the child feel about it?"

activities are "walking through" the activity, reading the directions completely, and having all the necessary physical equipment.

Although young children naturally compare their work with other children, competition is not necessary or helpful in creative activities. It is important that young children learn that personal feelings are normal and acceptable. Sometimes the expression of these feelings may cause problems and, therefore, may need modification. Sensitive answers to the questions, "How is the child being creative?" and "How does the child feel about it?" can help guide the teacher in facilitating creative behavior.

STUDENT ACTIVITIES

- Check the list of attitudes found in this unit which help in facilitating creative behavior in young children.

    A. Choose one example of each from your personal life in which you demonstrate the attitude.

  B. Decide whether this is an attitude you already possess or one that you need to work on in order to improve.

  C. For those attitudes that need improvement, consider how you plan to go about doing this.

- Make a list of feelings which often occur in your daily life. Then reflect on situations where expression of these feelings got you into some form of trouble or difficulty. What do these forms of expression have in common? Discuss this with classmates. What can be done about these forms of expression?

REVIEW

A. Define "facilitate."

B. List the necessary steps in preparing for a creative activity.

C. In relation to young children, discuss the difference between having feelings and expressing feelings.

PART II

Building and expanding on the theory presented in Part I, the many and varied activities given in Part II actually put this theory into practice. Numerous seasonal and general art activities and finger plays are presented to help children develop small motor skills. Varied games and movement activities are provided which are not only fun for young children, but also help build large motor skills. Additional resource/ideas units include topics such as reading readiness, cooking experiences, environmental education, music, and poetry. All of the activities presented are soundly based in developmental theory, yet simple to reproduce and expand upon.

To my Family
In loving appreciation for their support in my second circle.

Mary Mayesky

Unit 23 AUTUMN

This is the time of year when nature takes its last fling. The landscape is brilliant with raw and muted colors ranging from bright yellow to red-orange to red; from red-brown to red-violet.

The young child is naturally sensitive to the wonders and beauty of nature: the colors and rhythm of leaves whirled by autumn winds, the texture of dried seeds and weeds, the form and color in the harvest. There are a number of things a teacher can do to enlarge children's understanding of their world and to encourage them to learn to look, feel, and think:

- Begin a collection of objects from nature for classroom use. Encourage closer observation of design in nature.

- Take children on walking trips to discover and observe the colors, shapes, and textures in trees, plants, clouds, buildings, and vehicles. Individual observation can be shared with others at "see and tell" time.

The children draw and paint the beauty of nature as they each see it, using their own feelings and ideas. Their growing visual awareness is gradually reflected in picture-making, as they mature in the ability to interpret their environment. Some topics for drawing and painting include:

- Leaves in autumn
- Birds flying south
- A rainy day in fall
- The fall harvest
- Raking fall leaves
- My neighborhood in autumn

Other suggested art activities:

- A fall bouquet
- An autumn collage
- Playing store
- Nature prints
- Papier-maché harvest
- Cut-paper mural

ART ACTIVITIES

- **Leaf People and Animals**

Procedure:

1. Have children collect autumn leaves on a class walk, or on their walk to and from school.

Fig. 23-1 Leaf people.

2. Children then paste the leaves to a piece of brown, red, orange, or yellow piece of construction paper.

3. The teacher can show the children how the stem of the leaf is the first "leg" for a leaf person or animal. From that point on, the child's imagination aids the creation of the rest of the leaf picture.

4. After the leaf people and animals are completed, the children may want to fill in the background with crayons or chalk.

• **Leaf Tree**

Procedure:

1. Find a large branch about four feet tall with many twigs on it. Stand it in a can of plaster of Paris for a firm base.

2. Children can cut, trace, or draw leaves and tie them on the twigs. They can be drawn freehand or traced from actual leaves. The name of the leaf can be written on each.

3. The tree itself can be reused for such activities as word games, for different seasons, and for many other kinds of activities.

Fig. 23-2 All seasons tree.

• **Cut-Up Puppets**

Procedure:

1. If you have a damaged or outdated copy of a book you still use with the children, cut the characters out and paste them on popsicle sticks to make puppets.

2. A few days before the book is given to the children, introduce the puppets to them. Place the puppets in a container where the children can play with them during the day.

3. After reading the book, the children can use the puppets to act out the story.

• **Autumn Leaves Mobile**

Materials: twigs, leaves, string or yarn, construction paper

Procedure:

1. On a class walk or on the walk to school, have each child collect about 6 leaves and a small branch, about 12 inches long. A branch with a few twigs makes the best kind of mobile.

2. Under the close supervision of the teacher, have each child press the leaves between two sheets of waxed paper, using an iron on the "low" setting. This preserves the leaves.

3. When the waxed paper has cooled, the children then cut around the leaves to separate them for the mobile. The waxed paper may be left on the leaves. However, if it does not stay attached, the wax coating left by the heat application is enough to harden and preserve the leaves.

4. Children then make holes in each leaf with a needle, hairpin, or even a pencil point. Instruct children to do this carefully.

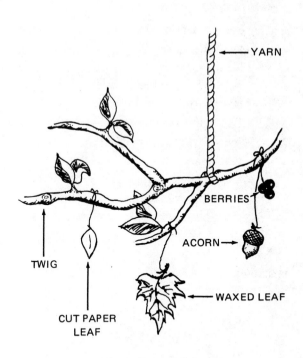

Fig. 23-3 **Leaf mobile.**

Fig. 23-4 **Transfer print.**

5. Children insert string or thin yarn into the holes in each of the leaves. The teacher may aid the children in knotting the string or yarn.
6. The children then attach a piece of string or yarn (about 12 inches long) to the branch. Help the children attach the string so that the branch hangs horizontally. (This is a good experiment in balance.)
7. Next, the children tie the leaves onto the branch in various places. Leaf shapes cut out of red, yellow, orange, and brown construction paper can also be attached to the branch with yarn.
8. Acorns, seeds, or even berries may also be strung and attached for added color and variety.
9. Mobiles may be hung on a string across a section of the room for an attractive fall display.

- **Nature Prints**

Children can make a splatter print of leaves, weeds, and grasses.

Procedure:

1. Rub a paint-filled toothbrush across a piece of wire screen, comb, or tongue blade. Create a transfer print by painting leaves and stamping them on paper.
2. Another transfer print can be made by arranging leaves, then covering them with paper. Rub over the paper with crayon. Make an overall design by moving the objects several times and repeating the rubbing. Colors may be overlapped and blended to create interesting effects.
3. For further suggestions, refer to the section on printmaking.

- **Center-of-Interest Autumn Collage**

Procedure:

1. Make an arrangement with objects of nature that can be pasted easily to a flat background such as a shallow box or box lid. Sheets of heavy construction paper or cardboard are also suitable. A variety of objects (different textures, shapes, and colors)

Fig. 23-5 Autumn collage.

are important in creating an interesting design.

2. Begin the collage by placing the most important object on the background. Then arrange the other objects around it so that it remains the center of interest. A collection of autumn collages makes an attractive classroom display.

• **Repeated Forms Autumn Collage**

Another nature collage can be made using seeds, pods, and other things scattered on the ground and left by the wind.

Procedure:

1. Children may classify the objects: large, small, round, straight, rough, smooth, hard, soft.
2. An egg carton is a good receptacle for small objects.
3. The objects may be arranged into a pattern of repeating forms, using contrasting shapes, textures, and colors. A group display tells the story of nature's materials.

• **Fall Bouquet**

When assembling objects of nature, try making a bouquet of dried flowers, weeds, twigs, and leaves.

Procedure:

1. Select a container such as a tin can, an old vase, or a paper cup. To hold objects in place, use sand, marbles, pebbles, oiled clay, play dough, or salt clay.
2. Begin the arrangement with the tallest pieces first; then use the short ones. Place objects at various heights and angles. Use different textures, colors, and shapes. If the bouquet is to be seen from all sides it must be interesting all around.

• **Papier-Maché Harvest**

Procedure:

1. Crumple newspaper into desired shapes (fruits or vegetables).
2. Cover each form with torn newspaper strips dipped into thin wheat paste. At least two layers of newspaper, with a generous use of paste, are needed to hold the form securely.
3. When thoroughly dry, fruits and vegetables can be painted in brilliant colors.

Fig. 23-6 Papier-maché harvest.

• **Play Store**

Procedure:

1. A miniature store can be set up on a spare table, or on some open shelves, or with a few large cartons.
2. Arrange papier-maché fruits and vegetables in baskets and boxes from the supermarket.
3. Children can play store, buying and selling with make-believe money.

• **Cut-Paper Mural**

This is another form of picturemaking in which each child can participate and make a contribution. Cut paper is a flexible technique that permits the child to arrange and rearrange objects on a background, grouping and overlapping them as desired.

Procedure:

1. After the topic is discussed, the children decide what they will each make, expressing their own ideas. A variety of papers may be used, such as colored construction paper, metallic foil, tissue paper, wallpaper, and illustrated magazine pages.

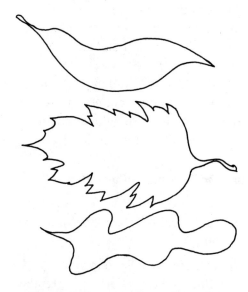

Fig. 23-7 Cut-paper leaves for mural.

2. In placing objects it must be remembered that to create depth, large shapes should appear in the foreground or bottom of the picture; smaller figures are placed toward the top.
3. From time to time, children should stop working and evaluate their progress.
4. When completed, the mural glows with autumn colors. It can be used together with any of the other suggested art projects on this general topic.

• **Painting with Weeds**

Procedure:

1. Some weeds can be used as brushes for painting, creating an interesting effect.
2. In the fall, many weeds are at maximum heights, and can be collected on class walks for later use in art activities.

• **Waxed Paper Pictures**

Procedure:

1. Place autumn leaves between two sheets of waxed paper, and press with a warm iron. (Shredded crayon pieces can be added before pressing for a more colorful effect.)
2. These leaf pictures can be hung on a window or wall, or used as placemats.

• **Leaf Rubbings**

Procedure:

1. Place leaves under a piece of thin paper.
2. Rub the side of an unwrapped crayon over the paper. The veins and outlines of the leaves will show up clearly.
3. Use different colors for each leaf to create a more colorful design.

ADDITIONAL FALL ACTIVITIES

• **What Happened?**

Procedure:

1. Take photographs during a fall walk. Try to take pictures that show a sequence of events.
2. Back in the classroom, arrange the photographs on display in sequence. Have the children think of captions for the pictures, then the story of the event, following the sequence shown in the pictures. Children who are not yet writing can dictate their captions and story to the teacher.

• **Bean Necklace**

Procedure:

1. Soak different kinds of dried beans in water that has been mixed with food coloring to soften and color the beans.
2. Thread a needle with heavy thread or twine. String the beans and let them dry.
3. The beans will shrink, so do not tie the necklace until the beans are dry.

• **What's the Weather?**

Procedure:

1. Ask the children to draw twin weather pictures. On the left side of the page, they can draw a familiar outdoor scene of any season of the year. On the other half of the paper, have them draw the scene as it would look at another time of year: for example, a crowded beach in summer and a lonely one in winter.
2. After they finish their drawings, encourage the youngsters to talk about seasonal differences.

• **Well-Preserved Beauty**

Here's a way to save some of the colorful beauty from autumn's fallen leaves.

Procedure:

1. Have each child choose a leaf for its color and shape, and place it on a piece of tagboard.
2. Trace the outline of the leaf with a crayon or paint the area inside with a bright fall color.
3. Label the leaf. Have the children look up the leaves they can not identify.

FINGER PLAYS, POEMS, AND SONGS

• **Safety — Finger Play**

Red says STOP
  (Hold right hand in "stop" gesture)
And Green says GO.
  (Extend right arm with index finger pointed)
Yellow says WAIT;
You'd better go slow!
  (With index finger extended, wave right hand across body from right to left and back to right)
When I reach a crossing place
  (Cross arms at wrists)
To left and right I turn my face.
  (Turn head to left and right)
I walk, not run, across the street
  (Demonstrate walking or use index fingers to show walking, then running)
And use my head to guide my feet.
  (Point to head then to feet)

• **Back to School — Finger Play**

(Have a calendar and clockface with movable hands ready before beginning this play.)

The calendar says September.
  (Point to the word "September" on calendar)

The clock says eight A.M.
   (Show clockface with proper line)
The school bus calls to take us
Back to school again!
   (Hold hands as though on steering
   wheel of bus)
When we see our friends, we'll wave
   (Wave hand and smile)
When we're in class, we will behave.
   (Fold hands in front — "good child"
   gesture)
We'll look at books and write our names
   (Pretend to hold an open book, and pre-
   tend to write in it)
And play some of our favorite games.
   (Pretend to throw a ball or jump rope)

- **Falling Leaves — Finger Play**

Red leaves falling down
Yellow leaves falling down.
   (Move fingers in falling leaves gesture)
Over all the town
Over all the town.
   (Make circle movements with arms)
Leaves are falling down
Leaves are falling down.
   (Move fingers in falling leaves gesture)
Red leaves, yellow leaves
All are falling down.
   (Children "fall" gently down to the
   floor)

- **The Apple Tree — Finger Play**

Way up in the apple tree
   (Point up)
Two little apples smiled at me.
   (Close thumb and forefinger of each
   hand)
I shook that tree as hard as I could
   (Grab imaginary tree and shake it)
Down fell the apples
   (Raise hands and arms high, then let fall)
M-m-m, were they good!
   (Rub tummy, satisfied smile on face)

- **Raking Leaves — Finger Play**

I like to rake the leaves
   (Raking gesture)
Into a great big hump.
   (Hands make hump)
Then I go back a little way,
   (Step back)
Bend both my knees, and jump!
   (Children jump)

- **Leaves Dance — Finger Play**

Leaves are floating softly down,
   (Waving fingers, like falling leaves)
They make a carpet on the ground.
   (Bend down, run hand close to ground)
Then swish, the wind comes whistling by
   (Stand up, raise hands above head)
And sends them dancing to the sky.
   (Dance)

- **Gray Squirrel — Action Poem, Song**

Gray squirrel, gray squirrel
Swish your bushy tail.
   (Children move "bottoms" pretending
   to move "tails")
(Repeat)
Hold a nut between your paws
   (Pretend to hold a nut with closed fists
   together)
Wrinkle up your funny nose.
   (Move nose like a squirrel)
Gray squirrel, gray squirrel,
Swish your bushy tail.
   (Pretend to move "tail")

- **Shuffling — Action Poem**

It's fun to shuffle on my way
   (Shuffle feet)
Through rustling leaves on an autumn day.
   (Shuffle feet)
The leaves aren't leaves at all to me;
   (Shake head)
They are cornflakes falling from a tree.
   (Pretend to munch and rub tummy)

- **Trees in Fall — Action Poem**

  The elm will stretch and stretch so wide
    (Children stretch arms out wide)
  It reaches out on every side.
    (Still stretching — horizontally)
  The pine will stretch and stretch so high
    (Now stretch arms vertically)
  It reaches up to touch the sky.
    (Still stretching)
  The willow droops and droops so low,
    (Droop down)
  Its branches sweep the ground below.
    (Fall softly to floor)

- **Come, Little Leaves — Action Poem**

  "Come, little leaves," said the wind one day.
    (Beckon with index finger)
  "Come over the meadows with me and play.
    (Beckon with arm)
  Put on your dresses of red and gold,
    (Pretend to dress)
  For summer is gone, and
  The days grow cold."
    (Rub arms to keep warm)

- **One Little Leaf — Finger Play**

  One little leaf, two little leaves,
    (Hold up 1, then 2 fingers)
  Three little leaves today.
    (Hold up 3 fingers)
  Four little leaves, five little leaves,
    (Then 4th and 5th fingers)
  Blow them all away.
    (Blow on fingers, and then put them
    down making them "blow" away)

FALL POETRY

- **A Leaf**

  If I were a leaf
  (But I wouldn't be),
  I'd have to be tied
  To a tree, tree, tree.

  I couldn't walk off
  (Or skip or run),
  And my nose would get burned
  By the sun, sun, sun.

  In summer, I'd roast,
  In winter, I'd freeze.
  And all through October,
  I'd sneeze, sneeze, sneeze!

- **Autumn Woods**

  I like the woods in autumn
  When dry leaves hide the ground,
  When the trees are bare
  And the wind sweeps by
  With a winsome, rushing sound.
  I can rustle the leaves in autumn
  And I can make a bed
  In the thick dry leaves
  That have fallen
  From the bare trees overhead.

- **Leaves**

  Down, down!
  Yellow and brown.
  The leaves are falling
  All over town.

- **Fall Bird**

  I saw a bird the other day,
  He sat upon a limb;
  He looked at me, then flew away,
  It was too cold for him.

  He flew away where the cotton grows,
  Where everything's bright, not dim;
  He flew away where it never snows,
  That bird upon the limb.

- **Autumn Bird Song**

  Over the housetops,
  Over the trees,
  Winging their way
  In a stiff fall breeze.

A flock of birds
Is flying along
Southward, for winter,
Singing a song.

Singing a song
They all like to sing,
"We'll see you again
When it's spring, spring, spring."

• **Dry Leaves**

Dry leaves in autumn
Go clicking down the street,
Like children playing dress up
With slippers on their feet.

• **Fall Insects Sleep**

What is under the grass
Way down in the ground,
Where everything is cool and wet
With darkness all around?

Little pink worms live there;
Ants and brown bugs creep
Softly round the stones and rocks
Where roots are pushing deep.

• **Frisky Squirrel**

Whisky Frisky,
Hippity-hop
Up he goes
To the treetop!

Whirly, twirly,
Round and round,
Down he scampers
To the ground.

Furly, curly,
What a tail!
Tall as a feather,
Broad as a sail!

Where's his supper?
In the shell;
Snap, cracky,
Out it fell.

• **Happy Leaves**

Little *red* leaves are glad today
    (Also substitute brown and yellow)
For the wind is blowing them off and away.

They are flying here, they are flying there.
Oh little *red* leaves, you are everywhere!
    (Also substitute brown and yellow)

• **I Saw a Squirrel**

I saw a little squirrel,
Sitting in a tree;
He was eating a nut
And wouldn't look at me.

• **Wind**

I like the wind
When I play out;
It blows the leaves and me about.
I like the rain upon my nose;
Of course, it's not so good for clothes.
The sun comes out most every day;
Sometimes, you know, it hides away.

• **The Milkweed**

In a milkweed cradle snug and warm
Baby seeds are hiding safe from harm.
Open wide the cradle!
Hold it high!
Come, Mr. Wind, help them fly.

• **It's Raining Gold**

It's raining gold
And red and brown,
As Autumn leaves
Come falling down!

COOKING EXPERIENCES

Picture Recipes

As children gain experience in cooking, they begin to see that specific directions are followed in recipes. It is then fun to write out recipes in picture form for children to

Fig. 23-8 Picture recipe for applesauce.

more quickly about proper measurements. Match the color of the picture to the color of the real spoon or cup.

- **Applesauce**

Ingredients:

4 to 6 medium apples
1/4 cup sugar
1/2 stick cinnamon (or 1–2 whole cloves, if desired)

Materials: apple corer, vegetable peeler, cooking pot, food mill (if available)

Procedure: (if food mill is not used)

1. Peel and core the apples.
2. Cut apples into quarters, and place in pot.
3. Add a small about of water (about 1 inch).
4. Cover the pot and cook slowly (simmer) until apples are tender. The cooked apples can then be mashed with a fork, beaten with a beater, or put through a strainer.
5. Add sugar to taste (about 1/4 cup to 4 apples), and continue cooking until sugar dissolves.
6. Add 1/2 stick of cinnamon (or 1 to 2 cloves) if desired.

Note: If a food mill is used, it is not necessary to peel and core the apples. After the apples are cooked as above, they are put through the food mill. Children enjoy turning the handle and watching the sauce come dripping out of the holes.

7. For fun, add a few cinnamon candies. What happens to the color of the applesauce? Is the flavor changed? Be sure to add them while the applesauce is still hot.

read by themselves. To make such recipes, simply cut out pictures of ingredients and utensils from magazines or make rough drawings. The children will learn that each picture stands for a particular food or utensil. They will soon be able to tell the teacher which ingredient is used next.

A plastic set of measuring cups and spoons should be available. Each size should be a different color, to help the children learn

- **Vegetable Soup**

Ingredients:

1 soup bone
1 onion
1 cup peas
3 diced potatoes
1/2 quart tomatoes
1/2 cup celery diced
1/2 cup shredded cabbage (optional)
1 cup corn
1 cup lima beans
salt and pepper to taste
macaroni alphabet letters

Procedure:

1. Cook the soup bone in enough water to completely cover it.
2. When tender, remove meat from broth and add diced vegetables, and more water if needed. Add macaroni letters.
3. Continue to cook for 20 minutes.
4. Seasoned, canned vegetables may be substituted for fresh vegetables; add just before serving. Instant vegetable soup may be used for broth, if desired. It is faster.

- **Baked Apples**

Ingredients:

6 red baking apples
1 tablespoon butter
6 tablespoons sugar
1 teaspoon cinnamon
1/3 cup water
1/2 cup dark molasses or sorghum

Procedure:

1. Wash apples. Remove cores (teacher).
2. Place apples in a buttered flat baking dish.
3. In center of each apple, put 1/2 teaspoon butter and 1 tablespoon sugar and cinnamon mixture. Combine water and molasses and pour over apples.
4. Bake at 350 degrees for approximately 45 minutes. Baste occasionally.
5. Raisins may be added to apples, if desired.

- **General Vegetables Preparation**

Green or wax beans – Cut in 1-inch pieces; cook in boiling salt water 15 to 20 minutes in a covered saucepan.

Beets – Wash and cut off tops; cook beets whole without salt 30 to 60 minutes, until tender. Drain; drop in cold water; slip off skins with your fingers. Cube or quarter.

Broccoli – Cut off large stems; cook (covered) 10 to 20 minutes. Cut into bite size pieces.

Cabbage – Shred with long sharp knife. Cook in small amount of water 5 to 15 minutes; red cabbage 20 to 25 minutes.

Carrots – Cut into sticks; cook 10 to 25 minutes in boiling water.

Celery – Cut into 1-inch pieces; cook in small amount of water 15 minutes.

Peas – Shell just before cooking time. Cook in small amount of water. Cover and cook until tender but not mushy.

Squash – Cut in half or pieces; remove seeds and fibers; bake 35 to 45 minutes until soft. Season with brown sugar or molasses. Cut into small pieces for tasting.

Asparagus – Wash; cut up. Cook covered in a small amount of boiling salted water for 5 to 10 minutes.

Other vegetables that might be cooked include:

Lima or any beans
Brussels sprouts
Cauliflower
Corn on the cob

Okra   Turnips
Potatoes   Greens
Spinach   Peppers
Tomatoes

- **Apple Cake**

Ingredients:

1 1/2 cups cooking oil

3 eggs

2 cups sugar

2 teaspoons vanilla

3 cups presifted flour

1 teaspoon baking soda

2 teaspoons cinnamon

1/2 teaspoon salt

2 cups peeled, chopped apples

1 cup chopped walnuts

Materials: knife for peeling and chopping apples, flour sifter, measuring cup, measuring spoons, 2 loaf pans, large and small mixing bowls, mixing spoon

Procedure:

1. Help the children flour and prepare the apples.
2. Grease the loaf pans.
3. Sprinkle a little flour in each pan and shake it until the pan is dusted with flour.
4. Measure the sifted flour into the small mixing bowl.
5. Stir in the baking soda, cinnamon, and salt.
6. In the big mixing bowl, mix the sugar, oil, eggs, and vanilla.
7. Add the flour mixture to the egg mixture and stir well.
8. Add the apples and nuts and stir gently.
9. Pour the whole mixture into loaf pans.
10. Bake for 1 1/2 hours at 350 degrees. (Makes 2 loaves.)

- **Hot Apple Cider**

Procedure:

1. Heat cider or apple juice.
2. Add a pinch of cinnamon or nutmeg, or both.
3. How does it smell?

- **Vegetable Dip**

Dip celery, cucumber, or carrot sticks into peanut butter, sour cream, yogurt, or cottage cheese that has been mashed with a fork.

LANGUAGE ARTS

Apple Story

Have an apple ready to cut in half across the width, at the end of this story. When cut widthwise, the apple seeds look like the "star" in the story.

The Star in the Apple

Once upon a time there was a little boy who couldn't find anything to play with. He was tired of all his toys and asked his mother if she could please help him find something to do. She thought and thought and finally said, "Why, I know what you can do. You can go outside and look for a little red house that is round and shiny, has no doors and windows, and has a star inside." He thought it sounded like fun, and easy to find, so outside he went. He looked and looked but there was no such house to be found.

The little boy met a dog and said, "Mr. Dog, would you help me find a little house that is red and shiny, has no doors or windows, and has a star inside?" The dog said, "Surely," and they went together to find the house. (They meet a cat, a horse, a cow, and a chicken, and go through the same routine.) The whole procession at last met a little old woman who had a knife in her hand. The little boy asked her if she had seen a little house which was red and shiny, with no doors or windows, and with a star inside.

She answered, "Why, yes, come along with me and I will find it for you." The little old woman led them to a hill. Only an apple tree grew on the hill. The old woman said, "This is where the house is, little boy." The little boy and his friends looked and looked, but could not see a little red house. The old woman picked an apple and asked, "Isn't this round and shiny? It has no doors, and no windows. I wonder if there is a star inside."

With her knife, she cut the apple horizontally. There was the star! So the little boy found the little red house that is round and shiny, has no doors and windows, and has a star inside. It is an apple!

TAG GAMES FOR FITNESS

Children have a natural desire to chase and to be chased. Tag games help to satisfy this desire and at the same time encourage fitness. Here are 9 tag games and some tips to make the teacher's job easier.

Teaching Tips:

1. If possible, use an area with clearly marked boundaries.
2. Generally, the smaller the area of play, the more active the game. In a smaller area, players are nearer the child who is "it," and thus have to run more.
3. To settle disputes over whether a player was tagged, make a rule that the word of the tagger counts.
4. If a player has been "it" for 30 seconds and cannot catch anyone, have another child help chase.
5. Limit vigorous tag games to 10 or 15 minutes.

• **Boundary Tag**

This is the simplest type of tag game. Any number of children may play, but the game is best when limited to no more than 15 children. Use any clearly marked area about the size of a basketball court. One player is selected to be "it" while the rest of the group spreads out within the play area. "It" chases until someone is tagged. The person tagged becomes the new "it," and the game continues. A player who runs out of bounds to avoid being tagged will also become "it."

• **Skipping Tag**

This tag is played the same way as boundary tag, except that all players must skip. (It is a good game for checking motor coordination of four and five year olds.) This is good for teaching fundamental movements such as skipping, galloping, and hopping. A player becomes "it" when tagged or when moving any way except skipping. (A variation of this game is walk tag, where players must walk. This is a good game to use following a vigorous tag game.)

• **Imitation Tag**

This is identical to the other tag games, except that the person who becomes "it" selects the type of motion (running, skipping, etc.) to be used. Then the player who is "it" tries to catch the other players. If no one is caught, "it" may change the motion being used one time, and then if no one is caught, someone else becomes "it."

• **Rope Tag**

Use no more than 15 players per game, with a 10- to 15-foot jump rope. With 30 in a class, use two ropes and play two separate games. The playing area can be any area with clearly marked boundaries. One player is selected to be "it" and is given a rope. All other players spread out within the playing area. The person who is "it" attempts to tag one of the other players, but must drag the rope at all times. The other players may tease "it" by stepping on the rope. The rope gives less aggressive players courage to play. A player who runs out of bounds or is tagged becomes "it."

• **Chain Tag**

Having 10 to 20 players works best. If there are more children, start two games. Use an area about the size of a basketball court, with clearly marked boundaries. The one who is "it" chases until catching someone. The two join hands and try to catch more players. Each player who is tagged joins the chain. Only the end players of the chain may tag. If the chain breaks, no one may be tagged until the players rejoin hands. The players being chased may dodge under the arms of the players in the middle of the chain. The last player to be tagged becomes the new "it." Tagged players always join the end of the chain away from "it," thus "it" always remains at one end.

• **Raindrop Game**

Have the children sit in a circle on the floor with their eyes closed and one hand open behind their backs. Appoint one child the "rainmaker." This person carries a "raindrop" (pebble or button) around the circle and drops it into the hand of one of the other children, who then jumps up and tries to tag the rainmaker. If the rainmaker can reach the safety of the vacated seat, the chaser becomes the new rainmaker. Otherwise, the rainmaker must take another turn.

• **Who's Missing?**

The child who is "it" leaves the room. Another person either hides or leaves the room,

being careful not to be seen. "It" is called back and tries to figure out who is missing.

• **Blackboard Tag**

Choose a boy and a girl. A blackboard eraser is placed on each child's head. The boy stands at one end of the room and the girl at the other. At a given signal they start walking toward each other. The object of the game is for the girl and boy to try to tag each other without losing their eraser. If an eraser falls off, the other player is the winner.

• **Tadpole**

Two teams form circles. Each team gets one beanbag or playground ball. The object of the game is to see how many times the ball can make complete circuits of the circle by passing it to each player while the other team completes a relay by passing their ball. The ball may be handed or thrown or bounced from one player to the next, all the way around the circle. Each time the ball passes around the circle, the players count the number of times loudly. When the teacher calls, "Time," the team with the most circuits completed wins.

MOVEMENT EXPERIENCES
• **Eye-Foot Coordination Activities**
Activity 1

Equipment: lines can be placed on a floor (gym, multipurpose room or classroom), either with tape or liquid white shoe polish
Formation: one line for each child
Procedure: Place a line on the floor and have children:
1. Walk forward on the line, heel to toe.
2. Walk backward on the line, heel to toe.
3. Walk forward on the line, with giant steps.
4. Walk forward on the line, on tiptoes; backward.

5. Walk sideways on the line, (slide) on tiptoes in both directions.
6. Walk backward on the line.

Activity 2

Procedure:

1. Use tape, paint, chalk or rope to make specific patterns on the floor.

Examples:

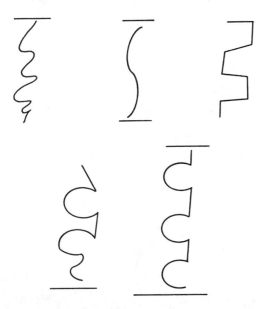

Fig. 23-9 This rope activity helps children develop eye-foot coordination.

2. Divide class equally among the number of shapes you have taped on the floor.
3. Have a relay with each line. The students can: walk the pattern; hop the pattern; skip the pattern; and crawl the pattern.

Activity 3

Procedure:

1. Use the patterns in figure 23-10. Show them to each child by drawing them on a chalkboard or on task cards.
2. The children then reproduce what they see through motions on the floor.

Fig. 23-10 Patterns for activity 3.

- **Frog and Lily Pads**

    Equipment: frogs with pictures of objects on them, one lily pad for each child

    Purpose: To develop visual discrimination, visual memory, and visual imagery.

Procedure:

1. Make a large number of frogs using the pattern in figure 23-11. On each frog will be pasted the picture of some object; each object will be in the shape of a square, oval, rectangle, triangle, or circle.

Fig. 23-11 Patterns for frog and lily pad activity.

2. Make a lily pad for each child.

3. Have the children sit in a circle with their lily pads in front of them. Place all the frogs in a pile, face down.

4. Pick up a frog and read the object on the frog out loud. Rotating around the circle, ask a child to tell what shape the object is. If the child answers correctly, he puts the frog on his lily pad. If he misses, or does not know, the next child guesses.

5. Keep rotating around the circle until all the frogs are sitting on lily pads. Examples of objects that may be used for the various shapes are as follows:

Square	*Oval*
dice	football
sugar cube	egg
carmel candy	links in a chain
record jackets	pecan
ice cubes	watermelon
	cigar

Rectangle	*Triangle*
chalkboard	"yield" sign
notebook paper	mountain peak
stick of gum	Christmas tree
door	sailboat sail
domino	tepee
brick	arrowhead

Circle

basketball
plate
jar lid
marble
record
person's head

• **Cotton Ball and Balloon Blowing**

Cotton balls and balloons can be blown across the floor between children as the children lie on their stomachs. Relay races can also be played by teams.

• **Animal Walking**

In the form of relay races, or simply moving about the room, have the children pretend to be different animals:

Kangaroo or rabbit — jump or hop
Duck — squat and walk
Elephant — clasp hands and hang them down in front for a trunk. Swing your trunk as you walk.
Dog, cat — crawl on hands and knees
Bird — fly with arms outstretched
Alligator, crocodile — lie on stomach and move across floor

• **Animal Cracker Charades**

Equipment: one box of animal crackers
Procedure:

1. Choose one child to pick out an animal cracker, so no one can see which one is picked. The child turns away from the others, and eats the cracker.

2. The child then "becomes" that animal and pretends to be it through motions.

3. The other children must guess what animal it is. The one who guesses correctly is the next cracker-eater.

• **Umbrella Game — For a Rainy Day**

Procedure:

1. One child walks around the outside of a circle, carrying an umbrella.

Fig. 23-12 Umbrella game.

Everyone sings to the tune of "Here We Go 'Round the Mulberry Bush," using the following verses:

What shall we do on a rainy day,
Rainy day, rainy day?
What shall we do on a rainy day,
When we can't go out to play?

2. As the verse ends, the child with the umbrella stops behind another child and asks whether the child wants to go for a walk under the umbrella.

3. If the second child accepts, they both go walking while the next verse of the song is sung:

We shall go for a walk today,
A walk today, a walk today.
We shall go for a walk today,
Under our big umbrella.

- **A Hunting We Will Go**

Procedure:

1. Children sit in a circle.

2. One child is the fox and walks around the circle while everyone sings:

A hunting we will go,
A hunting we will go
We'll catch a fox and put him in a box,
And then we'll let him go.

3. The fox taps another child on the head, who then tries to catch the fox as he runs around the circle back to his place.

4. If caught, the fox sits in the center of the circle (in a box, if one is available), while the game is repeated. Release the first fox when a second one is caught.

- **Jack Be Nimble**

Procedure:

1. The children sit in a circle, semi-circle, or line.

2. Set up a block for a pretend candle. (Two or three can be set up, if desired.) The children take turns jumping over the candle(s) while everyone sings:

Jack be nimble,
Jack be quick,
Jack jump over the candlestick.

(Children enjoy having their own names substituted for "Jack.")

3. Variation: To give everyone a chance to be more active, have the children form a circle holding hands and walk around "Jack" while he jumps over the candle.

- **Tommy's Going Fishing**

Procedure:

1. Make a fishing pole by attaching a piece of string to a cardboard tube or a yardstick. Tie a magnet to the end of the string.

2. Paper fish can be made using paper clips for mouths. (The paper clips will attract the magnet.)

3. Put fish on the floor in a "pond."

4. Children take turns walking around the fish carrying the fishing pole while others chant:

Tommy's going fishing,
Tommy's going fishing.
Tommy's going fishing,
What will he catch?

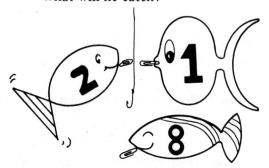

Fig. 23-13 Tommy's going fishing game.

5. The child with the pole catches a fish and then gives the next child a turn. If the fish are different colors, the children might enjoy naming the color of the fish that is caught. Or, write different numbers on the fish and see whether the children can identify them.

6. If the teacher puts dots on the fish to equal the number on the fish, children can count dots to check their answers.

CHILDREN'S BOOKS FOR AUTUMN

Ets, Marie H., *Play With Me.* New York: Viking, 1955.

Gray, Nicholas S., *Apples Stones.* New York: Hawthorn, 1969.

Hunt, Irene, *Trail of Apple Blossoms.* Chicago, Illinois: Follett, 1968.

Kane, Henry B., *Four Seasons in the Woods.* New York: Knopf, 1968.

Scheer, Julian, *Rain Makes Applesauce.* New York: Holiday, 1964.

Selsam, Millicent E., *See Through the Forest.* New York: Harper and Row, 1956.

Unit 24 HALLOWEEN

To young children, Halloween means dressing up in colorful costumes and playing trick or treat. The fastasy and tradition of Halloween have more meaning for children when they understand how this yearly festival began. The tale of how the Druids (people who lived many centuries ago) observed Halloween will unfold as a fascinating story.

"All Hallow's Even," as it was called, was the night when the Lord of Death called together the souls of the wicked who had died during the past year. The Druids believed that on this night, characters such as ghosts, fairies, and witches appeared from their hiding places to harm people. They thought that cats had once been human beings but were changed as punishment for evil deeds. An Irishman named Jack, who walked the earth at night carrying a pumpkin lantern, is credited with the origin of the "jack-o-lantern." From these early beliefs comes our tradition of using witches, ghosts, cats, and pumpkins as Halloween symbols.

Motivated by this exciting background and their own experiences, children will have individual ideas and feelings to express the weird, spooky fun of Halloween. They will welcome the opportunity to be inventive, and they do not need patterns to trace. Some suggested topics for picturemaking include:

- Halloween Spooks
- Shining Jack-O-Lanterns
- We Play Trick or Treat
- Happy Goblins
- Flying Witches
- A Halloween Party

Other suggested art activities:

- Spooks and Goblins
- Halloween Promenade
- Real Jack-O-Lantern
- Rattles and Noisemakers
- Witch-On-A-Stick
- Masks

ART ACTIVITIES

- **Tissue Ghosts**

  Materials: white facial tissues, rubber bands, popsicle sticks, cotton balls, magic markers

  Procedure:
  1. Wrap cotton balls into two white facial tissues, forming a rounded section.
  2. Wind a rubber band around the covered cotton balls to form the ghost's head on a popsicle stick.
  3. Use a black magic marker to make the ghost's features.

- **Painted Pumpkins**

  (Use a real pumpkin for display prior to this activity.)

  Procedure:
  1. Cut out a pumpkin shape on a large (18" x 24") piece of brown wrapping paper, manila paper, or construction paper.
  2. Have the children color their paper pumpkin according to how they observe the real pumpkins.

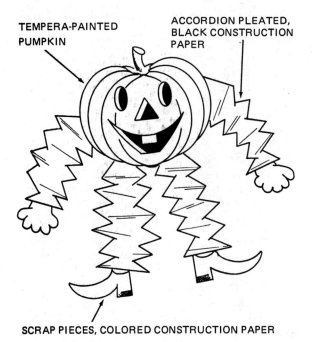

Fig. 24-1 Pumpkin accordion people.

Fig. 24-2 Spooks and goblins.

- **Pumpkin Accordion People**

  (Use the pumpkins painted in the above activity.)

  Procedure:
  1. Cut thin (1 1/2″ wide x 12″) strips of black construction paper — 4 for each pumpkin.
  2. Have the children accordion pleat these 4 strips.
  3. Attach two of the accordion strips for arms and the remaining two for legs.
  4. Shoes and hands (or gloves) cut from bits of construction paper may be added for fun. A cut-paper hat also makes an attractive addition.

- **Spooks and Goblins**

  Who knows what spooks and goblins look like? Children do! They can make many fantastic three-dimensional figures with paper and paste.

  Procedure:
  1. Odd shapes of paper from the scrap box can be used for the body and head.
  2. Paper strips for arms and legs can be curled, folded, twisted, crumpled, rolled, or cut to express movement.
  3. For variety of design, add a poncho, wings, antennae, floppy hat, or boots. Goblins may be attached to a stick (like a rod puppet), to do a goblin dance to recorded music.

- **Rattles and Noisemakers**

  Procedure:
  1. Use discarded crayon boxes or similar small boxes filled with seeds, beans, or tiny pebbles. Tape the box shut at either end.
  2. To depict a Halloween character, paint the box or decorate with pieces of cut paper. A tongue depressor or lollipop stick taped to the back of the rattle serves as a handle.

Fig. 24-3 Halloween rattle.

Fig. 24-4 Paper bag heads that can be mounted on a stick.

- **Halloween Promenade**

Most children enjoy getting dressed in costumes and playing make-believe. They need to make only those parts of the costume considered important; their imaginations can fill in the rest.

Procedure:
1. A partial costume may include an oatmeal box for a phantom's hat, a paper bag ghost mask, a paper tie for a pumpkin man, some yarn for a witch's hair or a cape of white roll paper for a spook who is getting ready to fly in the wind.
2. The Halloween "characters" may go for a walk around the school or make a brief visit to another classroom.

- **Witch on a Stick**

Procedure:
1. Paint or decorate a paper bag with cut paper. Children may want to add hair, a funny hat, or a bright color.
2. Stuff the bag with crumpled newspaper and attach it to a stick to be carried on Halloween night. Other Halloween figures may be made using the same method.

- **Real Jack-O-Lantern**

Carving a real pumpkin to make a jack-o-lantern is a project in which both children and teachers can participate.

Procedure:
1. The children can draw the features on the pumpkin. The teacher may want to do the carving.
2. Seeds can be roasted and salted for a tasty treat at home or left to dry in the classroom and used later for making necklaces or bracelets.
3. Another use for pumpkin seeds is saving them until early spring when children can plant them in individual containers, such as milk or cottage cheese cartons. Later, the small plants can be placed outdoors in warmer weather.

- **Construction Paper Masks**

Procedure:
1. Fold a piece of 9″ x 12″ construction paper vertically. Open the paper and

Fig. 24-5 Construction paper masks.

hold it against the child's face, marking the place for eyes, nose, and mouth.

2. Add cut-paper ears, eyebrows, hair, and whiskers. Roll paper strips over a pencil to create curly hair.

3. Features that pop out can be made of paper strips, accordion pleated. Or, cut paper can be folded and attached at only one point so that it protrudes.

4. Other masks can be made of boxes or paper plates.

- **Lining Them Up for Halloween**

  Procedure:

  1. Have each child make two sheets of striped paper by pasting strips of orange on black.

  2. Using one striped sheet as the background, paste on a Halloween figure cut out of the other striped sheet. Place the figure so that its stripes contrast with those of the background.

Making Costumes

Dressing up for Halloween offers children an opportunity to exercise their imaginations. Halloween should be a fun time, free from the experiences that often frighten small children. The costumes they wear should be safe, simple, and amusing rather than gruesome or grotesque.

When children make their own costumes, it becomes a wholesome, creative activity. To stimulate the children's imaginations, the teacher can have a variety of supplies available for the children. On one shelf might be various pieces of colorful cloth, and on another, a box of old jewelry, some feathers, artificial flowers, ribbons, laces, bits of fur, scraps of construction paper, grocery bags large enough to fit over a child's head, paper plates and cups, yarn, and string. On a third shelf might be scissors, tape, paste, glue, safety pins, crayons, rubber bands, a stapler, and paper fasteners.

The fun the children have in assembling their own costumes is part of the Halloween celebration. As children finish their work, they can join a group for storytelling and perhaps describe their costumes.

- **Pumpkin and Cat Costumes**

  Materials: 2 large sheets of brown wrapping paper for each costume, pencil, staples or paste, crayons or paints

  Procedure:

  1. Put 2 sheets of paper together and fold them lengthwise.

  2. Draw half the design against the folded edge, figure 24-6, page 234.

  3. Cut out the design.

  4. Unfold it.

  5. Decorate with crayons, or paste on pieces from cutouts.

  6. Staple or paste each costume together at the shoulders and sides. (Or make paper straps for the shoulders and sides.) Wear over jeans or leotards.

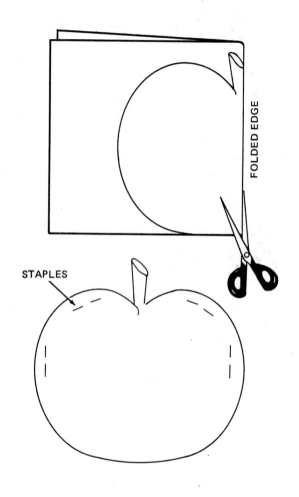

FOLDED EDGE

STAPLES

Fig. 24-6 Pumpkin costumes.

Fig. 24-7 Halloween mobile.

- **Halloween Mobiles**

Procedure:

1. Have each child cut the shape of a pumpkin, cat, witch, ghost, or goblin out of construction paper or tagboard.
2. Decorate both sides with cut-paper features. Small pieces of metallic paper, aluminum foil, or glitter will add interest.
3. Punch a hole in the top of the object and thread with black thread.
4. Hang on a wire across the room. Some children can tie two objects together (such as making a witch with a cat tied to her skirt).

- **Paper Pumpkin Chains**

Procedure:

1. As an addition to regular paper chains, add orange construction paper pumpkins to a black and orange paper chain.
2. Alternate pumpkins to every third link for an attractive party decoration.

- **Haunted Houses**

Materials: paper, scissors, glue or stapler, crayons

Procedure:

1. Discuss with the children what they think a haunted house might look like and what might be found in it. List their ideas on the board.
2. Distribute large pieces of paper and have the children draw haunted houses. In the space for the windows and doors, ask them to draw surprising or scary things that might be found in a haunted house.

3. From other paper, cut out window shades, shutters or curtains, and a door. Glue these on the house so that they can be folded back. Behind these glued-on sections are the children's drawings of ghosts, witches, and apparitions. Each child can then fold back the doors and shutters and show the class what is in the haunted house.

• Paper Bag Vests

Procedure:

1. Use a large grocery bag. Cut arm holes in the side. Then cut down the front of the bag.
2. Let the children decorate their vests with their own Halloween designs. This vest also makes a good Indian costume.

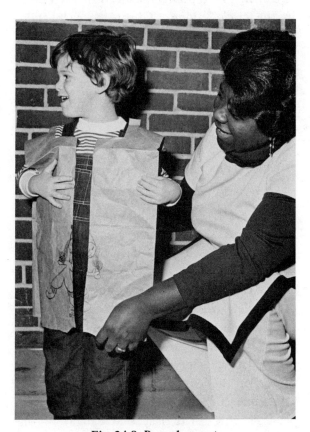

Fig. 24-8 Paper bag vest.

• Stand-Up Paper Pumpkins

Using a basic round shape, almost any kind of animal, bird, or face may be constructed.

Procedure:

1. Fold a 12″ x 18″ piece of construction paper in half. While still folded, turn up open edges about 3 inches, then turn down so that the crease can be seen.
2. Starting at the fold on both sides, draw a curved line down to the crease and then follow it to the edge of the paper. With the paper still folded, cut along the lines.
3. Add cut-paper features and details. It is easier to paste them in place while the paper is still flat.
4. Fold both bottom strips to the inside and paste one over the other.

GAMES AND MOVEMENT

• The Old Witch and the Cat

The children sit on the floor in a half-circle. They are the cats. One child, the witch, stands a short distance away, facing away from the cats. One of the cats meows. The witch turns quickly and tries to guess which cat it was. If the guess is correct, that

Fig. 24-9 Stand-up paper pumpkins.

cat (the one who meowed) becomes the witch. If not, the witch hobbles around the circle while the cats meow. A new witch is then chosen.

• Ghosts and Witches

Divide the group in half. Have the children line up on opposite sides of the room. These are the ghosts. Two children, one from each side, are selected to be witches. They are blindfolded and stand in the center of the room. The ghosts, one at a time, cross over to the opposite side. If a witch hears a ghost from the other side crossing, the witch calls, "I hear a ghost." If the witch is correct, the ghost drops out of the game. If the witch is wrong, a ghost from the witch's own side drops out. The side whose witch catches the most ghosts wins.

• Spiders and Flies

A group of 10 to 20 can play this game. Choose 3 to 4 "spiders" and the rest of the group becomes the "flies." The spiders stand in a line, a good running distance from the flies. (The distance depends on the age of the group. A greater distance is needed for older children.) The game begins when the spiders say, "We are the spiders," to the group of children playing the flies. The flies respond, "We are the flies." Then the spiders say, "We're going to catch you," and the flies say, "You just try!" When the flies say this, the spiders begin running toward the flies, trying to tag them. Once tagged, the flies are out. The spiders have to tag all the flies, before the game ends. The flies can only run toward the "safe" boundary in one direction. (No running back and forth.) The last 3 or 4 flies tagged become the new spiders for the next round.

• Popcorn Vendor

(See related cooking activity, Popcorn Balls.)

Children sit in a circle. Choose one child to be the "popcorn vendor." The child chosen bounces a ball in front of the three children saying, "Popcorn," while bouncing the ball. After the three are chosen, the popcorn vendor then says, "Start," or "Begin to pop." To "pop," the three children chosen by the popcorn vendor also hop, bouncing the ball, too. They must tag each child separately with the ball. The last child tagged with the ball is the new popcorn vendor. The circle of children represents the boundary. If one of the children steps out of the circle, the child is out.

• Ghost, Ghost, Witch

(A variation of Duck, Duck, Goose)

Have the children sit on the floor in a circle. Choose one child to be "it." The child who is "it" walks around the outside of the circle, lightly tapping the head of each child in the circle saying, "Ghost" to each child. When the child who is "it" taps a child's head and says, "Witch," the child named "witch" must get up and chase after "it." If "it" gets back to the proper place on the floor, then the "witch" becomes "it" and the game continues.

• Ghost Trap

(A variation of Mousetrap)

Select five or six children to be ghosts. The rest of the class forms a circle by joining hands (the ghost trap). When the arms of the ghost trap are *up,* the trap is open and the ghosts can run in and out as they go around the circle. When the teacher says, "Snap," the children who make up the ghost trap will lower their arms to catch the ghosts in the trap. The ghosts who are caught go to the center of the circle and have to stay there. The game continues until all the ghosts have been caught. The last one caught is the winner.

- **Bean the Pumpkin**

This Halloween game is a variation of beanbag. The target can be created by the children. The opening could be in the shape of a big jack-o-lantern on heavy posterboard or plywood. Secure the target at an angle so that the beanbag can go through the opening. Each child has a chance to throw from one to three beanbags at the jack-o-lantern. No score needs to be kept, but if the children decide to do so, they could get a point each time they hit the target. Eye-hand coordination is developed through this activity.

The game can be played with partners or with four or five players. Variations of the game can be made for other holidays. For example, a wreath for Christmas, a four-leaf clover for St. Patrick's Day, an egg for Easter, and a heart for Valentine's Day.

- **Pepper the Pumpkin**

Cut a large pumpkin face out of cardboard. Draw and cut out features. Paint and prop it against a wall. Children try to throw beanbags through the pumpkin's eyes, nose, or mouth.

A large pumpkin can also be drawn on the chalkboard and a damp sponge used. If the sponge touches any part of the eyes, nose, or mouth, the child scores.

- **The Goblin in the Dark**

(Use the melody for "A farmer in the dell")

> The goblin in the dark,
> The goblin in the dark,
> Hi, ho, on Halloween,
> The goblin in the dark.

Repeat, using Halloween creatures, such as: The goblin takes a witch; or the witch takes a bat; or the bat takes a ghost; or the ghost says, "Boo!" Children particularly enjoy one final chorus of:

> They all scream and screech,
> They all scream and screech,
> Hi, ho, on Halloween,
> They all scream and screech.

- **Here We Go 'Round the Jack-O-Lantern**

(Use the tune for "Here We Go 'Round the Mulberry Bush")

The children form a circle, holding hands, and walk around an imaginary jack-o-lantern. Everyone sings the chorus:

> Here we go 'round the jack-o-lantern,
> Jack-o-lantern, jack-o-lantern.
> Here we go 'round the jack-o-lantern
> So late on Halloween night.

Children stop walking, drop hands, and begin doing this action, while singing: "This is the way we take out the seeds."

Repeat the chorus and then another verse, substituting any action suggested by the children such as: carve the face, put in a candle, etc.

FINGER PLAYS AND POEMS

- **Mr. Pumpkin**

I am Mr. Pumpkin, big and round,
   (Use arms to show size of pumpkin)
Once upon a time I grew on the ground.
   (Point to the ground)
Now I have a mouth, two eyes, a nose,
   (Point to each feature on own face)
What are they for, do you suppose?
   (Right forefinger to forehead — thinking gesture)
When I have a candle inside shining Bright,
   (Hold up right forefinger)
I'll be a jack-o-lantern on Halloween Night.
   (Thumbs in armpits — bragging gesture)

- **Five Little Jack-O-Lanterns**

Five little jack-o-lanterns sitting on a gate
   (Put up five fingers)

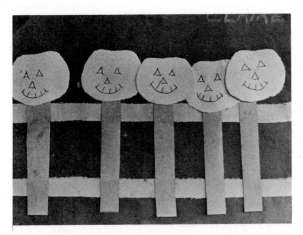

Fig. 24-10 Five little jack-o-lanterns.

First one said, "My it's getting late!"
  (Touch thumb)
Second one said, "It's cold out here."
  (Touch index finger)
Third one said, "There's witches in the air."
  (Touch middle finger)
Fourth one said, "Let's go away from here."
  (Touch fourth finger)
Fifth one said, "It's only Halloween night."
  (Touch fifth finger)
In came the wind, out went the light.
Now the fun is over for this year's Hallow-
  een night!

- **Mr. Pumpkin**

Smiling Mr. Pumpkin
With your great big shining eyes,
Will you be my jack-o-lantern
Before we make you into pies?

I'll put you in my window
To watch the children come,
And when they see your shining face
Oh, how they will run!

- **What Am I?**

They chose me from my brothers;
"That's the nicest one," they said.
And they carved me out a face
And put a candle in my head.

And they set me on the doorstep,
Oh, the night was dark and wild;
But when they lit the candle,
Then I smiled.

- **Halloween Time**

Halloween's the time for nuts,
    And for apples, too,
And for funny faces that
    Stare and stare at you.
Right behind them is a friend,
    Jack or Bob or Bess,
Isn't it the greatest fun
    When you try to guess?

- **What Is It?**

It will make a jack-o-lantern
Or a big Thanksgiving pie,
It's a big, round, yellow something,
You can guess it if you try.

- **Halloween Friends**

On Halloween my friends and I
Dress up in frightening clothes,
We each put on a funny face
With an enormous nose.

We ring our neighbors' doorbells
And they get an awful fright,
To see such scary creatures
Standing there at night.

- **Five Little Ghosts**

  (See related art activity, Tissue Ghosts,
  page 230.)

Five little ghosts dressed all in white,
Were scaring each other on Halloween night.
"Boo!" said the first one. "I'll catch you!"
"Wooooo," said the second. "I don't care if
  you do."
The third ghost said, "You can't run away
  from me!"

And the fourth one said, "I'll scare everyone
  I see!"
Then the last one said, "It's time to disappear,
See you at Halloween the next year!"

• How does a Goblin Go?

How does a goblin go?
Let me see.
He goes flip, flap, flip, flap, and floggle.

That must be
The way a goblin goes
With his leader heels and flat-top toes,
Flip, flap, flip, flap, floggle

Down in the marsh
Where bullfrogs goggle,
That's where he goes,
With a sway and joggle,
Flip, flap, flip, flap, flip, flap, floggle.

• Black and Gold

Everything is black and gold,
  Black and gold tonight.
Yellow pumpkins, yellow moon,
  Yellow candlelight.
Jet-black cat with golden eyes,
  Shadows black as ink.
Firelight blinking in the dark
  With a yellow blink.

Black and gold, black and gold,
  Nothing in-between . . .
When the world turns black and gold,
  Then it's HALLOWEEN!

• The Magic Vine

A fair seed I planted
So dry and white and old,
There sprang a vine enchanted,
With magic flowers of gold.

I watched it, I tended it,
And truly, by and by,
It bore a jack-o-lantern
And a great Thanksgiving pie.

• Pumpkin

A roly-poly pumpkin
Went traveling down the street.
It couldn't walk,
It couldn't run,
It hadn't any feet.

It rolled along
Til out of breath,
It stopped beside our door.
Cook spied it,
And alas, alack,
The pumpkin is no more.

• Little Jack Pumpkin Face

Little Jack pumpkin face
  Lived on a vine
Little Jack pumpkin face
  Thought it was fine.

First he was small and green,
  Then big and yellow,
Little Jack pumpkin face,
  Is a fine fellow.

They chose me from my brothers,
  "That's the nicest one," they said.
And they carved out a face
  And put a candle in my head.

They set me on the doorstep,
  And the night was dark and wild,
And when they lit the candle,
  Then I smiled and smiled and smiled.

This is the night of Halloween,
  When all the witches can be seen,
Some are small and some are lean,
  Some are tall as a cástor bean.

• The Popcorn House

(For related cooking activity, see "Popcorn
Balls," page 240.)

A mole, a rabbit, and a little grey mouse,
All lived together in a popcorn house.

The mole chose the cellar,
With its nice dirt walls.

The rabbit took the center,
With its cupboards and hall.

The attic was chosen
By the little grey mouse.

And all were very happy
In the popcorn house.

COOKING EXPERIENCES

• **Roast Pumpkin Seeds**

(A natural follow-up activity to the carving of a Halloween pumpkin.)

Ingredients: pumpkin seeds, 1 tablespoon butter for each cup of seeds, salt

Materials: measuring cup, measuring spoons, large saucepan, mixing spoon, cookie sheet

Procedure:
1. Wash the pumpkin seeds and let them dry.
2. Heat the oven to 300 degrees.
3. Melt the butter in the saucepan over low heat.
4. Add the seeds to the saucepan and mix.
5. Spread the pumpkin seeds on the cookie sheet.
6. Sprinkle with salt.
7. Bake in the oven until crisp and slightly brown.
8. After this activity, see the Mr. Pumpkin finger play for a fun language art experience.

• **Yummy Candy**

Ingredients: 1 pound milk chocolate, 12 marshmallows, 1 cup chopped nuts

Materials: knife, for cutting marshmallows, measuring cup, double boiler, mixing spoon, waxed paper, cake pan or pie plate

Procedure:
1. Let the children help cut the marshmallows into small pieces.
2. Melt the milk chocolate on top of the double boiler.
3. Line the cake pan or pie plate with waxed paper.
4. Pour in one-half of the melted chocolate.
5. Cover this portion of chocolate with nuts and marshmallows.
6. Pour over the rest of the chocolate.
7. Wait until it has cooled.
8. Break into pieces.
9. Read De Jong's *Journey From Peppermint Street* for a related story.

• **Popcorn Balls**

Ingredients: 1 popcorn popper full of prepared popcorn, 1 pound marshmallows, 1 stick margarine, 1 teaspoon vanilla

Procedure:
1. Melt marshmallows and butter, and add vanilla.
2. Pour over popcorn.
3. Have each child rub margarine on both hands and shape the mixture into individual popcorn balls.

• **Honey Balls**

Ingredients: 3 tablespoons honey, 4 tablespoons peanut butter, 1/2 cup nonfat dry milk, 1/2 cup dry cereal flakes (crushed)

Procedure:
1. Mix honey and peanut butter. Gradually add nonfat dry milk. Mix well.
2. Form into balls with greased hands.
3. Roll in dry cereal flakes.
4. Chill until firm. Makes 18 balls.

- **No-Cook Peanut Butter Fudge**

  Ingredients: 1 cup peanut butter, 1 cup Karo syrup, 1 1/4 cups non-fat dry milk solids, 1 cup sifted confectioner's sugar

  Procedure:
  1. Blend peanut butter and syrup in large mixing bowl.
  2. Measure nonfat dry milk solids and sifted confectioner's sugar, and add all at once. Mix all ingredients together — first with a spoon, then with the hands, knead in dry ingredients.
  3. Turn onto a board and continue kneading until the mixture is well blended and smooth. Press out with your hands or a rolling pin, making squares. Dough should be 1/2-inch thick.
  4. Cut into squares. Top with nutmeats, if desired. Makes about 2 pounds.

- **Caramel Apples**

  Ingredients: 1 pound small caramels, 1 stick margarine, 10 to 12 small apples, 10 to 12 popsicle sticks

  Procedure:
  1. Melt a stick of margarine in a 3-quart pan.
  2. Add caramels. Melt caramels and margarine over boiling water. Keep stirring.
  3. Push popsicle stick squarely into center of each apple.
  4. Have the children dip apples into the caramel. The caramel apples should be placed on waxed paper to dry.

CREATIVE MOVEMENT ACTIVITIES FOR HALLOWEEN

In a discussion with the children at Halloween time, make a list of feelings and objects that describe the holiday. Then have the children use movement to express these ideas. Encourage creativity.

Several ideas for children to act out include:

- black cat arching its back
- witch riding a broomstick
- owls and bats
- tricks
- full moon
- happy
- excited
- mysterious

Such words might also be used to stimulate creative art, stories, poetry, and songs.

- **Halloween Skits**

  Using some of the topics from the previous activity, divide the children into 3 or 4 groups. Give each group a topic to act out for the rest of the class. As each group performs, the rest of the class is the audience.

- **Mostly Jolly Jack-O-Lanterns**

  The following Halloween poem could be read by the teacher with the children acting out the five characters in the poem (Barney, Chester, Freddy, Harry, and Reuben).

  Five little jack-o-lanterns
  Lighted by a fairy,
  Most had funny faces,
  Some looked scary.

  These little jack-o-lanterns
  Shining yellow bright,
  Made some ghostly shadows,
  All through the night.

  Jack-o-lantern Barney
  Had a nose that wiggled,
  When children looked at Barney,
  They jiggled as they giggled.

Jack-o-lantern Freddy
His front teeth out,
Made those who saw him,
Holler and shout.

Jack-o-lantern Chester
Eyes stared at the night,
As children looked at Chester,
They laughed at the sight.

Jack-o-lantern Harry
His mouth with scowls would bend,
When children gazed at Harry,
Their hair would stand on end.

But jack-o-lantern Reuben
With kindly face aglow,
Brought smiles from all the children,
Because he loved them so.

- **Exploring the Jack-O-Lantern**

Each child should have an opportunity to feel, lift, thump, and smell the pumpkin before, during, and after carving. Weigh the pumpkin on a scale. If more than one pumpkin is involved, make weight comparisons as well as comparing size, shape, and color.

Other activities centered around the jack-o-lantern include:

- Allowing children to scoop out the seeds.
- Telling a story or singing songs about Halloween while carving the pumpkin.
- Passing out small cubes of raw, washed pumpkin for the children to taste.
- Baking small cubes in a buttered baking dish and serving them warm.
- Washing and drying the seeds.

- **Trick or Treat in Reverse**

One way to combat the "gimme" attitude at Halloween is to go trick or treating in reverse. Rather than asking for treats, the children can give treats to others. The children should help decide what the treats will be and to whom the treats will be given. One idea is for the children

to make an excess amount of whatever they are preparing for their own party, such as popcorn, cookies, or cupcakes. The extra food could be wrapped in a party napkin or small, decorated sack, and secured with a ribbon, string, or rubber band. This food would then be delivered around the school or neighborhood. On the package there could be a tag saying something like, "For your afternoon coffee. (signed) The Kindergarten." The children usually take particular delight in hanging the small package on a doorknob, knocking, and then crouching as if to hide until the occupant comes to the door, at which time they jump up and call, "Surprise!" — a voluntary action that seems to come naturally.

CHILDREN'S BOOKS FOR HALLOWEEN

Alexander, Lloyd, *The Marvelous Misadventures of Sebastian.* New York: Dutton, 1970.
Anglund, Joan W., *Nibble, Nibble, Mousekin: A Tale of Hansel and Gretel.* New York: Harcourt, Brace, Jovanovich, 1962.
Bonsall, Crosby N., *The Case of the Cat's Meow.* New York: Harper and Row, 1965.
Bright, Robert, *Georgie.* New York: Doubleday, 1959.
Child Association of America, *Holiday Storybook.* New York: T. Y. Crowell, 1952.
Eager, Edward, *Half Magic.* New York: Harcourt, Brace, Jovanovich, 1970.
Garfield, Leon, *Mister Corbett's Ghost.* New York: Pantheon, 1968.
Mitchell, Lucy Sprague, *Another Here and Now Story Book.* New York: Dutton, 1937.
Norton, Mary, *Bed-Knob and Broomstick.* New York: Harcourt, Brace, Jovanovich, 1957, 1975.
Sauer, Julia L., *Fog Magic.* New York: Archway, 1977.
Sendak, Maurice, *Where the Wild Things Are.* New York: Harper and Row, 1963.

Unit 25 THANKSGIVING

Thanksgiving is an American holiday that originated in the Plymouth Colony in the autumn of 1621. At that time and place, the Pilgrims and Indians joined in giving thanks for the year's harvest. To this day, people gather in the family circle for Thanksgiving celebrations at home. It is a time of merriment, hospitality, and gratitude for the day-to-day joys often taken for granted. Many families attend religious services and in some places, people of different religions worship together. All over the nation, parades take place on Thanksgiving. Some are patriotic or historic; others are more spectacular like Hudson's Thanksgiving Day/Santa Parade in Detroit. Teachers can help children learn the true meaning of Thanksgiving by making them more aware of the many things for which to be thankful and how to be helpful to others. The children can learn human values in everyday living by being involved in such creative art experiences as painting pictures, making cut-paper family portraits, or constructing models of their homes. During the discussion, the teacher helps students recall their own experiences and feelings about Thanksgiving and clarifies their thinking about the experiences.

The subject of Thanksgiving is broad enough to include a variety of topics for picturemaking:

- Some Things I am Thankful For
- Eating Thanksgiving Dinner
- The Thanksgiving Day/Santa Parade
- Getting Ready for Thanksgiving
- My Family on Thanksgiving
- Helping Mother at Home
- A Visit with Friends

ART IDEAS

• Holiday Nut Cups

Nut cups for a colorful Thanksgiving table can be made by cutting and folding construction paper into a little container. Small boxes, cupcake cups, cardboard tubes or metallic foil pressed into a cup shape are also suitable.

Decorations may consist of cut-paper designs with a seasonal theme.

• Vegetable Creatures

Creating animals and creatures for a barnyard scene or party table centerpiece is a challenge to the child's imagination. Features can be cut from paper scraps and pasted onto a potato, beet, squash, or cucumber body.

Fig. 25-1 Holiday nut cups.

Fig. 25-2 Vegetable creatures.

Fig. 25-3   Turkey farm.

Fig. 25-4   Paper bag turkey.

Toothpicks may be used for legs. Beet or carrot tops create a tail or mane.

• Turkey Farm

Using colored construction paper, children can create their own impression of turkeys, all sizes and shapes, to make an attractive bulletin board. Tail feathers may consist of real feathers (found objects) or fringed paper. A cut-paper fence may surround the turkeys.

• Indian Headdress

Cut a two-inch strip of heavy paper or cardboard long enough to fit around the child's head. Staple the ends together. Add colorful cut-paper feathers or those that have been painted or drawn in crayon. The headband may be decorated with Indian symbols.

• Thanksgiving Table

Turn a cardboard box upside down. Draw and cut legs at the corners. Benches or chairs can be made by folding small strips of paper or cardboard. Make a tablecloth with white roll paper or paper napkins. Plates may consist of jar lids, with food from clay or salt clay. Figures of people such as Pilgrims and Indians can be drawn on paper or cardboard and bent into a sitting position.

• Paper Bag Turkeys

Pinch one corner of the bottom of a flat paper bag. Shape it into a head and tie. Stuff the bag half full with crumpled newspaper and tie, leaving the open end fringed and cut for tail feathers.

Additional feathers can be attached to the body. Staple cardboard feet at the base to allow the bird to sit upright. Accordion pleat a strip of red paper for the wattle. The turkeys make an attractive table centerpiece and may be combined with crumpled paper fruits and vegetables.

• Pilgrims and Indians

Begin by stuffing a small grocery bag half full so that it is flat at the bottom. Staple the bag closed across the top and attach the head. Fasten cut-paper feet at the bottom. Paper strips stapled into the folds at the sides form the arms. The body can be painted or finished with cut paper for a costume.

Fig. 25-5 Pilgrims and Indians.

- **Large People**

Although drawing people can be done any time of the year, making Pilgrims is good to start with. Be sure children are familiar with Pilgrim dress. Talk about how people look. Start with a discussion of the head, which the children can see is not round; then talk about the neck and shoulders. The body gets smaller at the waist. When standing, the elbows come to the waistline and the hands do not reach the knees. The arms come from the shoulders.

Now the children can begin to make their people. The head and the neck are made first. Then the clothing, bodies, arms, and legs are made. When finished, the figures are cut out and tacked to a bulletin board.

- **Egg-face Pilgrims**

Glue hard-boiled eggs into nut cups with rubber cement or paste. Children can decorate the eggs with yarn or curled paper as hair. Cut paper makes faces, collars, and hats.

- **Dollhouses**

Suggestions for a homemade dollhouse include:
— a cardboard carton, turned on its side; cut windows and doors; add carpet scraps for rugs; decorate the walls with paper or the child's artwork.

— an orange crate, decorated similarly.
— rooms drawn on a piece of cardboard for a floor, but no walls.
— carpet scraps for rooms, but again, no walls.

- **The Furniture**

Paste magazine pictures on the cardboard floor. Or use match boxes, small boxes, pieces of wood, blocks, spools, plastic lids from aerosol cans, etc., to make beds, tables, sofas, chairs, kitchen appliances, bathroom fixtures, and so on.

- **The People**

Possibilities include:
— wallpaper and stick puppets.

Fig. 25-6 Wallpaper and stick puppets (a) front.

Fig. 25-6 (b) back.

– spools of various sizes and heights with faces drawn or glued on; add pipe cleaners for arms and legs, and yarn for hair.

– clothespins, decorated similarly.

- ● **Handkerchief Puppets**

Draw a face on a handkerchief. Put it over your hand to make it move. Or, draw a face in the center of a handkerchief, stuff cotton or cloth inside, and tie it with string or ribbon around the neck. (These also make great ghost puppets!)

Fig. 25-7 Styrofoam cup puppets.

- ● **Styrofoam Cup Puppets**

Draw a face on a cup, or glue on facial features using colored paper, felt, etc. Or, make an animal, gluing ears to the top of a cup and a tail to the back, using a pipe cleaner or a strip of paper.

- ● **Styrofoam Ball Puppets**

Make a face with felt-tip pens or by gluing eyes, nose, and a mouth made of paper to the ball. Insert a pencil in the bottom of the ball or make a hole to put a finger in.

Fig. 25-8 Styrofoam ball puppets.

- ● **Paper Bag Puppets**

Draw or glue paper on the bottom of the bag to make a face. Insert one hand in the bottom fold of the bag to make the face move. It's fun to glue a felt or paper tongue under the flap and a tail on the back of the bag.

- ● **Pilgrim Mobile**

Let each child trace a Pilgrim pattern on a piece of construction paper. Decorate both sides with cut-paper features. Punch a hole in the top of the object and thread it. Hang it on a wire across the room.

Fig. 25-9 Paper bag puppets.

Fig. 25-10 Pilgrim pattern.

FINGER PLAYS AND POEMS

• Thanksgiving Feast

Thanksgiving table? This is it;
> (Hands side by side, palms down, resting on thumbs)

And a chair where each may sit.
> (Left hand up, right hand bent, fingers of right hand touching palm of left hand)

For each, a plate, a cup,
And spoon,
> (Make circle with thumbs and forefingers for "plate," cup the right hand for "cup," lay forefinger on table for "spoon")

We'll eat and eat till
Afternoon.
> (Eating gesture)

And everyone will chatter,
> ("Chattering" motion with first two fingers and thumb of each hand)

The turkey will rest on a platter.
> (Hands together, palms up, for "platter")

The gravy will be in a boat-shaped bowl,
> (Cup two hands together for "bowl")

And I will have a drumstick — whole!
> (Make "drumstick" with left fist and right index finger)

I'll drink milk from a pretty glass
> (Indicate shape of glass with two hands)

And only let the celery pass.
> (Show shape of celery with index fingers and thumbs touching)

And then I'll have a piece of pie,
> (Make pie wedge shape with index fingers and thumb)

I can eat it if I try!
> (Rub tummy with right hand)

• The Baby Brother

I am the sister of him
And he is my brother.

He is too little for us
To talk to each other.

So every morning I show him
My doll and my book,
But every morning he still is
Too little to look.

• Grandma's Glasses

These are Grandma's glasses
> (Bring index finger and thumb of both hands together and place against eyes as if wearing glasses)

This is Grandma's hat,
> (Bring fingertips together in a peak over head)

This is the way she folds her hands
> (Clasp hands over head)

And lays them in her lap.
> (Lay hands in lap)

• Houses

This is a nest for Mr. Bluebird
> (Cup both hands, palms up, little fingers together)

This is a hive for Mr. Bee,
> (Both fists together, palm to palm)

This is the hole for bunny rabbit,
> (Fingers clasped together to make a hole)

And this is a house for me.
> (Fingertips together to make a peak)

• Our House

Our house is like no house I know
On any street in any row;
For brick or shingle, tall or wide,
A house is yours when you're inside.

• This House So Good

This is the roof of the house so good,
> (Make peaked roof with both hands)

These are the walls that are made of Wood.
> (Palms vertically parallel)

These are the windows that let in the Light,
> (Join thumbs and index fingers — two windows)

This is the door that shuts so tight.
  (Palms together)
This is the chimney so straight and tall
  (Arm up straight)
Oh, what a good house for one and all!
  (Arms at angle for roof above head, one
  hand extending for chimney)

COOKING EXPERIENCES

• **Pudding Cookies**

This recipe is so easy that, once familiar with it, children can make these cookies all by themselves.

Ingredients:
1 cup Bisquick
1 small package instant pudding — any flavor that appeals to the cooks!
1/4 cup salad oil
1 egg
chocolate chips, raisins, shredded coconut, or 1/3 cup peanut butter (all optional, use if desired)

Procedure:
1. Mix ingredients together.
2. Roll the dough into balls and put them on an ungreased cookie sheet.
3. Dip the bottom of a glass in sugar and press it on each ball until flattened. If making plain dough, cookies may be decorated with red cinnamon candies or chocolate chips before baking.
4. Bake at 350 degrees for 8 minutes. Makes 2 to 3 dozen cookies.

• **Good Potatoes**

Ingredients: baking potatoes, butter, sour cream, parsley or chives
Equipment: baking dish, fork, knife for cutting potatoes
Procedure:
1. Heat oven to 425 degrees.
2. Wash potatoes and let them dry.

3. Grease potatoes with butter.
4. Bake potatoes in baking dish for 40 minutes to 1 hour.
5. When they are half-cooked, prick each one with a fork to let out the steam. Then, finish baking.
6. When the potatoes are done, help the children cut a cross in each potato and push the potato open.
7. Into the opening in each potato, put some sour cream or butter with salt and pepper.
8. Sprinkle with parsley or chives.

• **Candied Sweet Potatoes**

Ingredients:
6 sweet potatoes
salt
paprika
1/3 cup maple syrup
1 1/2 teaspoons lemon juice
1/2 teaspoon grated lemon rind
2 tablespoons butter

Equipment: grater, measuring cup, measuring spoons, mixing spoon, small mixing bowl, large saucepan, baking dish, fork, knife for cutting sweet potatoes in half

Procedure:
1. Grate the lemon rind.
2. Boil the sweet potatoes in covered saucepan. Use enough water to cover the sweet potatoes.
3. When the potatoes are a little soft, prick them with a fork, and pour off the water.
4. Heat the oven to 375 degrees.
5. Let the sweet potatoes cool.
6. Take off the skins.
7. Help the children cut each sweet potato in half.
8. Put potatoes in a baking dish and sprinkle with salt and paprika.

9. Mix the maple syrup, lemon juice, and lemon rind in a small mixing bowl.
10. Pour the mixture over the sweet potatoes.
11. Dot with small pieces of butter.
12. Bake uncovered for 20 minutes.

- **Orange Nut Bread**

Ingredients:

2 1/2 cups sifted flour
2/3 cup sugar
1 teaspoon salt
2 1/2 teaspoons baking powder
1/2 cup chopped walnuts
1 egg
1 cup milk
1 tablespoon grated orange peel
1/4 cup orange juice
2 tablespoons cooking oil

Equipment: flour sifter, grater, measuring cup, measuring spoons, large mixing bowl, small mixing bowl, egg beater, loaf pan

Procedure:

1. Help the children sift the flour.
2. Grate the orange peel.
3. Butter the loaf pan.
4. Mix together the flour, sugar, salt, and baking powder in the big mixing bowl.
5. Stir in the chopped nuts.
6. Beat the egg in the small mixing bowl.
7. Add the milk, orange peel, orange juice, and oil to the egg.
8. Add the egg mixture to the flour mixture. Do not stir too much, just until everything is wet.
9. Pour into loaf pan.
10. Bake in oven for one hour and 15 minutes at 350 degrees.

- **Cranberry Bread**

Ingredients:

1 cup sugar
1/2 teaspoon salt
1 1/2 teaspoons baking powder
2 cups flour
1/2 cup orange juice
1/2 teaspoon baking soda in 2 tablespoons hot water
2 tablespoons melted butter
1 egg
1 cup cranberries
1 cup chopped pecans

Equipment: measuring cup, measuring spoons, large mixing bowl, small mixing bowl, mixing spoon, egg beater, small pan for melting butter, loaf pan

Procedure:

1. Grease the loaf pan.
2. Melt the butter in a small pan.
3. Heat the oven to 325 degrees.
4. Dissolve the baking soda in the hot water.
5. Beat the egg in the small mixing bowl.
6. In the large mixing bowl, mix the ingredients in the order they are listed — all except the cranberries and nuts.
7. Mix well.
8. Add the cranberries and nuts, and mix again.
9. Pour mixture into loaf pan.
10. Bake in oven for one hour and 15 minutes.

CHILDREN'S BOOKS FOR THANKSGIVING

Families

Potter, Beatrix, *The Tale of Peter Rabbit.* New York: Western Publishing Co., 1970.
Zolotow, Charlotte, *Do You Know What I'll Do?* New York: Harper and Row, 1958.

Parades

Dr. Seuss, *And to Think I Saw It On Mulberry Street.* New York: Vangard, 1937.

Ets, Marie H., *In the Forest.* New York: Viking, 1944.

McCloskey, Robert, *Lentil.* New York: Viking, 1940.

Books Which Develop Concepts

— *Brotherhood*

Beim, Jerrold, *Swimming Hole.* New York: Morrow, 1951.

Brenner, Barbara, *Faces.* New York: Dutton, 1970.

Guggenheim, Hans, *The World of Wonderful Difference.* Japan: Publisher Friendly Hse, 1972.

Salazar, Violet, *Squares are not Bad.* New York: Western Publishing Company, 1967.

— *Consideration*

Stover, Jo Ann, *If Everybody Did.* New York: McKay, 1960.

— *Cooperation*

Evans, Katherine, *A Bundle of Sticks.* Englewood Cliffs, New Jersey: Hall, 1962.

— *Family Enjoyment*

Fischer, Aileen, *In the Middle of the Night.* New York: T. Y. Crowell, 1965.

Goudey, Alice, *The Day We Saw the Sun Come Up.* New York: Scribner, 1961.

— *Family - Reassurance*

Zolotow, Charlotte, *The Storm Book.* New York: Harper and Row, 1952.

— *Friendship*

Anglund, Joan, *A Friend is Someone Who Likes You.* New York: Harcourt, Brace, Jovanovich, 1958.

Anglund, Joan, *Love is a Special Way of Feeling.* New York: Harcourt, Brace, Jovanovich, 1960.

Miles, Miska, *Having a Friend.* New York: Knopf, 1959.

— *Gifts from the Heart*

Zolotow, Charlotte, *Mr. Rabbit and the Lovely Present.* New York: Harper and Row, 1962.

— *Greed*

Lionni, Leo, *The Biggest House in the World.* New York: Pantheon, 1968.

— *Happiness*

Beim, Jerrold, and Beim, Lorraine, *Two is a Team.* New York: Harcourt, Brace, Jovanovich, 1974.

Fatio, Louise, *The Happy Lion's Treasure.* New York: McGraw Hill, 1970.

Wondriska, William, *Mr. Brown and Mr. Gray.* New York: Holt, Rinehart, and Winston, 1971.

— *Importance of Community*

Lionni, Leo, *Swimmy.* (Pinswheel Books) New York: Pantheon, 1963.

— *Importance of Individual*

Lionni, Leo, *Tico and the Golden Wings.* New York: Pantheon, 1964.

— *Sacrificial Giving*

Ness, Evaline, *Josefina February.* New York: Scribner, 1963.

GAMES AND MOVEMENT EXPERIENCES

• Turkeys, Trot

The children stand and face a child selected as the leader. The leader says, "Turkeys, trot," and runs in place. The class is to copy this motion. If the leader says, "Desks, run," "Rabbits, run," or "Turtles, run," the players stand still. Those who kept running must sit down. A new leader may be chosen by the old leader after a while.

• Hit the Basket

Form 4 lines of children behind a foul line. Put a wastebasket or box in front of each line, about 8 to 10 feet from the foul line. Each team has three balls or beanbags. The team who throws the most balls into the basket wins.

• **Book Relay**

Divide the class into equal teams. The first person on each team puts a book on their head and walks to the front of the room and back to the second person in line who repeats the act. The first team to finish wins the relay.

• **Motion**

Players are seated or standing in a circle around the room. The one who is "it" closes both eyes as the teacher points to a leader who stays in place and all players clap. The player who is "it" stands in the center so it is not possible to see everyone at once. The leader changes the motion from clapping to another motion, and the rest of the class follows. "It" has three guesses to find the leader. Change "it" and the leader for a new game. Hint: Players should not show they know who the leader is by staring. Indoor desk exercises can also be used as motions and the game may be played from the desk.

• **Self-awareness Activity**

Purpose: To be able to identify body parts.
Formation: all children scattered
Note to the teacher: Ask the children to touch the various body parts as you call them out loud. The children should be in scatter formation, looking at the teacher. Note whether the children are touching the correct body parts without looking at their classmates. Proceed slowly.
Teacher instructs children to touch their own:

A. Head
   1. Hair
   2. Forehead
   3. Eyebrows
   4. Eyelashes
   5. Eyes
   6. Nose
   7. Nostrils
   8. Cheeks
   9. Lips
   10. Tongue
   11. Teeth
   12. Chin
   13. Ears
   14. Earlobes
   15. Neck

B. Trunk
   1. Chest
   2. Stomach
   3. Hips
   4. Waist
   5. Side

C. Arms and Hands
   1. Shoulders
   2. Elbows
   3. Forearms
   4. Hands
   5. Fingers
   6. Thumb
   7. Palm
   8. Wrist
   9. Knuckles
   10. Finger

D. Legs
   1. Thighs
   2. Knees
   3. Calves
   4. Ankles
   5. Heels

• **Body Awareness**

Purpose: To identify verbally the missing parts from an incomplete face.

Equipment: flannel board, two circles cut from felt, two sets of eyes and ears, etc., all made of felt

Procedure:
1. Have all the children seated around a small table. Put the flannel board in front of you and the two circles and facial features in a box in front of you on the table. Put the circle on the flannel board. Then put the pieces of facial features in their proper places. Have children name them as you do so. Say, "I am going to put these on first (eyes). What am I putting on now? Yes, the eyes." Follow this procedure as you put on the nose, mouth, and other features.

2. Put the second circle on the flannel board under the first face. This time, leave off the mouth. Say, "Look at this. I have another face here. Something is missing on this face. Can you see what is missing?" If the children cannot discover the missing part, say, "He has hair (point to hair) and he has two eyes (point). Where is his mouth? Do you see his mouth? No? His mouth is missing. Let's put his mouth on."

3. The teacher says, "Now, let's play another game. (Have all parts on the two faces.) See, all of the parts are on the two faces. You will close your eyes and I'll take one of the parts off the face. Then you will open your eyes, look at the face, and find a part that is missing. Ready?"

   Note: The children can make a face from the back of a paper plate. Cut eyes, ears, nose, and a mouth for the children to paste on in the proper place. Give them yarn for the hair. Check to see if the features are pasted in the right places.

• **Simon Says**

Purpose: To identify body parts in a game situation.

Formation: all children scattered

Note to the teacher: This is an old game which children still enjoy. The leader gives commands such as, "Simon says touch your toes." Whenever the leader says, "Simon says" do something, the group must do it. If the leader says, "Touch your toes," without first saying "Simon says," the group must *not* do it. The person who moves when the leader does not say "Simon says" is out. The last one left becomes the new leader.

• **Pop Goes the Weasel**

Note to the teacher: Sing the song, "Pop Goes the Weasel" once. Explain to the children that the next time you sing it, they are to jump up when they hear the word "pop."

'Round and 'round the mulberry bush,
The monkey chased the weasel.
The monkey thought it was all a joke.
Pop! goes the weasel.

• **Old McDonald**

Purpose: To promote good body part identification.

Formation: children in circle, or scattered

Note to the teacher: The children sing the tune, "Old McDonald," using a new format. Use the children's names and different body parts.

Example:

Suzy, Suzy had a body, e - i - e - i - o.
And on her body she had a foot, e-i-e-i-o.
With a (stomp), (stomp), here and a (stomp), (stomp), there
Here a (stomp), there a (stomp),
Everywhere a (stomp), (stomp),
Suzy, Suzy, had a body, e - i - e - i - o.

Repeat the song using various body parts.

• **Imitation of Postures**

Note to the teacher: The children stand in front of the teacher and attempt to imitate the teacher's arm and leg movements.

Variations: Have the children get a partner with whom they will take turns imitating postures.

• **If You're Happy**

Purpose: To play act musical games that use body parts.

Formation: all children scattered

Note to the teacher: Sing the song, "If you're happy and you know it," using body part movements in the verses.

Example:
I. If you're happy and you know it, shake your head.
II. Repeat
III. If you're happy and you know it and you really want to show it
IV. If you're happy and you know it, shake your head.

For other ideas, instead of "shake your head," substitute:

a. Clap your hands.
b. March in place.
c. Shake your hips.
d. Touch your toes.
e. Roll your head.
f. Wiggle your nose.
g. Smile really big.

The children really enjoy making up their own verses.

• Moving the Beach Ball

Note to the teacher: Divide the class into two groups, the X's and the O's.

Purpose: Have the children work together to keep a large beach ball up in the air. They should use their fingers and stay under the ball to try to hit it. The X's try to hit the ball to the O's. This is important as a large group activity.

• Spatial Orientation

Purpose: To promote body awareness.
Formation: children scattered
Note to the teacher: This is a lesson on spatial orientation. The children should be in a scatter formation with adequate room between each child.

Challenges: Teacher says,
a. Show me how small you can be (also, how tall, wide, thin, and long).
b. Point to the farthest wall; touch it and return to your place.
c. Point to the nearest wall; touch it and return to your place.
d. Standing in your place, make your feet move fast; slow.
e. Move your hands fast; slow.
f. Show me how slow you can walk.
g. Show me how fast you can walk.
h. Be a tree, wall, ball, river.

Guide children to look at objects in the room where they are located. Have the children close their eyes and then point to the objects in the room that the teacher calls out. Point to the door, flag, chalkboard, window, wastebasket, floor, ceiling, playhouse area, wagons, play toys, hoops, teacher's desk, outside play area, and so on.

• Exercising

Purpose: To conduct physical fitness activities which will reinforce body image.

Equipment: record player, records:

Learning Basic Skills Through Music, Volume II, AR 522, Activity Records, Educational Activities, Inc., Freeport, NY., Original Words and Music by Hap Palmer.

Perceptual Motor Rhythm Games, Jack Capon and Rosemary Hallum, with special material by Henry "Buzz" Glass, Educational Activities, Inc., Freeport, NY.

Rhythmic Rope Jumping, Kimbo Records, Created by Dr. Annelis Hoyman, Kimbo Educational Records, Box 55, Deal, NJ.

Rhythmic Activity Songs for Primary Grades, L. P. 1055, Vol. I, Kimbo Educational Records, Box 246, Deal, NJ.

Rhythmic Gymnastics (Hoops and Indian Clubs), Created by Dr. Annelis Hoyman,

Kimbo Educational Records, Box 55, Deal, NJ.

And The Beat Goes On (For Physical Education), L. P. Album 5010 Elementary, Produced by Educational Activities and Kimbo Educational Records, Narrated by Ambrose Brazelton, Arranger and Conductor Edward Shanaphy, Recorded at Fine Recording, New York, NY, engineered by Rich Mays.

Formation: all children scattered

Procedure: Have the children follow the teacher and do exercises involving different body parts.

Examples:

1. Rotating the head.
2. Head bouncing up and down.
3. Toe touches.
4. Windmills (alternate toe touches).
5. Stretch for an imaginary star (tip toes).
6. Jumping up and down involving the whole body.
7. Running in place.

The children can really loosen up using the song, "Spanish Flea." Sitting on the floor, they can start moving toes, then feet, then knees, then fingers, hands and on to include the whole body. They can creatively move either in their personal space or in general space.

Unit 26 WINTER

Young children greet winter with delight. It means ice-skating and sledding, rolling snowballs to make a snowman, sliding on the ice, jumping in snowdrifts, and catching snowflakes on warm mittens.

Winter offers many stimulating subjects for creative art activities. Children can experiment with paints to depict the gay color of winter clothing and the active lines seen in outdoor sports. The delicate textures can be created by painting with bits of sponge, crushed paper, or old toothbrushes. White chalk is another medium that works well for winter pictures. It may be used alone, on colored paper, or in combination with crayon. Some topics for picturemaking are:

- Playing in the Snow
- Our Street in Winter
- Feeding the Birds
- Riding on my Sled
- We Play Safely in Winter
- Ice-Skating with my Friends
- Building a Snowman
- Dressing for Winter Weather

Other suggested art activities include:

- Paper Snowmen
- Snowflakes
- Toboggan Run
- Winter Mobile
- Winter on our Street
- Skating Pond

- **Snowflakes**

The individual patterns of snowflakes vary greatly, but all have six points. Some flakes are finely cut; others are fringed like delicate feathers.

Procedure:
1. Using tissue paper or other fine paper, begin by cutting a circle, then fold it in half.
2. Fold the half-circle into three parts, then in half again.
3. Make cuts along the folds but leave solid areas between, making the pattern as delicate as possible. Snowflakes can be used decoratively on a bulletin board or added to a winter mural.

Fig. 26-1 Winter on our street.

- **Winter on Our Street**

Procedure:
1. Cover a table or counter top with white roll paper, sheet, or fireproof cotton.
2. Use discarded cardboard boxes painted or covered with construction paper to make buildings and cars.
3. Sprinkle glitter or spray snow on rooftops for a frosty effect.
4. Trees may consist of twigs stuck in clay. Arrange houses and mark streets.

- **Skating Pond**

Procedure:
1. Ice for a skating pond may be cut from aluminum foil.
2. Draw colorful action figures on newsprint. Cut out and paste onto a narrow ring of toweling roll for support.

- **Toboggan Run**

Procedure:
1. Create slopes for sleds, snowmobiles, toboggans or skis by placing crumpled paper underneath white roll paper.
2. Make toboggans from a used toothpaste tube, cardboard, or aluminum foil curled at one end. Sleds and snowmobiles can be made from small boxes.

- **Paper Snowmen**

Procedure:
1. Large or small paper bags can be stuffed with newspaper, tied at the neck and head, and then painted. While the paint is wet, sprinkle with glitter for a frosty look.
2. The snowman's hat may be made of construction paper. A broom, shovel, and scarf may be added. Other snowmen may consist of marshmallows or cotton balls fastened together with glue or toothpicks.

- **Winter Mobile**

Procedure:
1. Mobiles may consist of two- or three-dimensional objects of paper, cardboard, or metal foil tied with string or thin wire. They can be hung from a small tree branch, coat hanger, or embroidery hoop.
2. Several objects can be made to balance a large one.
3. A winter mobile may contain icicles, snowmen, snowflakes, winter birds, or abstract shapes.
4. Add glitter or sequins to create lights and shadows as objects move with the air current.

Fig. 26-2 Paper snowmen.

Fig. 26-3 Winter mobile.

5. In designing objects to hang, children need to think of how objects look as they turn and move. Creating a mobile helps children develop an appreciation of sculpture in motion and helps them grow in the ability to select, arrange, design, and create in space.

• **Soapy the Snowman**

Procedure:

1. Pour a box of soap flakes into a large container.
2. Add water slowly until the mixture is the consistency of paste.
3. Roll into balls. Put two balls together for the body and add a smaller one for the head.
4. Toothpicks help hold the balls together. Use pipe cleaners or toothpicks for arms, and buttons for features. After

Christmas, the decorations can be removed and the balls used for hand soap.

• **Indoor Snow**

Procedure:

1. Collect some snow in containers and bring it back into the classroom.
2. Mark the snow line on the container and note the difference after the snow melts. Discuss why this happens.
3. Note any pollutants in the melted snow.
4. Place some containers near the heat and others farther away from the heat. Compare the time each takes to melt. If you don't live in an area where it snows, conduct the same experiments using ice cubes.

• **Snow Pictures with Cotton**

Procedure:

1. Try this idea on the day of the first snow, or just after a big storm. Talk about snow and the way it piles up on roofs, trees, cars, and so on.
2. Each child then paints a picture on colored construction paper. Pictures should contain three or four large objects such as a house or a tree.
3. Cotton is added to represent snow. The children will find they can roll it into small balls to make it look like snow falling, snowballs, or snowmen. Or, it may be piled loosely on housetops.
4. Glue is put on the paper and the cotton laid on top of it. Children should be cautioned to keep glue away from fingers since the cotton will stick to them.

• **Snowstorm**

I love to see the snowflakes fall
And cover everything in sight.

The lawn and trees and orchard wall —
With spotless white.

- **Chalk Art**

Procedure:

1. Read the poem, "Snowstorm," to the children once. Then ask what they "saw in their minds" when they heard the poem.
2. Read it again and ask how many others saw pictures of the scene in their minds.
3. After a short discussion of individual children's "mind pictures," they can draw the "pictures in their mind" on paper. Give each child a large (18" x 24") piece of dark-colored construction paper, crayons, and one piece of white chalk. Now let them draw what came to their minds when they heard this poem.

- **Snow Clowns**

I watched the snow come tumbling down,
  Each flake a tiny circus clown.
They chinned themselves along the eaves,
  The clothesline made their gay trapeze.
And then they waltzed in jeweled frills,
  Upon the edge of windowsills.
They played leapfrog just everywhere,
  And ran in circles here and there.
The raindrop soldiers march and pound,
  But snow clowns never make a sound.

(Follow same procedure for drawing pictures as in "Snowstorm" poem.)

- **Snowflake Figures**

Materials: white paper, pipe cleaners, some nonhardening clay

Procedure:

1. Let everyone cut out circles, tracing them from bottles, cans, and other round objects if desired.
2. Fold the circles in half twice.
3. Cut slits and notches of different sizes from both folds, then open and there is a delicate snowflake. (Someone may want to make cuts along the rounded edge as well.)

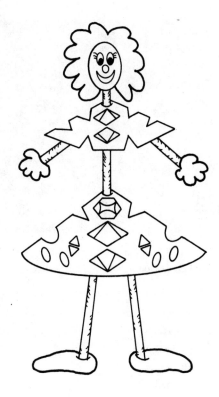

Fig. 26-4 Snowflake figure.

4. The figure is made from two pipe cleaners. Slits are cut in the center of the snowflake so it will slide over the figure. Glue the snowflake back together to make a skirt. A smaller snowflake makes a collar or cuffs.
5. To make the figure stand, push one foot (pipe cleaner) or both into a piece of clay. Some paper and yarn may be glued to the pipe cleaner head to make a face and hair.

FINGER PLAYS, POEMS, AND SONGS

- **The Mitten Song**

Thumbs in the thumb place,
  (Put up thumbs)
Fingers all together!
  (Put up all fingers, together)
This is the song
We sing in mitten weather.

Fig. 26-5 Group finger plays provide a social experience as well as fine motor skills practice.

When it is cold.
   (Hug self with arms, in "cold" gesture)
It doesn't matter whether
   (Shake head)
Mittens are wool,
Or made of finest leather.
   (Put out hand)

This is the song
   (Keep hands up)
We sing in mitten weather:
Thumbs, in the thumb place,
   (Put up thumbs)
Fingers all together!
   (Put up all fingers, together)

- **Icy**

(Children particularly enjoy "acting out" this poem)

   I slip and I slide
   On the slippery ice;
   I skid and I glide,
   Oh, isn't it nice!
   To lie on your tummy
   And slither and skim,
   On the slick crust of snow
   Where you skid as you swim.

- **Winter**

There's wind in the chimney
And snow in the air
And frost on the pane
And cold everywhere.

So wear your long leggings
And wrap up your throat
And pull on your mittens
And button your coat.

And do be careful
And don't freeze your noses
You'll need them next summer
To smell the red roses.

- **First Snow Of the Season**

Silently, softly, and swiftly
   (Make motion of falling snow with fingers
   of both hands)
It falls to the earth and lies
In heaps and drifts and hummocks —
   (Show heaps by motions of hands)
A wintertime surprise!

Get out your sled and boots
   (Pretend to pull a sled and put on boots)
Get out your mittens and cap,
   (Pretend to put on mittens and cap)
You can coast a long, long hour,
And then take a nice long nap.
   (Fold hands under cheek; close eyes and
   pretend to sleep)

- **Little Snowflakes**

Merry little snowflakes,
Dancing in the air;
Busy little snowflakes,
Falling everywhere.

Blowing in our faces,
Falling at our feet,
And kissing all the children
As they run along the street.

- Snow

Snow makes whiteness where it falls,
The bushes look like popcorn balls.
And places where I always play,
Look like somewhere else today.

- Bed in Winter

(A good poem to recite at rest time while
the children are on cots, and can put out
their feet to act out this poem.)

At night I reach down with my feet
    Just to see,
Then I curl up quickly instead.
For every place, except right under
    Me,
Is terribly cold in my bed!

- Snowballs

I had a little snowball once,
It was so round and white,
I took it home with me and tried
To keep it overnight.

But when next morning I awoke,
Just at the break of day,
I went to get it and I found,
It had melted all away.

- Chasing Snowflakes

(Children enjoy "chasing snowflakes" after
this poem. Gentle, soft "chasing" generally
fits the poem best. Even better — go out in
a snowfall and *really* chase snowflakes!)

    I had a snowman
    Fat and gay.
    I had him all
    One Winter's day.
    I have him yet,
    Because I took his picture
    For my snapshot book!

- The Snowman

(Let the children act out this poem. They
especially like wearing a top hat as a prop.
Have one child play the snowman and another
the north wind.)

Once there was a snowman
Who stood beside the door,
Thought he'd like to warm himself
By the firelight red,
Thought he'd like to jump upon
    The big, white bed.
So he called to the north wind —
    "Help me, wind, I pray,
I'm completely frozen, standing here
    All day."
So the north wind came along, and
    Blew him in the door,
And now there's nothing left of him,
But a puddle on the floor!

- Falling Snow

See the pretty snowflakes,
    Falling from the sky;
On the walk and housetops,
    Soft and thick they lie.

On the window ledges,
    On the branches bare;
Now how fast they gather,
    Filling all the air.

Look into the garden,
    Where the grass was green;
Covered by the snowflakes,
    Not a blade is seen.

Now the bare black bushes
    All look soft and white;
Every twig is laden —
    What a pretty sight!

- A Joke

(A natural follow-up to this activity is a winter
walk, to see if our breath comes out like "little puffs of smoke." Try taking a picture of
the puffs of smoke.)

When I am outdoors in the cold,
Isn't it a joke
How my breath comes out of me
Like little puffs of smoke?

• Snow Under My Feet

(A natural follow-up to this activity is a winter walk, to see if our feet make the sound, "crickery, crackery, creek.")

Crickery, crackery, creek,
The snow is talking under my feet.
Ice and snow and hail and sleet,
Talk crickery, crackery, creek.

• Winter is Coming

(Let the children play all the parts in this poem: bear, leaf, frog, bird, chipmunk, caterpillar.   It could also serve as a short play, with costumes, for a parent's meeting.)

Winter is coming, and what will you do?
"Sleep," said the bear, "the cold season
  Through."
"Float," said the leaf, "right down from
  The tree,
This wind in the branches is too much for me."
"Sink," said the frog, "I shall drop into bed,
In the mud of this pond I shall cover my head."
"Fly," said the bird, "the summer is old.
I am going south before it gets cold."
"Dig," said the chipmunk, "a hole in the
  Ground.
Till spring comes again, that's where I'll
  Be found."
"Spin," said the caterpillar, "weave a cocoon,
Tied to this twig I shall go to sleep soon."
"In the spring," said them all, "we shall
  Start life anew,
But when winter is coming these things
  Must we do."

• Signs of Winter

(Same note as for "Winter is Coming" poem)
On a big gray cloud away up high,
Sat a soft little snowflake in the dark sky.
"I must fall," said the snowflake white.
"I must fall down to the earth tonight."
Said the big gray cloud, "Oh, please don't go.
Something might happen to you, you know."
But the little snowflake with a tear in his eye,
Said, "Good-by, good-by, I am leaving the sky."
Then off he went, and he floated down
Till he came to a quiet New Hampshire town.
And there on the hard brown earth he lay.
The next day, some children came out to play.
They said, "A snowflake has come to stay,
And winter is at last on its way.
Good-by to summer, good-by to fall,
Good-by to little leaves one and all."
That day, from the clouds came snowflake
  mothers
And snowflake fathers and sisters and brothers.
Oh, hundreds of snowflakes came fluttering
  down,
Covering rooftops all over the town.
The children laughed for they had a plan.
From mounds of snow, they would make a
  man.
Then all that day they worked very hard,
And they made a snowman out in the yard.

• My Zipper Suit

My zipper suit is bunny brown,
The top zips up, the legs zip down,
I wear it every day.
My daddy brought it out from town,
Zip it up, and zip it down,
And hurry out to play!

• Snow

The more it snows,
The more it goes,
The more it goes
  On snowing.

And nobody knows,
How cold my toes,
How cold my toes
Are growing.

— A. A. Milne

CREATIVE MOVEMENT ACTIVITIES

• **Icicles**

We are little icicles
Melting in the sun.
Can't you see our tiny tears
Dropping one by one?

Say the poem aloud to and with the children a few times until they can repeat it with you. Then ask the children if they can be like little "icicles." How would icicles stand — straight or slouchy?

Discuss what happens to icicles in the sun. Then ask the children to show with their own bodies what happens to icicles in the sun. Reinforce the concept of the relaxed melting motions of icicles on a winter class walk. Be sure to point out some real icicles!

• **Silent Snowfall**

Read this poem to the children once. Discuss how they think snowflakes "sounded" in the poem. Discuss how snowflakes would move. Read the poem again.

The snow fell softly all the night
It makes a blanket soft and white.
It covered houses, flowers, and ground.
But did not make a single sound.

Now let the children move (softly, slowly) like the snowflakes in the poem.

• **Skaters' Waltz**

You don't have to live in a cold climate to ice skate. Mark off an irregular shape on the classroom floor with tape to create an "ice skating pond." Let the children go "skating" in their stocking feet. A few grains of very fine sand or cornmeal sprinkled on your classroom "pond" enables the children to feel the movement and rhythm of skating as they alternately slide on either foot.

• **Snow Fun**

If you live in a snowy area, let the children have fun outdoors as often as possible. (Tell your plans to parents and ask them to dress the children suitably with extra mittens, scarves, etc.) Walk around in the snow, shovel paths through it, build snowmen, look for tracks in the snow, watch the snowplows at work, play "angels in the snow." If there is a hill nearby, children can go sliding on the seats of well-padded snowsuits or use big pieces of cardboard for sleds.

• **Blow, Melt, and Trickle**

Dramatizations can be stimulated by using phenomena that exists in our everyday world. Encourage the children to pretend (by acting with their body movement) to be any of the following:

- leaves waving in a gentle wind, a heavy wind, and then eventually flying through the air
- snow falling softly, being made into a snowman, and then melting
- an ice cream cone or icicle melting in the sun
- rain trickling down, running into a swift stream, the sun coming out, and a rainbow appearing
- an icy hill that is hard to walk up
- a thick fog to find one's way through

The children and teacher may think of others.

GAMES

• **Freeze**

It is important for children to be able to stop and start quickly. Their locomotor skills are somewhat limited, so they need to use them. This activity gives them that opportunity. At the word *freeze,* they stop and hold the position until the word *go.* Continue the game, using different body parts.

If space permits, have the children get up and move about, using those locomotor skills which are possible in terms of space and ability.

> Walk! — Freeze!
> Hop! — Freeze!
> Run! — Freeze!
> Move any other way that you can! — Freeze!

At different times, use levels (high, low), speed (fast, slow), and size (large, small).

- **Chips Off the Ice Block**

Each child has a large block. Lay blocks in spaces so the children have room to move around without touching anyone.

Exploration (Be sure to give children time to explore.)
- Go over the block as many different ways as you can.
- Go around the block as many different ways as you can.
- Push the block with as many different parts of your body as you can.

Exploration with limitations
- Place one foot on the block and move over and around it without touching it with the other foot.
- Place one hand on the block and go over and around it.
- Do the same thing with two hands on the block, or one foot and one hand.
- Sit on the block and push with your feet.
- Lie on the block and push with your hands.
- Get on the block and try to move it without using your hands or feet.
- Jump up on the block and then off.

- Jump off the block and touch the floor with your hands as soon as you land.

- **Ball Freeze Game**

In their own spaces, have the children do as many things with a ball as they can, without losing control of it. This can be done while standing or seated. Stress keeping control of the ball. At the word, freeze, the children stop and hold the ball in whatever position they may be.

- **Snowmen Game**

Divide the class into two groups. One group lines up across the room and pretends it is a group of snowmen. The other group hops on one foot (or two) across the room and attempts to get through the line without being stopped. All hands must be kept close to the body. Then the groups exchange sides.

- **Snowball Through the Wreath**

Players throw "snowballs" (cotton ball, sponge, old socks made into balls) through a large Christmas wreath, suspended from the ceiling. The group may be divided into two teams. Each time a player throws a snowball successfully through the wreath, a point is scored for the team. A cluster of bells may be hung at the top of the wreath. If the bells are hit, an extra point is scored.

- **Charlie Over the Ice**

Have the class divide into groups of 8 or 10. One person in each group is "Charlie." This person squats down with the others circling around him. As they circle, they sing, "Charlie over the ice, Charlie over the sea, Charlie can catch a blackbird — but he can't catch me!" At the word, "me," Charlie tries to catch as many as possible before they can reach home. Home is any place where they can touch wood, iron, glass, or some material agreed upon by the players.

• **Cat and Mouse (Snow) Ball**

Everyone forms one large circle. The children pass a ball around the circle with each child holding it for a second. Then, introduce a second ball. Each person passes the first ball to the next person, and then turns the other way to look for the next ball. After a few turns, make this game a winter game by having the second ball be the sun trying to shine on the snowball (other ball) and melt it.

COOKING ACTIVITY

• **Snow Ice Cream**

Right after a snowfall, when the snow is clean, collect a pailful of snow. In a big bowl, combine a large can of evaporated milk and several cups of superfine sugar, mixing until the sugar is dissolved. Stir in one tablespoon of vanilla extract. Add large amounts of snow and stir quickly, adding more snow until the mixture looks like and tastes like vanilla ice cream. (For additional activities, see December Holidays unit.)

CHILDREN'S BOOKS FOR WINTER

Burton, Virginia L., *Katy and the Big Snow.* Boston, Massachusetts: Houghton Mifflin, 1974.

Keats, Ezra J., *Snowy Day.* New York: Viking, 1962.

Tresselt, Alvin, *The Mitten.* New York: Lothrop, 1964.

Tresselt, Alvin, *White Snow, Bright Snow.* New York: Lothrop, 1947.

Unit 27 DECEMBER HOLIDAYS

December is a month of holidays, a time for lighting candles, feasting, giving and receiving gifts, and caroling. Whether children look hopefully for Santa Claus, Father Christmas, Pere Noel, or Saint Nicholas, people of many countries anticipate the season in much the same spirit. Various customs have developed throughout the world, such as the celebration of Christmas in Mexico beginning on December 16. Children participate in fiestas and play "breaking the pinata" for candies and good luck charms. In Norway, even the birds have their own Christmas trees. On Christmas morning, children tie sheaves of wheat or other grain to poles or spruce trees for the winter birds to eat. In England, under lofty arches of great cathedrals, children join processions at Christmas Eve services to sing carols and hymns.

Christmas customs also vary in different parts of the United States. In Williamsburg, Virginia, the old English tradition of bringing in the Yule log and lighting it is carried on as it was in the time of George Washington. Fireworks fill the skies the night before Christmas over states farther south. In New England towns, caroling is done in neighborhoods on Christmas Eve. Homes throughout the nation are decorated with greens.

While Christian children light their Christmas candles, Jewish children gather with their families around the Hanukkah candles and attend services in the synagogue (temple). Hanukkah, often called the Festival of Lights, symbolizes religious liberty. It lasts eight days and is celebrated each night by placing a lighted candle in the Hanukkah lamp (called the menorah), until all eight are burning on the last day. Evenings are festive with storytelling, gift giving, and feasting. Children play a game with a top called a dreidel, which has four Hebrew letters on it. As it spins around, the children sing a song about the dreidel. Clubs and groups celebrate with plays, concerts, and parties.

In picturemaking, children will have many ideas to paint about their own holiday experiences when they are inspired. Some ideas are

- A Beautiful Christmas Tree
- Christmas Angel
- Decorating Our House at Holiday Time
- A Trip to See Santa
- Lighting the Hanukkah Candles
- The Holiday Feast
- Playing Hanukkah Games

Other suggested art activities:

- Holiday Greeting Cards
- Christmas Characters
- Holiday Door Decorations
- Glittery Baubles
- Toy Shop Window
- Miniature Trees

- **Holiday Greeting Cards**

Procedure:

1. Techniques for making greeting cards may include cutting and folding, stenciling, or printing. Holiday designs are as varied as the number of children in the class.

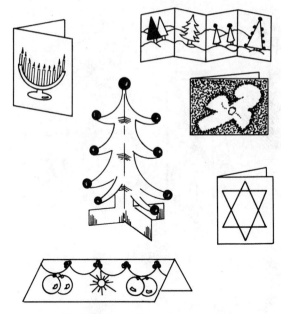

Fig. 27-1 Holiday greeting cards.

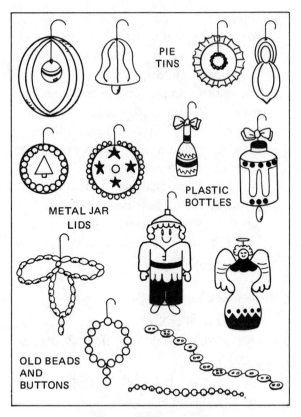

Fig. 27-2 Glittery baubles.

2. Children should be encouraged to explore the scrap box for sparkling materials such as metallic foil, gum wrappers, wrapping paper, old greeting cards, and bits of discarded ribbon.

• **Glittery Baubles**

Children make decorative holiday objects for use as tree ornaments, mobiles, bulletin board displays, and party favors. A variety of found objects can be used such as nonflammable pie tins, detergent bottles, plastic squeeze bottles, metal jar lids and bottle tops, or discarded pieces of styrofoam.

Procedure:

1. Tins and plastic bottles may be used in their original shape or cut and bent into desired forms.

2. If objects need a covering, use construction paper, wallpaper, metallic foil, or newspaper.

3. Sparkling trimmings include beads, buttons, glitter, sequins, or discarded holiday decorations. Baubles can be hung with ornament hooks or thin wire.

Fig. 27-3 Toy shop window.

• **Toy Shop Window**

A bright holiday bulletin board brings the color and spirit of the season into the classroom.

Procedure:

1. Arrange strips of construction paper over background paper on the bulletin board to indicate windowpanes.
2. For a three-dimensional effect, pull the paper strips out to the head of the pins. Colorful toys made from children's drawings, paintings, or cut paper can be placed in the windows.
3. A brightly painted paper awning may protrude from the storefront by fastening it in several places to strips of cardboard pinned at right angles to the background.

• Christmas Characters

Figures such as Santa and his elves, dolls, and toys decorate tables for holiday parties.

Procedure:

1. Use cardboard boxes of various sizes to form the foundation.
2. Decorate boxes with scraps of construction paper or felt for clothing.
3. Add bits of cloth, braid, feathers, yarn, string, or ribbon for color and texture.
4. Elflike features can be created with buttons, beads, or sequins.

• Holiday Door Decorations

Procedure:

1. Bend a thin wire coat hanger to form a desired shape, such as triangular Christmas tree, Santa Claus, fanciful angel, toy head, or wreath.
2. After covering the coat hanger with construction paper, complete the design with a variety of paper scraps, ribbon, yarn, metallic foil, felt.

• Miniature Trees

A number of techniques for making miniature Christmas trees are suitable for young children.

Fig. 27-4 Christmas characters.

Fig. 27-5 Holiday door decorations.

Cone-shaped tree. This consists of a rolled piece of construction paper stapled firmly in place. Several cones, graduated in size, can be stacked one on top of another and fringed along the edges.

Three-sided tree. This can be made by first folding three pieces of construction paper in half. Then, paste them back-to-back. Cut in

Fig. 27-6 Miniature trees.

the desired shape, leaving enough space at the base for standing.

Flat cardboard tree. To make this free-standing tree, sink the base in a lump of clay or piece of discarded styrofoam.

Tree branch. A tree branch can be anchored in a small flowerpot, box, or milk carton filled with clay or styrofoam.

Decorations. A variety of odds and ends left over from previous holidays can be used for decorations, but unusual materials make the most interesting trees. Children can collect such found objects as feathers, yarn, sequins, metallic foil, felt, and shells. They may want to make a candy tree using gumdrops or marshmallows.

- **More Decorations**

Spirals. The spiral is made by cutting a circle of paper round and round from the edges toward the center. Variations of the spiral could be squares or triangles cut in the same way. Spirals may be hung from ceilings or on trees; two of them may also be

Fig. 27-7 Spiral decorations.

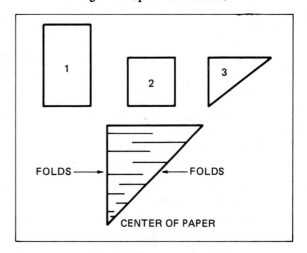

Fig. 27-8 Birdcage ornament.

glued together at the widest ends and an ornament hung through the center.

Birdcage. Foil paper or poster paper should be used for this decoration since it is easier to cut when folded. The paper is first cut in squares about 6″ by 6″ or larger. A square is folded three times to form a triangular shape. Cuts are made from one fold almost all the way over to the opposite fold, alternating first from one side to another, down to the tip of the triangle. Open carefully and pull the center upward to form a cage. Hang the decoration by the center from the ceiling or from a tree branch.

Balls. For this decoration, cut five circles all the same size from construction paper or foil paper. Fold them in half both ways. Cut another small circle, about half the size of the others. Cut a slit across the center of the five circles and slide them on the smaller circle, making a ball. Glue the sides of the circles together, string them, and hang them on a tree or from the ceiling. Interesting variations of this decoration can be made by using square shapes, diamond shapes, and so on, instead of circles.

Pinwheel. The pinwheel is made from a square piece of paper. The paper is creased from corner to corner. The creases are cut almost to the center. Then all left or right corners are glued to the center of the paper. A pinwheel can be hung from one of its points, or a series of them strung through the center and graduated in size. Glitter, cotton, yarn, sequins, and other decorations make the pinwheels attractive.

Star fan. Make two fans out of two long pieces of paper, the length at least three times the width of the paper. Cut notches along the folded sides to make a pattern. Cut one end to a point to make pointed edges. Unfold and glue the sides of the two fans together to make a circle. The centers may be sewn together to keep the folds tight. The star fan is then strung and hung from the ceiling or from a branch of a tree.

To do with dough. Use up modeling dough as it begins to dry out. Form it into balls and have the children stick small pebbles, beads, buttons,

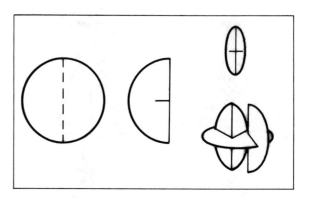

Fig. 27-9 Balls.

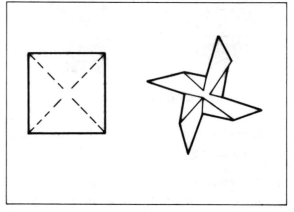

Fig. 27-10 Pinwheel.

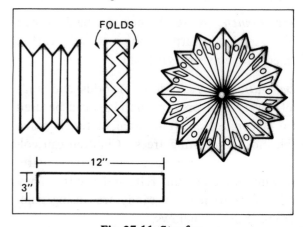

Fig. 27-11 Star fan.

or sequins into the surface of the balls. Hang them as mobiles or holiday decorations.

• **Snowflakes**

Snowflakes are easy to make and may be used as mobiles, window decorations, or bulletin board decorations.

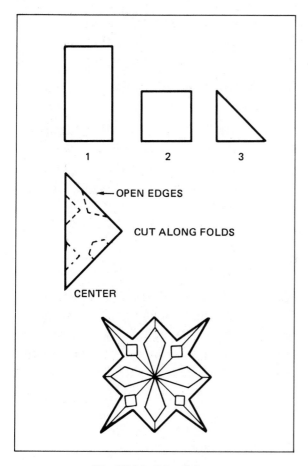

Fig. 27-12 Snowflakes.

Fig. 27-13 Santa on a stick.

Procedure:

1. Cut foil paper, tracing paper, poster paper, or any decorative wrapping paper into squares of many sizes.
2. Fold the squares in half twice, then fold to make a triangle. Keep in mind where the center of the paper is.
3. Cut a "V" shape into the open edges, to get the points of the snowflakes.
4. Cut notches of different sizes along the two folded edges. The more pieces cut out, the fancier the snowflakes will be.

• **Pine Cone Centerpiece**

Procedure:

1. Cut small logs, about 3" in diameter and 12" long.

2. Gather acorns and pine cones of all sizes.
3. Glue the cones and acorns on the log. Some of the larger cones may be pulled apart and the petals used to make floral designs.
4. Holes may be drilled in the log to fit the candles.
5. After the log is covered with the cones and acorns, spray the entire piece with silver or gold paint.
6. The decorated logs make attractive and lasting holiday centerpieces.

• **Santa on a Stick**

Rows of Santas in the window box or stuck in mounds of clay are creative room decorations.

Procedure:

1. Double heads and bodies of Santas are cut from heavy tagboard and painted.
2. Cut-paper and cotton faces, beards, hats, buttons, boots, and mittens are added.
3. The figures are then glued back-to-back with a thin, flat stick or piece of No. 4 reed between them.
4. Christmas trees, snowmen, or other figures can also be made the same way.

• **Gift Making**

Gifts are fun to make and give. Children can participate in planning and creating presents for others. An example of what happened in one kindergarten follows:

Teacher: (Reading from a chart upon which the children's plans for holidays have been written) Our third plan says, "We can make holiday presents for other people." Who could we make presents for?

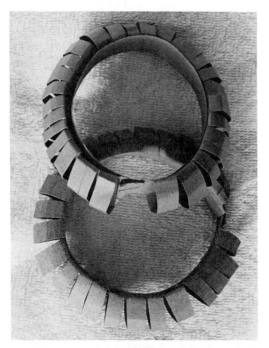

Fig. 27-14 One present a child can make is a cut-paper wreath.

Mary: Our mothers.
Sue: Our fathers.
John: I could make one for my brother.

As the children talk, the teacher makes a list of the people they suggest.

Teacher: That's a good list. What kinds of things do we have in our class that we could use to make gifts for these people?
Jill: We have paper.
Teacher: What could we make out of paper, Jill?
Jill: We could make a picture for our mothers.
Teacher: (Nodding) That's a good idea. (Under the title, "Kinds of Presents We Could Make," she writes, (1) We could make pictures.) The list continues as the children and teacher think of things that could be made out of the paper, clay, lumber, cloth, and waste materials that are available.

Some possibilities for presents include:

• Drawing, painting, or chalking a picture. Give children a variety of kinds, colors, and sizes of paper to choose from. Have the children sign and date their pictures. Mount each picture on another sheet or on cardboard for stiffness.

• Making booklets of various sizes for writing memos, notes, telephone numbers, or grocery lists. Books can be made in various ways, by folding single sheets in half and stapling, or fastening with a paper fastener. Different shapes and ways of folding them together can be discovered by the children. They can then complete the books by designing the cover. It might have a title, or a design made of colored paper, paint, or crayon.

- Making bowls, paperweights, candle holders or pencil holders out of clay. The children decide what they will do and how to do it. Dried objects may be fired if a kiln is available. The objects can be painted with tempera paints, varnished, or shellacked by the children.

- Making hot-dish stands or spindles out of lumber. Each child can saw a piece of soft pine, 3/4″ thick, into a shape that they like and paint it in a solid color or in a design. For a spindle, drive a large nail up through the center. For safety while taking it home, have the child cover the nail with a sheaf made by rolling corrugated cardboard into a coil, securing it with tape, and pressing it over the nail.

- Boxes and cans of all shapes and sizes can be painted or covered with cloth or decorative paper. Contact paper and shelf paper are good for this. The containers can be used to hold yarn, knitting, buttons, pencils, paper clips, jewelry, or handkerchiefs. They can also be used as drawer organizers.

As the children construct these gifts, the teacher will tactfully channel their thinking along workable ideas, while at the same time encouraging their creative talents and active participation in the planning.

To prevent the children from becoming discouraged, the teacher might send a tactful letter to parents explaining how to understand and accept a child's gift. An example of such a letter follows:

Dear Parents,

Your child will soon be bringing home holiday presents for his family. To you, they may look different than the item usually looks because after all, they are the work of a very young child. But no matter how they appear, your child has put his best efforts into planning and making the gifts and they are all his own creation.

When you receive the gifts, you might ask how to use them if the gift is not immediately identifiable. Point out something of special interest to you and actually make some use of the gifts. This will be the best kind of encouragement that you could possibly give.

Happy holiday!

- **Greeting Cards**

Greeting cards are usually sent to friends and relatives to celebrate holidays, birthdays, anniversaries, births, and other memorable occasions. Making such cards offers children an opportunity to do something thoughtful for others; to plan, organize, and complete a piece of work; and to exercise creative self-expression.

Children can make birthday cards for classmates, Thanksgiving greetings, Christmas cards, Mother's Day cards, Father's Day cards, Saint Patrick's Day greetings, valentines, Easter greetings, sympathy cards, thank-you notes, get-well cards, congratulations cards, and so on. To construct and illustrate the cards, children can use paper of different types, chalk, paint, crayon, scissors, paste, scotch tape, paper punch, stapler, ribbon, collage material, paper fasteners, and similar materials.

The following are some of the techniques that are used:

Finger painting. Have each child make a large painting, then cut up the painting to use for individual cards.

Collage. Arranging scraps of paper, cloth, and so on, in a colorful design.

Spatter painting. Child cuts a shape, places it on a background sheet of paper, and spatter paints it by rubbing a toothbrush dipped in paint over a screen. When the shape is removed, its outline remains.

String painting.   String, yarn, or roping is dipped in paint and dragged across the paper, making a colorful design.

Straw painting.   Blobs of paint are dripped on the paper and the child blows through a straw into the blobs to create interesting shapes.

Block painting.   Wooden blocks or shapes cut from vegetables such as potatoes or carrots are dipped in paint and transferred to paper.

Crayon resist.   Draw a design with crayon and then paint over it with thin watercolor.

Rubs.   Put the paper on a patterned surface such as over a piece of wire netting, or a leaf, or an arrangement of strings.   Color with the side of a crayon or chalk, pressing down hard on the paper.   The design from underneath will come through.

Chalk on wet paper.   Dip a piece of paper in a pan of water.   (Any paper will do; even newspaper looks interesting with chalk colors added.)   Spread the wet paper on a flat surface and draw designs with chalk.   Hang up to dry.   If the paper wrinkles, press with a hot iron.   If the chalk is likely to rub off, set it with hair spray.

For the greeting or message the card carries, children might dictate appropriate thoughts to the teacher, who could type them on a primer typewriter or write them in script and duplicate a copy for the children to paste or staple to the card.   The more mature children can copy their own messages if the messages are kept very short and simple.   "Hi!" is an easy word for even the youngest.   "Hello," "Mom," "Dad," and "Love" are meaningful words that many children might like to copy.

- **Easy, Decorative Christmas Trees**

Procedure:

1. Cut quarter-circles from colored construction paper.   Glue the sides together to form cones, and place over dowels stuck in spools to make tall, slim trees.

2. Spirals may be added for decoration.   To make a spiral, start with a circle slightly larger than the base of the cone and follow directions for Spiral Ornaments, page 269.   The center of the spiral is placed on the point of the cone and the rest circles around the cone.   Glue at the top and bottom.

3. A small cone placed over the top of a large cone will help hold the spiral in place until the glue dries.   Or, add glitter, cotton, foil paper, yarn, and so on, as decorations for these easy-to-make, attractive trees.

- **Stone Paperweight**

Have everyone bring to class medium-sized stones of interesting shapes.

Procedure:

1. Paint them with tempera, making unusual designs, faces, or figures suggested by the shape of the stone.

2. When the paint is dry, the stones are shellacked.   A felt base may be glued on the bottom, if desired.   The stones make useful and decorative paperweights — gift items for parents.

- **Christmas Boxes**

Read this poem aloud once to the children.   Discuss how they "see it" in their minds.

Read it again.   Then have the children draw and color what they "see" in the poem.

Big boxes, little ones,
Some in-between;
All holding presents that
Cannot be seen.

Boxes with ribbons,
Boxes with string;
Boxes with wrappings
That don't tell a thing!

Boxes with lids on,
Boxes that fold;
Boxes that whisper
Of treasures they hold.

Green boxes, red boxes,
Silvery ones, too;
Under the Christmas tree,
Waiting for you!

- **Paper Batik**

Here's an interesting variation of the "resist" technique. After completing your drawing with crayons, soak the paper in water and crumple into a ball. Then uncrumple the paper, flatten it out, and blot off the excess water.

Flow a watercolor or a diluted tempera over the surface with a wet brush. Because the color will be more intense in the creased area, the finished drawing will have dramatic contrasts.

MOVEMENT AND GAMES

In a discussion with the children at holiday time, make a list of feelings and objects that describe the holiday. Then have the children use movement to express these ideas. Encourage creativity.

Christmas:

opening packages	Santa Claus
reindeer	trimming the tree
shopping	toys
making a snowman	

Hanukkah:

candles	seder
Menorah	joyous
dreidel	

- **Story Plays**

Some ideas to stimulate imaginations: bring home a Christmas tree; activities in Santa's toyshop; falling snowflakes; such winter sports as skiing, skating, and sledding; shoveling snow; carrying in firewood for the fireplace; Washington riding his horse over the plantation. Let children develop these ideas through rhythmic movements, pantomimes, or simple one-act plays.

- **Here We Go 'Round the Christmas Tree**

(Variation of "Here We Go 'Round the Mulberry Bush.")

Several verses that can be used for this song include:

"Here we go 'round the Christmas tree" etc.
"This is the way we hang a star (icicle, ball, candy cane, light, etc.)"

- **Rug in the Center**

A small rug is placed in front of the room or in the center of the room. Individuals take turns dramatizing characters in a familiar holiday song or story. Children guess who is being depicted. For another twist, select different children to pantomime zoo animals. Then have an animal parade.

HOLIDAY CANDLES

> Caution: There must be adult supervision at all times during the wax melting.

Materials: baby food jars, colored tissue, liquid starch, heavy string (cord) for wicks, bar of paraffin, colored dye powder

Procedure:
1. Decorate baby food jars with pieces of colored tissue. Attach to jar by brushing on liquid starch.
2. Let jars dry.

Fig. 27-15 Stocking patterns.

3. Candles are simple to make using household paraffin wax gaily colored with dye powder. (Do not use liquid dye as this will not mix with the wax.)

4. For larger candles, insert the wick before adding the wax. Punch a hole in the center of the bottom of the mold, no larger than the cord. Run the cord through the hole and up through the mold. Tie the end to a pencil or stick placed across the top of the mold. Pull the cord taut and secure the other end by knotting and taping. For wicks in smaller candles, dip the cord (which is cut one inch longer than the depth of the mold) into the melted paraffin and set aside to harden.

5. To make colorful candles, melt paraffin wax in top part of a double boiler. Never use direct heat as the wax is flammable. Add dye powder, using about 2 teaspoons for each pound of paraffin. Remove the pan from the boiling water, stir thoroughly for 2 to 3 minutes, and let stand. Since dye is made to be soluble in water, not wax, some residue will remain in the pan after pouring. Simply discard. Pour wax carefully into molds from a height of one to two inches.

6. When the wax begins to harden in the small molds, push in the prepared wicks. Remove the tape holding the wicks for larger molds, when the molds have hardened. To unmold, dip metal molds quickly in very hot water to loosen; then shake out. Peel off cardboard from carton molds.

• **String Balls**

Procedure:
1. Soak string, cord, yarn, or twine in paste. Wrap around and around, crisscross fashion, on large, blown-up balloons.

2. Scatter on glitter to give sparkle, and allow to dry.

3. Pop the balloons and pull away. Hang decorations with string or ribbon tied through the top.

• **Spatter Printing**

Create unique and original designed fabric for use as wall hangings or for covering and decorating items such as wastebaskets, screens, and lamp shades.

Procedure:
1. Begin with a washable fabric — an old sheet, piece of burlap, or unbleached muslin are suggestions.

2. Place material on a flat surface with protective paper around the work area.

3. Mix 1/4 cup liquid dye or 1/2 package of dye in 1 pint of hot water.

4. Spatter dye the solution onto the fabric with a brush. Use two or three colors for interesting patterns.

5. Allow the fabric to dry.

6. If the fabric is to be used for covering items, a protective coat of clear shellac should be brushed or sprayed on.

7. Note: Do not use spatter-dyed fabric for articles that would come in direct contact with other articles (for example, pillow covers), because of possible rub-off from dye.

• **Rope Tricks**

Procedure:
1. Make colorful jump ropes by dunking ordinary clothesline, cut the proper length, in a solution of dye.

2. Finish the ends by tying on empty thread spools that have been tinted matching or contrasting colors.

- **Colorful Animals**

Procedure:
1. Dye socks following directions on dye container.
2. Fit ball snugly into toe of sock making sure that fabric covers the ball smoothly. Secure the ball with string or needle and thread. Leave body limp.
3. Finish raw edges as desired.
4. Make animal faces with embroidery thread or paint in features. Use yarn in loops, or pieces of bias tape to make ears, mane, or other animal features.

- **Play Clay**

Ingredients:
1 cup Argo cornstarch
2 cups baking soda (1 pound package)
1 1/4 cups water

Procedure:
1. Combine cornstarch and baking soda thoroughly together in a saucepan.
2. Mix in water. Bring to a boil over medium heat, stirring constantly, until mixture reaches a moist mashed potato consistency.
3. Remove immediately from heat. Turn out on a plate and cover with a damp cloth until cool.
4. When easy to handle, knead like dough. Shape as desired or store in a tightly closed plastic bag for later use.
5. Note: For solid colored play clay, add a few drops of food coloring or tempera paint powder to water before it is mixed in with starch and soda. Objects may be left white or painted when dry.

- **Play Clay Creations**

Holiday ornaments. Roll out play clay to 1/4 inch thickness on waxed paper. Cut out shapes with cooky cutters of all sizes, bottle tops, or with a knife. Use a sharp needle or pin to make a hole for string or yarn to hang on the Christmas tree.

Beads. Shape the play clay into small balls or ovals. Using a long pin or wire, make a hole through each bead for later stringing.

Sculpture. Use as a clay, shaping into all sorts of objects.

Pendants, pins, and buttons. Roll out play clay. Cut into circles or other designs, moistening each piece slightly so the pieces will stick together or glue in place when dry. For buttons, glue a safety pin on the back when dry, for wearing.

To dry: Play clay objects will dry and harden at room temperature in approximately 36 hours depending on thickness. To speed drying, preheat oven to 350 degrees F.; turn oven off and place objects on a wire rack or in a cardboard box on the rack. Leave in the oven until the oven is cool.

To finish: Paint dried play clay with watercolors, poster paints, or felt-tip pens. Spray with clear plastic, dip into shellac or coat small pieces with clear nail polish.

- **Papier-Maché**

Ingredients:
instant laundry starch
cold water
tissue paper, facial tissue, newspaper
string, cotton, etc.

Procedure:
1. Make a paste by mixing equal parts of instant laundry starch and cold water until the starch is dissolved.
2. Let stand a few minutes to thicken.
3. Dip in desired materials.
4. Shape as desired, molding over a balloon, wire, or cardboard frame for interesting forms.

5. Allow to thoroughly dry on waxed paper for rigid finished objects. Drying time varies depending on object size. Allow 2 to 3 days for hats and balloon decorations.

• **Papier-Maché Magic — Cheerful Hats**

Procedure:

1. Dip torn pieces or strips of rice paper or newspaper into paste and mold over blown-up balloon for basic hat shape.
2. Dip colored pieces of crushed tissue paper into paste; cluster over hat shape to give flowered appearance.
3. When dry, slowly let air out of balloon and gently pull away from hat.

• **Mosaics**

Here's a good way to use the leftover stubs and pieces of crayons instead of discarding them.

Procedure:

1. Peel off the wrappers of crayon stubs and experiment with arranging them in designs and patterns.

2. Use them as they are, or cut them to fit.
3. Glue the pieces to a stiff cardboard backing. The result: a beautiful mosaic.

POEMS, FINGER PLAYS, AND SONGS

• **Around the Corner**

Christmas is coming,
Around the corner.
It's time to be good,
Like little Jack Horner.

• **Christmas Morning**

At last it's Christmas morning!
So I'm up and ready for fun.
And I think, as I greet my family,
"Merry Christmas to everyone!"

• **A Package**

If you see a package
Gaily wrapped and tied,
Don't ask too many questions
Cause the secret's inside!

Fig. 27-16 Mosaic.

- **Waiting**

We've hung our Christmas stockings,
They look so long and thin;
And now we're waiting in our beds,
For morning to begin.

It's black outside the window,
It rattles at the door;
Oh, will tomorrow ever come?
Or won't it anymore?

- **Christmas Goodies**

It's hustle and bustle at our house,
So I try to keep out of the way.
But I sniff with delight at the goodies
That are baking for Christmas Day.

- **A Jolly Time**

Oh, Christmas is a jolly time
    No matter where you're living —
A time for songs and lights and fun
    And getting gifts — and giving.

- **Just for You**

Do you know what I'd like to do
When Santa Claus comes knocking?
I'd like to squeeze up a little
And hide behind my stocking.

And then when he opened his pack,
 I'd say, "Boo," just for fun,
And maybe it would scare him so
He'd drop his pack and run.

Now wouldn't that be fun?

- **Christmas Toys**

A ball, a book, and a tooting horn
    (For ball, make ball shape; for book, put

palms together as for a prayer gesture; for
horn, put fists together)
I hope I'll get on Christmas morn.

A ball to bounce,
    (Pretend to bounce an imaginary ball)
A book to read,
    (Put palms together and then open like a
    book)
And a horn to toot.
    (Hold fists up to mouth like a horn)

When I see Santa I'm going to say,
"Please bring me these toys on Christmas Day."

- **Santa's Visit**

When you are fast asleep in bed
Santa comes in his suit of red;
From his heavy bag he takes
A doll, a ball, a pair of skates.

Then up with his pack and out of sight.
Away he goes into the night.
If you want Santa to visit you,
These are the things that you must do:

Always listen to daddy and mother,
Be kind to your sister and brother.
And at the end of a busy day,
Pick up your toys and put them away.

If all these things you really do,
Santa Claus will visit you.

- **What Santa Brought**

Vacation time went by on wings,
Santa brought me lots of things.

A drum to beat,
    (Pretend to beat a drum and to spin a top)
A top to spin,
A puzzle to fit pieces in.

A telegraphic key to click
  (Use index finger of hand to make "clicks")
And best of all, a pogo stick!
  (Pretend to grasp pogo stick and jump)

Next Christmas I hope I get
  (Pretend to type on imaginary typewriter and to press with hand stamp)
A typewriter and a printing set,

An easel and palette of paint.
  (Hold imaginary palette in left hand, imaginary brush in right; pretend to paint on canvas set on imaginary easel)
Oh, dear! It seems so long to wait.

• **Pine Tree — Christmas Song**

(To tune of Little Teapot)

I'm a little pine tree tall and straight
Here are my branches for you to decorate.
Don't forget to put the star on top
Just be careful the balls don't drop.
Now be sure to plug in all the lights
So I will look very gay and bright.
Then put all the presents under me
I'm all set for Christmas as you see.

• **Peanut Butter Song** (See related food experience, Peanut Butter, page 282.)

Peanut, peanut butter
and JELLY (in a deep voice)
Peanut, peanut butter
and JELLY (in a deep voice)

First, you take the peanuts and you pick 'em, pick 'em, pick 'em, pick 'em (Picking gesture)
Then you smash 'em, smash 'em, smash 'em, smash 'em, smash 'em (Smash hands together)
Then you spread 'em, spread 'em, spread 'em, spread 'em (Spreading on bread gesture)
Peanut, peanut butter
and JELLY (In a deep voice)

Then you take the berries and you pick 'em, etc. (Picking gesture)
Then you smash 'em, etc. (Smash hands together)
Then you spread 'em, etc. (Spreading on bread gesture)
Peanut, peanut butter,
  and JELLY (In a deep voice) (2 times)

Then you take the sandwich and you bite it, bite it, bite it, bite it, bite it, (Biting gesture)
Then you chew it, chew it, chew it, chew it, chew it.
(Hum Peanut Butter chorus)
(Hum in a deeper voice, the JELLY part)

• **I'm Giving Some Presents**

I'm giving some presents for Christmas,
And I know I'll receive more than one.
It's not what I get that makes Christmas,
But the things that I give, that make fun.

• **A Present for Me**

When Santa comes down our chimney
With presents for under our tree,
I hope he'll remember I live here
and leave a nice present for me!

• **When Santa Claus Comes**

A good time is coming, I wish it were here,
The very best time in the whole of the year.
I'm counting each day on my fingers and thumbs,
The weeks that must pass before Santa Claus comes.
Then when the first snowflakes begin to come down.
And the wind whistles sharp and the branches are brown,
I'll not mind the cold, though my fingers it numbs,
For it brings the time nearer when Santa Claus comes.

CHILDREN'S BOOKS FOR CHRISTMAS

Carroll, Latrobe, and Carroll, Ruth, *Christmas Kitten.* Portland, Maine: Walck, 1970.

Duvoisin, Roger, *Christmas Whale.* New York: Knopf, 1945.

Lipkind, William, and Mordvinoff, Nicholas, *Christmas Bunny.* New York: Harcourt, Brace, Jovanovich, 1953.

Moore, Clement C., *The Night Before Christmas.* New York: Random House, 1962.

COOKING EXPERIENCES

- **Chocolate Walnut Balls**

Ingredients:
1 1/2 cup ground walnuts
2/3 cup confectioners' sugar
1 egg yolk
3 ounces semisweet chocolate, grated
1 teaspoon grated orange peel
2 egg whites

Materials: measuring cup, measuring spoons, large mixing bowl, small mixing bowl, grater, egg beater, mixing spoon

Procedure:
1. Grate the chocolate and the orange peel. The children can do this well under supervision.
2. Separate the eggs.
3. Beat the egg yolk in the small mixing bowl.
4. In the large mixing bowl, mix 1 cup walnuts with the sugar, egg yolk, chocolate, and orange peel.
5. Roll the mixture into balls about the size of walnuts.
6. Beat the egg whites until foamy.
7. Dip the balls into the egg whites.
8. Then roll them in the remaining ground walnuts.
9. Let them dry two hours before serving.

10. Read Robert Dahl's, *Charlie and the Chocolate Factory,* as a natural ending to this activity. Do this as the children are tasting their work.

- **Peanut Butter**

(Put in baby food jars, with a bow on top — Makes a great child-made Christmas gift.)

Ingredients:
fresh or salted peanuts
1 1/2 to 3 tablespoons corn oil to 1 cup peanuts
if nuts are unsalted, use 1/2 teaspoon salt for each cup

Materials: measuring spoons, measuring cup, blender

Procedure:
1. Shell the peanuts.
2. Put all ingredients in the blender and turn on at low speed until the peanut butter is smooth.
3. The Peanut Butter song would be an enjoyable enrichment activity after making the peanut butter, or while it is being made.

- **Santa Apple**

Santa apples make excellent table decorations, party favors, and gifts.

Materials: toothpicks, large red apples, marshmallows, gumdrops

Procedure:
1. Five marshmallows, stuck to the apple with toothpicks, make the head, arms, and legs.
2. A large red gumdrop is stuck to the head for a hat, black gumdrops make boots, red are hands.
3. Small bits of gumdrops make the features.
4. A small bit of cotton makes Santa's beard.
5. Use tiny bits of toothpicks to hold all things in place.

Unit 28 VALENTINE'S DAY

Valentine's Day began in the days of the ancient Romans who celebrated it with a festival on February 15. Young people chose partners for the festival and exchanged gifts as a sign of friendship. Around the year 500, the festival was given a religious meaning by changing the name to Saint Valentine's Day in honor of two men named Valentine, and the date was changed to February 14. In the United States, Valentine's Day became popular during the 19th century. Many valentines of that period were handpainted and elaborately decorated with ribbons and lace. Some had dried flowers, feathers, tassels, imitation gems, and even seashells. People displayed their valentines and saved them among the family keepsakes.

Some suggested topics for picturemaking include:

- I Like to Make Valentines
- Fun at a Valentine Party
- Mailing my Valentines
- Making a Valentine Box
- My Valentine Friends
- A Valentine Surprise for Mother
- Painting a Valentine

Other suggested activities:

- Valentines
- Paper Lace
- Cut-paper Hearts
- Valentine Trees
- Valentine Container
- Playing Mail Carrier
- King and Queen of Hearts
- Party Favor
- Place Mats

- **Valentines**

Procedure:
1. Design hearts using cut paper, crayon, and paint. Use brilliant colors, or pastel shades of yellow, pink, or blue.
2. Some hearts may have faces or a pattern of stripes or dots to be pierced by cupid's arrows.
3. Hearts can be used either alone or combined to form animals, people, and flowers.

- **Valentine's Day**

Procedure:
1. To cut a heart shape, first fold paper in half.
2. Then, keeping the center of the heart along the fold, cut both sides of the heart at the same time.

Fig. 28-1 Ideas for valentine's day cards.

3. Hearts attached to background paper may be decorated with bits of ribbon, yarn, paper lace, sequins, and discarded cloth flowers.

4. Valentine cards can be folded at the side, top, in accordion style or in three parts to form a window. The folding technique depends on the shape desired, such as a house, basket, flower, or bird.

- **Paper Lace**

Procedure:

1. Cut-paper lace can be made of tissue paper, paper napkins, or other thin paper.

2. Fold the paper into four or eight parts.

3. The lacy design is created by shapes cut here and there along the folds; the more cuts, the finer the design.

4. Outside edges may be scalloped or cut in a zigzag pattern.

5. Small figures of birds, flowers, or stars can be added to complete the design.

- **King and Queen of Hearts**

Procedure:

1. For the figure of the king, use a toweling roll covered with construction paper and crowned with little paper hearts.

2. A piece of paper rolled into a cone shape forms the queen's body. Make a tiny slit at the top to hold a heart-shaped head, with paper lace for the crown.

3. Royal robes may be made of paper or cloth, trimmed in sequins, hearts, metallic foil, or paper lace.

- **Playing Mail Carrier**

Young children enjoy dramatizing everyday experiences. They can play-act mailing valentines and delivering them by a mail carrier.

Fig. 28-2 Paper lace.

Fig. 28-3 King and queen of hearts.

Procedure:

1. A sturdy cardboard box with half the top closed and the other half folded back makes a good mailbox when painted appropriately.

2. A mail carrier's bag may consist of a large, heavy paper sack with an old belt for the shoulder strap.

3. Half an oatmeal box painted with a visor of construction paper can serve as the mail carrier's hat.

Fig. 28-4 Valentine containers.

Fig. 28-5 Gumdrops and marshmallow tree.

• **Valentine Containers**

Procedure:

1. Begin the project with a large cardboard box, tin can, or basket.
2. Decorate the containers with bits of ribbon made into bows or cut-paper hearts, paper lace, and discarded trimmings such as flowers, feathers, and sequins.
3. Boxes can be made into a house, truck, or train loaded with valentines.

Fig. 28-6   Paper hearts, toothpick and marshmallow decorations.

• **Valentine Tree**

A decorative centerpiece may be a group project.

Procedure:

1. The tree consists of a small tree branch set in sand or clay.
2. Trim the tree with paper flowers, hearts, birds, and ribbons.

Fig. 28-7 Gumdrop and toothpick animals.

• **Party Ideas**

— Fasten little, red gumdrops to a small twig stuck into a marshmallow.

— Paste paper hearts onto a toothpick and insert it into a marshmallow or gumdrop.

— Create little heart figures with gumdrops and toothpicks.

— Use a heart-shaped lollipop for the head and body of a valentine figure. For dresses, use paper lace fastened with pipe cleaners at the base of the heart. Paste little paper

Fig. 28-8 Valentine figures.

hearts to the ends of the pipe cleaners for hands. The lollipop may be set into a gum-drop for a base.

- **For a Party Table**

— Decorate the edges of paper plates with hearts or flowers from cut paper.

— Make place mats of white roll paper decorated with valentine designs.

— Use one of the candy treat ideas for place cards.

— Make candy cups from: egg cartons, match boxes, paper cups, frozen pie tins.

- **Painted Valentines**

Procedure:

1. Cut a large heart from a piece of brown wrapping paper.
2. Have the children paint these large hearts red.
3. Colored construction paper scraps may be pasted on for decoration.

- **Valentine Greeting Cards**

For making valentine cards, use the basic techniques for making holiday greeting cards at the beginning of unit 27.

Fig. 28-9 Painted valentine decorated with cut paper.

PERSONALIZED VALENTINE GIFTS

- **Have a Ball**

Procedure:

1. Have the children make their own balls from old socks filled with rags or packing materials.
2. Seal them with masking tape.

- **Hands and Feet**

Procedure:

1. Place a large sheet of paper on the floor.
2. Have the children dip their hands in finger paint and make handprints on the paper.
3. Label each pair of hands with the child's name.
4. Have the children take off their shoes and socks and do the same with their feet.
5. Make sure a pail of water and paper towels are ready to use for cleanup.

- **Mosaics on the Roof**

Here's a unique, yet easy to obtain, raw material that can liven up mosaics.

Procedure:

1. Tiny granules that have fallen off roofing shingles are available in many colors from roofing and construction supply companies.
2. Have the children draw designs, put glue on the area to be covered, and sprinkle on the granules. They look great on valentines.

- **Cleanup Paintings**

One art form can lead to another. Did you ever think of cleaning up excess paint from a dripped paint mural with a blotter?

Procedure:

1. If the paint is thick, it will not dry quickly. Use a large blotter to soak up the excess paint from the mural.

2. Then, cut the blotter into smaller panels.

• Sponge Print Valentines

Procedure:

1. Add natural sponges to your printing supplies.
2. Put primary colors in two pie pans.
3. Have each child dip a sponge in one and then the other color.
4. Print on construction paper. The sponges will mix the colors and print interesting, irregular patterns on a paper heart of any size.

• Decorated Doilies

Materials: paper doilies (which can be purchased inexpensively in a dime store), coloring materials, red construction paper, paste

Procedure:

1. Distribute the doilies.
2. Let the children decorate them with color. The intricacy of the doily lends itself to beautiful color designs.
3. For a variation, a red paper heart may be pasted in the center before coloring the doily.

• Love Puzzles

Materials: heavy paper, scissors, coloring materials

Procedure:

1. Draw fairly large hearts.
2. Have the children decorate them.
3. On the back, draw lines to create a jigsaw-type puzzle. Cut along the lines to make the puzzle.

• Valentine Creatures

Procedure:

1. Cut one large red construction paper heart for the body, and a smaller one for the head.

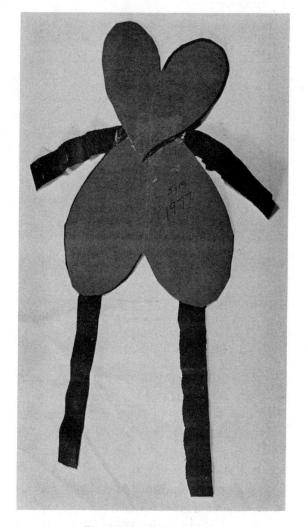

Fig. 28-10 Kitten valentine.

2. Use thin (1/2″) strips of 3″ long black construction paper for arms and legs.
3. Accordion pleat (fold) these strips and attach them at the sides and bottom of the body for arms and legs.

• Valentine Boxes

These boxes make good 3-dimensional bulletin board displays or boxes to hold valentines. They may also be hung as mobiles.

Procedure:

1. Cut two hearts the same size from oak tag or colored bristol. (If you use oak tag, it should be covered with paper

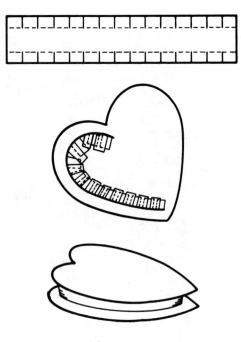

Fig. 28-11 Valentine boxes.

rather than painted, since paint tends to warp this material.)

2. Cut long strips of construction paper in the same color, making the strip as wide as you want the box deep, plus an extra inch for tabs.
3. Measure one-half inch in on each side.
4. Fold and make slashes to the creases.
5. Fold tabs and glue around the edge of one heart. Glue the second heart to the tabs on the other side and decorate.
6. To make a box that opens, fold the strips only on one side and attach to one heart. Then attach another strip to the second heart. (Attach it a little further in from the edges so that this side will fit inside the other.)

FINGER PLAYS AND POEMS

• **Be My Valentine**

Do you know what this is?
  (Put thumbs and forefingers together to make a heart shape)
Yes, a heart. Pretend it's mine.
  (Point to self)

I'll put it on a paper,
And make a valentine.
  (Make heart again and pretend to put it on an imaginary piece of paper on the desk or table in front of you)
Into an envelope it will go,
  (Pretend to grasp paper in one hand and slide it into imaginary envelope held in fingers of the other hand.)
With address written clear.
  (Pretend to write address with imaginary pen.)
Soon you'll pull it out and read:
  (Reverse pantomime for placing letter in envelope)
"To my valentine so dear."
  (Pretend to hold up a valentine and read its message)
That's you!
  (Point to someone)

• **Valentines**

Valentines, valentines
How many do you see?
Valentines, valentines
Count them with me.

One for father
  (Put up thumb)
One for mother
  (Put up index finger)
One for grandma
  (Put up third finger)
One for sister
  (Put up fourth finger)
One for brother
  (Put up pinkie finger)
And here is one for you!
  (Blow a kiss)

MOVEMENT GAMES

In a discussion with the children, make a list of objects that describe Valentine's Day. Have the children use movement to express these ideas. Encourage creativity. Some ideas that could be used include:

- Making valentines
- Delivering valentines
- Heart shapes
- Mailing valentines

- **Valentine Game**

(Variation of Button Game)

Use a red button, if possible. Children pretend it is a tiny valentine heart. (The teacher may wish to use a candy heart instead.)

One child has a large red button or valentine. The rest of the children fold their hands and close their eyes. The one with the button goes to each person, dropping the button into one closed hand along the way. When the child has gone to everyone in the class, someone else asks who has the button. This child asks another until the button has been found.

Insist on clear speech, for example,

Question: "Billy, do you have the valentine?"
Answer: "No, Jane, I do not have the valentine."

- **Valentine Relay**

Divide the class into equal teams. Paste a large valentine heart up on a wall or chalkboard for each team.

The first child in line runs (walks, hops, crawls, etc.) from the line to the valentine, touches the valentine (or for older children, puts his initial on it), and returns to the end of his team line (using the same movement). The next child in line repeats the process. The first group finished is the winning team. The prize: valentine candy hearts.

Unit 29 EASTER

Easter is a festival celebrating the end of winter and the coming of spring. Traditional Easter customs include the visit of the Easter bunny, having baskets heaped with candy, decorating brightly colored eggs, feasting with family and friends, and hunting for Easter eggs.

People dressed in spring clothes attend church services or join the Easter parade, while children in the nation's capital participate in the egg-rolling race on the lawn at the White House. Some topics for picture-making include:

- Decorating Eggs for Easter
- Shopping for Easter
- A Beautiful Egg Tree
- A Visit from the Easter Bunny
- My Easter Basket
- Walking in the Easter Parade

Other suggested art activities:

- Decorating Eggs
- An Egg Tree
- Easter Parade
- Chick in an Egg
- Mr. and Mrs. Rabbit
- Easter Baskets
- Egg Portraits
- Funny Bunny

- **Decorating Eggs**

Several ideas for egg decorations include:

1. Make an interesting line design on an egg by wrapping rubber bands or string around the hard-boiled egg, dipping it in dye or paint, and removing it when dry.

Fig. 29-1 Easter egg decorations.

2. Stipple design the egg with a piece of cotton or a sponge dipped in dye or food coloring; more than one color may be used. This can complete the decoration, or be the beginning of a more elaborate design.
3. Decorate eggs with ribbon, braid, sequins, little beads, or metallic foil.
4. Draw directly on eggshells with crayon, then dip eggs in dye to create a resist effect.
5. Paint free spontaneous designs in brilliant colors.

290

Fig. 29-2 Egg tree.

Fig. 29-3 Mr. and Mrs. Rabbit.

- **Egg Portraits**

Procedure:

1. Make the facial features with crayon or cut paper.
2. Make ears, hair, collar, and hat with scraps of cloth, yarn, string, or paper to complete the design.
3. Eggs can be displayed sitting in a section of an egg carton, in a bottle cap, or in a ring of construction paper.

- **Egg Tree**

Procedure:

1. Place a small branch in a vase or set it into a box of sand or plaster of Paris.
2. The tree can be trimmed with eggs cut from construction paper decorated with metallic foil, tissue paper, or paper lace.
3. Hard-boiled eggs can be hung when wrapped with ribbon or string, leaving a loop at one end.
4. To blow out an egg, shake it a few times to loosen the membrane. Make a hole at either end, and blow steadily into one of the openings. (See page 294, "Blown Eggs")

5. Insert a piece of string or wire through the holes making a knot or loop at one end. If eggs are to be dyed, this must be done before removing the contents.

- **Mr. and Mrs. Rabbit**

Procedure:

1. Use small, cardboard towel tubes for bodies.
2. Decorate with construction paper.
3. Add ears, whiskers, and a tail to complete the design.

- **Easter Baskets**

Suitable containers include oatmeal boxes cut in half, plastic tomato racks or berry boxes, small food cartons, frozen pie tins, and plastic detergent bottles cut down to a basket shape.

Procedure:

1. Decorate baskets with construction paper, wallpaper, ribbon, braid, discarded flowers, or feathers.
2. Interesting objects found in Easter baskets may include chicks, bunnies, and eggs modeled in clay or made of cut paper, settled in curled tissue grass.

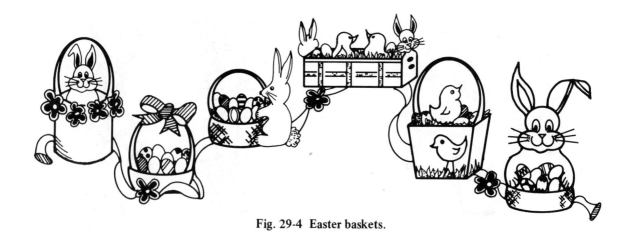

Fig. 29-4 Easter baskets.

• **Easter Parade**

Procedure:

1. Draw figures dressed in their Sunday best, and cut them out.
2. Cut cardboard tubes into sections and fasten them to the base of the parade figures, so they can stand freely.
3. Display the Easter Parade on a table or counter top.
4. Make a background for the figures by folding construction paper in accordion folds.
5. Cut rooftops along one end to indicate a city scene.

• **Chick in an Egg**

Procedure:

1. Use the upper half of an empty eggshell leaving enough room to hold a little chick.
2. Fasten the shell to sit upright in a ring of paper and fill the shell with paper grass.
3. Chicks may be modeled in clay or made of cut paper.

• **Funny Bunny**

Procedure:

1. Model a bunny from a large wad of shredded paper.

Fig. 29-5 Chick in an egg.

2. Wind white thread or string around to hold the shape of the body, head, legs, and tail as they are formed.
3. Ears, eyes, and whiskers can be made of cut paper glued in place.

• **Polish Paper Cutting**

Paper cutting is an Easter tradition in Poland. Children can make similar paper cuttings for cards and decorations.

Procedure:

1. On a folded piece of lightweight white paper, have each child draw a design. Traditional designs include roosters, flowers, stars, and eggs.

2. The cutouts can be mounted on construction paper, folded to make a card, or left flat for a wall decoration.

• **Egg Hangers**

Procedure:

1. Cut free-form shapes or spring shapes such as chicks, bunnies, and flowers from dark-colored tissue paper.
2. The children select a shape and glue it on pastel-colored tissue paper.
3. Bend coat hangers to form egg shapes.
4. The children place their coat hanger on tissue so that the hanger encircles the shapes.
5. Over the hanger, lay another sheet of the same-color tissue paper.
6. Mix one part white glue with one part water. The children paint the mixture over the tissue paper and across the parts that cover the hanger frame.
7. The children trim the tissue extending beyond the frame after the tissue dries.

• **Easter Bunnies**

Materials: paper, scissors, colored paper, staples, glue

Procedure:

1. Take a rectangular-shaped piece of paper and roll it into a cylinder.
2. Staple it or paste it together.
3. From another piece of paper, cut out ears and attach (paste) them to the cylinder. The ears will look more realistic if they are creased down the center before attaching them.
4. Using colored paper, add eyes, nose, mouth, eyelashes, and a tail. (Cotton balls are even better for tails!)

• **Cut-Paper Bunnies and Baskets**

Procedure:

1. Have children either cut or tear colored construction paper into egg shapes.

Fig. 29-6 (a) Cut-paper bunny.

Fig. 29-6 (b) Torn-paper basket.

2. Children fill a paper basket with the colored paper eggs.

- **Blown Eggs for Easter**

"Blown" eggs decorated by the children and hung on a small tree or branch make a lovely center of visual interest.

Procedure:

1. To "blow" an egg, puncture a small hole in each end of the egg with a sharp instrument, such as a large needle.
2. Insert the needle into one hole and wiggle it around a bit to break up the egg mass.
3. Blow into the top hole while holding the the egg over a bowl. The yolk and white will drain out leaving the shell intact. (This is fun for children to watch, but usually too difficult for them to do! They can color the shell, however.)
4. To hang the shell on the branch, tie a thread to one-half of a toothpick, making a loop. Drop the toothpick in the hole while holding the thread. When the thread is pulled up, the toothpick catches at right angles to the hole, and forms an anchor for the loop.
5. The tree can be made by selecting a branch of the desired shape and size, and standing it upright in a container of sand or hanging it, like a mobile, from the ceiling. The branch can be painted or wrapped in foil, if desired.

- **Miniature Easter Hats**

Procedure:

1. Save the empty plastic cream containers provided by restaurants.
2. Cut small (1 1/2" – 2" diameter) circles out of colored paper.
3. Glue the cream container onto these circles.
4. A small artificial flower may be glued on for an added decoration.
5. These may also be hung on the Egg Tree, described on page 291.

Fig. 29-7 Miniature Easter hats.

Fig. 29-8 Paper plate bunny.

- **Paper Plate Bunnies**

Procedure:

1. Use plain, white, dinner-size paper plates.
2. Have the children cut ears, nose, eyes, mouth, and eyelashes from colored construction paper.

3. Paste the features onto the paper plate.
4. Punch a hole for string and hang for room decorations.

• **March Special**

Procedure:

1. Circle Easter on the calendar. Invite children to relate the events if their families have special activities at Easter time.
2. Display a large cutout of an Easter basket.
3. Give the children large paper egg shapes of different colors.
4. On the paper eggs, the teacher can write (older children may write their own) Easter activities such as going to church, visiting grandparents, dyeing eggs, etc. Then the children may decorate the eggs as they wish. Children pin their eggs on the basket.

• **Egg Shapes**

Procedure:

1. Collect 10 or more egg shapes, plastic Easter toys, panty hose packages, or egg cartons.
2. Mark a different numeral on the top half of each egg and the same numeral on its bottom half.
3. Separate the halves and mix them together. The children make eggs by finding the matching numerals.

• **Easter Egg Drawings**

Materials: paper, coloring materials, scissors, glue or staples, 8 1/2″ x 11″ pieces of paper (two for each child)

Procedure:

1. On one piece of paper, each child creates an overall design.
2. The child folds the other paper in half. On the fold, have each child draw half an oval. (The teacher may need to assist younger children with this.)

3. When the paper is cut along the half-oval, it will make the shape of an egg. This paper is glued or stapled over the design paper. It creates a framed Easter egg that can be used as a greeting card.

• **Different Easter Baskets**

Procedure:

1. For each basket, cut a 12-inch square from brightly colored construction paper. It is best if the teacher cuts enough squares for each child who wants to make a basket. (The squares will be more accurate and easier to fold.)
2. The children then fold the paper in half, unfold it, and fold each side into the center fold.

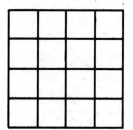
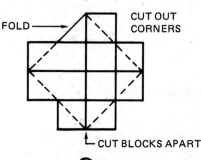

Fig. 29-9 A different kind of Easter basket.

3. Unfold the paper and turn it a quarter turn. Repeat the process. There are now 16 squares.
4. Cut out the corner squares.
5. Then separate the two remaining squares on each side by cutting on the crease down to the next fold. Fold these two squares diagonally towards each other so each makes a triangle.
6. Overlap the triangles and glue.
7. Add a paper or pipe-cleaner handle and decorate.

• **Easter Baskets**

Procedure:
1. Easter baskets can be made from many different kinds of materials: for example, paper cones or box shapes constructed from paper; plastic or wax cardboard refrigerator containers such as margarine or cottage cheese tubs; plastic bottles cut to various shapes; milk or orange juice cartons cut down; paper baking or drinking cups.
2. String, yarn, pipe cleaners or construction-paper strips can be used as basket handles.
3. Any type of scrap materials make good decorations, along with dried macaroni, egg shells, and many other items.

• **Paper Bag Bunnies**

Procedure:
1. Stuff two large paper bags with crumpled newspaper, ending up with rounded shapes.
2. Partially fill two other paper bags and twist for ears.
3. Cover with layers of papier-maché, using a flour and water paste and strips of newspaper. Be sure the strips dry between layers.
4. Cover with cotton tufts.

5. Poke holes in the rabbit's head and insert ears (also covered with papier-maché). Add construction-paper features.

• **Egg Personalities**

Procedure:
1. Egg personalities can be made from hard-boiled eggs that are painted, bewigged, and dressed with cloth or paper scraps.
2. Make stands from inverted sections of an egg carton.
3. Construction-paper rings or decorated small juice cans complete the project.

• **More Baskets**

Procedure:
1. Have the children cut basket shapes from construction paper and paste them onto a different colored background.
2. Fill the baskets by: (a) drawing and painting flowers in them, (b) cutting stems and flowers from paper and pasting them on, or (c) by collecting grasses, leaves, or twigs from outside and gluing them on.

MOVEMENT AND GAMES

In a discussion with the children at Easter time, make a list of feelings and objects that describe the holiday. Then have the children use movement to express these ideas. Encourage creativity. Several ideas include:

rabbits	spring flowers
eggs	windy
nests	coloring

• **Egg Roll**

Have the children curl up into balls as round as they can, and roll on the floor, trying to roll forward, sideways, and backward.

• **Easter Parade**

Wearing Easter hats, decorated by themselves, the children march around the room to the music of a radio or record player. Next, have the children "dance" to the music. Children enjoy waving old scarves, flags, feathers, or bells as they dance. Each child can move about in his own particular way. An old pair of tap shoes adds an exciting variation.

• Everyone Do This

Children take turns doing something active (hopping like a bunny, clapping hands, turning around) while others imitate. Everyone sings:

Everybody do this, do this, do this,
Everybody do this, just like me.

Variation: Same action, but different words:

Simon says do this, do this, do this,
Simon says do this, just like me.

• Here We Go 'Round the Bunny's House

(Variation to "Here We Go 'Round the Mulberry Bush")

Modify the song and games as follows:

Here we go 'round the bunny's house (etc.)
This is the way we color eggs (etc.)
This is the way we dress so nice (etc.)

• Bunny Top Game

The group is lined up across the room. One player is "Bunny Top." He stands about 5 feet in front of and facing in the same direction as the rest of the group. At the signal, all the players jump forward in response to the chant, "Hippity, hippity — hop," hopping on each word. Bunny Top then says, "You're not allowed to stop," as he hops forward 3 times. This continues back and forth, first the group hopping, then Bunny Top. At the end of any phrase, Bunny Top may whirl around and hop back, attempting to touch the other players. Those he catches before they get back to the starting line, become his helpers.

FINGER PLAYS AND POEMS

• The Easter Rabbit

The Easter Rabbit keeps a very
Cheerful hen that likes to lay
Blue and red and green and yellow
Eggs for him on Easter Day.

He puts the eggs inside his basket
With a lot of other things,
Bunnies with pink ears and whiskers,
Little chicks with tickling wings.

Then on tip-toe he comes hopping
Hiding secrets everywhere,
Speckled eggs behind the mirror
Sugar bird nests in the chair.

If we saw him we would give him
Tender lettuce leaves to eat.
But he slips out very softly
On pussy-willow feet.

• The Bunny

Tall ears,
Twinkly nose,
Tiny tail,
And hop he goes!

His ears are long,
His tail is small,
And he doesn't make
Any noise at all.
(Repeat the first verse.)

• Easter

I'm sure a bunny
Must remember
Everything he's told
Because his ears
Are oh, so large,
Just think how much they hold!

• April First

Little bears have three feet;
(Hold up three fingers or touch a flat surface with three fingers)

Little birds have four;
  (Use four fingers in same way)
Little cows have two feet;
  (Use two fingers in same way)
And girls and boys have more.
  (Use five fingers in same way)
Do you believe my story?
  (Point to "you," then point to own fore-
  head, then mouth)
Do you believe my song?
  (Point to "you," then point to own fore-
  head, then throat)
I'll tell it only once a year,
  (Hold up index finger for "once")
When April comes along.
APRIL FOOL!
  (Clap hands to express pleasure)

• **The Bunny**

Here is a bunny, with ears so funny
  (Fingers form ears, hands for head)
And here is a hole in the ground.
  (Hand on hip forms hole in ground)
When a slight noise he hears,
He pricks up his ears,
And jumps in the hole in the ground.

• **Wiggle Song**

(Children sitting very quietly at beginning)
My thumbs are starting to wiggle,
  (Wiggle thumbs)
My thumbs are starting to wiggle,
My thumbs are starting to wiggle,
    Around, around, around.
My hands are starting to wiggle (3 times)
  (Wiggle hands)
    Around, around, around.
My arms are starting to wiggle (3 times)
  (Wiggle arms)
    Around, around, around.
My head is starting to wiggle (3 times)
  (Wiggle head)
    Around, around, around.

Now all of me is wiggling (3 times)
  (Wiggle entire body)
    Around, around, around.

(Children can suggest other parts of the body
— nose, feet, etc. — to add to the song.) Read
Humbug Rabbit, by Lorna Balian (Abingdon,
1974).

CHILDREN'S BOOKS FOR EASTER

Dr. Seuss, *Horton Hatches the Egg.* New
  York: Random House, 1940.
Friskey, Margaret, *Chicken Little, Count to
  Ten.* New York: Children's Press, 1946.
Lefevre, Felicite, *The Cock, the Mouse, and
  the Little Red Hen.* New York: Dufair,
  1959.
McCloskey, Robert, *Make Way for Ducklings.*
  New York: Viking Press, 1941.
Potter, Beatrix, *The Tale of Peter Rabbit.*
  New York: Western Publishing Co., 1970.
Zolotow, Charlotte, *Mr. Rabbit and the
  Lovely Present.* New York: Harper and
  Row, 1962.

COOKING EXPERIENCES

• **Cole Slaw**

Ingredients:
a small head of cabbage, grated
1 small onion, chopped fine (or 1 tablespoon
  dried, chopped onion)
1 tablespoon sugar
2 tablespoons mayonnaise
salt and pepper to taste

Materials: knife for chopping onion, grater,
        measuring spoons, mixing spoon,
        mixing bowl

Procedure:
1. Chop the onion (in an onion chopper).
   If dried onions are being used, simply
   measure the amount needed.
2. Grate the cabbage.

3. Put everything in the mixing bowl and mix well.
4. Chill before serving.

(A good story to read in association with this activity is *The Tale of Peter Rabbit* by Beatrix Potter.)

• **Cheesey Carrots (Snack Time)**

Ingredients:

yellow cheese, grated (cheddar, American, colby, etc.)

cream or mayonnaise

Materials: grater, mixing bowl, mixing spoon

Procedure:

1. Let the children grate the cheese into the mixing bowl. (A blender can be faster, but less fun.)
2. Mix the shredded cheese with just a little cream or mayonnaise until the mixture can be shaped with the hands.
3. Shape into tiny carrots.
4. Put a sprig of parsley on the end of each cheese carrot.

(A natural follow-up to this activity is to read the book, *The Carrot Seed* by Ruth Krauss, Scholastic Book Services.)

• **Carrot Salad**

Ingredients:

4 large carrots

1/2 cup seedless raisins

1/2 cup chopped peanuts

3/4 teaspoon salt, dash of pepper

1 tablespoon lemon juice

1 cup sour cream

Materials: knife for chopping peanuts (or a nut chopper), vegetable parer for scraping carrots, grater (or blender), measuring cup, measuring spoons, mixing bowl

Procedure:

1. Let the children chop the nuts in a nut chopper or even in a blender.
2. Wash and scrape the carrots.
3. Grate the carrots.
4. Mix everything together and serve with sour cream, or mix a few tablespoons of sour cream into the salad before serving.

(Read *The Carrot Seed* for this activity, too.)

Unit 30 SPRING AND SUMMER

The gradual coming of spring brings many signs of beauty, such as the color and texture of flowers in the sunlight or the pattern of delicate leaves against the sky. Children can share their experiences during a class discussion or they can bring in objects of nature for closer observation. Objects may include a bouquet of dandelions, a piece of moss, some pussy willows, or a budding tree branch. These discoveries motivate children to learn by stimulating their curiosity about the world around them and arousing new interests and ideas.

In picturemaking, children can express their feelings and understanding of the beauty of spring and summer in many ways. Some topics include:

- Spring Flowers
- Walking on a Windy Day
- Flying Kites
- Birds in Spring
- Planting Seeds in the Garden
- Playing Outdoors in Spring and Summer
- Helping with Spring Cleaning
- My New Spring and Summer Clothes

Other suggested art activities:

- Flowers
- Birds
- Toy Kites
- Butterflies
- Miniature Garden

- **Spring Flowers**

Procedure:

1. Paper can be rolled, twisted, fringed, curled, or folded into a desired flower shape.
2. Suitable papers include: newsprint, construction paper, tissue paper, metallic foil, cellophane, gift wrapping. Discarded materials are also useful, such as paper cupcake liners, small frozen pie tins, paper cups, toweling tubes, egg cartons.
3. Stems can be made from pipe cleaners, toothpicks, wire, tongue depressors, paper drinking straws, popsicle sticks.
4. Small discarded flower pots, egg carton, plastic bottles, juice cans, or rolled corrugated cardboard can be used for

Fig. 30-1 Spring flower designs.

flower containers. They can be covered with paper or painted.

5. Use paper flowers in decorative ways, such as a flower show, store or garden in a bulletin board display or three-dimensional exhibit.

- **Butterflies**

Procedure:

1. Fold a sheet of paper in half, then open it and place generous spots of paints on one side of the paper.
2. Fold the blank side over the wet, painted area and press.
3. Cut or tear the paper into a desired shape while folded. Open and allow to dry.
4. Add a body and antennae with cut paper. Wings may be cut in lacy designs. Then fill the open area with various colors.

- **Birds**

Procedure:

1. Draw the body and head on one piece of paper and cut it out.
2. Repeat the design on the other side.
3. Colorful wings and tail feathers can be folded, curled, or fringed, and then attached to the body.

Fig. 30-3 Bird and insect designs.

4. Another bird can be made by folding a piece of paper in half and cutting a half-circle with the center along the fold.
5. Cut along the fold about halfway, and fold back pieces to form the wings.
6. Add a design in crayon or cut paper.
7. Use sequins, glitter, and metallic foil when making birds and butterflies, to create unusual textural effects.
8. Display birds singly or group them on a tree branch inserted in a box. Butterflies may be added to the exhibit.

- **Miniature Garden**

Procedure:

1. Suitable containers include frozen pie tins, or a discarded dish or bowl. Other possible containers are empty tin cans, cheese cartons, or cut down plastic bottles covered with colored paper or metallic foil.
2. Fill containers with soil and plant whatever seeds are available such as grass seed, lentil beans, and carrot seeds for the tops.

Fig. 30-2 Bird and butterfly mobile on branch.

Fig. 30-4   Toy kites.

3. Add a few small stones or pebbles for texture.
4. Add a small clay turtle, frog, or bird; or make a cut-paper butterfly or ladybug fastened to a stick.

• **Toy Kites**

Procedure:

1. Begin with a piece of 12″ x 18″ construction paper, or use newsprint if a larger size is desired.
2. After making the design in crayon or paint, the paper can be folded and stapled with all corners toward the center in a diamond shape.
3. Strips of masking tape may be crisscrossed on the back for reinforcement and a string fastened in the center.
4. A tail can be added using several bow ties of cloth or paper tied to a length of string.
5. Smaller kites make colorful room decorations when used on bulletin boards or strung across open areas.

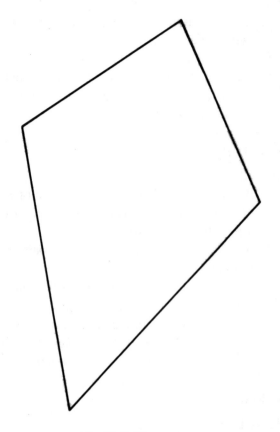

Fig. 30-5   Kite pattern.

• **Windswept**

Procedure:

1. Spread newspaper on the floor.
2. Give each child a full sheet of white or pastel construction paper.
3. Place the papers on the newspaper.
4. Put a dab of red, yellow, blue, and white tempera paint on each paper.
5. Give each child a small piece of cardboard.
6. The children push, pull, turn, and twist the cardboard through the paint puddles to create windswept strips and patches of color.
7. Do this activity outside for the best results.

• **Blow Painting**

Procedure:

1. Place sheets of typing paper on a flat surface.

2. Give each child a small amount of watery tempera paint in a container and a plastic spoon.

3. The children spoon a very *small* puddle of tempera on the paper.

4. They use a straw to blow the paint in various directions, creating a variety of patterns.

5. To create interesting wind patterns, have the children experiment with blowing gently, hard, and so forth.

- **Windy Day Painting**

Procedure:

1. Wet white construction paper with water.

2. Give each child a small amount of red, yellow, blue, and white *dry* tempera and several small strips of cardboard.

3. The children use the cardboard strips to paint a windy day by quickly brushing the dry tempera onto the wet surface. Encourage the children to mix and blend the colors.

4. Wind motion can be used to create unusual effects with the strips. Push, pull, and twist the paint over the surface.

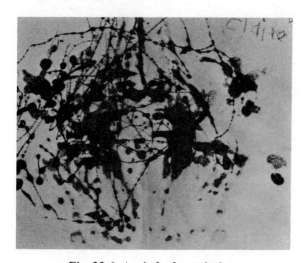

Fig. 30-6 A windy day painting.

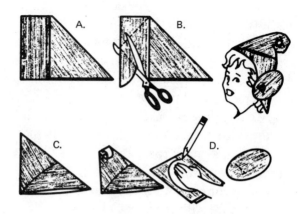

Fig. 30-7 Making a leprechaun hat.

- **Leprechaun Hat**

Procedure:

1. Fold a 12″ x 18″ sheet of green construction paper to form a triangle.

2. On the portion of the paper extending beyond the triangle, pinch the edge at the center.

3. Draw a diagonal line from that center to each upper corner of the triangle.

4. Cut along the two lines.

5. Fold and paste down the triangle flap.

6. Curl the pasted peak with the scissors blades.

7. To make leprechaun ears, trace the child's hand on folded paper. (Fingers should be close together with the thumb tucked underneath.) Cut the hand shape from the folded paper to make a pair of ears. Cut a narrow hole in the center of each ear shape.

8. The children put on their hats and then slip on their "ears."

- **Peekers**

Procedure:

1. Mount pictures of familiar objects (elephant, rabbit, dog, airplane, orange, etc.).

2. Help children identify the pictures.

3. Take three pieces of cardboard, each large enough to cover the pictures.

Cut a few small holes in one piece of cardboard, medium-size holes in the next, and large holes in the third cardboard.

4. Place the cardboard with the small holes over a selected picture.
5. A child guesses what the picture is from the parts seen through the holes. If the child can't guess correctly, place the cardboard with the medium-size holes over the picture, and if necessary, use the cardboard with the large holes.

• **Peek-A-Boo**

Procedure:
1. Cut out a large magazine picture of an object or animal.
2. Cut the picture into narrow strips.
3. Place the strips in a large envelope.
4. The children pull out one strip at a time and try to guess what the picture is.
5. When they think they have guessed correctly, they put all the strips together to check their response.

• **Color of Spring**

Procedure:
1. Cut out color pictures of spring scenes and hang them around the room.
2. Ask the children why they think these particular pictures were hung around the room today.
3. Encourage the children to see on the calendar that March 21 is the first day of spring, and that these are pictures of spring.
4. Ask volunteers to point out areas of red, blue, and yellow in the pictures.
5. Help the class determine which color is used most in spring pictures, and which color is second.
6. Provide time for the children to draw their own spring pictures.

• **The Greens**

Purpose: To sharpen color discrimination.

Preparation: Circle Saint Patrick's Day on the calendar. Show and discuss the color (green) associated with this occasion.

Procedure:
1. Pin a piece of green paper on a bulletin board.
2. Have the children find green cloth and paper to cut pieces from and pin on the board. Allow the pieces to overlap to create a green collage.
3. Magazines and old wrapping paper provide good sources for "greens."
4. As a variation, use the previous three steps, but increase the level of difficulty. When the children find a green color, they must compare it with each cloth and paper piece on the board to make

Fig. 30-8 Saint Patrick's Day hat.

sure that the sample is not the same shade already displayed. If it is, then the color cannot be added to the collage.

- **Saint Patrick's Day Hat**

Procedure:

1. Attach an 8" x 10" piece of green construction paper to a 2" wide band cut to fit around the child's head.
2. A small square may be pasted on to be a buckle ornament.

- **Bird Mobiles**

Procedure:

1. Each child cuts the body of a large bird from oak tag or a double thickness of construction paper.
2. The tail and wings are made by folding pieces of paper like fans. The tail is one fan stapled to the body. The wings are a single fan pinched in the middle to make both wings.
3. To attach, cut a hole in the body and push the wings through.
4. The birds are strung and hung from the ceiling, a wire, or a large tree branch set in plaster of Paris.

5. Air currents in the room will keep the birds moving.
6. For a variation, attach cut-paper birds to a twig (with string), and tie on cut-paper leaves. Hang with yarn as a mobile.

- **Easy 3-Dimensional Flowers**

Procedure:

1. Cut colored construction paper into squares of different sizes. Each square can be made into a 3-dimensional flower.
2. To make one flower, for example, fold the square in half two times and around the outside edges (those with no folds) to create a circle.
3. Fringe the rounded edge and unfold.

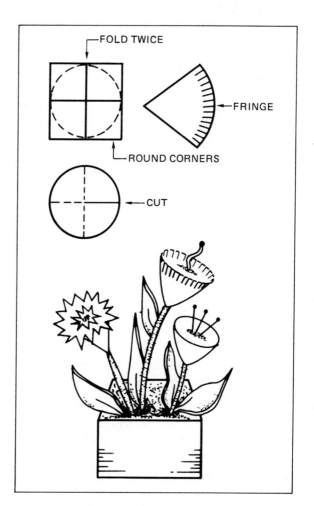

Fig. 30-10 3-dimensional flowers.

Fig. 30-9 Bird mobile on string.

Fig. 30-11 Cut-paper toothpick flowers in egg carton.

4. The flower can then be decorated with crayon lines, spots, or other touches.
5. Now cut from the outside to the center on one fold.
6. Overlap one side over the other and paste.
7. A pipe cleaner with one end folded over may be pushed down through the center for a stem.
8. Small boxes filled with sand and painted or decorated make attractive flowerpots.

Note: Another cut-paper flower activity is shown in figure 30-11.

- **Stand-up Painted Faces**

Procedure:
1. Small children can easily roll a piece of paper to form a cylinder. Let them start with paper about 12″ x 12″.
2. Paste the edges and fasten, pressing from the inside to make the paste hold securely.
3. Stand the cylinder on end.
4. Paint eyes, nose, mouth, teeth, glasses, freckles, cheeks, ears, hair, mustache, and any other features desired. Do not forget to paint the back of the head.
5. Cut-paper shirts, collars, and ties can also be added.
6. Each child will have an individual "face" and will be pleased that it is three dimensional.

Fig. 30-12 Stand-up painted faces.

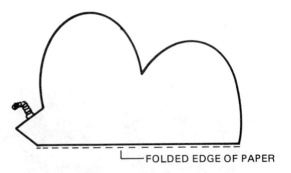

Fig. 30-13 Butterfly pattern – beginning.

- **Paper Butterflies**

Procedure:
1. Have children draw butterflies (or use the butterfly patterns in figures 30-13 and 30-14).
2. Use finger paint, regular tempera paint, or crayons to decorate the butterflies.

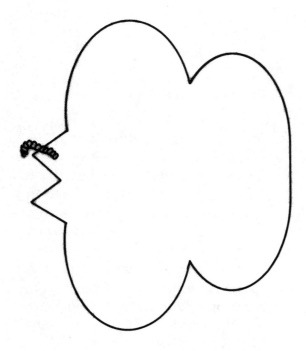

Fig. 30-14 Butterfly pattern — end.

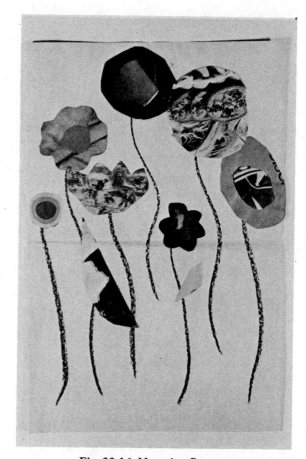

Fig. 30-16 Magazine flowers.

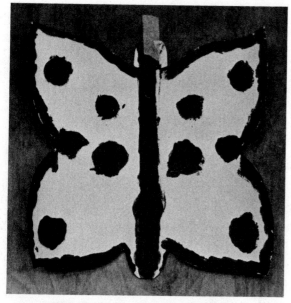

Fig. 30-15 Brush-painted butterfly.

- **Magazine Flowers**

Procedure:

1. Cut out the top of flower shapes from colored pictures in shiny-paged magazines. Simple, rounded-type shapes are good.

2. Children glue the flower shapes to a piece of colored construction paper or manila paper.
3. The stems and leaves as well as the background can then be colored in.

- **Cupcake Liner Flowers**

Procedure:

1. Use multicolored cupcake pan liners to make flowers.
2. Glue the liners to a piece of construction paper.
3. Decorate the centers of the flowers by gluing on (with white glue) bits of colored paper, popcorn, sawdust, etc., for a textured effect.
4. Color on the stems and leaves, or glue on cut-paper pieces.

Fig. 30-17 Paper plate clown face.

Fig. 30-18 Mother's Day card.

- **Paper Plate Clown Faces**

Procedure:
1. Use a white paper plate for the clown's face.
2. Paste on cut-paper features for eyes, hair, nose, and mouth.

- **Mother's Day**

Procedure:
1. The children can give "themselves" to their mothers for Mother's Day by making silhouette patterns on newsprint.
2. Use a filmstrip projector to cast each child's shadow on paper attached to the wall.
3. Another child can draw the outline of the shadow.
4. Have the youngsters cut out and decorate the silhouettes.

5. The large "cards" can then be rolled up and tied with a ribbon and bow for attractive delivery.

- **A Rainbow in Your Room**

Procedure:
1. Make a rainbow in the classroom. All that is needed is a glass of water and a sunny day. (Be sure to use a clear glass. The wider the mouth, the better.)
2. When the glass is placed in sunlight, there should be a rainbow where the shadow would fall.
3. What is made is a simple prism, which can be used in lessons about the color spectrum. Point out to the children that a rainbow forms outdoors when drops of water in the air act as prisms.

- **Spring is Sprung**

Procedure:
1. Discuss the look, feel, sound, and smell of spring and the other seasons as they happen.
2. How do the children know that it is spring in their neighborhood? By the green grass and pussy willows? Mud? Reruns on television? Different clothes? Baseball?
3. Divide the bulletin board into four areas: "My Eyes See Spring," "I Feel Spring," "I Hear Spring," and "My Nose Knows It Is Spring." Have the children draw pictures to illustrate each theme.

- **Window Gardens**

Procedure:
1. Draw outlines of stems and leaves on the windows and ask each child to add a flower.
2. Have the children work out their patterns on paper or on the chalkboard first.

3. Have each child use a black crayon to trace the outline on top of a stem on the window.
4. Mix thick tempera paint in various colors with detergent, so the paint will stick to the window, and have the children fill in their outlines.
5. Keep plenty of rags on hand for clean up.

• **Flying Fish**

Materials: a strip of paper 11″ x 1 1/2″ (any thin paper will do), scissors, pencil, ruler, felt pen

Procedure:
1. Cut a slit about half way through the strip of paper, about 3″ from each end of the paper strip.
2. Decorate the strip in bright colors.
3. Roll the strip around and slide slits into each other.
4. Pinch lightly in the center.
5. Reach up and "drop" the flying fish in the air. It will twirl down.

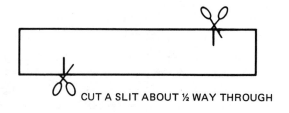

CUT A SLIT ABOUT ½ WAY THROUGH

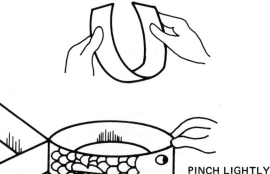

PINCH LIGHTLY
IN CENTER

Fig. 30-19 Flying fish.

• **Egg Carton Zoo**

Many innovations in art come from the use of discarded materials. Parts of egg cartons can be used to create real and imaginary animals for a "big city zoo."

Procedure:
1. Begin by cutting the cartons into separate parts to use either the inside or the outside of the egg cup.
2. Turn a cup upside down to make the body and legs of an animal.
3. Make the head with construction paper or use part of another cup and attach with glue.
4. Paint the features and body.
5. Add paper ears, horns, or hair.
6. The project can be extended to include little trees made of twigs and stuck in clay; painted "pools" for the animals and rocks can be made of crumpled paper.

Fig. 30-20 Egg carton zoo characters.

- **End-of-the-Year Fun**

Why not have a hose and sprinkler party? Ask each child to bring a bathing suit and make arrangements to have a hose and sprinkler available. On the first warm day during the final weeks of school, have a splash party.

- **Magical Mystery Paints**

Here's an art project with a touch of mystery.

Procedure:

1. Have the children place waxed paper over drawing paper and use sharp pencils to make pictures or designs.
2. The wax will be "invisibly" transferred to the drawing paper.
3. Attractive drawings magically appear when the children brush on watercolor paints. (Since the lines of the pictures will appear the same color as the drawing paper, it is best to use dark paint on white paper.)

- **A Marvelous Mess**

Was there a mess left after some of your more successful art projects? Here's a way to turn the leftovers into another fun time for the children.

Procedure:

1. Collect the colorful bits from each art project — glitter, hole-punched paper, fine-colored gravel, paper, cloth scraps.
2. When you have a good selection, roll out a large sheet of draft paper on the floor.
3. Place one large puddle or several small puddles of glue on the paper.
4. Have the children place their left-over scraps wherever they want on the paper.
5. Sprinkle the finished design generously with glitter or confetti.

- **Footprints in the Sands**

Procedure:

1. Try a foot mural. Spread out a long roll of wrapping paper.
2. Have the children take off their shoes and socks and trace around their feet with magic markers.
3. Label each pair of feet with the child's name.

- **Pipe Cleaner Dancers**

Procedure:

1. Obtain extra-fluffy pipe cleaners.
2. Shape them into dancing figures. (This is a good activity to do when a dancer visits the class.)
3. Dip the characters into a mixture of one cup soap powder and four table-spoons plastic starch, and sprinkle with glitter.
4. After they dry, hang them as mobiles.

- **Recycled Paint**

Procedure:

1. Scrape the dried paint from containers used at the easel and save them.
2. Squeeze glue onto construction paper, making any kind of design.
3. Sprinkle with paint chips. Shake off the excess.

- **Sawdust Sculpture**

Procedure:

1. Mix wheat paste and water to a thick consistency.
2. Add sawdust until the mixture can be formed into a ball.
3. Give each child a lump of the mixture to mold into any shape.
4. Dry the shapes for two or three days. They can be painted with tempera.

• **Pom-Poms**

Procedure:

1. Fold a sheet of tissue paper lengthwise.
2. Paint about an inch border of paste near the end of an empty paper towel cylinder.
3. Wrap the folded tissue around the end of the cylinder.
4. Tape the wrapped tissue in place.
5. Fringe the end of the tissue by cutting slits about 1/4 inch apart.
6. Have the children shake their pom-poms to music.
7. Play recorded selections that suggest wind sounds.

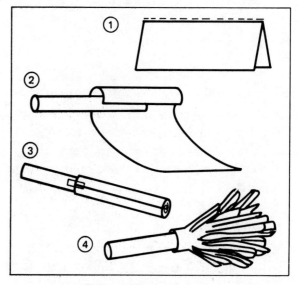

Fig. 30-21 Pom-Poms.

Unit 31 MORE SPRING AND SUMMER ACTIVITIES

There are so many good activities to use in spring and summer that they require two units. This unit contains more activities for these seasons, including art experiences, poems, finger plays, songs, games, books, and cooking activities.

- **Bumblebees**

Materials: 2 strips of black construction paper (18" long x 3" wide), 2 strips of yellow construction paper (9" long x 2" wide), 2 strips of black construction paper (9" long x 2" wide), pipe cleaners, paste, crayons

Fig. 31-1 (c)

Fig. 31-1 Bumblebee art activity (a)

Fig. 31-1 (d)

Fig. 31-1 (b)

Fig. 31-1 (e)

Procedure:

1. One long (18″ x 3″) black strip of construction paper is the bee's body. Loop one end for the head.
2. To the long black strip, have the children glue the shorter strips of yellow and black, alternating the colors.
3. Make a loop by pasting together the ends of the last long black strip.
4. Glue this loop behind the head for the bee's wings.
5. Poke holes in the construction paper head strip, for the pipe cleaner antennae.
6. After the paste dries, children can put their arms through the bee's wings and "fly" the bees.

- **Bee Mobiles**

Procedure:

1. Use the bee pattern in figure 31-2.
2. Follow the instructions in Unit 24 for making Halloween mobiles.

- **Walnut Smile/Sad Faces**

Procedure:

1. Save walnut half-shells.
2. Make a knot in the center of a piece of yarn. (Make sure the yarn is longer than the size of the child's neck.)
3. Set the knot between the two walnut shells, and glue them together.
4. When the glue has dried, use nail polish to paint a smiley face on one side and a frown on the other side of the walnut shells. Children can show their moods by exhibiting either the smile or the frown side of the walnut.

- **Pinwheels**

Procedure:

1. Follow directions in Unit 27 (figure 27-10) for making pinwheel ornaments. Substitute wallpaper samples (oilcloth) for regular paper so pinwheels will be strong enough for outdoor use.

Fig. 31-2 Bee pattern.

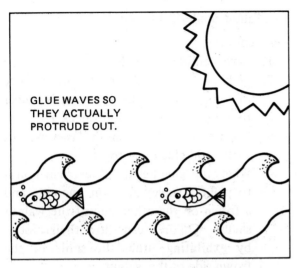

GLUE WAVES SO
THEY ACTUALLY
PROTRUDE OUT.

Fig. 31-3 3-Dimensional water pictures.

2. Hold the pinwheel together with a straight pin, stuck through the pinwheel center and into a pencil eraser.

- **3-Dimensional Water Pictures**

For a summer art activity, use manila drawing paper for a background, and paste light blue construction paper on it for waves.

Procedure:

1. First cut the blue paper in a wave shape.
2. Then glue it in a few places, allowing it to "bump out" in other places, to create the effect of real waves.
3. The children can fill in the rest of the water scene with crayons, markers, or cut-paper designs.

- **Accordion Pictures**

For an interesting effect, have the children accordion pleat (or fan) their colored pictures. It provides an unusual 3-dimensional effect.

- **Spring Flowers**

Materials: iron, paper, crayons

Procedure:

1. Fold the paper in half, then open it.

2. On one side of the fold, the children draw flowers: a single flower, or a bouquet.
3. When finished, they refold the paper, with the flower drawing on the inside, and bring it up to the teacher for ironing.

   Note: While children are working, set up an ironing station. On a desk, near an outlet, place several layers of newspaper, a magazine, or other paper. When ironing, place a piece of paper over the child's folded paper to prevent crayons from soiling the iron. The heat of the iron on the crayon creates an impressionistic-like flower picture.

4. These can be used for greeting cards or cut out and put on a class flower mural.

- **More Spring Flowers**

Materials: paper, felt pens or black crayons, watercolors

Procedure:

1. Another technique for making spring flowers is to use felt pens and watercolor. The idea here is to outline the flower with a felt pen (preferably) or a black crayon.
2. Then wash in with watercolors and *do not* try to keep within the lines.

- **Spring Murals**

Materials: see Easter activities in Unit 29.

Procedure:

1. The children can create a mural using the above techniques or other simple methods. First, discuss with them which things are to be included. (for example, birds, butterflies, insects, flowers, trees, grass).
2. Have the children decide which items they are going to prepare.

3. The children work at their own desks and cut out their finished pictures.
4. The pictures are then glued onto a larger paper.

POEMS, FINGER PLAYS, AND SONGS

• **It's Raining**

I wear a rubber raincoat
To cover up my clothes,
And some shiny, new black rubbers
To cover up my toes.

I hold a green umbrella
As I walk along to school,
And the raindrops make some splashes
In the little, muddy pools.

• **Rain**

Rain is falling down,
Rain is falling down.
Pitter, patter
Pitter, patter,
Rain is falling down.

• **A Kite**

I often sit and wish that I
Could be a kite up in the sky,
And ride upon the breeze and go
Whichever way I chanced to blow.

• **Kite Days**

A kite, a sky, and a firm breeze,
And acres of ground away from trees,
And one-hundred yards of clean, strong string
O boy, O boy! I call that spring!

• **No Drop of Rain**

It rained on Anne,
It rained on Fran,
It rained on Ara Bella,
  But - -
It did not rain on Mary Jane
She had a HUGE umbrella!

• **Dandelions**

Oh, dandelion, as yellow as gold,
What do you do all day?
"I wait and I wait in the tall green grass
Till the children come out to play."

Oh, dandelion, as yellow as gold,
What do you do all night?
"I wait and I wait in the tall green grass
Till my yellow hair turns white."

And what do the little children do
When they come out to play?
"They pick me up on their hands
And blow my white hair all away!"

• **The Earth**

The earth must be a lady;
She likes to change her clothes.
In winter time she loves to wear
The very whitest snows.
In spring she goes about in green,
In summer, flowers bold,
And in the fall she's very grand,
All dressed in red and gold.

                    —Hansi Chambers

• **Air**

Air, air — air.
Where? Where? Where?
I can't see it.
I can't feel it.
But I *know* it's there.

                    —M. Terwilliger

• **Thunder**

Black clouds are giants
Hurrying across the sky
And they slip out bolts of lightning
As they go racing by.

When they meet each other,
They shake hands and thunder
How-do-you-do
How-do-you-do
HOW-DO-YOU-DOOOOO!

- **Who Likes the Rain?**

"I," said the duck, "I call it fun,
For I have my little red rubbers on.
They make a cunning three-toed track
In the soft cool mud. Quack! Quack! Quack!"

"I," cried the dandelion, , "I.
My roots are thirsty, my buds are dry."
And she lifted her little yellow head
Out of her green and grassy bed.

"I hope 'twill pour!   I hope 'twill pour!"
Croaked the tree toad at his gray back door.
"For with a broad leaf for a roof
I am perfectly weatherproof."

Said the brook, "I welcome every drop;
Come, come, dear raindrops never stop
Till a great river you make of me.
Then I will carry you to the sea."

—Clara Doty Bates

- **Mud**

Mud is very nice to feel
All squishy-squash between the toes!
I'd rather wade in wiggly mud
Than smell a yellow rose.

Nobody else but the rosebush knows
How nice mud feels between the toes.

—Polly Chase Brown

- **The Wind**

Who has seen the wind?
Neither I nor you;
But where the leaves hang trembling,
The wind is passing through.

Who has seen the wind?
Neither you nor I;
But when the trees bow down their heads,
The wind is passing by.

—Christina Rossetti

- **Clouds**

If I had a spoon
As tall as the sky,
I'd dish out the clouds
That go slip-sliding by.

I'd take them right in
And give them to cook,
And see if they tasted
As good as they look.

- **Little Wind**

Little wind, blow on the hilltop,
Little wind, blow down the plain;
Little wind, blow up the sunshine,
Little wind, blow off the rain.

—Kate Greenway

- **Clouds**

White sheep, white sheep,
  On a blue hill,
When the wind stops,
  You all stand still.
When the wind blows
  You walk away slow.
White sheep, white sheep,
  Where do you go?

- **Windy Wash Day**

The wash is hanging on the line,
And the wind's blowing —
Dresses all so clean and fine,
Beckoning
And blowing.

Stockings twisted in a dance,
Pajamas very tripping,
And every little pair of pants
Upside down
And skipping.

—Dorothy Aldis

• The Wind

I saw you toss the kites on high
And blow the birds about the sky;
And all around I heard you pass,
Like ladies' skirts across the grass—
   O wind, a-blowing all day long,
   O wind, that sings so loud a song!
I saw the different things you did,
But always you yourself you hid.
I felt you push, I heard you call,
I could not see yourself at all—
   O wind, a-blowing all day long,
   O wind, that sings so loud a song!
O you that are so strong and cold,
O blower, are you young or old?
Are you a beast of field and tree,
Or just a stronger child than me?
   O wind, a-blowing all day long,
   O wind, that sings so loud a song!

        —Robert Louis Stevenson

• The Storm

From my bed so safe and warm,
I like to listen to a storm.

Thunder rumbling grand and proud,
Is louder than the rain is loud.

Bang it goes (like little boys)
But lightning doesn't make a noise.

Bright and quick and sudden though
It can cut the dark in two—

For just a second in its light,
My chair is red, my curtains white.

      —Dorothy Aldis

• I am a Tall Tree

I reach toward the sky
  (Both hands reach upward)
Where bright stars twinkle
And white clouds float by
  (Look upward, arms sway)
My branches toss high

As the wild winds blow
  (Arms wave wildly)
Now they bend forward
Loaded with snow
  (Arms out front swaying)
I like it best
When I rock birdies
To sleep in their nest.
  (Continue swaying while forming nest)
At the end of the poem, place hands at the side of the head and close eyes.

• Rain

The rain is falling all around,
It falls on field and tree,
It rains on the umbrellas here,
And on the ships at sea.

• The Secret

We have a secret
  Just we three,
The robin and I,
  And the sweet cherry tree.
The bird told the tree,
  And the tree told me,
And nobody knows it,
  Just we three.

But of course, the robin
  Knows it best,
Because he built the nest,
  I shan't tell the rest.
And laid the four little
  Somethings in it
I'm afraid I shall tell it
  Every minute.

But if the tree and the robin
  Don't peep,
I'll try my best
  The secret to keep;
Though I know when the little
  Birds fly about,
Then the whole secret
  Will be out.

• Pussy Willow

I have a little pussy
And her coat is silver gray,
She lives out in the meadow
And she never runs away.

She always is a pussy,
She'll never be a cat,
Because she's a pussy willow,
Now what do you think of that?

• Caterpillar

Fuzzy, wuzzy, creepy, crawly,
Caterpillar funny—
You will be a butterfly
When the days are sunny.

• Tenants

I printed a "For Rent" sign
For all the world to see.
Dad set it on the birdhouse
Up in the maple tree.
The robins like the birdhouse
Lived there the summer long.
And paid their rent each morning
By singing us a song!

• Butterfly

Up and down the air you float,
Like a little fairy boat.
    I should like to sail that sky
    Gliding like a butterfly.

• Wind on the Hill

No one can tell me,
    Nobody knows,
Where the wind comes from,
    Where the wind goes.

It's flying from somewhere,
    As fast as it can,
I couldn't keep up with it,
    Not if I ran.

But if I stopped holding
    The string of my kite,
It would blow with the wind
    For a day and a night.

But then when I found it,
    Wherever it blew,
I should know that the wind
    Had been going there too.

So then I could tell them
    Where the wind goes . . .
But where the wind comes from
    Nobody knows.

• Fog

The fog comes
On little cat feet.
It sits looking
Over harbor and city
On silent haunches
And then moves on.

—Carl Sandburg

• Whickety-Whack

Wind is a train
That goes so fast
You hold your hat
When it whizzes past.

Whickety-whack,
The wind goes by,
Whisking its car
Across the sky.

Whooshing past,
On a magic track,
Switching rails,
And swishing back!

• The Moon's the North Wind's Cooky

The moon's the North Wind's cooky
He bites it, day by day,
Until there's but a rim of scraps
That crumble all away.

The South Wind is a baker
He kneads clouds in his den,
And bakes a crisp new moon that . . . greedy
North . . . Wind . . . eats . . . again!

—Vachel Lindsay

• **The Tire**

I'll play that I'm a tire
And take a breath just so;
Pretend that I am filled with air
From my head down to my toe.
And then when I am very full,
I'll let it go like this:
Softly . . . slowly . . . softly . . .
    "Sssssssssss."

• **Rain Song**

The sky has shut its big blue eye,
    The trees are wet with seeping.
Oh, where's the bright and laughing sky?
    Sleeping,
        Sleeping,
            Sleeping.
Nothing but the river sings,
    Not a bee is humming.
Oh, where's the sun with yellow wings?
    Coming,
        Coming,
            Coming.

• **Tiny Tim**

I had a little turtle
    (Put thumbs and index fingers together)
His name was Tiny Tim.
I put him in the bathtub
To see if he could swim.
    (Make swimming motions with arms)
He drank up all the water
    (Head back, hands to mouth in drinking
    gesture)
He ate up all the soap
    (Chewing gesture)

He woke up in the morning
With bubbles in his throat.
    (Wave fingers in air above, from mouth, up
    to above head)

• **Birds Flying**

Up, up in the sky, the little birds fly
    (Fingers flying like birds)
Down, down in the nest, the little birds rest
    (Hands form nest)
With a wing on the left, and a wing on the right
    (Hands on each hip)
Let the little birds rest all the long night.
    (Head to one side like tucking under wing)

• **Winkie**

Winkie, the elephant, walks and walks
    (Arms in front to make a "trunk")
Never making a sound.
She moves her trunk from side to side
And it never touches the ground.

• **Little Turtle**

There was a little turtle
    (Make small circle with hands)
Who lived in a box
    (Hands form box)
He swam in a puddle
    (Hands swim)
He climbed on the rocks
    (Fingers climb up)
He snapped at a mosquito
    (Snap fingers)
He snapped at a flea
    (Snap fingers)
He snapped at a minnow
    (Snap fingers)
He snapped at me.
    (Snap fingers)
He caught the mosquito
    (Clap hands)
He caught the flea
    (Clap hands)

He caught the minnow
  (Clap hands)
But he didn't catch me!
  (Shake head no, no, and point to self)

• **Ten Red Balloons**

Ten red balloons flying in the air
  (Put 10 fingers in the air and wave them
  back and forth)
One went POP!
  (Clap hands)
and 9 were there.
  (Put 9 fingers in the air)
9 red balloons flying in the air
  (Wave them)
One went POP!
  (Clap hands)
and 8 were there.
  (Put 8 fingers in the air)
8 red balloons flying in the air
  (Wave them)
One went POP!
  (Clap hands)
and 7 were there.
  (Put 7 fingers in the air)
  (Continue counting down to . .)
One red balloon flying in the air
  (Put 1 finger in the air)
It went POP!
  (Clap hands)
and NONE were there.
  (Open hands, palms up to show "all gone")

• **From Seed to Seed**

See the little seed I brought
  (Hold up imaginary seed between left
  thumb and forefinger)
I'll dig a hole and plant it
  (Dig hole with right hand for trowel; "plant"
  seed with left hand)
I'll smooth the earth with little pats
  (Do so, using both hands on flat surface)
And water it with care
  (Pretend to hold watering can in right hand)

The sun will shine on it
  (Make "sun" with one or both hands held
  high)
And one day I will see
A tiny green shoot
  (Use right forefinger to represent the shoot)
Then a leaf or two
  (Bring right thumb up beside forefinger;
  bring up middle finger)
And finally a flower
  (Make circle of left thumb and forefinger;
  hold it above right forefinger)
It will nod in the breeze
  (Keeping the "flowers" just formed, wave
  it back and forth)
I will smell its perfume
  (Bend head over "flower" and sniff)
Then the petals will fall
  (Let fingers of left hand represent petals
  and flutter downward)
Soon the seeds will scatter
  (Let fingers of right hand be seeds; flutter
  fingers away from self)
Someday there will be more flowers.
  (Lift all ten fingers to represent flowers)

• **Kites**

"I can go higher than you,"
Boasted a dragon-shaped kite.
  (Make a rotating upward motion with the
  right arm and hand)
"But I am stronger than you,"
Answered a box-shaped kite.
  (Make a box with both hands)
"Well, I am prettier than you,"
Said a round-faced kite in the sky.
  (Make a circle with both hands)
"But I have a longer tail than you,"
Was a dainty kite's reply.
  (Make a streaking motion through the air
  with left hand)
The last little kite flew out of sight.
He didn't talk. He didn't boast.
  (Shake head in a negative motion)

He just did things.
(Raise the right hand higher and higher; drop both hands to rest in lap)

• **May Basket**

With my little scissors
I cut some paper strips.
(Cutting motion with index and middle finger of right hand)
Then I wove them in and out
(Suggest weaving by putting right index finger over and under fingers of left hand)
And pasted at the tips.
(Pretend to dip right index finger in paste; touch it to tips of fingers of left hand)
This became a basket
Pretty and gay
(Interlace fingers of both hands to make a basket shape)
In which to put flowers
On the first of May.
(With right forefinger and thumb, pretend to pick flowers and put them in a "basket" suggested by slightly cupped left hand)
I twisted pipe cleaners
(Make twisting motion with fingers)
To make a handle strong.
(Over "basket" suggested by left hand, curve right thumb and forefinger for a handle)
And left it at your house
(Point to someone on the word, "your")
When May Day came along.

• **Tulips**

(Attach tulip shapes to each fingernail — red ones on the little fingers, purple on the fourth fingers, and so on.)
In Holland the beautiful tulips grow.
(Hold both hands on flat surface in front of you, palms up, as though looking at nails)
Red and purple, white, yellow, pink.
(Show little fingers first, fourth fingers next, and so on, until all "tulips" are visible to the children in front of you)

Each flower is like a cup.
(Put forearms together for a flower stem; cup hands for blossom)
Someday I think I'll take a drink.
(Pretend to drink from cupped hands)

GAMES

• **Raindrops are Falling**

Have the children sit in a circle on the floor with their eyes closed and one hand open behind their backs. Appoint one child to be the "rainmaker," to carry a "raindrop" pebble or button around the circle and drop it into the hand of one of the other children, who then jumps up and tries to tag the rainmaker. If the rainmaker can reach the safety of the vacated seat, the chaser becomes the new rainmaker; otherwise, the rainmaker must take another turn.

• **"Be A"**

Make flashcards containing the words "Be a . . ." Paste pictures on the cards to complete the statement. Mix the cards in a bag. The children take turns pulling cards from the bag. Without showing their cards to others, each child performs actions that help the class guess what the child is. The more varied the pictures, the greater the challenge and the fun will be; so include pictures of a portable electric fan, an electric can opener, an alligator, a kite, a leprechaun, an alarm clock, and a door.

Sing "The Wind" from *The Spectrum of Music 2,* by Mary Val Marsh and others (MacMillan, 1974). Have the children use the pom-poms from page 311 to provide an interesting background effect.

Read *Look Around and Listen,* by Joy Troth Friedman (Grosset and Dunlap, 1974). Help the children become aware of the sights and sounds in their surroundings.

- **May Day Flowers**

    Pictures of various flowers are cut from magazines or flower catalogs. (You may wish to let the group do this preparation.) Then cut across each picture in an irregular line and pass out all the pieces. Each child tries to find the part that will form a complete flower, and piece it together to form the whole flower. Completed flowers may be pasted on large construction paper to form a spring poster.

- **The Caterpillar**

    Players form a single line, each player putting his hands around the waist or on the hips of the player ahead. The leader walks around the room with the rear of the "caterpillar" trailing behind. The leader then starts in a circle, making the circle smaller and smaller. When the leader gets inside, he reverses and leads out again. It is important that the players do not let go at any time.

- **Jump the Brook**

    Draw two lines on the floor, starting them only about two feet apart, and gradually widening so they are about eight feet apart. These lines form the bank of the brook. In turn, the players run and jump over the brook starting at the narrow end. Those stepping in, "get their feet wet" and must "go home and change their shoes" (lose a turn). The successful jumpers move to a wider spot in the brook and continue until they get their feet wet. At the wider end, stepping stones can be drawn in the brook so that players can hop from one to the next to get across. If there is no room for running, a standing jump may be used.

- **Dumping Ground**

    Two areas are marked on the floor quite far apart. The class divides in half, one half putting as many books in one area as there are children in the group. The other half does the same at the other area. On a signal, everyone carries one book at a time to the opposite area, walking not running. Stop them a minute later. Let the children count the books to see which area has the least books when time is called.

- **Balloon Throw**

    Everyone stands behind a chalk line and sees how far they can throw an inflated balloon. A mark is made where the balloon first touches the floor, and the child's initial put on it. The player who throws the balloon the farthest is, of course, the winner.

- **How Many Fingers**

    To review the numbers one to five, play this guessing game. The person chosen to be "it" is blindfolded. The rest stand at their seats. At a signal from the leader, everyone stretches a number of fingers. "It" tries to guess the number of extended fingers, calling the number aloud. The object is to see how few guesses "it" needs. After five turns or when "it" has guessed correctly, this child chooses a new "it."

- **Mickey Mouse**

    The group joins hands in a circle. Each child is given a letter to remember – A, B, C, or D. When the leader says a letter, everyone with that letter turns right and walks around the outside of the circle. The first child to walk around the circle, back to his place, and then into the center mark (make a small circle with chalk in the middle of the circle of children) becomes Mickey Mouse. That child then says a letter and the game continues. If there is a question as to who gets to the center first, Mickey Mouse decides.

- **Ring Around the Rosy**

The group forms a circle with two players, a girl and boy, standing in the center. The others circle around, singing:

Ring around a rosy,
A pocket full of Posy!
The one who stoops last
Wants to be your Beau-sy!

As the verse ends, the children stoop quickly. The last to stoop must join the pair in the center. If it's a boy, then the original boy in the center leaves; if it's a girl, then the girl leaves. Then the ring moves around again. In this way there's always a girl and a boy in the center. Or, give the children numbers — alternating ones and twos. Play the same way so there is always a "one" and a "two" in the center.

- **One Pin Bowling**

A milk carton makes a good bowling pin. Any size ball is satisfactory for this activity, but stress the point that the ball must be rolled smoothly to the pin. Each child has five rolls. Scores are kept. Groups of three children work well in playing this game — one bowls, one keeps score, and one sets the pin. Then players change places so another can bowl.

- **Call Ball**

Divide the class into groups of six to eight players. Each group forms a circle with a player in the center. The center player has a ball. This player tosses the ball straight in the air so that it comes down to bounce inside the circle. As the ball is tossed, the center player calls the name of a circle player, who must catch the ball before it bounces a second time. If the person catches it, that person becomes the tosser. If the ball is not caught, the first person has another turn.

- **Steal Ball**

Line up the group in two rows approximately 20 feet apart, and place a large ball on the floor between the two teams. The teacher says the name of two children, one from each side. The object is to see who can steal the ball from the center and get it "home."

- **On My Way to School**

The children are seated in a circle or at their desks. A player starts the game by imitating something that might be seen on the way to school — such as a paper boy, a dog, an airplane, or anything else that can move. The leader says, "On my way to school, I saw . . . " and then dramatizes what was seen. The player who guesses correctly becomes the new leader and the game continues.

- **Spring Picking Flowers**

Form three teams and line up behind a line. Draw a circle. Each team has a beanbag (flower) in the circle and the second person picks the "flower" up and tags the next person in line, who puts the "flower" down again. The first team to finish wins.

- **Inchworm**

Have the children begin in a kneeling position and push themselves up, so their weight is supported on both their hands and feet. They then move both hands forward at the same time, supporting themselves on their toes. After their hands are repositioned, tell the children to bring their feet forward together, while they support their weight on their hands.

- **Busy Bee**

Half the children form a large circle facing in and are designated as the stationary players. The other children seek partners from this group, and each stands in front of one of the stationary players. An extra child is in the center and is the "Busy Bee." The Bee calls out directions which are followed by the children ("back to back," "face to face," "take hands," "kneel on one knee," "hop on one foot," etc.) The center child calls out "Busy Bee." Stationary players stand still and all inner circle players seek another partner while the center player also tries to get a partner. The child without a partner becomes a Busy Bee. (After a while, let the active and stationary players rotate.)

● **Moving Music**

Play selections from the record "Creative Movement and Rhythmic Explorations," by Hap Palmer (Educational Activities). Encourage the children to move as they think the lyrics indicate. Or, play any song the children can move to without demonstration.

● **Spring Has Come**

Sing the Japanese folk song, "Haru Ga Kita" from *Expressing Music/New Dimensions in Music,* by Robert A. Choate and others (American Book, 1940). For a follow-up activity, have the children paint pictures of spring coming to the hills, to the city, or to a village.

● **March Wind**

The March wind roars loudly,
"Winter can't stay!"
Wind murmurs through branches
While Sun warms the day.

Wind purrs through the treetops
And as branches sway,
Wind whispers this secret,
"Spring's not far away!"

—Billie M. Phillips

Next, let the children act out this poem.

● **Wind Words**

Read "The Wind," by Robert Louis Stevenson. Create a windy day with an electric fan. Or, take the children outside on a windy day. Have them close their eyes and feel the wind in their faces and at their backs. Hold up a strip of tissue and watch its movements. Encourage the children to call out words that describe how the wind feels to them and how it moves.

● **Balloon, Feather, and Bubble Chasing**

Balloons and very light feathers can be batted into the air with the hands or fists, then chased and caught. Children can also run after bubbles, trying to pop them before they get away.

CHILDREN'S BOOKS FOR SPRING AND SUMMER

Brown, Marcia, *Three Billy Goats Gruff.* New York: Harcourt, Brace, Jovanovich, 1957.

Daugherty, James, *Andy and the Lion.* New York: Penguin Books, 1970.

Ets, Marie H., *Play with Me.* New York: Viking Press, 1955.

Fatio, Louise, *The Happy Lion.* New York: McGraw Hill, 1954.

Flack, Marjorie, *Tim Tadpole and the Great Bullfrog.* New York: Doubleday, 1959.

Freeman, Don, *Come Again, Pelican.* New York: Viking Press, 1961.

Garelick, May, *Where Does the Butterfly Go When It Rains?* New York: Scholastic Book Service, 1970.

Getz, Arthur, *Hamilton Duck's Springtime Story.* New York: Western Publishing Company, 1974.

Green, Carol, *The Truly Remarkable Day.* St. Louis, Missouri: Concordia, 1974.

Gunthorp, Karen, *The Wonderful Ball.* New York: Doubleday, 1968.

La Fontaine, Jean de, *The Lion and the Rat,* New York: Watts, 1963.

Langstaff, John, and Rojankovsky, Feodor, *Over in the Meadow.* New York: Harcourt, Brace, Jovanovich, 1971.

Lionni, Leo, *Swimmy.* New York: Pantheon, 1963.

McCloskey, Robert, *Blueberries for Sal.* New York: Penguin Books, 1976.

Sendak, Maurice, *Pierre.* New York: Harper and Row, 1962.

Tresselt, Alvin, *Rain Drop Splash.* New York: Lothrop, 1946.

Wright, Ethel, *The Saturday Walk.* Reading, Massachusetts: Addison-Wesley Publishing Company, 1954.

Yashima, Taro, *Umbrella.* New York: Penguin Books, 1977.

ANNOTATED LIST OF BOOKS FOR YOUNG CHILDREN

Adamson, Joy, *Elsa.* New York: Pantheon Books, 1963.
An extraordinary true story of lion cubs in the "wild," yet friends of mankind.

Beskow, Elsa, *Pelle's New Suit.* New York: Harper and Row, 1929.
The story of how wool from a lamb becomes a suit for a little boy, who is surprised that he has grown bigger.

Carle, Eric, *One, Two, Three to the Zoo.* Cleveland, Ohio: Collins, William, and World, 1968.
Each double page spread contains a numeral and corresponding number of zoo animals.

Colby, C. B., *Big Game: Animals of the Americas, Africa, and Asia.* New York: Coward, McCann and Geoghegan, Inc., 1967.
Pictures of some famous big game animals with simple text.

Cosgrove, Margaret, *Eggs and What Happens Inside Them.* New York: Dodd, Mead and Company, 1966.
A look at what happens inside eggs.

Epple, Anne O., *Beginning Knowledge Book of Ants.* New York: Macmillan, 1969.
Beginning Knowledge Book of Fossils. New York: Macmillan, 1969.
Two books which introduce children to ideas about ants and fossils.

Fisher, Aileen, *We Went Looking.* New York: T. Y. Crowell, Co., 1968.
A glimpse of wild creatures as they really are.

Hammond, Winifred, *The Riddle of Seeds.* New York: Coward, McCann, and Geoghagan, Inc., 1965.
A story of seeds and their importance in the world.

Hess, Lilo, *Animals that Hide, Imitate and Bluff.* New York: Charles Scribner's Sons, 1970.
This story tells and shows (in photographs) how camouflage enables many animals to survive.

Hutchins, Pat, *Rosie's Walk.* New York: Macmillan, 1971.
Rosie walks around the barnyard unaware she is being followed by a sly and greedy fox.

Kohn, Bernice, *Chipmunks.* Englewood Cliffs, New Jersey: Prentice-Hall, 1970.
A story of chipmunks, told through words and pictures.

Mari, Iela and Mari, Engo, *The Chicken and The Egg.* New York: Pantheon, 1970.
Wordless book, beautifully illustrating the hatching of a chick.

Newberry, Clare Turlay, *Widget.* New York: Harper and Row, 1958.
A naughty kitten is rescued by his mother.

Posell, Elsa, *The Beginning Knowledge Book of Seashells.* New York: Macmillan, 1969.

  A child's introduction to seashells.

Rey, H. A., *Curious George.* Boston, Massachusetts: Houghton, Mifflin, 1973.

  The tale of an adventurous monkey named George.

Sauer, Petter, *Seashell Towns.* New York: Coward, McCann, and Geoghegan, Inc., 1968.

  A description of snails, mussels, and barnacles.

Schima, Marilyn, *Something Grows.* Englewood Cliffs, New Jersey: Prentice-Hall, 1969.

  The story of how each seed is special; how living seeds are able to change and grow until they are like the plant or animal from which they came.

Schwartz, Elizabeth, and Schwartz, Charles, *When Water Animals are Babies.* New York: Holiday House, 1970.

  Accurate drawings in soft colors; describes wide variety of ways that water mothers care for their young.

Selsam, Millicent, *All Kinds of Babies.* New York: Scholastic Book Service, 1967.

  Picture book about baby animals.

Steig, William, *Sylvester and the Magic Pebble.* New York: Simon and Schuster, 1970.

  Family love demonstrated through a donkey named Sylvester.

Tresselt, Alvin, *The Beaver Pond.* New York: Lothrop, 1970.

  Story of beavers — the dams they build and their effect on the streams.

Wong, Herbert, and Vessel, Matthew, *Our Terrariums.* Reading, Massachusetts: Addison-Wesley, 1969.

  The excitement of catching and caring for an animal is expressed in this story.

Wong, Herbert, and Vessel, Matthew, *Pond Life: Watching Animals Grow Up.* Reading, Massachusetts: Addison-Wesley, 1970.

  Two boys observe aspects of pond ecology — how animals grow and how animal parents treat their young.

COOKING EXPERIENCES

(All of the following recipes have been used in actual day care centers and kindergartens.)

For additional cooking activities, see Unit 19, Foods: A Creative Approach.

- **French Toast**

Ingredients:

2 eggs
1/2 teaspoon salt
2/3 cup milk
1/2 teaspoon vanilla
1 tablespoon butter
4 slices of bread

Materials: measuring spoons, mixing bowl, egg beater, large frying pan, spatula

Procedure:

1. Melt the butter in the frying pan over low heat.
2. Put eggs, milk, salt, and vanilla in mixing bowl.
3. Beat well with an egg beater.
4. Soak slices of bread in the mixture.
5. Brown the bread in the frying pan.
6. Use a spatula to turn the bread over so that it will brown on both sides.
7. Sprinkle with sugar and cinnamon or serve with maple syrup.
8. This makes enough servings for 4 people.

(Maurice Sendak's, *In the Night Kitchen,* is a good story to read with *any* cooking activity.)

- **Hawaiian Toast**

Ingredients:

4 slices white bread
2 eggs

1 cup pineapple juice (if fresh pineapple is used, save the top to grow later)

1/2 teaspoon salt

8 slices bacon

4 slices pineapple

Materials: measuring spoons, measuring cup, spatula, egg beater, mixing bowl, paper towels, large frying pan (preferably electric)

Procedure:

1. Cook the bacon in a frying pan until crisp.
2. Use a spatula to turn the bacon over so that it will be crisp on both sides.
3. Drain the bacon on paper towels.
4. Put the eggs, pineapple juice, and salt into a mixing bowl.
5. Beat well with egg beater.
6. Soak bread in the mixture.
7. Brown the toast in bacon fat in a frying pan.
8. Turn with a spatula to brown on both sides.
9. Put toast and bacon on plates.
10. Fry the pineapple slices in a frying pan.
11. Put one slice of pineapple on each piece of toast.

• **Zoo Sandwiches**

Ingredients:

several slices of bread

cream cheese

cream (use 1 tablespoon cream for a 3-ounce package of cream cheese)

food coloring

Materials: animal cookie cutters, mixing bowl, measuring spoons, mixing spoon, table knife

Procedure:

1. Put the cream cheese and cream into a mixing bowl.

2. Mix together with a mixing spoon until the cream cheese is soft.
3. Add a few drops of food coloring (if desired), and stir well.
4. Cut out the bread with animal cookie cutters.
5. Spread on the cream cheese mixture with a knife.

Variation: Try spreading whole wheat bread with honey and peanut butter.

• **Orange Crush**

Ingredients:

1 1/2 cups orange juice

1 pint soft vanilla ice cream

orange slices, cherries

Materials: knife for slicing oranges, measuring cup, mixing bowl, mixing spoon, 3 glasses

Procedure:

1. Let the children slice the oranges.
2. Put ice cream and orange juice in the mixing bowl.
3. Stir with the mixing spoon until smooth.
4. Pour it into glasses.
5. Decorate each glass with orange slices and cherries.

• **Little Pizzas**

Ingredients:

1 English muffin for each child

cheddar cheese (or American, colby, or mozzarella)

tomatoes

salad oil

oregano

Materials: knife for slicing tomatoes and cheese, and a cookie sheet

Procedure:

1. Heat oven to 400 degrees.
2. Have the children help slice the tomatoes and cut the cheese into strips.

3. Split each muffin in half.
4. Put the halves on the cookie sheet.
5. Put a slice of tomato on each one.
6. Put some cheese on top of the tomatoes.
7. Sprinkle a few drops of oil on each.
8. Sprinkle with a bit of oregano.
9. Bake in the oven for about 6 or 7 minutes.

- **Pancake People/Animals**

Ingredients:
ready-mixed pancake batter
raisins
syrup

Materials: electric frying pan, mixing bowl, mixing spoon, measuring cups

Procedure:
1. Mix batter, adding water as directed on the package.
2. Pour enough batter in the frying pan to make a medium-sized pancake.
3. Drop a small amount of batter at the top of this pancake to make "ears" on both sides.
4. Flip over the pancake to complete cooking.
5. Place raisins for eyes, nose, and mouth.
6. Some other "animals" to try: elephant, cat, dog. Simple, round pancakes can be made into "faces" by decorating with raisins.

- **Peach Crisp**

Ingredients:
1 cup oatmeal
1/2 cup presifted flour (children should do the sifting)
1/2 cup brown sugar, well packed
1/2 teaspoon salt
1/2 cup melted butter
1 teaspoon lemon juice
4 cups peeled, sliced peaches
ice cream (vanilla or peach)

Materials: knife for peeling and slicing peaches, flour sifter, measuring cup, measuring spoons, mixing bowl, mixing spoon, glass baking dish, small pan for melting butter

Procedure:
1. Help the children sift the flour and prepare the peaches.
2. Melt the butter over low heat.
3. Heat the oven to 350 degrees F.
4. Put oatmeal, flour, sugar, and salt into a mixing bowl.
5. Mix well with a mixing spoon.
6. Pour in melted butter and beat into the mixture.
7. Butter a glass baking dish.
8. Spread the sliced peaches on the bottom of the dish.
9. Sprinkle peaches with lemon juice.
10. Spread oatmeal mixture over the peaches.
11. Bake for 30 minutes or until brown.
12. Serve with ice cream (or liquid cream).

(A good story to use for a supplement to this activity is Robert Dahl's, *James and the Giant Peach*.)

Special Projects

Unit 32 CLEANUP WEEK
ECOLOGY AND ENVIRONMENTAL EDUCATION

CLEANUP WEEK ECOLOGY

Helping children to see beauty, or the lack of it, in our environment is vital in helping children develop visual sensitivity when responding to everyday experiences. Hopefully, this new awareness means that children are able to relate to the problem of improving the visual quality of the world around them .

Geared to children's ages and levels of understanding, there are a number of art experiences that can involve children in the personal aspect of the total environment. Stimulus for creative visual expression may come from any area of the child's daily life at home, in school, and in the neighborhood. With motivation and encouragement, many ideas about ecology and the preservation of nature will come from the children themselves. Some suggestions for picturemaking include:

- Walking in the Fresh Air
- Before and After — Cleaning Up the Yard
- Keeping Our School Beautiful
- The Living Creatures of the Earth
- A Clean City Street
- Don't Be a Litter Bug
- Fixing Up the Playground
- Plant a Garden

Other suggested art activities:

- Assemblage
- Posters
- Litter Pig
- Parade — Floats
- Collographs
- Mini-Park

- **Assemblage**

Encourage children to make a collection of found objects of all sizes, shapes, colors, and textures including cans, bottle caps, discarded toys, scrap lumber, and household items. Arrange the objects in containers, such as cardboard boxes, egg cartons, and berry boxes that have been painted or covered with paper. Rearrange the objects, if necessary, until the desired composition is achieved. Fasten objects in place with glue or staples. An assemblage design may represent something in real life, or may be abstract, depending on the child's imagination and ideas.

Fig. 32-1 Children may want to draw pictures of their environment as a response to their surroundings.

Fig. 32-2 Assemblage.

Fig. 32-3 Litter pig.

• Posters

Posters that promote ideas leading to a better environment can help to spread the word when placed throughout the school. The message may begin with a bold, simple drawing or painting, or even a magazine picture illustrating the main idea. The slogan should be short with words that are easily understood by young children. Cut-paper letters or printed words from magazines or newspapers are suitable. When possible, children can letter their posters in crayon.

• Litter Pig

Another way to dramatize the importance of each child's help in cleaning up the environment is to create an unusual trash collector for everyone to fill. Assemble some boxes and arrange them in the shape of an animal such as a pig. Leave a large opening at the mouth or top to collect litter. Attach boxes together with tape. Paint the animal in bold colors to attract attention.

• Collographs

Make a print (collograph) using a collage as a printing plate. First collect a variety of textural materials from the environment. Discarded items may include: cardboard, corrugated board, string, keys, rubber bands, buttons, and burlap. Or, children may want to use natural forms such as leaves, bark, twigs, shells, grasses, and weeds. Arrange materials on a cardboard background and glue them securely. When the plate is thoroughly dry, spread paint over the entire surface and place the slightly dampened printing paper over it. Press carefully with the fingertips, a spoon, tongue depressor, or spatula. Paper will be less likely to crinkle by rubbing from the center outward.

• Mini-Park Model

Design a small, restful, open green area needed for recreational use in a commercial and industrial community. Plans may include such items as trees, shrubbery, grass, flowers, a rock garden, pool with a fountain, sculpture, benches and walkways. Table models may be made from cardboard, twigs, paper, sponges, or clay.

Fig. 32-4 **Mini-park models.**

• **Parade Floats**

Begin construction of the base of a float with a vehicle such as a wagon, a bike, a baby's stroller, a wheelbarrow, or anything that can be pulled along or driven easily. The base can be covered with cloth, paper, or boxes, forming an animal, person, or other figure to dramatize the idea. Banners, posters, and sandwich boards add further meaning to the parade; children may design hats or carry objects depicting the theme.

ENVIRONMENTAL EDUCATION

• **Action 1**

Go outside and collect materials from your environment and make art objects with them. Each piece of art should show one of the following:

— Ugliness in your environment

— Beauty in your environment

— How the environment makes you feel

— The joy of your environment

— The sadness of your environment

— How time changes your environment

Variations:

Determine a quality of your environment that you want to portray and then do it. Children work in groups and repeat the assignment.

• **Action 2**

Go outside and do something that you really want to do. Some ideas include:

— Watching ants

— Reading outside

— Working with the custodian

— Taking pictures

(This activity is a great "trust builder" between teacher and child. When the children believe in their teacher, the way may be paved for openness in the classroom. The teacher should do this, too.)

Variation: How did you feel about "doing your thing" while doing it? How were your feelings involved in what you did? What can be done to let more of this kind of thing happen in a school?

• Action 3

Go outside and collect materials with which you can make a tool to use in creating an art form. Then create the art form. Some things that may be collected include:

— sticks	— grass
— bottles	— dirt
— leaves	

Media that you might have on hand:

— fingerpaints	— temperas
— oils	— acrylics
— chalks	— charcoal
— India ink	— mud

(The key to success is invention. This activity invites the invention of something that is ordinarily quite familiar. Encourage divergent and different solutions.)

• Action 4

What are the youngest and the oldest things in the school? (Photography optional)

Youngest	*Oldest*
paint	building stone
repairwork	bricks
planks	sidewalks
animals	trees
books	chalk
bulletin boards	chalkboard (slate)

Rank these things in order by age. How is age determined? Do you like newness or oldness best?

• Action 5

Take a picture that is positive evidence that something natural happened. Several things that may be suggested are

- Roots cracking the sidewalk (caused by nature)
- Paint peeling (caused by nature)
- Litter on the school grounds (natural condition)
- Car fenders bent (natural condition)

(Note: "Caused by nature" versus "natural condition" — Some students may have a problem in determining what is "natural." Part of this assignment is to let them clarify this point. After the assignment is finished, discuss it and repeat it if desired.)

• Action 6

Blindfold the students. Form groups of three. Pass out a variety of objects for the students to touch: vegetables, fruits, paper, tacks, feather, marshmallows, sandpaper, small animals, steel ball, cloth, raw meat, and so on. Variation: Have the students bring things from home to repeat the assignment. Try blindfolded touch-tours of the school.

• Action 7

Go outside and find objects in your environment that are representative of the following pairs of words: hard/soft, ugly/beautiful, big/small, important/unimportant, high/low, on/off, threatening/calming, useful/wasteful, like/dislike, happy/unhappy, funny/sad, justice/injustice, wise land use/poor land use.

Variation: Children choose word pairs of their own and find objects to represent them.

• **Action 8**

Choose a series of pictures that were taken for previous assignments that show a variety of things. Children take pictures of something that is the opposite of each of the original pictures. (This activity helps bring out the idea that many things that are opposites also have some things in common.)

Variations:

— Children invent a "same" game.

— They exchange the pictures they took and repeat the assignment.

— They guess what each other's photograph represents.

— Try some opposite word plays (hot/cold, hard/soft, mild/strong).

• **Action 9**

Go outside and prove that living things in your environment change, such as trees, ants, pets, people, and so forth.

• **Action 10**

Take some art materials of your choice outside and use them on some aspect of the environment, so that you actually bring some of the environment back inside. Materials that could be used include paper, finger paints, charcoal, and clay. Some things to do are wall rubbings, street rubbings, and textures in clay or fingerpaints.

• **Action 11**

Go outside and count something so you know more about it after you have counted it than you did before you counted it. Things to count: bricks, windows, sand grains, how much garbage is produced by the school, how much gasoline is sold at a service station, number of cars at a busy intersection, insects, leaves, etc.

Variations:

— How can the various things that were counted be related?

— Should any of the things counted increase or decrease?

— How can they be made to increase or decrease?

• **Action 12**

Go outside on the school grounds and find something to make a kite from. Materials that can be found include: brown paper bags, rubber bands, strings, cans, and plastic bags. (This assignment calls on the inventiveness of the children. They learn a lot about air in motion doing this exercise, and can create wind maps after it is over.)

Variation: Whose kite flies the longest, the highest, the prettiest, the slowest, and so on? What kind of wind is needed for a kite to fly? Where is it the windiest on the school grounds?

• **Action 13**

Go outside with a tape recorder and find and bring back sounds you like and dislike. Also, find and bring back morning, day, and night sounds. Some possible sounds to record: traffic noises, school announcements, birds, donut shop sounds, police whistle.

This is an invitation to explore the environment with basically one sense.

Variations:

— How does a sound make you feel?

— Record sounds of work.

— Record sounds of play.

- **Action 14**

    Children select one quality of themselves and record the change. Some possible variables to use are

    — height   — attitudes

    — weight   — feelings

    — sizes

(Children seldom include themselves as part of a changing environment. They may not think about changes in themselves very often, and therefore, are sometimes unaware of growth in their personal qualities and characteristics. This is a continuing activity so children should make entries in their "see me" log.)

Variations:

- What can you do to speed up or slow down the change?

- What changes would you like to have?

- **Action 15**

    Obtain any ten photos taken at random, from the old picture box, and write the children's dictated story that includes all the pictures.

What they do:

- Personal stories about the people in the pictures

- Stories about the neighborhood

- Stories about a theme such as love, hate, trees

- Conservation, pollution, etc.

Variation: Use the same pictures and write a different story. The entire class uses the same set of pictures.

Notes: This is great for a rainy day and when a camera is running out of film. Since these are the children's pictures, they usually like to talk about them. With many children, talking about the photos helps them develop better verbal communication. This assignment is also a way to collect personal data from the children.

- **Action 16**

    Define "predator" and "prey" for the children. The assignment is to find out who in the community are predators and who are preyed upon:

- cats and rats

- birds and bees

- gulls and fish

- robins and worms

Variations:

- Find out how these relationships can be changed.

- Discuss if they can be changed.

- Will the balance of the environment be affected if any of the predators or prey are removed?

- What happens when the predator and prey change places?

CHILDREN'S BOOKS ABOUT ECOLOGY AND ENVIRONMENT

Picture Books

Bartlett, Margaret, *The Clean Brook*. New York: T. Y. Crowell, 1960.

Carrick, Carol, *Swamp Spring*. New York: Macmillan, 1969.

Clymer, Eleanor, *A Big Pile of Dirt*. New York: Scholastic Book Service, 1972.

Fisher, Aileen, *We Went Looking*. New York: T. Y. Crowell, 1968.

Freschet, Berniece, *The Old Bullfrog*. New York: Charles Scribner's Sons, 1972.

Garelick, May, *Where Does the Butterfly Go When it Rains?* New York: Scholastic Book Service, 1970.

Hurd, Edith, *Wilson's World,* New York: Harper and Row, 1971.

Keats, Ezra, *The Snowy Day.* New York: Viking Press, 1962.

Keith, Eros, *A Small Lot.* New York: Bradbury Press, 1968.

Lionni, Leo, *Inch by Inch.* New York: Astor-Honor, 1962.

Lubell, Winifred and Lubell, Cecil, *The Tall Grass Zoo.* Chicago, Illinois: Rand McNally, 1960.

McCloskey, Robert, *Time of Wonder.* New York: Viking Press, 1977.

Mendoza, George, *The Hunter I Might Have Been.* New York: Astor-Honor, 1968.

Miles, Miska, *Apricot ABC.* Boston, Massachusetts: Little, Brown, and Company, 1969.

＿＿＿＿ *Nobody's Cat.* Boston, Massachusetts: Little, Brown, and Company, 1969.

＿＿＿＿ *Hoagie's Rifle Gun.* Boston, Massachusetts: Little, Brown, and Company, 1970.

Mizumura, Kazue, *If I Build a Village.* New York: T. Y. Crowell, 1971.

Peet, Bill, *Wump World.* Boston, Massachusetts: Houghton Mifflin, 1970.

Piatti, Celestino, *The Happy Owls.* New York: Atheneum, 1964.

Schoenherr, John, *The Barn.* Boston, Massachusetts: Little, Brown, and Company, 1968.

Udry, Janice, *A Tree is Nice.* New York: Harper and Row, 1956.

Zolotow, Charlotte, *Storm Book.* New York: Harper and Row, 1952.

Nonfiction

Bendick, Jeanne, *A Place to Live: A Study of Ecology.* New York: Parents, 1970.

Bloome, Enid, *The Air We Breathe.* New York: Doubleday, 1971.

＿＿＿＿ *The Water We Drink.* New York: Doubleday, 1971.

Busch, Phyllis, *Puddles and Ponds: Living Things in Watery Places.* Cleveland, Ohio: Collins, William, and World, 1969.

Goetz, Delia, *Rivers (How Pollution Develops).* New York: William Morrow and Company, 1969.

Guilcher, Jean, and Noailles, R. H., *A Tree is Born.* New York: Sterling, 1960.

Haley, Gail, *Noah's Ark.* New York: Atheneum, 1971.

Hoover, Helen, *Animals at my Doorstep.* New York: Parents, 1966.

McCord, David, *Every Time I Climb A Tree.* Boston, Massachusetts: Little, Brown, and Company, 1967.

Parnall, Peter, *The Mountain.* New York: Doubleday, 1971.

Podendorf, Illa, *Every Day is Earth Day.* Chicago, Illinois: Childrens, 1971.

Selsam, Millicent, and Morrow, Betty, *See Through the Sea.* New York: Harper and Row, 1955.

Tresselt, Alvin, *The Beaver Pond.* New York: Lothrop, 1970.

Webber, Irma, *Bits That Grow Big.* Reading, Massachusetts: Addison-Wesley, 1949.

HEALTH AND SAFETY

It is important that children learn good habits of health and safety. In school, children are taught how to cross streets safely, to eat a healthy breakfast before going to school, to keep themselves clean, and to help keep their environment clean and attractive. These lessons are clarified and become more meaningful and lasting when accompanied by creative art experiences. Children are more aware of the importance of practicing safety at the crosswalk when they can create a puppet show and dramatize a safe practice (such as helping the safety patrol person), or when they can make a picture on how to stop, look, and listen before crossing streets.

Some additional suggestions for picture-making topics on health and safety:

- Brushing My Teeth
- I Walk Across the Street
- Safe Places to Play
- A Healthy Breakfast
- How I Keep Clean and Neat
- Helping Mother Clean House
- At the Doctor's Office

Other suggested art activities:

- Cross with Safety
- Food Montage
- Toothful Tommy
- Posture Silhouette
- Set a Healthy Table

• Cross with Safety

Figures of a safety patrol person and children at a corner can be made of toweling rolls. The children use the figures in play-acting, to show how to cross a street safely. They can thus learn the correct safety practice through a fun activity.

Toweling rolls can be painted to depict the characters. Arms may be made by cutting a narrow strip of paper and attaching it to the back of the figure. For rounded arms, use pieces of soda straws, inserted into holes made on both sides of the toweling roll. Mark streets on a table-sized piece of paper. Then the figures can be arranged and moved as they dramatize the safe way to cross the street.

• Food Montage

Good eating habits can be illustrated by creating a montage. Cut out random illustrations of healthful foods from magazines, or cut out foods that are only from certain categories (dairy, meat, etc.), or special meals. Arrange cutouts in a pleasing design onto a paper or cardboard background, and paste them down.

• Toothful Tommy

Puppets can be useful in dramatizing the importance of dental care. Fold a paper plate in half to create a large "mouth." Cut two strips of heavy paper to act as straps in order to operate the puppet. Fasten one at the top and one at the bottom of the plate on the outside, leaving room for four fingers to slip into the strap at the top, and the thumb at

Fig. 32-5 Safety patrol roll figures.

Fig. 32-6 Toothful Tommy.

the bottom. Add cut-paper eyes and a nose along the top edge of the plate. Paper teeth and tongue can be attached along the inner edge of the "mouth." Use a long sock with a slit in the toes allowing room for the hand to slip through and operate the paper plate puppet.

• Posture Silhouette

Using a projector, children can easily check their posture. Stretch some white roll paper along an empty wall space. As one child stands in the beam of light, another traces his silhouette. Using a number of silhouettes is a good way to create a group portrait.

• Set a Healthy Table

Oiled clay, salt clay, or crumpled paper are suitable for modeling three-dimensional objects, such as meats, fruits, and mashed potatoes or other vegetables. Crumpled paper objects can be painted in appetizing colors. White paper cups may suggest glasses of milk. Children can create a decorative table by printing colorful designs on napkins and

placemats made of white roll paper. Cardboard is suitable for plates and silverware. In this way, children learn how to set the table; they can arrange and rearrange the "food" in various combinations, and enjoy learning good health habits at the same time.

• Stop! Look! Listen!

Stop! Look! Listen!
Before you cross the street.
Use your eyes; use your ears;
Then use your feet.

• Stop and Go

The traffic lights we see ahead
Are sometimes green and sometimes red.
Red on top and green below,
The red means stop, the green means go.
Green below, go – go – go,
Red on top, stop – stop – stop!

• Stop! Yield!

Most traffic signs have their own distinctive shapes. Cut out the shapes from construction paper in appropriate colors and have the children fill in the words. Ask them to note traffic signs on the way home and duplicate as many of them as they can remember the next day.

• Walkabout to Reinforce Safety Habits

There are many interesting spots in your school, the playground, or the neighborhood where teacher and children can visit. The children may enjoy seeing the school's library, the nurse's and principal's offices, the kitchen, and the gym. (Arrange each visit beforehand.) Is there a tree, a big rock, or a view of interesting traffic near the playground? Is there a bakery store, a supermarket, a pet store, a construction site, trees to watch in various seasons, a vacant lot with weeds and bugs to collect, or gardens to look at nearby?

Fig. 32-7 Setting a healthy table.

Unit 33 READING READINESS

WAYS TO HELP CHILDREN LEARN TO READ

It is the job of the preschool teacher to help a child get ready to read. Although regular reading lessons should not be presented too early, there are many things a preschool teacher can do to prepare a child for future academic situations. Learning to read in the regular classroom is not a simple operation, like learning to hammer a nail. It is made up of a number of smaller skills, habits, attitudes, and abilities that enable a child to see the differences in the shapes of letters and word forms, to get ideas from symbols, and to enjoy the learning process. Here are some ways the early childhood teacher can help develop these skills.

Teach the Child How to Listen

Play the letter game. In this simple but helpful game, the teacher says, "I went to the store and bought butter, beans, and blocks." The child then adds a word beginning with the same letter.

Fig. 33-1 In helping children develop reading readiness skills, a teacher can provide equipment for listening activities.

To reinforce letter sounds in an art activity, cut large letters out of paper. Talk about each letter and its sound. Then have the children list all the things they can think of which start with that letter. The large paper letter can then be filled in with pictures of the words suggested by the children. Or, the children can draw the objects inside the letter. Over the course of a month, semester, or year, the room can be decorated with these large alphabet letters filled with pictures of objects with that sound.

Play "What Did I Do?"

Make a sound and have the children guess what you did. For example, while the children hide their eyes or look the other way, move a chair, stir something in a bowl with a spoon, close a door, etc.

Read Poetry to the Children

Read nursery rhymes, nonsense rhymes, and the "fun poems" listed on page 339. Children in preschool enjoy hearing strange, musical, and funny sounding words.

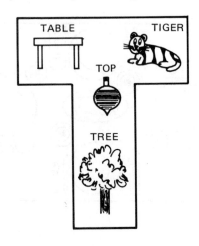

Fig. 33-2 Letter "T" of the letter game.

Good poetry for children:

Belloc, Hilaire, *The Bad Child's Book of Beasts.* New York: Knopf, 1965.

Ciardi, John, *The Man Who Sang the Sillies.* Philadelphia, Pennsylvania: Lippincott, 1961.

Dr. Seuss, *And To Think That I Saw It on Mulberry Street.* New York: Vangard, 1937.

Lear, Edward, *The Jumblies.* Boston, Massachusetts: Waine, 1907.

McCord, David, *Every Time I Climb a Tree.* Boston, Massachusetts: Little, Brown, and Company, 1967.

Milne, A. A., *Now We are Six.* New York: Dell Books, 1975.

          When We Were Very Young. New York: Dutton, 1966.

O'Neill, Mary, *Hailstones and Halibut Bones.* New York: Doubleday, 1961.

Tap Out Rhythms

Use a pencil or coin to tap out a short, simple rhythm on the table. Ask the children to tap out the same pattern. This helps train children to listen carefully and to remember what they heard. These skills are necessary for learning the phonics and sounding patterns of reading.

Give the Children Simple Verbal Directions

Give the children simple directions. At first, ask the child to perform one familiar task. Then, gradually add another and another until each child is able to remember them and do them in order. This develops alert listening and auditory memory. For example, you can say, "David, please close the door." When he can perform one direction, give him two. "Please close the door and then bring me the paper." When he can perform three directions in the correct order, the child has developed his auditory memory as well as that of the average beginning reader.

Play Restaurant

The teacher sits at the table and lets one child be the waiter or waitress. The teacher gives the order verbally, and makes sure that the "food" served is the same as ordered. Pictures of food cut from magazines or even "play food" from the doll corner can make this activity more fun.

Develop Children's See-Ability

In order to learn to read, children must be able to distinguish small differences in the objects they are looking at — differences in size, shape, position, and color.

Provide picture puzzles. Start with very simple puzzles for the younger children. The pieces should be large and easy to fit together.

Play color detective. To sharpen the children's sense of color, ask the children to point out all red objects in the room, all blue objects, and so on.

Helping Children Learn to Speak Fluently

Encourage conversation on the toy telephone. If a child mumbles, the teacher can say, "Speak more clearly, sir. We seem to have a bad connection!" The teacher plays announcer; the children can give a weather report or report the "news."

Ask children to tell a story. After the teacher has read or told a story, ask the children to help tell a story. The teacher starts with a sentence and lets each child continue it, in turn, from there. For example, "There was once a brown dog running along a country road and all of a sudden he barked at a _____ ." The child makes up the rest of the story.

Find the missing parts. Old pictures from magazines or coloring books, or even torn reading books can be used. Parts of the pictures are removed and the child is asked what is missing. Some things to remove: tails of animals, the engine off of a train, wheel off of a car, etc.

ADDITIONAL READING READINESS ACTIVITIES

- Have the children count balls, each other, or anything else they think of, always counting from left to right. Encourage them to count with just their eyes.

- Show a picture of a child performing a skill, such as throwing a ball. Encourage the children to talk about the picture. Put the word "throw" on the board, or on a large piece of paper. Everyone then pretends to do it.

- Place various kinds of balls in the center of a circle. Talk about how they are alike and how they are different: size, color, texture, etc. Pass the balls around the circle and let the children see and feel the differences.

- Say a number of words beginning with the same sound; then one with a different sound. Children indicate when they hear the different word by jumping up and down.

- Have half of the children jump, skip, hop, and so on, a number of times. The others listen, count mentally, and then tell the number. Vary the procedure by having the children perform slowly, quickly, and in an irregular rhythm.

- Play picture hunt to develop visual awareness. Cut out or draw pictures of several objects such as a car, a tree, a telephone, or the moon. Use any number, and place them side by side on the chalk tray or on the desks. Divide the children into teams of four or five members. Each child has a picture magazine, old mail order catalog, etc. The leader points to one picture object (the car). The children quickly thumb through the magazines to see who can come up with another picture of the car first. The winner takes the picture that was put up by the teacher. The game continues until all the pictures are gone. The team with the most pictures wins. After several turns, the magazines are traded. If no one can find a picture, choose other magazines and try again.

- Match the sound game. Make cards with pictures of simple objects, such as a fish, a broom, or a hat on one side, and the letter the object starts with on the other. Make about 30 cards with each letter of the alphabet represented. Then make another set of cards with a letter of the alphabet on each card. Spread out the alphabet letter cards in rows between the players (4 players at the most). One player begins the game by placing one of the picture cards in the middle, and tries to put the right alphabet letter card with it. To check if the letter is correct, the player turns over the picture card to see if the right letter was matched with the right picture. If the cards were matched correctly, the player gets the picture card. The next player tries to match the next picture card with the correct letter of the alphabet, and so on until all the picture cards are won. The winner is the one with the most picture cards.

LISTENING EXERCISES FOR READING READINESS

- **Hearing Sounds**

Purpose: auditory perception; to be able to tell sounds apart. This is necessary before discrimination of letter sounds can be developed.

Equipment: two pieces of sandpaper (to rub together), scissors and paper (to cut), marbles (to roll), a clock (for the winding sound), a rattle, a ball (for bouncing), etc.

Directions: The children listen while the teacher demonstrates what is to be done with each item. Then one child is chosen to be "it," and another is chosen to make a sound. The child who is "it" either turns away or is blindfolded. The teacher or child sounds each item and "it" has to identify the object.

- **Clap Hands Clap**

Directions: Child number 1 closes both eyes. Child number 2 goes to a place in the room and the teacher tells child number 1 that number 2 is ready. Child number 1 then says, "Clap hands clap," and child number 2 claps hands. The first child must point in the direction of the sound. If the child guesses correctly, he gets to take the second child's place. If he does not guess correctly, another child takes his place.

- **Warm-Up Hearing Exercise**

Purpose: auditory perception

Equipment: various small musical instruments

Directions: A child is blindfolded and seated. Other children are stationed at different places in the room. On a signal from the teacher, a designated child talks, sings, or plays an instrument. The blindfolded child must identify the child who is talking, or the song being sung, or the instrument being played.

Variations:

- The instrument is sounded and the blindfolded child must tell if the instrument is near or far away.

- The instrument is sounded and the blindfolded child must say if it is loud or soft.

- Children are placed at various points in the room with the same instruments. The teacher indicates which children are to play loudly and which are to play softly. As each is heard, the blindfolded child must point to the place where the sound came from and tell if it is loud or soft.

- **Dog and Bone**

Directions: One child is selected to be the dog. This child sits on a chair facing away from the other children, who are sitting at their desks. The "dog" closes both eyes. The dog's bone (which is an eraser or any small article) is placed near the dog's chair. Another child, selected by the teacher, tries to sneak up to the dog and get the bone. The child who tries to get the bone then barks, with a disguised voice. This player returns to his seat, and the dog has three tries to guess who has the bone. If the dog does not guess correctly within three tries, the player who has the bone becomes the dog.

- **Hot and Cold**

Purpose: auditory perception

Equipment: something to hide

Directions: Hide an object somewhere in the room, while "it" is not looking. "It" attempts to find the object by moving around the room and listening to the loudness or softness of the clapping. As "it" approaches the object, the clapping becomes louder. As "it" moves away from the object, the clapping becomes softer.

- **Hands**

Directions: One child is blindfolded and must guess what another child is doing. The second child is using his hands in some way, such as clapping, snapping, rubbing, scratching the desk, or tapping the chalk-board. If "it" can't guess what is being done by the child after two tries, the other child becomes "it."

• **Echo**

Directions: The teacher claps out a simple rhythmic pattern and the children repeat it. Progress from short rhymes to more complex and longer patterns.

• **Auditory Activities**

Purpose: to give children the opportunity to develop coordination between hearing and movement, and to tell the difference between sounds

Equipment: balls for each child and a whistle or a musical instrument

A. Drop and catch exercise.

A child closes both eyes while holding a ball with the hands, arms in front of chest. On the command "Drop," the child drops the ball. On hearing the ball hit the floor, the child opens both eyes and catches the ball on the rebound.

B. Drop and catch exercise (back of body).

Child closes eyes, holds the ball behind the neck and away from the body. On the command, "Drop," the child drops the ball. Hearing the ball hit the floor, the child makes a half-turn and catches the ball on the rebound.

C. Bounce and count exercise.

Children turn their backs to the teacher. The teacher bounces a ball a number of times. The children count the number of bounces and duplicate the number of ball bounces they heard.

D. Ball bounce, clap, and catch exercise.

The children turn their backs to the teacher. The teacher claps hands a number of times. The children are asked to clap their hands the same number of times between the time they drop and catch the balls.

E. End of lesson – auditory memory

1. On a long whistle blow, be "tall." (Children stretch arms high in air.)
2. On a short whistle blow, be "small." (Children curl up in a small position.)
3. On two long whistle blows, be "thin." (Children stand with arms and legs very close to body.)
4. On three short whistle blows, be "wide." (Children stand with arms and legs spread out.)

OTHER ACTIVITIES FOR READING READINESS

• **Visual Training**

Directions: Children are instructed to move their eyes without moving their heads.

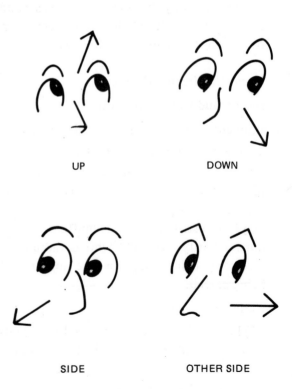

UP   DOWN

SIDE   OTHER SIDE

Fig. 33-3 Visual training.

- **Sam Smith's Suitcase**

Purpose: auditory perception

Directions: The first time, the teacher is the leader. The leader says, "My name is Sam Smith. I'm going to take a trip and take along a suitcase. I'll take some of you with me, but only if you take the right thing with you. Remember, I'm going to take a suitcase."

Each of the young players is then asked what they will take along. Thomas says, "My name is Thomas and I will take along ties." "You may come," says the teacher. Jane says, "My name is Jane. I'll bring along a ribbon." "I'm sorry," says the leader, "you must stay home this trip." (It may be necessary to tell the children that the only ones who can go on the trip are those who name objects which begin with the first letter of their name. Be sure to go on a second trip so that those who couldn't go on the first trip get a chance to go.

- **Color Relay**

Equipment: four large sheets of white paper

Directions: Draw identical sets of fruit forms. (Draw bananas, apples, oranges, grapes, lemons, plums, etc., on each piece of paper. Tack or tape the papers to the wall, far enough apart so that the children can color without interfering with one another.) Provide a box of crayons for each group.

Procedure: Divide the children into teams and line them up. Children can start the game from their seats and each row can be a separate team. Hand a box of crayons to the first child of each team. At the signal each child dashes up and colors any one of the fruit forms with the appropriate crayon. When finished, the child hurries the box of crayons to the next player on the team. Dropped crayons must be picked up by the racing player, not by teammates.

- **Pantomime Common Activities**

Purpose: kinesthetic, gross motor movement

Directions: Show children how to pantomime an activity, for example, jumping rope. Then have the children take turns pantomiming some activity while the others guess what it is. Examples: putting on and tying a shoe, combing hair, filing nails, throwing a ball, playing musical instruments, and so on.

Variation: Name the activity and have the child act it out. For example, have the child demonstrate what it is like to walk through water, mud, or snow; what it would be like to be a fly on sticky paper, a camel in the sand, an old man on ice, or an astronaut in space.

- **Heap Big Smoke**

Purpose: auditory perception, rhythm, and listening

Formation: children in circle

Directions: Children sit cross-legged (Indian fashion) in a circle. Begin by tapping palms on the floor twice, then on the knees twice, then raise hands in the air while shaking fingers. This is done to the words, "Heap big smoke and no fire." Hands are in the air with "No fire." This is repeated once. Then, with the left hand on the hip and the right hand behind the ear, they say, "Oh, they talk a lot, but they're not so hot!" They then return to the original movements and "Heap big smoke and no fire." The first line is repeated with the same movement, but in a louder voice. Then the second line is said in a quiet voice, and finally the third, "Heap big smoke and no fire," is said very loudly. After putting hands in the air and shaking fingers, they finish by bringing hands down in front along with bowing the head to the floor.

Chant complete, no movements:

Heap big smoke and no fire.
Heap big smoke and no fire.
Oh, they talk a lot, but they're not so hot!
Just, heap big smoke and no fire!
Heap big smoke and no fire.
Heap big smoke and no fire.
Heap big smoke and no fire.

- **Auditory Memory Exercises**

Directions: Both the teacher and the children are sitting on the floor. The teacher says sentences similar to the following: "Birds fly," "Cows swim under water," and "Snakes drive cars." If the children think the statement is true, they sit still; however, if they think the statement is false, they imitate what the subject of the sentence really does.

MORE LISTENING EXERCISES

- **What Is It?**

Equipment: glass, bell, block, tin can, glass of water, book, paper clip to strike a comb with, and drum

Purpose: auditory perception and auditory discrimination

Directions: Place a number of objects on a table. Tap these objects so that the children become familiar with the sounds produced. Have the children put their heads down. Tap an object and ask "What is it?" After the children have become familiar with the objects, tap several of the objects and ask which one was tapped first, which second, and so forth.

- **Where Is the Bell?**

Equipment: two or three little bells
Directions: Seat the children in a circle. Have one child leave the room. Give one of the children in the room a bell which is small enough to hide in one hand. Ask the child who left the room to come back in. When the child has returned, have all of the children stand and shake their fists above their heads. You may use more than one bell when the children become accustomed to the game. The player who is "it" will have three chances to locate the bell.

HEARING AND REMEMBERING EXERCISES

Purpose: auditory discrimination and auditory memory

Equipment: various musical instruments

- **Warm-up Rhythm**

Directions: When the music plays slowly, the children should move slowly; as it speeds up, so should they. Begin this activity with a drum. Each time the teacher beats the drum, the children should take a step. At first, the beat will be slow and even. Later, it should be faster and the children should be running. Then, more complex musical pieces can be introduced as the children gain the ability to interpret tempo in music into a corresponding tempo in movement.

- **Simon Says**

Directions: Have children stand so that they can all see the leader (the teacher or another child). The leader gives specific directions, actually doing them while saying them. For example, when the leader says, "Simon says touch your head," the leader touches his own head, too. Children are to follow all directions that begin with "Simon says . . ." If the leader gives a direction but does not say "Simon says . . . ," the children should not follow the direction. Later, the teacher advances to giving two directions.

- **Shapes**

Equipment: various shapes, two of each

Directions: The teacher says, "Now, I want you to listen very closely. I am going to call out three different shapes. Then you will tell everyone the names of those shapes and hold up the shapes in the order they were named. Darlene, a rectangle, a triangle, a circle. Now, you say them. Now hold them up — first, the rectangle. That's it." Give each child a turn. The child holds up the shapes after the teacher has given the auditory commands.

- **Listening Games**

Purpose: auditory discrimination and auditory memory

Area: classroom

Equipment: blindfold, pin, paper clip, rubber ball, pencil, blown-up paper bag, tin pan, castanets, a rattle, pebble, etc.

GAME 1:

Purpose: to identify an animal sound and tell the direction from which it comes

Material: blindfold

Directions: Have the children imitate various animal noises (dog, cat, cow, sheep, etc.). Make sure the noises they make are recognized by the other children. Then blindfold one child while others are positioned around the room. Have one child make an animal noise. The child who is blindfolded must identify the sound and the direction from which it comes. When the blindfolded child gets three right, another child becomes "it."

GAME 2:

Purpose: to identify an object by listening to its sound when dropped

Materials: something one can stand behind and not be seen, a pin, a paper clip, a rubber ball, a pencil, a blown-up paper bag, a tin pan, a rattle, a pebble, castanets, etc.

Directions: Ask children to close their eyes. Stand behind the screen and drop one of the articles on the floor. Ask, "What did you hear?" The performance may need to be repeated several times. Children may take turns dropping the object. Without a screen, children should close their eyes while an object is dropped and then replaced on the table.

GAME 3:

Purpose: to identify children in a classroom by their voices

Equipment: blindfold

Formation: children form circles

Directions: Form a circle of several children. Blindfold one child and have this child stand in the middle. Have the children regroup so that each will be in a different place in the circle. Then have each child make a simple statement, such as "I like to play games." The child in the center then points to one child and identifies this child or asks questions (up to three) that must be answered in a sentence. If the child who is "it" guesses correctly, or fails to after three times, "it" returns to the circle and another child becomes "it." To make the game more difficult, have children disguise their voices.

(The class can be divided into two or more circles instead of one big circle.)

Variation: Blindfold one child, point to another who taps several fingers on the table, floor, etc. The child who is blindfolded says "Who's knocking at my door?" The child who knocked says, "It is I." The person who is "it" has three turns to guess correctly. This game, too, may be made more difficult by having children disguise their voices.

GAME 4:

Equipment: loud ticking clock or timer

Directions: Hide the clock or timer in the classroom while children close their eyes. Then have the children point to where they believe the clock to be.

Allow about 15 minutes for this activity.

Variation: This can be done in the gym using bread drums. The child crawls in the drum. The teacher or another child rings a bell and the child rolls in the direction of the sound.

• Touch Me Box

Cut holes in opposite sides of a cardboard box — large enough for a youngster to put a hand through. Each day place a variety of things inside the box and ask the children to touch the objects. Ask them to describe what they have touched. When selecting objects for the box, try for a good mix of textures — hard, soft, rough, smooth, squishy. Also strive for varied textures that inspire colorful descriptions — velvet, bark, a sponge, sandpaper, cotton, a powder puff, a feather.

• Tick Tock

Many children first learn about time through television. They may know the hour of a favorite television program long before they know when school begins. Ask the children what television programs they watch. Make a wall chart and draw a clock face beside each program showing the time it begins.

• Togetherness

Help children sort objects by like qualities. Ask them: "In what ways is this table like that table?" "In what way is this chair like that table?" (They are both made of wood. They both have four legs.) Have the children suggest things that are alike in some ways. Ask: "How many things in the room are made of wood?" "Which are made of plastic?"

• Sorting Practice

Glue different buttons into the bottom sections of egg cartons. Have several extras of each button so the children can place the matching buttons in the right cup.

• Classification

Introduce the concept of classification, using everyday objects in the classroom. After explaining that things can be classified in any number of ways, ask the children for suggestions on things they can classify. Accept all suggestions. Start with simple objects — blocks, coins, colored paper — that the children can classify using just one criterion (size, shape, color, etc.). Gradually move into two criteria, such as size and color. Make circles, squares, and triangles from construction paper. First ask the children just to name shapes, then add color, size, and so on.

• Are You Listening?

Fill eight margarine tubs (with plastic lids) with different materials: for example, two with flour, two with buttons, two with nails, two with pins. Have the children find the two that sound alike by shaking them.

• Tape That

Tape a story all of the children have read but make some mistakes, changing words here and there. Have the children listen to the tape and pick out the errors.

• Spiderman Starts With "S"

Many children like comic books. Capitalize on it. Ask the children to bring in old copies and make a bulletin board comic book collage, with the names of all their favorite characters printed clearly and spelled correctly.

- **What's in the Bookstore?**

Is there a bookstore in your neighborhood? Take the children on a trip there. (Call ahead to arrange the best time.) Show them some of the most interesting books, especially inexpensive paperbacks. If there is no bookstore nearby, is there another store that sells books? Find out about different book clubs for children.

- **Fast — Slow**

Ask two children to stand side by side. Have one walk and one crawl for a certain length of time — perhaps to a count of 10. Mark how far each has traveled and measure the distance. Discuss other fast/slow relationships — car versus bicycle, airplane versus train, an ice cube melting versus a match burning, building a house versus painting a house.

- **Following Directions**

Divide the class into pairs. Have one member of each pair give directions to the other to get to the front door; the other member of the pair should follow the directions exactly.

- **I Can Read Pictures**

Gathering information from pictures is a useful skill. Have the children look at some pictures in a book. How much can they learn about the characters without reading any of the words? Do the words and pictures always agree? Could the children make up a different story to go with the pictures?

- **A Hoarse Horse**

Have the children collect words that sound the same and draw pictures that illustrate each meaning: horse, hoarse; ball, bawl; pail, pale; rap, wrap; wait, weight; stake, steak; Sunday, sundae; knight, night; I, eye; eight, ate; toe, tow.

- **Library Lessons**

Do all of the children in the class have a library card? Plan a trip to the public library and ask the librarian to speak to them about all the services the library offers. When the children return to class, ask them to tell about all the services they remember, and to explain how to join the library.

- **Not Alike**

Ask the children to tell how things in the room are not alike. "How is a table different from a chair?" "How is this block different from that block?" Use colored construction-paper shapes and ask: "Find two triangles that are different colors," or "Find three different shapes."

- **Color Relay**

From cardboard or oak tag, cut out identical sets of fruit forms, such as bananas, apples, oranges. Mount each set on a large sheet of wrapping paper and fasten the sheets securely on the chalkboard. The class is divided into two teams. They may be lined up or numbered for turns.

The first player on each team has a box of crayons. At the signal, this player goes to the board, colors any one of the fruits on his paper, and returns, giving the box of crayons to the next player. This continues until all of the fruits are colored. The first team to complete all colored fruit is the winning team. Any crayons dropped must be picked up by the player who drops them.

- **Touch**

The group is divided into 2 teams. Each team lines up facing each other, but as far apart as possible. The leader says "Everyone touch wood" (or anything the leader calls). Each child must find wood, touch it, and return to his original place. The first team to do this is the winning team. The leader, or teacher, should try to think of many different things to touch (such as cloth, things made of glass, paper).

• **Who is That?**

Tape voices; radio and television are good sources as well as people you know. Tape voices of people the children know: the custodian, the principal, other children. Tape singers, news announcers, political figures, comedians, cartoon characters, movie stars. Play the voices back and have the children identify them.

• **Sound Idea**

Use a tape recorder and some imagination to create activities to stimulate children's perceptions and imaginations. Tape all kinds of sounds for the children to identify and describe. Tape individual sounds, such as an alarm clock, a police siren, a piano, a flute, a baby crying, a cat meowing, a dog barking. Play the tape and ask the children to identify the sounds and describe the sound makers.

• **Nonverbal Communication**

Not all language is verbal. Have the children act out the following phrases silently: "Stop!" "Just a minute!" "Yes!" "No!" "I'm tired." "I have a headache." "That smells good." "What a surprise!"

• **Words and Music**

Ask the children to bring some of their favorite records to class. Play them and have the children sing the words. Start a class songbook with the words of songs, clippings about favorite singers, and so on.

• **Dream a Dream**

Have the children lie on the floor or put their heads on their desks and close their eyes. Then take them on an "imaginary journey." For example, say: "Imagine you are floating on a river. The river is winding through a beautiful forest. You can see the trees, the golden flowers and the blue sky." Then, let them continue the journeys on their own and discuss their imaginings afterwards.

• **Mat Stunts**

Purpose: kinesthetic awareness and tactile awareness

Equipment: mat for safety

Directions: Divide 8 children into squads of four each. For a "dog run relay," children are on hands and feet (4-legged run with weight distributed evenly on hands and feet). For "lame dog relay," children are on two hands and one leg (3-legged run with weight on hands, and hopping with one leg forward).

• **Hoop Pattern with Ball Bouncing**

Equipment: 10 hoops, 2 balls, 2 sets of number cards 1–5

Directions: There should be two squads of four children each. Each child holds a ball, jumps into each hoop, and bounces and catches the ball a directed number of times inside each hoop. The first team to be completely sitting wins.

• **Rhyming Game**

Directions: Children are seated in a circle formation. The teacher says to a child, "Say may, day, play. Do these words sound the same?" (Yes)

Note: At first, the child may have difficulty understanding the concept of rhyme. In the beginning, it might be easier to offer two choices. Once several children understand what a rhyme is, a game can be made out of it. The first player says a word. The second player says the first player's word and another word that rhymes with it. Continue around the circle in this manner. The third player has to repeat the first two players' words, plus make up a third word which rhymes with the first two. The last child left is the winner.

• **Textures**

Purpose: follow-up to tactile activities in previous lessons; auditory memory

Equipment: various items with different textures: such as salt, flour, rice, beans, water, or ice; several small bowls

Vocabulary: touch, soft, silky, smooth, rough, bumpy, cool, warm, icy, sticky, hard

Directions: The child places a hand in the first bowl and feels what is inside. The teacher says, "How does the flour in this bowl feel?" The child may answer that it feels "fine." The teacher says, "Doesn't it feel soft and smooth?" After two or three different things are felt and described, ask the child to close both eyes. Place one of the three bowls in front of the child. Say, "Let's play a touching-guessing game. What does this feel like?" The child may be able to remember from the feel of it, what is in the bowl and be able to describe it. If the child has trouble, give some hints. Let the child try the guessing game with the teacher. The teacher closes both eyes and the child places a bowl under the teacher's hand, for the teacher to guess the contents. More items can gradually be added to the game. The children can play the guessing game with each other, too.

• **Touch and Tell Game**

Vocabulary: soft, hard, rough, smooth, heavy, light, big, small, thick, thin

Directions: Ask a child to sit down, close his eyes, and open his hands in front of him. Place an object (stone, pencil, leaf) in his open hands. Ask him questions about the object: "What does it feel like? Is it hard or soft? Is it thick or thin? What is it used for? Where is it found? What does it do?" The last question should be "What is it?" The goal of the game is for the child to figure out what the object is without opening his eyes. Let each child take turns holding an object and answering questions about it.

Note: This game can be played anywhere, indoors or out. Play it with one or more children. Once they learn the game, the children can play it with each other.

• **Stimulate Tactile Awareness**

Directions: Children pair off in scatter formation. Child A closes both eyes and stretches both hands flat on the knees, palms down. Child B taps one of Child A's fingers and asks Child A to move the finger tapped. After five minutes, children reverse roles.

• **Colors**

Purpose: visual discrimination

Equipment: five or six colors of construction paper cut into shapes (circles, squares, triangles), one piece per child

Directions: The children are seated in a circle. They each place a marker in front of themselves. The teacher calls out one of the colors. All children having that color run around the circle in the same direction and back to their places. The first one seated upright and motionless is the winner.

Different kinds of locomotor movements can be specified (skipping, galloping, walking, hopping, etc.).

Variations: Use shapes instead of colors.

• Put in Order

Materials: objects of various sizes, textures, and shapes

Directions: Scatter several objects on the floor. Blindfold the children and tell them the type of object they must locate. Begin with three types. Have them locate the objects and place them in order. For example, tell them to find something round, then something hard, then something smooth.

• Memory Ball

Materials: football, basketball, baseball, softball, soccerball, volleyball, kickball, tennis ball, and whiffle ball

Directions: Place the balls in different locations on the floor. Have the children, blindfolded (or with their eyes closed), locate and name the various balls and tell what they are used for.

Fig. 33-4 In the memory ball game, a large playground ball is one type that can be placed in a corner of the room, for children to find and identify.

• Mystery Box or Bag

Purpose: tactile discrimination

Equipment: box or bag, and geometric block shapes which are made of various types of material (kindergartens should have various parquetry shapes that would be excellent for this activity; also wooden letter shapes)

Directions: Construct a "feel" box. This is a cardboard box with a hole cut into the top. Into the box are put objects of different geometric forms, which are made of various types of materials. The child must reach in, feel an object, and identify its shape by touch. The object may then be removed from the box, and the child can see if the guess was correct. This can be done with the children seated in a circle on the floor.

• Walking and Feeling

Purpose: tactile discrimination

Materials: 1 or 2 pans of wet textures of mud, sand, moist clay
1 or 2 pans of dry mixtures of sand, dirt, grits, pebbles

Directions: Blindfolded, the children place their feet in different wet textures and dry textures, and make basic forms and free designs with their feet.

• Footprints and Handprints

Materials: fingerpaint and fingerpaint paper

Directions: Children step in fingerpaint and print their right feet and left feet, and then their hands. This work could be saved and used in social studies for a book "all about me."

• Temperature Identification

Materials: four bowls of water (cold, hot, cool, warm)

Directions: While blindfolded, the child uses an elbow to identify hot, cold, warm, and cool water temperatures.

• **Matching Game**

Materials: a box with a piece of cloth attached to the front, shapes (two of each), and other symbols (letters, numbers, two of each)

Directions: The child matches basic symbols inside a cloth-draped wooden box.

• **Fruit Guess**

Materials: blindfold and various pieces of fruit (orange, apple, pear, banana); vegetables can also be used.

Directions: One child in the group is blindfolded. The leader of the group hands the blindfolded child a piece of fruit. The child tries to guess the name of the fruit.

• **Identifying Body Parts**

Purpose: develop tactile perception by identifying and matching objects by touching and feeling

Equipment: a blindfold for each child (tear up an old sheet)

Formation: scatter formation in pairs

I. Children will identify body parts while blindfolded.
  1. Touch your toes.
  2. Touch your knees.
  3. Touch your elbows.
  4. Touch your shoulders.
  5. Touch your ankles.
  6. Touch your heels.
II. Back writing
  1. Divide the children into pairs.
  2. Child A writes a letter or numeral on Child B's back, and Child B tries to guess what this letter or number is.

3. Children change roles: Child B writes on Child A's back.

III. Blind crawl using ropes

Equipment: a blindfold for every child (or just have the children close their eyes), a jump rope for every child

Directions:
  1. Can you crawl over the rope blindfolded or with your eyes closed?
  2. Can you jump over the rope blindfolded or with your eyes closed?
  3. Can you crawl up and down the rope blindfolded or with your eyes closed?
  4. Can you crawl on your back up and down the rope?
  5. Can you hop over the rope blindfolded or with your eyes closed?
  6. Can you jump rope blindfolded or with your eyes closed?

• **Fine Motor Exercises**

Purpose: kinesthetic (fine – motor)

Equipment: fingerpaint, fingerpaint paper or glossy shelf paper

Directions: Let the children squeeze the fingerpaint through their fingers until they get the "feel" of it. Then show them how they can make designs with their fingers, thumbs, palms of their hands, arms, knuckles.

Hint: Use fingerpaintings as covers for collections of the children's own artwork or stories they have composed.

• **Hand Tracing**

Equipment: paper, pencil, inkblot pad

Directions: Have a child place one hand firmly in the center of a 9″ x 12″ sheet of paper. Using the other hand, the child traces one on the paper. Make sure the child realizes that the hand must be held firmly. If desired, the child may take each finger, put it in ink, and paint in the corresponding finger on both right and left hands.

- **Tracing**

Materials: crayons, large manila paper

Directions: Children will make a certain letter with one color crayon. Then tell them they can make letter "rainbows" by tracing over the letter. Then have the children outline letters and make their names or certain vocabulary words which are giving the children problems.

- **Comparing Shapes and Sizes**

Materials: a variety of objects familiar to the child: button, bead, peg, ball, etc.

Directions: A leader blindfolds each child. Place an object in one hand for the child to feel. Ask the child to identify the object. Then put it on a table with two other objects and ask the child to find it. Gradually increase the difficulty of the task by adding more shapes and sizes. Examples: a round bead and an oval bead, a small ball and a large ball, a square box and a rectangular box.

Unit 34 MOVEMENT

• **Hula Hoops**

Each child has a hula hoop. Have the child place it on the floor, leaving enough space so movement around it will be safe.

Directions:

I. Have the children:

1. Move around their hoops. When the teacher calls out a part of the body, the children stop and put that part (hand, foot, elbow, etc.) in the hoop.
2. Go over the hoop as many different ways as they can.
3. Go around the hoop as many different ways as they can.
4. Touch the hoop with as many parts of the body as they can at the same time: hand, foot, knee, etc.
5. Make the hoop twirl in as many ways and with as many different parts of their body as they can.

Fig. 34-1 Hoops provide large motor fun for all ages.

6. Roll the hoop and run beside it.
7. Roll the hoop and run past it.
8. Roll the hoop and go through it.
9. Roll the hoop in a circle.

II. Ask the children if they can:

1. Jump in and out of the hoop? Front, side, and backward . . . ?
2. Hop in and out of the hoop? Front, side, and backward . . . ?
3. Run around the outside of the hoop? Change directions . . . ?
4. Put both hands inside the hoop and both feet outside the hoop . . .? Circle around the hoop in this position?
5. Put both feet inside the hoop and both hands outside? Circle around the hoop in this position?
6. Roll the hoop and keep it from falling over?
7. Spin the hoop away from you so that it will return?
8. While the hoop is rolling, make it turn without having to stop it? Spin the hoop like an egg beater?
9. Throw the hoop into the air and catch it before it hits the ground?
10. Jump the rope like a hoop? Make your hoop turn around your neck? Around your waist? Around your arm?
11. How many different things can you do with the hoop while you are walking the balance beam?
12. What can you do with two hoops?

• **Tin Can Stilts**

(Simple to construct — children love them!)

Materials: 2 no. 10 tin cans, nylon cord, 4 nails

Directions:

1. To secure the cord to the cans, punch two holes in the top of the cans.
2. Tie the cord to the middle of the nails and insert through the hole in the can. The nail will keep the cord from pulling out of the can. Do this in all four holes (2 cans).

• **Rope Skills**

Directions:

1. With the rope laid in a straight line on the floor, can you walk it as if it were a tight rope? Can you do this while moving backward?
2. Who can walk the "tight rope" with their eyes shut?
3. Can you jump from side to side across the rope without touching the rope?
4. Can you hop from side to side without touching the rope?
5. Can you straddle the rope, jump in the air, turn around, and land on your feet straddling the rope?
6. Lay your rope in the pattern of a circle. Can you get inside the circle, taking up as much space as possible, without hanging over the edges?
7. Make several little circles with the rope. Can you put one body part in each circle and balance?
8. If your rope were shaped as the letter "V," could you jump over the "V" without touching the rope? See how close you can come to jumping or leaping over the widest part of the "V."
9. Can you go over your rope by placing both hands on one side and swinging your legs across? How high can you swing your legs as you bring them across?
10. Place the rope on the floor in a long curved shape. Can you begin at one end and travel to the other end by kicking your feet in the air and doing most of the traveling on your feet?
11. Take one end of the rope in each hand (step over the rope so that it is behind you). Now, pull the rope over your head and see if you can jump it as it comes down to your feet. Can you jump it one time? Two or three times without stopping? How many can you do without having to stop?

• **More Rope Skills**

Give each child a short rope. Find an empty space in the classroom. Pull hard on both ends of your rope. See how many places you can take your stretched rope in your own space. Try to keep moving your rope all the time: up, down, front, forward, back, side to side. How far from the middle of your body can you stretch your rope? How far in front? How far behind you? Keep pulling and stretching. Can you bend your body sideways and keep stretching the rope? Bend backward? Feel how strong your muscles are as you pull on the ends of your rope.

Variation: Try standing with your feet wide apart. Then, with your feet close together, which way can you get a stronger and longer bend in your body and stretch on your rope? Sit down and see how many places you can stretch your rope: high over head and down near the floor. Try kneeling. How far to the side can you bend your body and still keep moving the rope? Can you feel the tightness of the muscles when you pull hard on the rope?

• **Circles**

Set up four groups of imaginary circles on the floor, with six to eight short ropes in each circle. Have one child to each rope.

The problem is spacing. The purpose is to develop an awareness of when to speed up and when to slow down in order to keep an even distribution around the circle. The children will have to be stopped and started several times so their positions can be checked, and explanations can be given. This will be a difficult concept for children to master but it should be introduced and practiced· often thereafter.

The teacher can ask the children if they can move forward, backward, and sideways over the ropes, or go over each rope in some other different way. How high can they get into the air as they go over the rope? How softly can they land? The teacher then changes directions on the call. Everyone forward over two ropes in different ways; everyone backward over 3 ropes in as many ways as they can; then forward. Can everyone turn halfway around as they jump over each of the 3 ropes . . . and so on.

• **Partners**

Pick partners who have about the same level of skills.

Directions:

1. How many can face their partner holding the end of the rope in one hand and turn it slowly? When they can do this, try the same thing with the other hand.
2. Have partners facing each other across the rope. While each partner holds the other partner's hands, can they both jump at the same time so that they land straddling the rope? How many can give a bigger jump and land on opposite sides of the rope while still holding hands?
3. Can the partners do the same thing from a stoop position?
4. Have partners facing each other across the rope again. Can they jump across the rope, turn and jump again, doing this at the same time? If successful, they can try the same routine with hopping and leaping.

Fig. 34-2 Children enjoy using old tires to climb and swing on as playground equipment.

• **Movement Experiences with Tires**

Purpose: to develop agility and stamina

Equipment: old bus tires

Note: There may be a storage problem. Tires will leave marks on floors unless polyethylene is placed under them. For inside storage, do not stack tires more then five high. *Caution:* do not let children play inside the tires when they are stacked. When tires are stored outside, stand them upright and next to each other against a tree, post, or fence.

Run a lightweight chain through the middle of the tires, over the top and around the post. Lock the free ends together. This will prevent them from being rolled all over the school grounds.

Outside tires should also be covered with polyethylene to keep water out. Be certain the tires are dry on the surface before the children use them.

• Single Tire Routines

Directions:

1. Walk around the rim of the tire.
2. Spread feet on the rim of the tire and jump around the circles.
3. Jump in and out of a tire using various rhythms.
4. Can you get into the "push up" position and move around your tire keeping your back straight? How many times?
5. Jump out, in, out, in, etc.
6. Stand inside a tire. Jump upward as high as you can. At the top of your jump, spread your feet as wide as you can. Then, quickly bring them back together again and land inside the tire.
7. Stand with feet spread on the edge of the tire. Jump upward. Click your heels together and land with your feet spread on the edge of the tire as in the beginning.
8. Get into the push-up position again, this time with your feet on the tire. Keep your back straight. Can you walk around the tire in this position using your hands and feet?
9. From the frog jump position, can you jump and turn halfway around on your tire? Both feet and hands must be off the tire while you are turning.
10. Feet spread, jump up, then turn halfway, and land! (Can you turn all the way around?)
11. From a stand, do a tuck, a pike, and then a spread eagle.

• The Box

Find a large cardboard packing box, large enough for children to crawl in and out of. Cut four openings, one on each side, in the shape of a triangle, a square, a rectangle, and a circle. Make openings large enough for the children to crawl in and out of the box.

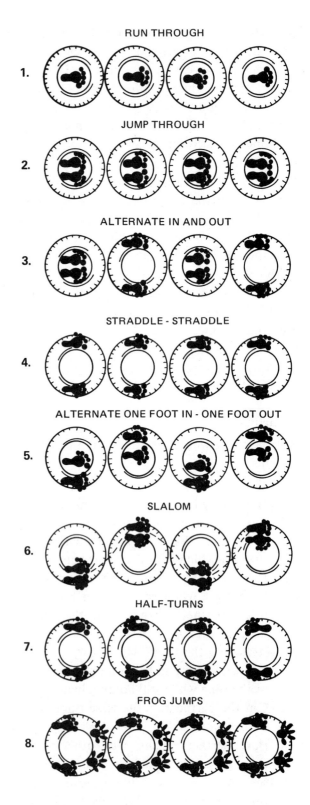

Fig. 34-3 Tire techniques.

Set up problems for the children to solve such as:

1. Identify all openings.
2. Crawl in the box head first through the circle, and come out feet first through the square.
3. Crawl in head first through the rectangle. Now head out of the triangle, then the square, and then the circle.

• **I Can**

Here's an action poem that leads to a lot of fun and movement.

Like a bunny I can hop
I can spin like a top.
I can reach way up high
And I almost touch the sky.
In a boat I row and row
Sometimes fast and sometimes slow.
Now a bouncing jumping jack
I pop up and then go back.
Then sway gently in the breeze
Like the little forest trees.
Make silly faces like a clown
And then I quietly settle down.

• **Three-Quarter Time**

Bring in some old and new dance records — a waltz, a tango, a foxtrot, ragtime, the twist, and some popular songs. Let the children make up their own dances to suit the way the music makes them feel. Then sit in a circle and clap to the dance rhythms.

• **How Do You Feel?**

Many children know only a few verbal expressions for their feelings, for example, happy, sad, mad. A good way to sharpen their awareness of emotions and increase their vocabulary is to have them pantomime stories. Tell a story about a commonplace activity, such as going to the store, or riding the bus. Make sure to introduce incidents that produce different emotions. As you get to each incident, name the emotion (puzzlement, frustration, joy, weariness, annoyance) and have the children act it out.

• **It's How It's Said**

Have the children act out the following phrases as they would be said by different people: "I'm thirsty," as said by an athlete who has run a mile, by Count Dracula, and by a whiny child. "Oh," as said by someone in pain, in surprise, in admiration, in disbelief.

• **Use the Tube**

Long cardboard tubes, like the ones used for wrapping paper, can be imaginative props for pantomime. Have each child use a tube in a way that suggests an action. As each child performs the pantomime, have the others guess what is being done. Some obvious uses are a telescope, cane, sword, etc., but children can come up with such variations as a straw for a "giant soda" or a dispenser for paper cups.

• **Ring Around the Rosy — Leader**

This game is a combination of Ring Around the Rosy and Follow the Leader. The group joins hands in a circle. The leader says, "Circle left" or "Circle right." As they walk around they sing "Ring around the rosy, a pocket full of posies. Ashes, ashes. Leader, what do we do?" After the words, "Ashes, ashes" everyone stops to see what the leader will do. Everyone follows the actions of the leader. A new leader is chosen by the previous leader each time.

• **Keep the Basket Full**

Take a basket of balls and pour them out on the floor. The children, who are scattered around the room, run after the balls, bring them back, and put them in the basket. The teacher should keep pouring them out for a few minutes to give all the children an opportunity to get one or more balls.

This active game helps develop space awareness, quick change of direction, and moving in a straight line.

• **Turk Stand**

The children are standing scattered around the floor. Have them cross their legs (Indian style), cross their arms, and try to sit down without uncrossing either arms or legs. Then ask the children to stand up without uncrossing either arms or legs or touching knees to the floor. Suggest that they keep their feet as flat as they can if they are having trouble standing up. Have the children try the exercise several times during this activity period, and frequently throughout the year. It is an excellent way to develop coordination and a sense of balance.

• **Follow the Ropes**

Give each child a rope and make sure each is positioned so there is plenty of space between children. Say, "Pull on the rope as hard as you can and move the stretched rope as many places as you can." (For example, they may extend their arms overhead with the rope stretched in their hands; try to get the rope behind their back, etc.)

Lay out the ropes and ask the children to follow you and do as you do. As you go over each rope, do something different, such as hop.

Unit 35 COOKING EXPERIENCES

Cooking is usually a favorite activity with preschoolers. They like to help prepare foods as well as eat what they have made. There are many simple projects which three- and four-year-olds can handle by themselves. But even when using more complicated recipes, children can do most of the work. Let them do the pouring, dumping, or stirring, for example, while you hold the bowl.

Children can help prepare family meals at home. Think of simple tasks for them to do, such as tearing lettuce for a salad, buttering dinner rolls, or frosting cupcakes. To young children, helping prepare a family meal can be very special. Praise the child's efforts, even if the job isn't up to adult standards. More important than perfection is the child's sense of pride as he presents the family with his contribution to the meal. A child may be more willing to try new foods if he has helped prepare them.

Cooking can also be a good learning experience. It is fun to watch the amazement on a young child's face as he discovers that orange juice can be squeezed from real oranges and that bread does not always come from the grocer's shelf. A set of measuring cups and spoons provides early learning about measurement. Counting the number of teaspoons needed is a good way to introduce numbers. For preschoolers, perhaps the most exciting part of cooking is watching what happens as ingredients are mixed, new ones are added, and the food changes as it is cooked. This is an excellent time to compare colors, sizes, and textures. Be sure to do lots of tasting, smelling, and feeling as you go along!

It is a good idea to cover the work area with a plastic tablecloth or a piece of newspaper. Part of the fun of cooking is being a bit messy, and an occasional accident may occur. Also, if keeping clothes clean is necessary, the child can wear an old shirt, smock, or apron.

Fig. 35-1 Cooking with young children provides a pleasant combination of social, math, and science experiences.

FOODS FROM DIFFERENT CULTURES AND GEOGRAPHICAL AREAS

Southern spoon bread, hush puppies

Chinese steamed rice

Mexican tortillas

Italian spaghetti and meatballs

Swedish pancakes; meatballs

Irish or Scotch stew

Spanish rice

Danish apple pudding

Guacamole

English muffins (toasted, with jelly or honey)

Scotch shortbread

California hamburger

Puerto Rican green beans

Hot German potato salad

French bread (buttered and warm)

Italian bread sticks, fortune cookies (buy)

"HEALTH FOODS"

Whole grains

Wheat germ

Seeds

Honey (instead of sugar)

Carob (instead of chocolate)

Fresh or dried fruits

Molasses

Nuts

SENSORY EXPERIENCES WITH FOOD

- Sight — bread rising
- Hearing — popcorn popping
- Taste — sweetness of maple syrup
- Smell — bacon frying
- Touch — coolness of ice cream

THINGS TO REMEMBER WHEN WORKING WITH FOODS

1. Work out a sequence of steps.
2. Write the steps on the blackboard or make a wall chart.
3. Plan a series of projects which are gradually more complex.
4. Encourage the children to talk about what they are doing.
5. Relate the activity to home experiences.
6. Label new foods, processes, equipment.
7. Ask children and parents for ideas about things to make.

8. When appropriate, involve the children in getting supplies.
9. Encourage discussion of what has been done. Allow time for tasting and touching.
10. Keep in mind the different kinds of learnings involved in cooking — science, math, language arts, understanding of community and home.
11. Use supplementary and follow-up activities to reinforce learning.

USING FOOD IN SCIENCE ACTIVITIES

- Plant an outdoor or indoor garden.
- Have a tasting party.
- Arrange unusual foods on a science table.
- Place carrot, beet, or pineapple tops in a shallow bowl of crushed stones or pebbles covered with water.
- Cut off the top 1/3 of a sweet potato and put it in water. Allow sprouts to vine at the top. Hold the potato part way out of the water.
- Examine a coconut. Break it open.
- Examine and cut a fresh pineapple.
- Taste baby foods.
- Place seed catalogs on the reading shelf.
- Make apple sauce, butter, ice cream, jello.
- Sip orange juice with a straw.
- Vegetable or fruit dyeing (cranberry or beet juice and white cloth or feathers).

WHAT YOUNG CHILDREN ENJOY ABOUT FOOD

- Bright colors
- Mild flavors
- Different textures (try a variety in each meal — crisp, smooth)
- Finger foods (small pieces are easier to eat)

- Lukewarm foods
- Unmixed, simple foods (foods easy to place in a spoon or fork)
- Consistency (children like moist and smooth foods)

TABLE ACTIVITIES — FOOD EXPERIENCES

- Sewing cards with food pictures
- Teacher-made "move forward" games (ice cream store, hot dog stand)
- Lotto games — teacher-made or store bought
- Set out dishpans of beans with funnels, cups
- Food scale with beans for weighing
- Balance with beans
- Commercial puzzles with food parts
- Placemats
- Flannel board activities with food cutouts
- Classification games

FIELD TRIPS — FOOD EXPERIENCES

- Grocery store
- Vegetable garden
- Fruit orchard
- School kitchen
- Bakery
- Restaurant
- Pizza parlor
- Ice cream store
- Fruit and vegetable stand
- Bottling company
- Dairy
- Canning factory
- Hatchery
- Cornfield, strawberry or melon patch
- Kitchen of one of the children's families

EXAMPLE OF A COOKING EXPERIENCE

Materials: rotary eggbeater in fitted bowl (or pint jar with screwcap), mixing bowl, wooden spoon, salt, whipping cream (1/2 pint of cream, with a minimum of butterfat content, makes 1/3 cup of butter)

Procedure:

1. Remove the cream from the refrigerator 10 minutes before churning.
2. Beat or shake until small lumps of butter form throughout the cream (20 to 30 minutes).
3. Pour off buttermilk and work the remaining buttermilk out of the butter.
4. Wash the butter several times and add 1/4 teaspoon salt for each cup of cream.

COMMERCIAL EQUIPMENT FOR COOKING EXPERIENCES

Egg Carrier, Creative Playthings
Apple Differences, Puzzles, Creative Playthings
Wood Cash Register, Creative Playthings
Aluminum Utensils, Constructive Playthings
Birthday Party Puzzle, Playskool
Baker Party Puzzle, Playskool
Fruits I Like Puzzle, Playskool
I Set the Table Puzzle, Playskool
Milkman Puzzle, Playskool
Grocer Puzzle, Playskool
Waitress Puzzle, Playskool
Gingerbread Boy Puzzle, Constructive Playthings
Making Maple Syrup, Judy See-Quees, Constructive Playthings
Apple Tree, Judy See-Quees, Constructive Playthings
Story of Milk, Judy See-Quees, Constructive Playthings
Grocery Shopping, Judy See-Quees, Constructive Playthings

Foods, 32 Photographs, Constructive Playthings

Plants and Foods, Instructo Flannel Board Aids, Constructive Playthings

Nutrition, Instructo Flannel Board Aids, Constructive Playthings

Balanced Meals, Constructive Playthings

Supermarket, Senior Puzzle, Constructive Playthings

Pears or Apples, Difference Puzzles, Constructive Playthings

Apple Puzzle, Judy See-Quees, Constructive Playthings

Milk Carrier Puzzle, Constructive Playthings

Milk Wagon Puzzle, Fisher Price, Constructive Playthings

Aluminum Liquid Measures, Constructive Playthings

Nutrition Bulletin Board Aids, Constructive Playthings

Time to Eat, Golden Block Book, Constructive Playthings

RELATED RECORDS FOR COOKING EXPERIENCES

No. 1023 Sugar Lump Town, Constructive Playthings

No. 1003 Carrol Seed, Constructive Playthings

No. 7070 The Downtown Story (Department Store and Supermarket)

No. 7071 The Laundry and Bakery Story

Gingerbread Story Sets, Educational Testing Aids Division

Food Market Classification Game, Educational Testing Aids Division

Food Set, 32 Cards, General Learning Corporation

Supermarket, Judy Puzzle, Educational Testing Aids Division

Baking a Cake, Judy See-Quees, Educational Testing Aids Division

Apple, Judy Puzzle, Educational Testing Aids Division

Apple Traction Set, Educational Testing Aids Division

GAMES FOR COOKING EXPERIENCES

1. Farmer Plants His Seeds (corn, oats, beans, carrots, etc.)
2. Farmer Picks His Corn (beans, radishes, turnips, etc.)
3. Can you Remember? (display foods on a tray, cover, try to remember where each is)
4. How Many? (different foods, etc.)
5. Which? (foods that can be eaten raw, foods that are yellow, etc.)
6. Grouping (those that are yellow, those that are eaten for breakfast, etc.)
7. Which Came First? (orange, orange juice; egg, fried egg)
8. What's Its Name?
9. Scrabble (place in a row, identify; rearrange, identify)
10. I See A Food; Do You See One?
11. Touch and Tell (place food in a bag; have child feel and try to identify)
12. Smell and Tell (have child close eyes and try to identify food by smelling)
13. Guess What? (describe the characteristics of food and children try to identify)
14. Hot Potato (choose an object that is light and easy to pass; pretend it is a hot potato; have children sit in a circle; pass the hot potato quickly around the room; ring a bell to catch someone with the hot potato)

CREATIVE ART ACTIVITIES WITH FOOD

- Macaroni collage
- Fruit-colored playdough
- Instant potato finger paint (water and instant potato)
- Spaghetti painting
- Stringing cheerios/fruit loops

Supermarket	Grocery boxes, cash register, play money, paper pads, pencils, paper sacks, empty food cartons, grocery carts, grocery aprons, cans with smooth edges, food posters, food scale, bread sacks stuffed with paper, plastic foods, number stamps and stamp pads, telephone.
Dairy store or milkman	Plastic bottles, milk cartons, wagon or cart, white hat and coat, ice cream cartons, ice cream scoop, ice cream cones, ice cream posters, malt/milk shake cups, sundae dishes.
Restaurant	Order pads, dishes, tablecloth, silverware, chef's hat, cash register, hot dog stand, menus, napkin dispensers, aprons, waitress hats, disposable containers, paper bags from drive-ins.
Cooking	Pots, dishes, egg beater, toy toaster, aprons, spoons, pitchers, rolling pin, flour sifter, empty spice containers, funnel, salt boxes, empty food containers, skillet, pancake turner, ice cube tray, pictures of food mounted on cardboard, TV dinner trays, plastic foods, measuring cups, cookie cutters.

Fig. 35-2 Learning centers related to food experiences.

- Potato printing
- Stringing macaroni
- Printing with cabbage, lemons, oranges, celery, carrots, onions, peppers
- Seed collage
- Jello finger painting
- Rice and felt collage (color rice)
- Broken eggshells on paintings
- Child-made food books
  Foods I Like
  Fruits I Like
  Foods My Daddy (or Mommy, Sister, etc.) Likes
- A mural made of pictures of foods
- Salt trays (place salt in shallow box, child may write with finger in it)
- Creating flannel board pictures (have foods cut from flannel for child to arrange on table, on plate, in basket)
- Cut food pictures from newspaper ads to paste on colored paper
- Colored cornmeal (mix cornmeal and dry tempera; sprinkle on glue designs)
- Have children paste pictures of foods on a chart with area for fruits and vegetables, breads, milk, meats

ADVANTAGES OF COOKING EXPERIENCES FOR CHILDREN

1. Easy to provide.
2. Basic to life and related to everyday experiences.
3. Cooking is an activity where emotions can be involved.
4. To young children, food may have special meaning.
5. Provides an opportunity for children to try out adult roles.
6. It is a way to include children in home activities.
7. Cooking is work which results in a worthwhile product.
8. These experiences can be used to achieve a variety of objectives.
9. Provides opportunities to learn about different cultures.
10. Encourages children to use all senses.

Level	Medium	Title	Color Cir.	Sound	Date	Price	Source	Size
Preschool-Kindergarten Primary 1,2	Cards	Concept Builders-Foods	C	-	P69	$ 4.95	Instructo	32 ea.
"	Sound Filmstrip	Foods to Help Us Grow	C	Record	68	$12.50	RMI Film	Approx. 9 min.
"	Transparency	Foods	C	-	67	$ 7.00	Creative Visuals	1 ea.
"	Study Print	Food and Nutrition (12)	C	-	69	$ 2.25	David C. Cook	1 ea.
"	Study Print	Miniature Take-home Pictures	C	-	69	$ 1.50	David C. Cook	5 ea.
"	Filmstrip	Indian Food (American Indian)	C	-	69	$ 6.00	Curriculum Materials Corp.	—
"	Filmstrip	Wholesome Living	C	-	P69	$ 7.25	Bailey Film Assn.	Approx. 20 frames
"	Movie 8 mm.	Frozen Foods	C	Sound	P69	$89.00	Bailey Film Assn.	11 min.
"	Videotape	Roundabout: Baking	-	Sound	P69	$35.00	Natl. ITV Center	15 min.
"	Transparency	Mother & Daughter Preparing Food	C		P68	$ 4.00	GAP Reprographic	1 ea.
"	Game	Floor Puzzle-Breakfast	C	-	P70	$10.20	Scott Foresman	1 ea.
"	Record (33)	How to Use Food & Stay Healthy	-	-	69	$11.50	Society for Visual Ed.	12 slides

Fig. 35-3 Audiovisual media for food experiences.

11. It is a way to teach good nutrition, and expose children and parents to healthy foods.

12. Through cooking experiences, customs and holidays can be celebrated.

FOOD BIBLIOGRAPHY FOR PRESCHOOL CHILDREN

Arnold, Pauline, *Food Facts for Young People*. New York: Holiday House, 1968.

Beck, Barbara L., *The First Book of Fruits*. New York: Franklin Watts Inc., 1967.

Berenstein, Stanley, *The Big Honey Hunt*. New York: Beginner Books, 1961.

Best, Allena, *Eating and Cooking Around the World, Fingers Before Forks*. New York: John Day Company, 1963.

Brown, Marcia, *Stone Soup*. New York: Charles Scribner's Sons, 1947.

Brown, Myra, *Company's Coming for Dinner*. New York: Franklin Watts, Inc., 1959.

Brown, Myra, *Ice Cream for Breakfast*. New York: Franklin Watts, Inc., 1963.

Buehr, Walter, *Bread, the Staff of Life*. New York: Morrow, 1959.

Buehr, Walter, *Food from Farm to Home*. New York: Morrow, 1970.

Eberle, Irmengarde, *Basketful, The Story of Our Foods*. New York: Thomas Y. Crowell Company, 1946.

Edlin, Herbert Leeson, *Plants and Men; The Story of Our Basic Food*. Garden City, N.Y.: Natural History Press, 1969.

Edwards, D., *Growing Food*. New York: John Day Company, 1969.

Esterer, Arnulf K., *Food: Riches of the Earth*. New York: Messner, 1969.

Fenton, Carroll L., *Fruits We Eat*. New York: John Day Company, 1961.

Fenton, Carroll L., *Plants That Feed Us*. New York: John Day Company, 1956.

Goldman, Ethel, *I Like Fruit*. Minneapolis, Minnesota: Lerner, 1969.

Graham, Ada, *The Great American Shopping Cart*. New York: Simon and Schuster, 1969.

Green, Mary, *Everybody Has a House and Everybody Eats*. New York: Young Scott Books, 1961.

Hoban, Russell, *Bread and Jam for Frances*. New York: Harper and Row Publishers, 1964.

Johnson, Lois S., *What We Eat: The Origins and Travels of Foods Round the World*. Chicago, Illinois: Rand McNally, 1969.

Leonni, Leo, *Swimmy*. New York: Pantheon, 1963.

Lerner, Sharon, *I Like Vegetables*. Minneapolis, Minnesota: Lerner Publishing Company, 1967.

Lewis, Alfred, *The New World of Food*. New York: Dodd, Mead, 1968.

Riedman, Sarah R., *Food for People*. New York: Abelard-Schuman, 1961.

Rothschild, Alice, *Fruit is Ripe for Timothy*. New York: Young Scott Books, 1963.

Scheik, Ida, *The First Book of Food*. New York: Franklin Watts, 1956.

Selsam, Millicent, *Peanut*. New York: William Morrow and Company, 1969.

Selsam, Millicent, *Plenty of Fish*. New York: Harper and Row, 1960.

Sendak, Maurice, *In the Night Kitchen*. New York: Harper and Row, 1970.

Trisselt, Alvin, *Autumn Harvest*. New York: Lothrop, Lee and Shepard Company, 1966.

Watson, Aldren, *My Garden Grows*. New York: Viking Press, 1962.

Weldsmith, Brian, *Fishes*. New York: Franklin Watts, 1968.

Wise, William, *Fresh Canned and Frozen: Food from Past to Future*. New York: Parents Magazine Press, 1971.

Zim, Herbert S., *Your Food and You*. New York: W. Morros, 1957.

SONGS, FINGER PLAYS, POEMS

Some well-known poems to use:

Pat-a-Cake
Muffin Man
Little Jack Horner
Mulberry Bush
Cats, Peas, Beans, and Barley
To Market, To Market
Peas Porridge Hot
Little Tommy Tucker

• **Two Little Apples**

Two little apples hanging on a tree
  (Arms out with hands turned down)
Two little apples smiling at me
  (Turn hands up)
I shook that tree as hard as I could
  (Shaking motion)
Down came the apples. Mmmmmm —
Were they good!
  (Falling motion: rub tummy)

• **Pumpkins**

A pumpkin is big
  (Circle arms over head)
A pumpkin is round
  (Circle arms in front)
A pumpkin has a great big smile
  (Outline smile on mouth)
But doesn't make a sound.

• **My Pumpkin**

Here's my orange pumpkin
  (Have hands outspread)
Big and fat and round
  (Hold hands above one another, outspread and extended; then make circle with hands)
It's the very best one
I could find downtown
  (Point in that direction)

Now I need to make a nose
A mouth, some eyes
  (Pretend to cut)
Or mother'll want to use it
  (Motion to remove)
To cook and bake some pies
  (Act like stirring)

See my jack-o-lantern
Smiling right at you
  (Smile)
You don't need to be afraid
  (Look frightened)
He can't holler "Boo!"

- **Making Cookies**

I am making cookie dough.
Round and round the beaters go.

Add some flour from a cup,
Stir and stir the batter up.

Roll them; cut them; nice and neat;
Put them on a cookie sheet.

Bake them; count them; one, two, three.
Serve them to my friends for tea.

- **Hot Cross Buns**

Hot cross buns,
Hot cross buns,
One-a-penny, two-a-penny,
Hot cross buns.

- **I'm a Little Teapot**

I'm a little teapot, short and stout.
This is my handle,
This is my spout,
When I get all steamed up, then I shout.
Just tip me over and pour me out.

- **Bananas**

When I first saw bananas grow
  (Bend and stretch fingers of both hands)
I couldn't help but frown.
I thought I was mistaken, but

The fruit hung upside down.
  (Make hands into cluster, holding the fingers down)

When I first saw potatoes grow,
  (Form a potato with both hands)
I had a big surprise —
I found them growing underground.
How could they use their eyes?
  (Point to eyes)

- **5 Currant Buns**

5 currant buns in the baker's shop.
Big and round with sugar on the top.
Along came (*name of child*) with a penny one
  day,
She/he bought one and took it away.

- **Lickety-lick**

Likety-lick, lickety-lick.
The batter is getting all thickety-thick.
What shall we bake?
What shall we bake?
A great big beautiful, chocolate cake!

- **Pancakes**

Mix a pancake,
Stir a pancake,
Pop it in the pan;
Fry the pancake,
Toss the pancake,
Catch it if you can.

- **Apple Tree**

This is the tree
With leaves so green
  (Make leaf with hand; fingers outstretched)

Here are the apples
That hang in between.
  (Make fists)

When the wind blows
The apples will fall
Here is the basket to gather them all.

SUGGESTIONS FOR SUCCESSFUL COOKING EXPERIENCES

1. The first experience should be very simple with no hazardous steps or dangerous materials.

2. The first time the teacher may measure ingredients.

3. Make the same food several different times, adding something new and more complex each time.

4. The teacher should try the recipe first.

5. Some children will enjoy cooking but will not want to taste the product.

6. Cooking experiences should not interfere with eating at meal times.

7. Some parents and children may be anxious about the use of a stove. Help them understand that school is a different situation.

8. Involve children in the clean-up process as well as the preparation.

9. Limit the number of children for most experiences.

10. Be aware of food allergies to such things as milk, milk products, orange juice, and so on. Also be aware of dangers from choking on nuts, celery, carrots, and popcorn.

11. Have enough equipment and plan the experience so that more children can participate.

12. Use portable appliances rather than a stove when possible.

13. Use tools and equipment that can be safely used by children — plastic bowls, scissors, blunt knives, paper cups.

14. Wash hands before starting and control such practices as tasting from the same bowl and using the same eating utensils.

15. Children should sit down to eat food that they have prepared.

16. Make sure that handles of pans are turned away from the children and caution the children about a hot stove, hot plate, or hot utensils.

17. The teacher should remain near the cooking experience at all times. Have all equipment and supplies within reach.

Toast	Cinnamon, orange, honey and butter, variety of toppings, french.
Fruits	Fresh fruit salad, apple crisp, baked apples. Prepare orange juice. Peel oranges and count segments. Pomegranate—cut open and examine the seeds. Put coconut in a "feel bag." Open it and share the milk. Bring in shredded coconut for comparison. Peel bananas. Compare dried, canned and fresh. Cut apple cross-wise. Count the seeds. Good lesson in fractions. Make lemonade, orangeade, limeade. Clean and hull strawberries. Make jam. Plant seeds of any fruits. Make apple sauce. Bake pumpkin seeds with butter and salt. Cut and taste fresh pineapple. Cut and serve melons.
Sandwiches	Many varieties! Let each child make a small hamburger patty.
Icings	Start with basic white icing made from soft butter, powdered sugar, milk, and vanilla. Let each child add his own food coloring to a small amount of icing in his own paper cup. Add raisins or chocolate bits. Spread on cookies or graham crackers.
Instant Puddings	Add chocolate bits, raisins, small pieces of peppermint candy, pieces of canned fruits, whipped cream.

Fig. 35-4 Cooking ideas for preschool and early childhood classrooms. (Continued on following page)

Vegetables	Make stew. Scrub potatoes or carrots. Shell peas. Snap beans. Cook vegetables and compare with uncooked. Clean radishes. Bake pumpkin seeds with salt and butter. Clean and stuff celery with peanut butter, cheese.
Soup	Canned soup. Packaged dehydrated soup. Add noodles and macaroni. Clean vegetables for soup.
Pudding	Tapioca, chocolate, rice, bread.
Pancakes	Mix batter and use electric skillet. Spread with jelly and roll up to eat.
Cookies, cake, cupcakes	Start with mix or slice and bake. Frost and/or decorate.
Candy	Use simple recipes.
Jello	Add fresh fruit or tiny pieces of marshmallow or whipped cream.
Special Projects	Make butter using churn or by simply shaking cream in covered jar. Make popcorn. Make meatballs. Freeze ice cubes or popsicles of fruit juice. Make blueberry muffins.
Crackers	Spread saltines with cheese, peanut butter, or butter. Spread graham crackers with frostings.
Cottage cheese	Mix with pineapple tidbits.
Ice cream	Make in freezer. Top with sauce or strawberries.
Milk	Add chocolate. Make milk shakes, cocoa
Eggs	Scramble. Eat hard-boiled.

Fig. 35-4 (Continued from previous page)

RECIPES FOR COOKING EXPERIENCES

- **Cheesy French Fries**

Ingredients:

1 package (9 ounces) frozen french fried potatoes
1/2 teaspoon salt
dash pepper
1/2 cup grated sharp cheese

Procedure:

1. Preheat oven to 450° F.
2. Arrange potatoes on cookie sheet.
3. Sprinkle with salt and pepper.
4. Bake uncovered 15 minutes.
5. Sprinkle cheese over potatoes.
6. Bake 2–3 minutes longer or until cheese is melted.

- **Turtle Cookies**

Ingredients:

1/3 cup margarine
2 beaten eggs
1 cup flour
2 squares chocolate
3/4 cup sugar
1 teaspoon vanilla

Procedure:

1. Melt butter and chocolate in a pan. Let cool.
2. In another bowl, mix the eggs, sugar, vanilla, flour; then add the melted chocolate mixture.
3. Bake in waffle iron, 1 teaspoon batter for each turtle. Bake 2–3 minutes.

- **Cocoa Mix**

Ingredients:
4 cups dry milk
1 cup cocoa
1 1/2 cups sugar
pinch of salt

Procedure:
1. Stir until well mixed.
2. Pour mix into a jar or can with a lid.
3. When ready to use, fill glass about 1/4 full of cocoa mix.
4. Pour hot or cold water over cocoa and stir until mixed.

- **Chocolate Milk Shake**

For each serving:
1/2 cup cold milk
3 tablespoons syrup
2 scoops vanilla ice cream

Mix just to blend.

- **Lemonade**

For each serving:
juice of 1 lemon (about 1/3 cup)
1 cup water
5 teaspoons sugar

Combine; pour over ice in tall glass.

- **Apple Sauce**

Ingredients:
2 1/2 pounds apples, cooking variety
1/2 cup water
1/2–2/3 cup sugar

Procedure:
1. Peel apples, cut into quarters, and remove cores.
2. Put in metal saucepan, add water, and cover.
3. Cook over medium heat until it boils, then simmer over low heat for 20 to 25 minutes until the apples are tender. (May be necessary to add more water.)
4. Beat apples until smooth with spoon.
5. Stir sugar in until it dissolves. (It may require more sugar depending on the tartness of the apples.)
6. Serve warm or cold. Makes 10 servings.

- **Orangeade**

For each serving:
1/3 cup fresh orange juice
2 tablespoons lemon juice
2 cups water
1 tablespoon sugar

Combine. Pour over ice.

- **Limeade**

For each serving:
juice of 1 lime
1 cup water
5 teaspoons sugar

Combine. Pour over ice.

- **Fruit Sun**

Ingredients:
grapefruit, sections
muskmelon, balls
cherries
raisins

Procedure:
1. Arrange grapefruit sections in a ring around muskmelon balls.
2. Cherries and raisins may be used to make a face.
3. Amounts depend on the number to be served. 1/2 cup servings are appropriate.

- **Pigs in a Blanket**

Ingredients:
frankfurters
bread slices
American cheese
butter
mustard

Procedure:
1. Spread butter on bread.
2. Place bread slices on ungreased baking sheet and top each with a slice of cheese.
3. Place frankfurters diagonally on cheese.

4. Fold bread over to form triangle. Brush with butter.
5. Set broiler at 550° F.
6. Broil about 2 minutes.

- **Muffins**

Ingredients:
2 cups flour, sifted
3 teaspoons baking powder
1 egg beaten
1/2 teaspoon salt
1 cup milk
1/4 cup fat, melted or cooking oil
1/4 cup sugar

Procedure:
1. Sift dry ingredients together into a large bowl; make a well in the center.
2. In another small bowl, beat the egg until foamy; add the milk and melted fat.
3. Add the liquid ingredients to the well in the dry ingredients. Stir until the dry ingredients are moist, but still lumpy. DON'T OVER MIX.
4. Fill greased muffin tins 1/2 full.
5. Bake at 400° F for 15-20 minutes. Makes 12.
6. To vary, add 1/2 cup chopped nuts, 3/4 cup fresh blueberries, 1/2 cup halved cranberries, or 3/4 cup cut-up dates.

- **Fruit Tapioca**

Ingredients:
2 cups fruit
2 cups water
4 tablespoons minute tapioca
1/2 cup to 1 cup sugar

Procedure:
1. Place ingredients in saucepan.
2. Put over low flame. Stir frequently.
3. Boil until clear.
4. Use tart fruit: apples, apricots, cherries, rhubarb, pineapple, raspberries.

- **Bread Pudding**

Ingredients:
6 slices bread
2 cups milk
1/4 cup sugar
3 tablespoons butter
1/2 teaspoon salt
3 eggs
1 teaspoon vanilla
1/2 teaspoon nutmeg

Procedure:
1. Place day-old bread in buttered baking dish.
2. Scald milk.
3. Add butter, sugar, and salt.
4. Beat eggs and slowly pour milk over eggs. Mix thoroughly.
5. Add flavoring.
6. Pour mixture over bread.
7. Bake at 350° F for 1 hour.

- **Meatballs**

Ingredients:
1 pound hamburger
1 cup bread crumbs
1 or 2 eggs
3/4 teaspoon salt
1/8 teaspoon pepper
1/4 cup milk

Procedure:
1. Mix ingredients well.
2. Shape into small balls.
3. Brown until cooked through in electric skillet.

- **Carrot and Raisin Salad**

Ingredients:
3 cups shredded carrots (teacher)
3/4 cup raisins
juice of one lemon
3 tablespoons sugar
dash of salt

Procedure:
1. Thoroughly mix ingredients.
2. Serve immediately.

- **Double Orange Pops**

Ingredients:
1 package (3 ounces) orange gelatin
2 cups water
1/2 cup sugar
2 cups orange juice

Materials: ice cube tray, small paper cups, frozen pop molds, wooden sticks, plastic spoons

Procedure:
1. Dissolve gelatin and sugar in boiling water.
2. Add orange juice.
3. Pour into trays, cups, or molds.
4. Insert wooden sticks or plastic spoons diagonally in each ice cube section, or at an angle in molds or cups for handles. Freeze until firm — 2 to 3 hours. Makes 20 to 24 pops.

- **Banana Bake**

Ingredients:
1 banana, peeled
butter, melted

Procedure:
1. Place peeled banana in shallow baking dish and brush with melted butter.
2. Bake in moderate oven (375° F) from 10 to 15 minutes (until tender).
3. Serve hot as a vegetable.
4. Yield: 1 serving.
5. If used as a dessert, sprinkle with lemon juice and powdered sugar.

- **No-Cook Peanut Butter Fudge**

Ingredients:
1 cup peanut butter
1 cup Karo syrup

1 1/4 cups nonfat dry milk solids
1 cup sifted confectioners sugar

Procedure:
1. Blend peanut butter and syrup in large mixing bowl.
2. Measure nonfat dry milk solids and sifted confectioners sugar and add all at once.
3. Mix all together — first with a spoon and then with the hands, knead in dry ingredients.
4. Turn onto board and continue kneading until mixture is well blended and smooth.
5. Press out with the hands or a rolling pin into square.
6. Dough should be 1/2-inch thick.
7. Cut into squares.
8. Top with nutmeats, if desired. Makes about 2 pounds.

- **Muffins**

Ingredients:
2 cups self-rising flour
2 cups softened vanilla ice cream
1 egg and 2 tablespoons cooking oil (optional)

Materials: muffin tins, mixing bowl

Procedure:
1. Combine in mixing bowl self-rising flour and softened vanilla ice cream. Beat until smooth.
2. Fill lined muffin tins three-fourths full.
3. Bake at 425° F for 20 to 25 minutes, or until golden brown.
4. Yield: 12 large or 24 small muffins.
5. For richer muffins, add egg and cooking oil.

- **Honey Balls**

Ingredients:
3 tablespoons honey
4 tablespoons peanut butter
1/2 cup nonfat dry milk
1/4 cup dry cereal flakes, crushed

Procedure:
1. Mix honey and peanut butter.
2. Gradually add nonfat dry milk; mix well.
3. Form into balls with greased hands.
4. Roll in dry cereal flakes.
5. Chill until firm. Makes 18 balls.

• **French Toast**

Ingredients:
8 slices bread
4 eggs
1/4 tablespoon salt
2 cups milk

Procedure:
1. Slightly beat eggs. Add salt and milk.
2. Dip slices of bread in egg mixture and fry in electric skillet.
3. Serve hot with jelly, honey, or syrup.

• **Potato Candy**

Ingredients:
1/3 cup mashed potatoes
1 3/4 cups powdered sugar
1 teaspoon vanilla
2 cups flaked coconut

Procedure:
1. Mix ingredients thoroughly.
2. Shape into desired balls.
3. Place in refrigerator until very cool.
4. Roll candy in melted German or semi-sweet chocolate.

• **Chow Mein Granchies**

Ingredients:
1 package chocolate chips (or 1 package butterscotch chips)
1 can chow mein noodles
1 cup salted peanuts

Procedure:
1. Melt chocolate chips in a double boiler or in a saucepan over very low heat.

2. Add a can of chow mein noodles and a cup of salted peanuts.
3. Stir until the noodles are coated with chocolate mixture.
4. Drop by spoonfuls on waxed paper.
5. Place in refrigerator until cool.

• **Jam Brown-n-Serve**

Ingredients:
6 brown-n-serve rolls
1 teaspoon melted margarine
6 teaspoons apricot preserves

Procedure:
1. Brush butter over top of rolls.
2. Make lengthwise cuts in top of roll.
3. Insert 1 teaspoon of preserves.
4. Bake in greased shallow pan at 200° for 10 to 12 minutes.

• **Cottage Cheese Cookies**

Ingredients:
1/4 cup butter
1/2 cup sugar
1/2 cup cottage cheese
1 teaspoon vanilla
1 cup flour
1/4 teaspoon salt
1 teaspoon baking powder

Materials: fork, cookie sheet

Procedure:
1. Mix butter and sugar.
2. Add cottage cheese and vanilla.
3. Add flour, salt, and baking powder.
4. Stir. Smooth into balls.
5. Put on greased cookie sheet. Flatten with fork. Bake at 375° for 10 to 15 minutes.

• **Stir-n-Drop Cookies**

Ingredients:
2 eggs
2/3 cup cooking oil

2 teaspoons vanilla
3/4 cup sugar
2 cups flour, sifted
2 teaspoons baking powder
1/2 teaspoon salt

Materials: cookie sheet, fork

Procedure:
1. Break the eggs. Beat with a fork.
2. Stir oil and vanilla into egg mixture.
3. Blend in sugar until mixture thickens.
4. Add baking powder, flour, and salt to egg and sugar mixture. Stir.
5. Drop by teaspoonfuls 2 inches apart on ungreased cookie sheets.
6. Press round with bottom of a glass dipped in sugar.
7. Bake at 400° F for 8 to 10 minutes.

• Scrambled Eggs

Ingredients:
eggs, one per child
milk, salt, pepper as desired

Materials: fry pan or electric skillet

Procedure:
1. Permit each child to break an egg into a bowl.
2. Beat the egg with a fork.
3. Add milk, salt, and pepper as desired.
4. Cook in fry pan or electric skillet.

• Uncooked Fondant

Ingredients:
2 1/3 cups confectioners sugar
1/2 cup sweetened condensed milk
1 teaspoon vanilla

Procedure:
1. Put sugar into bowl.
2. Slowly add milk and vanilla.
3. Mix until smooth.
4. Tint with food coloring.
5. Drop in flat pieces on waxed paper.
6. Press walnut piece on top of each.

• Ice Cream

Ingredients:
4 eggs
2 1/2 cups sugar
6 cups milk
4 cups light cream
2 tablespoons vanilla
1/2 teaspoon salt

Procedure:
1. Beat eggs until light.
2. Add sugar gradually, beating until mixture thickens.
3. Add remaining ingredients; mix thoroughly.
4. Freeze in ice cream freezer. Makes 1 gallon.

• Flavored Milk Drinks

For each serving, add the following syrups, fruits, or flavorings to a tall glass. Fill glass with cold milk and stir thoroughly. Serve.

Maple: 2 tablespoons maple syrup
Caramel: 1/2 to 2 tablespoons caramel syrup
Berry: 2 teaspoons strawberry or raspberry jam or ice cream topping or thawed frozen berries, and 2 to 3 drops red food coloring

• Caramel Syrup

Ingredients:
1 cup brown sugar
3/4 cup hot water
1 teaspoon vanilla
1/8 teaspoon salt

Procedure:
1. Melt sugar over low heat until smooth, light brown syrup forms.
2. Remove from heat.
3. Add water.
4. Heat.

- **Mints**

Ingredients:

2 ounces cream cheese

1 2/3 cups powdered sugar

1/2 teaspoon mint or peppermint flavoring

Procedure:

1. Mash cheese.
2. Add flavoring and food coloring if desired.
3. Mix in the sugar.
4. Knead and roll into little balls about the size of marbles.
5. To vary, instead of mint flavor, you can substitute three teaspoons cocoa and 1/2 teaspoon vanilla.

- **Doughnuts**

Ingredients:

1 1/2 cups oil, heated

1 can prepared biscuits

Procedure:

1. Heat pan to 350° F.
2. Fry biscuits in oil.

- **Turtle Pancakes**

Ingredients:

pancake or biscuit mix

1/3 cup nonfat dry milk

2 cups milk

Procedure:

1. Follow package directions. (For extra nutrition, add 1/3 cup nonfat milk to the standard recipe calling for 2 cups milk.)
2. The batter should be in a bowl rather than in a pitcher; the child puts the batter on the griddle by spoonfuls, sometimes deliberately dribbling for effect.
3. A turtle is made by adding four tiny pancakes (the legs) around the perimeter of one round pancake about 3 inches in diameter.

- **Raisin Cornflake Cookies**

Ingredients:

2 eggs

1/3 cup sugar

2/3 cup walnuts, chopped

2/3 cup raisins

salt (pinch)

1/2 teaspoon vanilla

cornflake crumbs

Procedure:

1. Grease a baking sheet.
2. Beat eggs until foamy.
3. Stir in sugar.
4. Fold in cornflake crumbs, nuts, raisins, salt, vanilla. Stir until well blended. Let mixture stand for 30 minutes.
5. Preheat oven to 350° F.
6. When mixture has been standing for 30 minutes, drop by teaspoonfuls onto greased baking sheet; bake 10 minutes or until delicately browned.
7. When still warm, remove the cookies from the pan. Cool.

- **Oatmeal Drop Cookies**

Ingredients

1/2 cup butter or margarine, soft

1 cup sugar

1 egg

1 1/2 cups flour (all purpose) sifted with:

1/2 teaspoon salt

1/2 teaspoon baking soda

3/4 teaspoon cinnamon, ground

1/2 teaspoon cloves, ground

1/2 teaspoon allspice

Stir in:

1 3/4 cups rolled oats, quick cooking

2/3 cup raisins, chopped

1/2 cup nuts, chopped

1/3 cup milk

(Yield: 3 dozen)

Procedure:

1. Cream butter until light and fluffy.
2. Gradually beat in sugar.
3. Add egg and beat until light.
4. Sift flour with salt, baking soda, and spices; add to first mixture alternately with milk and mix well.
5. Drop by teaspoonfuls onto greased cookie sheets.
6. Bake in preheated moderate oven (350° F) for about 15 minutes.
7. Teach the children new vocabulary words by explaining the baking and measuring terms. Let them mix and drop the dough onto the cookie sheets.

Unit 36 MUSICAL INSTRUMENTS, SONGS, AND ASSORTED ART PROJECTS

RHYTHM BAND INSTRUMENTS

Creating rhythm instruments from found objects gives young children another opportunity for self-expression. They receive satisfaction and pleasure from beating rhythmic sounds and keeping time to music on the radio or record player.

Materials:

paper plates	bottle caps
empty spools	small boxes or
pebbles	cartons
nails	dried beans
toweling rolls	peas or corn
sticks	wire
old Christmas bells	

Suggested Art Activities:

shakers	clappers
cymbals	tambourines
beaters	drums

Note: The instruments discussed below are illustrated in figure 36-1.

• Bottle Cap Shaker

Remove corks from bottle caps. Punch a hole in the center. String on a string and attach to a package handle. Paint if desired.

• Spool Shaker

Paint designs on a large spool. Force four pipe cleaners through the center of the spool. Attach a Christmas bell to the end of each cleaner by bending.

• Plate Shaker

Decorate two paper plates with crayons or paint. Put pebbles, dried corn, peas or beans between them and staple or sew the plates together with bright yarn or string. Bend wire

as shown in figure 36-1 (c). Fit the ends inside with a loop protruding to form a handle.

• Box Shaker

Place small pebbles, beans, or seeds in a small box or empty clean milk carton to make a shaker. It can be used with or without a handle. Decorate as desired.

• Sandpaper Blocks

Paint two small wooden blocks. Place a strip of sandpaper on the surface allowing an overlap on each end for fastening with thumbtacks. Sandpaper may replace carpet on old eraser blocks. Rub together to make a sound.

• Clappers

Nail bottle caps to a painted eraser block.

• Cymbals

Decorate two lids from tin cans. Fasten a small spool or block of wood on for a handle.

• Tambourine

Hang bottle caps by thin wire, pipe cleaners, or string to a decorated paper or tin foil plate.

• Hummer

Decorate a tube from waxed paper or paper toweling roll. Fasten a piece of waxed paper over the tube. Humming through the waxed paper is fun.

• Drums

Glue the lids to salt boxes, cereal boxes, or ice cream boxes and decorate with paint to use as drums. Older children may make drums from restaurant-size tin cans with canvas or heavy paper stretched and laced to cover the ends.

• **Drumsticks**

Mold balls of paper pulp on the end of two sticks. When this is dry, paint the sticks and use them for drumsticks.

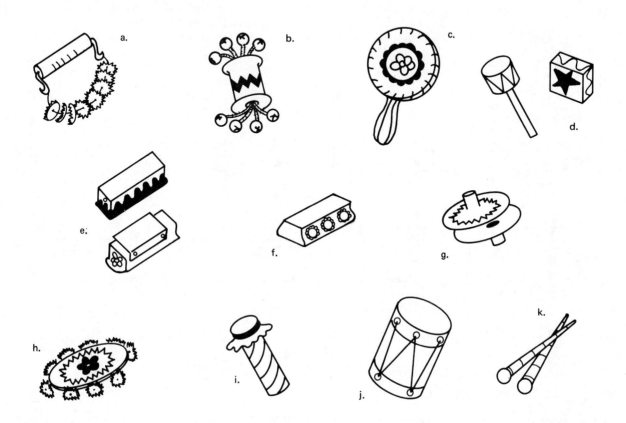

Fig. 36-1 Rhythm band instruments: (a) bottle cap shaker, (b) spool shaker, (c) plate shaker, (d) box shaker, (e) sandpaper blocks, (f) clappers, (g) cymbals, (h) tambourine, (i) hummer, (j) drums, (k) drumsticks.

MISCELLANEOUS SONGS

One, Two, Three, Four, Five

Ella Jenkins

One, two, three, four, five, I caught a fish alive. Six, seven, eight, nine, ten, I let him go again.
Why did I let him go? 'Cause he bit my finger so. Which finger did he bite? The little one on the right.

Mary Mack

Ella Jenkins

Mary Mack, dressed in black. Buttons all up and down her back. (Hi Yo 4x)
Give me a nickle, give me a dime. See my sugar baby all the time. (Hi Yo 4x)
Went to the river, couldn't get across. Got into trouble with my boss. (Hi Yo 4x)

The Man in the Moon

The man in the moon looked out of the moon, looked out of the moon and said,
" 'Tis time for all children on the earth to think about getting to bed!"

Tic Toc

Tic   toc   tic   toc   goes   the   clock.   Tic   toc   tic   toc   tic   tic   toc.

See My Pony

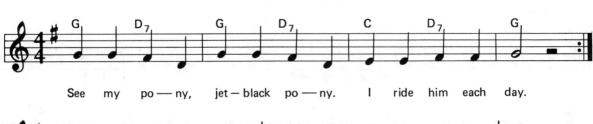

See   my   po — ny,   jet — black   po — ny.   I   ride   him   each   day.

When   I   give   him   oats   to   eat,   trot – ting   trot – ting   go   his   feet.   *Repeat 1st line once*

Fingers Are Very Smart

Did   you   know   your   fin — gers   can   tap   tap   tap?   Did   you

know   your   fin — gers   can   clap   clap   clap?   Yes   they   can,   yes   they

can, 'cause your   fin — gers   are   ver — y   smart.   Wiggle, wiggle, wiggle,   *Make up*
                                                            Jiggle, jiggle, jiggle   *your own*

Indian Song

1.)   1, 2, 3, 4, side 2, 3, 4,   2.)   Up 2, 3, 4, down 2, 3, 4,
        1, 2, 3, 4, side 2, 3, 4,   Up 2, 3, 4, down 2, 3, 4,

3.)   Look 2, 3, 4, look 2, 3, 4,   4.)   Listen to the 3, 4, listen to the 3, 4,
        Look 2, 3, 4, look 2, 3, 4,   Listen to the 3, 4, listen to the 3, 4,

Indian sound

This is how the great big In-di-an beats upon his drum. Hi   Ho   Hi   Ho   Hoooooooo!

Big Indians

*Note: Fingers of one hand represent Indians; the other hand is cupped to form the canoe.

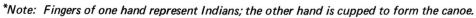

There were 5(4, 3, 2) great big   In ——— di —— ans.   They
was   one   He

stood so straight and tall.   They tried to fit in a
(last time) And   he   did fit in the

lit — tle can — oe and   one   of them did   fall.
lit — tle can — oe and   pad — dled the boat right home.

My Tambourine

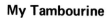

Shake shake,   knock knock,   shake shake,   knock knock.   I

play   on   my   tam — bou ——— rine.   rine.

ASSORTED ART PROJECTS

Art experiences can relate to and help clarify facts learned in other school studies. Experiences and learning acquired in other areas in the curriculum offer ideas for visual art expression in picturemaking, construction, modeling, puppetry, printmaking, and calligraphy. These ideas may be developed in relation to science, social studies, health and safety, music, and language arts.

Science

Art activities help children understand and interpret the many wonders found in science. Children can

- Paint pictures about plants, showing leaves, stems, roots, flowers.
- Cut a snowflake with its six points out of paper.
- Make designs of sun, moon, and stars.
- Construct sailboats of scrap materials.
- Plan and paint a seasonal mural on "out-of-doors" — fall, winter, spring, summer.
- Make a stencil of an insect design for the cover of a folder on science notes.
- Make prints with objects of nature, such as weeds, stones, twigs, leaves.
- Draw and illustrate a poster: Poison Ivy is a Dangerous Plant.
- Make and decorate envelopes to contain seeds collected from home gardens.
- Make a cut-paper aquarium shadow box showing stand-up water plants growing from the bottom of the box and fish suspended by thread from the lid.
- Decorate a tin can or plastic container with cut-paper for a Christmas plant.
- Bring in objects from fall gardens, fields, and woods in the area. Arrange and label a table exhibit in the classroom.

- Create an environmental assemblage with a variety of natural objects.
- Paint or draw murals on The Importance of Water in Our World.
- Collect flowers and leaves; arrange as desired and press between two sheets of waxed paper with a lukewarm iron.
- Draw or paint about travel in space.
- Construct miniature space people using toweling rolls for the figures.
- Make a diorama of the astronauts on the moon.
- Use paint or felt markers to create designs on stones to be used as paperweights.
- Draw plans for vegetable or flower gardens.
- Decorate a wooden box or flowerpot for window gardens.
- Make a mural showing animals important to people.
- Construct barnyard scenes for a table or showcase.
- Draw or paint about ecology.
- Experiment with found items to illustrate recycling objects of everyday use.

Social Studies

- Illustrate in crayon or paint: My Neighborhood, Our Family at Home, Shopping with My Parents, Going on a Picnic.
- Paint portraits of: Me, Mother, Father, Classmate, Teacher.
- Construct paper furniture for a shoe box house.
- Weave a paper rug.
- Make figures of cut paper for a family group.
- Paint or draw about: How We Work Together, How We Play Together.

- Make dioramas showing community helpers and what they do.

- Paint a mural of people working.

- Make posters on Ecology in our Neighborhood, Improving Our Community, Helping My Neighbor.

- Draw or paint about a family in another country.

- Make a foreign family grouping showing their native costumes.

- Construct dioramas showing how people obtain food by farming, fishing, and hunting in different countries and in the United States.

- Use papier-maché to construct a Mexican pinata.

Fig. 36-2 Construction paper family.

- Make puppets and dramatize how children from foreign lands play.

- Make box scenes illustrating the children's own city and foreign cities.

- Create masks for use in dances of different cultures.

- Make models of cars and other vehicles in clay to show various modes of transportation.

- Construct an Indian village in paper sculpture.

- Model fruits and vegetables in papier-maché and dramatize shopping at the supermarket.

- Make potato prints based on designs from foreign cultures.

- Model (in clay and papier-maché) foods native to specific geographical areas.

- Assemble ethnic costumes from discarded clothing for dancing and dramatization.

Reading Readiness

- Make a scrapbook about pets using crayons or paint. Build a pet shop; create animals and birds to "sell."

- Model clay figures of characters in favorite stories.

- Draw or paint portraits of storybook friends.

- Paint a mural about a trip taken to a zoo, farm, post office, dairy, or firehouse. Make a torn-paper picture of a scene from the trip.

- Make puppets and give a play about a favorite part of a story or poem.

- Children make illustrations for original stories or poems.

- Construct a table scene or diorama depicting the theme of a story.

- Make masks representing characters in stories for dramatization.

- Construct circus tents and cages. Model animals of clay or paper pulp. Arrange the exhibit on a table or in an exhibit case.

- Illustrate favorite poems about the holidays.

- Make cut letters from magazine illustrations to spell the name of a storybook character.

- Select some interesting or unusual words in a story or poem. Cut them out from magazines or newspapers. Arrange them in a collage.

- Draw or paint a character in a story. Then use free-style lettering within the form.

- Use children's drawings of events in sequence for a roller movie.

Unit 37 ROOM AND YARD ORGANIZATION, EXHIBITIONS, AND DISPLAYS

ROOM AND YARD ORGANIZATION[1]

Large Cardboard Cartons

Puppet theaters, post offices, and stores are easily constructed by slicing or sawing out a rectangular portion in the top half of the front section of a large carton. When folded to the inside, the flap can be cut back to the desired width for a stage or shelf. The flap is supported by a dowel or a length of heavy cord strung from one side of the box to the other. Leftover latex wall paint is ideal for painting these large structures. This type of paint conceals advertising, does not smear when dry, and can be washed off a brush or child's hands with water. Use old postage stamps, greeting cards, and envelopes if this is to be a post office. Paper tickets, signs, money (bottle tops, etc.) can be used if the structure is to be a theater.

Cable Spools

Empty cable spools are fun additions to the outside play area. A slat can be removed from the core creating a hiding place for the children or a climbing device. Two or three spools may be secured one on top of another with a plumber's pipe inserted through the center of each; a second pipe can be sunk in concrete close enough to the structure to be used as a fire fighter's pole. A rope ladder attached to the top spool adds to the climbing challenge.

Cardboard Boxes

To create a table easel from a large cardboard box, measure one side the equivalent length of the bottom and mark. Cut diagonally across from this mark to the bottom corner on both sides. This produces a sturdy cardboard triangle that serves as a table easel once two slits have been made for clothespin clips at the top. The children, themselves, will be able to remove or replace newsprint for paintings.

The same triangular arrangement covered with a piece of flannel makes a nontipping flannel board for children's and teacher's use. A show box containing flannel board figures may be stored beneath the triangle for the child's convenience. It can be used for retelling stories or reworking number experiences in small groups or as a solitary, self-selected activity.

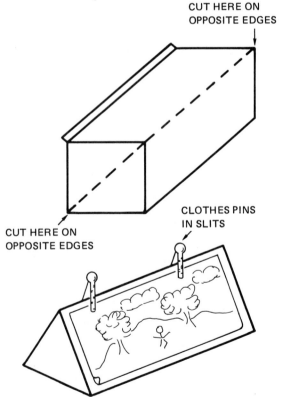

CUT HERE ON OPPOSITE EDGES

CUT HERE ON OPPOSITE EDGES

CLOTHES PINS IN SLITS

Fig. 37-1 Cardboard box easels.

[1]These suggestions are taken from Jean W. Quill's *A World of Materials.*

Wooden Crates

During cantaloupe season, grocery stores will supply empty cantaloupe crates. These are durable and good for school use. At a minimal cost, these crates may be transformed into a stove, sink, sofa, work bench, or locker arrangement. To form a solid front, it is only necessary to tap the wooden slats loose, add a few additional slats, and replace side by side. To create a stove, individual pie tins can be turned upside down to simulate gas burners. These are especially effective when painted black to look like "grating." Painted bottle tops add stove controls. A spool set on top of a scrap of wood and painted silver makes a faucet; the entire "sink" may cost little more than the price of the required pan. Many aluminum foil pans, left over, are suitable for this purpose. The ends of the cantaloupe crates make sturdy frames for children's drawings or trays for the doll corner or science table.

Window Shades

The discarded portion of the rollers make good instruments. Several roofing washers or bottle caps can be secured on a nail driven into the roller segment. This results in an effective shaking instrument.

Wooden and Plastic Soft-Drink and Milk Crates

These crates, sometimes available at a small charge, are excellent substitutes for commercial hollow blocks. Paint them bright colors with latex paint. A set of casters on one crate can produce a durable wagon for hauling friends or blocks. Set the casters far enough in to allow stacking at those times when the crates are not in use. They also make excellent "cubby holes" for storage.

Fig. 37-2 Plastic milk crates provide an inexpensive practical storage area.

Fig. 37-3 A recycled canoe can be suitable playground equipment.

Boats

At the beginning or end of the boating season, some rowboats may be destroyed or abandoned as no longer seaworthy. These boats are often donated by marina managers to a school or playground, if transportation is provided by the school. When stored safely, these boats can be made into useful playground equipment.

Junked Tires

Used tires, hung either horizontally or vertically, make excellent swings.

Fig. 37-4 Recycled tires give new life to an old swing set.

Fig. 37-5 Ice cream cartons bolted together make an unusual, yet practical wall storage unit.

Inflated tubes can be rolled from place to place, bounced on, and used for various movement games.

Ice Cream Containers

A circular, spatter-paint screen may be created from the three-gallon containers discarded by ice cream stores or restaurants. Cut the bottom from one of these containers, leaving only a narrow edge to which the edges of a circular piece of screen may be glued. A matching narrow circle, cut from another piece of cardboard, placed over the first and glued down, will secure the screen. A paint-dipped toothbrush is scraped across the screen;

any object placed beneath will leave a design on the paper on which it is resting. The carton should be cut down to leave approximately one-quarter of its original length; this gives a satisfactory height for spatter painting.

Ice cream containers can also be converted to wastebaskets, space helmets, and divers' masks. To make the latter, simply remove an area from an upside-down carton large enough for the child's face to appear. Allow the child to paint in a choice of colors. Ice cream containers can also be used as storage space, when bolted together.

Sawdust

Sawdust is available from the lumber mill for use in making sawdust clay. Simply mix a small amount of wallpaper paste in water and add sawdust until a pliable consistency has been reached. This clay hardens over a period of time.

EXHIBITIONS, DISPLAYS

It is stimulating and educational for children to see their work displayed. Whether the purpose of the exhibit is to introduce new ideas and information, to stimulate interest in a single lesson, to show the children's work, or to provide an overview of the semester's work, the subject of the exhibition should be directly related to the children's interests. Exhibits should be changed often to be of educational and decorative value.

Labels

- Make large, bold letters that can be easily read.
- Keep titles brief. Descriptive material should be in smaller letters.
- Label children's work with their names and grades as a means of creating pride through recognition of their work.

Fig. 37-6 Cut-out individual crayon drawings make an interesting display.

- Vary the material in making letters. In addition to paper letters, labels can be made of paint, ink, crayon, chalk, cloth, fancy papers, string, rope, yarn, and other three-dimensional materials.

Color

- Choose a basic color scheme related to the visual material displayed. Seasonal colors can be used, such as warm colors for fall (yellow, orange, red), cool colors for winter (blue, blue-green, gray), and light and cool colors for spring (colors with yellow in the mixture, such as yellow-orange).

- Use colors for mounting that are more subdued than the materials mounted. This may be accomplished by using lighter color, darker color, or grayer color.

- Select a bright color for accent, as in bands or other pleasing arrangements on the larger areas of grayed, lighter, or darker colors.

- Create a contrast to emphasize or attract attention. Intense color makes a visual impact, such as orange against black.

- Use both light and dark color values.

- Create color patterns that lead the eye from area to area.

Balance

Balance can be achieved formally or informally. To create formal balance, the largest piece of work may be placed in the center with similar shapes on either side. Informal balance is more interesting, subtle, and compelling. Material may be grouped in blocks of different sizes, colors, or shapes, and still be balanced. Margins of the bulletin board should be wider at the bottom.

Unity

Unity in design is the quality that holds the arrangement together in harmony.

- Ideas can be unified with background paper, lettering, strips of construction paper, yarn, or ribbon.

- Repetition of similar sizes, shapes, colors, or lines can help to create harmony.

- Shapes can be arranged to lead the eye from one part of the board to another.

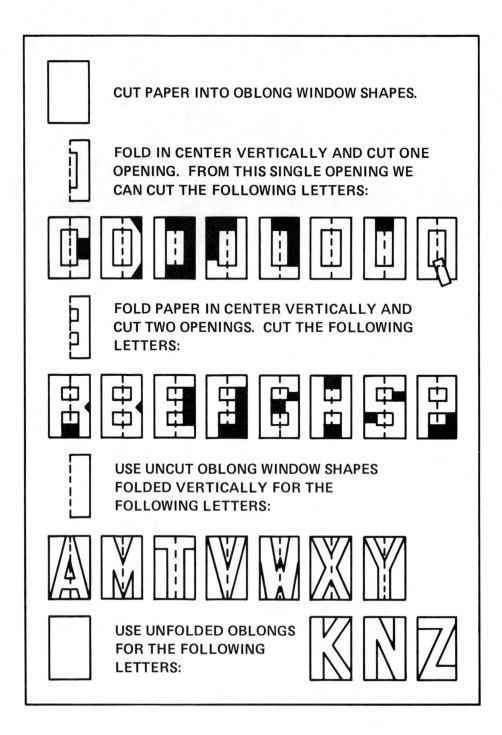

CUT PAPER INTO OBLONG WINDOW SHAPES.

FOLD IN CENTER VERTICALLY AND CUT ONE OPENING. FROM THIS SINGLE OPENING WE CAN CUT THE FOLLOWING LETTERS:

FOLD PAPER IN CENTER VERTICALLY AND CUT TWO OPENINGS. CUT THE FOLLOWING LETTERS:

USE UNCUT OBLONG WINDOW SHAPES FOLDED VERTICALLY FOR THE FOLLOWING LETTERS:

USE UNFOLDED OBLONGS FOR THE FOLLOWING LETTERS:

Fig. 37-7 Cut-paper letters.

- One large unusual background shape helps to unify the design.
- Avoid cluttering the display; items placed at all angles destroy the unity.

Variety

Variety in arrangement prevents monotony. Use interesting combinations of color, form, line, and texture.

Emphasis

Emphasis is the main idea or center of interest. This can be achieved by using larger letters, a brighter color, a larger picture, an unusual shape, texture, or three-dimensional object. Other material should be grouped into subordinate areas.

Line

Line is used to draw the eye to a specific area, suggest direction, action, and movement, and to hold the display together. Use thick or thin lines; solid, dotted, or dashed lines. Diagonal lines are used to show action, zigzag lines suggest excitement; slow-moving curves are restful. Lines may be painted, cut from paper, or formed with string, yarn, ribbon, or tape.

Texture

Texture may be created with a variety of materials:

- Paper and cardboard — textured wallpaper, sandpaper, metallic foil, egg containers, corrugated cardboard.
- Fabrics — netting, flannel, burlap, fur, felt, carpet remnants, assorted felt scraps.
- Miscellaneous — chicken wire, metal screen, sheet cork.

Three-Dimensional Effects

- Pull letters or objects out to the head of the pin.
- Staple a shallow box to the board as a shelf to hold lightweight three-dimensional items.
- Mount a picture on a box lid and fasten it to the board.
- Use shallow boxes as buildings, animals, and people.
- Pleat a strip of paper in an accordion fold with pictures attached.
- Use paper sculpture — strips of paper can be twisted, curled, folded, rolled, fringed, perforated or torn. Puppets, animals, birds, flowers, people, abstract forms, and masks can also be made.
- Use three-dimensional materials in displays — styrofoam, egg cartons, paper plates, paper cups, soda straws, cupcake cups, paper lace, toweling tubes, and other discarded materials.
- Use objects from nature — branches, shells, bark, driftwood, feathers.

Background Materials

- Display paper, tissue paper, burlap, corrugated cardboard, construction paper.
- Egg carton separators, blotters, textured wallpaper, shelf paper.

Display Boards for Two-Dimensional Work

- Standard cork boards or sheet of plywood to which cork tiles have been glued.
- Builder's wall board with wood strip nailed to the top with hooks for hanging.
- Thick cardboard that will hold pins.
- A pasteboard box opened for standing on a table or the floor, depending on size.
- A folding screen made from an old crate or packing box.

- Wide strips of binding tape attached along a blank wall; pin pictures to tape.
- Wire stretched across an empty space with pictures attached to it.

Display Areas for Three-dimensional Work

- Tops of cupboard or built-in shelves.
- Build shelves with boards supported by cigar boxes or brick, used permanently or temporarily.
- Attach a shelf of wood or beaverboard underneath a bulletin board.
- Cigar boxes nailed together make display shelves.
- Dioramas are especially useful where exhibit space is limited.
- A card table can be used for temporary exhibits, then folded up when not in use.
- If obtainable, a small showcase is valuable for displaying museum-type objects.
- Cardboard boxes fastened to bulletin boards make a display place for light-weight objects.
- Use driftwood as an interesting display for weaving and jewelry.
- Puppet display rods can be made with a board and some dowel sticks.
- Mobiles are attractive display devices. Coat hangers can also be used.
- Cover cardboard or cigar boxes and use them as bases for displaying art objects.
- Pegboard with brackets.

BIBLIOGRAPHY — ART EDUCATION FOR YOUNG CHILDREN

Books

Betts, Victoria, *Exploring Papier-Maché.* Worcester, Massachusetts: Davis Publications, Incorporated, (revised edition), 1970.

Bland, Jane Cooper, *Art of the Young Child.* New York: Doubleday and Company, 1960.

Cole, Natalie, *Children's Art from Deep Down Inside.* New York: John Day Company, 1966.

Grater, Michael, *Paper People.* New York: Talpinger Publishing Company, 1970.

Greenberg, Pearl, *Art and Ideas for Young People.* New York: Van Nostrand-Reinhold Company, 1970.

Hoover, F. Louis, *Art Activities for the Very Young.* Worcester, Massachusetts: Davis Publications, 1963.

Horn, George F., and Smith, Grace S., *Experiencing Art in the Elementary School.* Worcester, Massachusetts: Davis Publications, Incorporated, 1970.

Leyh, Elizabeth, *Children Make Sculpture.* New York: Van Nostrand-Reinhold Company, 1972.

Lidstone, John, *Building with Cardboard.* New York: Van Nostrand-Reinhold Company, 1968.

Lindstrom, Miriam, *Children's Art.* Berkeley, California: University of California Press, 1967.

McIlvain, Dorothy, *Art for Primary Grades.* New York: G. P. Putnam's Sons, 1961.

Meilach, Dona, and Hoor, Elvie Ten, *Collage and Found Art.* New York: Van Nostrand-Reinhold, 1964.

Pickering, John M., *Visual Education in the Primary School.* New York: Watson-Guptill Publications, 1971.

Sunset Editors, *Things to Make for Children.* Menlo Park, California: Lane Publishing Company (revised 2nd edition), 1973.

Magazines

Arts and Activities, 8150 North Central Park Avenue, Skokie, Illinois 60076.

School Arts. The Davis Press, Inc., Printers Building, Worcester, Mass.

Guides

Art Lessons Guide for the Primary Unit. Departments of Art Education and Educational Broadcasting.

Art Education Guide, Grades 3–6. Department of Art Education.

Unit 38 POETRY RESOURCE UNIT

ANIMALS

The Animal Store

If I had a hundred dollars to spend,
   Or maybe a little more,
I'd hurry as fast as my legs would go
   Straight to the animal store.
I wouldn't say, "How much for this or that?"
   "What kind of a dog is he?"
I'd buy as many as rolled an eye,
   Or wagged a tail at me!
I'd take the hound with the drooping ears,
That sits by himself alone,
Cockers and cairns and wobbly pups
   For to be my very own!
I might buy a parrot all red and green,
   And the monkey I saw before.
If I had a hundred dollars to spend,
   Or maybe a little more.

My Rabbits

My two white rabbits chase each other
With humping, bumping backs.
They go hopping, hopping
And their long ears
Go flopping, flopping
And they make faces
With their noses up and down.
Today I went inside their fence
To play rabbit with them
And in one corner under a loose bush
I saw something shivering in the leaves.
And I pushed
And I looked
And I found
There in a hole in the ground,
Three baby rabbits hidden away
And they made faces
With their noses up and down.

If You Find a Little Feather

If you find a little feather,
A little white feather,
A soft and tickly feather
   It's for you.
A feather is a letter
From a bird
And it says,
"Think of me,"
"Do not forget me."
"Remember me always."
"Remember me at least until
   the little feather is lost."
So—if you find a little feather,
A little white feather,
A soft and tickly feather,
   It's for you.
Pick it up, and put it in your
   Pocket.

Duck Song

(Tune: "Bell Bottom Trousers")

Six little ducks went out
   for a swim,
Tall ones, short ones, fat
   and thin—
Four little ducks that I
   once knew,
Went out walking two by two —
Down to the river, they did go,
Wiggle, wobble, wiggle, wobble,
   to and fro—

Chorus:

But the one little duck with
   the feathers on his back,
He led the others with his
   "Quack, quack, quack."

There Once Was a Puffin

Oh, there once was a puffin
Just the shape of a muffin,
And he lived on an island
In the
    Bright
        Blue
            Sea!

He ate little fishes,
That were most delicious,
And he had them for supper
And he
    Had
        Them
            For tea.

But this poor little puffin,
He couldn't play nothin,
For he hadn't anybody
To
    Play
        With
            At all.

So he sat on his island,
And he cried for awhile, and
He felt very lonely,
And he felt
    Very small.

Then along came the fishes,
And they said, "If you wishes,
You can have us for playmates,
    Instead
        Of
            For tea."

So they now play together
In all sorts of weather
And the puffin eats pancakes
Like you
    And
        Like me.

Caterpillar

A fuzzy, wuzzy caterpillar
On a summer day
Wriggled and wriggled and wriggled,
On his way.

He lifted up his head
To get a better view.
He wanted some nice green
Leaves to chew.

He wriggled and he wriggled
From his toes to his head
And he crawled about until
He found a comfy bed.

He curled up tight
In a warm little wrap
And settled himself
For a nice long nap.

He slept and he slept
And he slept until
One day he awoke
And broke from his shell.

He stretched and stretched
And he found he had wings!
He turned into a butterfly
Such a pretty-colored thing.

Oh, how happily
He flew away.
And he flew and he flew
In the sun all day.

Polliwog

Little Mister Polliwog
You swim to and fro,
When you turn into a frog
You'll hop where'er you go.

Mice

I think mice
Are rather nice.
Their tails are long,
Their faces small.

Fig. 38-1 To accompany a poem about animals, a good art activity is to make an animal beanbag of found items, such as pieces of burlap, felt, and yarn.

They haven't any
Chins at all.
Their teeth are white,
They run about
The house at night.
They nibble things
They shouldn't touch.
And no one seems
To like them much.
But I think mice
Are nice.

The Snail

The snail is very odd and slow,
He has his mind up to go
The longest way to anywhere,
And then will not let you help him there.

The Woodpecker

The woodpecker pecked out a little round
    hole
And made him a house in a telephone
    pole.
The day when I watched, he poked out his
    head
And he had on a hood and a collar of
    red.

Ducks

A pillow's good for somersaults
Or a sofa, or a bed.
But when a duck stands upside down
He likes a puddle for his head.

The Goldfish

My darling little goldfish
Hasn't any toes;
He swims around without a sound
And bumps his hungry nose.

He can't get out to play with me.
Nor I get in to him.
Although I say, "Come out and play."
And he, "Come in and swim."

Mrs. Peck-Pigeon

Mrs. Peck-Pigeon
Is picking for bread,
Bob-bob-bob
Goes her little round head.

Tame as a pussycat
In the street,
Step-step-step
Go her little red feet.

And her little round head,
Mrs. Peck-Pigeon
Goes picking for bread.

If I Were a Fish

I like to play in water
And if I were a fish,
I'd have water all around me
In a big glass dish.

My tail would make it splatter
'Til it splashed the sky,
And the mother fish would only say,
"No, don't — get — dry!"

Bird

Once I saw a little bird
Come hop, hop, hop.
So I cried, "Little bird,
Will you stop, stop stop?"

And as I was going to the window
To say, "How do you do?"
He shook his little tail,
And far away he flew.

Tiny Tim

I had a little turtle.
His name was Tiny Tim;
I put him in the bathtub
    To see if he could swim.

He drank up all the water;
He ate up all the soap;
And woke up in the morning
    With bubbles in his throat.

Bugs

I like bugs!
Black bugs
Green bugs
Bad bugs
Mean bugs
Any kind of bugs!

A bug in a rug
A bug in the grass
A bug on the sidewalk
A bug in a glass
I like bugs!

Round bugs
Shiny bugs
Fat bugs
Buggy bugs
Lady bugs
I like bugs!

— Margaret Wise Brown

Legs

Two legs for birds
And you and me
Four legs for dogs
And for squirrels in a tree.
Six legs for beetles —
Away they go
Eight legs for spiders
What do you know!

— Aileen Fisher

The Grasshoppers

High
Up
Over the top
Of feathery grasses the
Grasshoppers hop.
They won't eat their suppers
They will not obey
Their grasshopper mothers
And fathers, who say:
"Listen, my children
This must be stopped —
Now is the time your last
Hop should be hopped;
So come eat your suppers
And go to your beds — "
But the little green grasshoppers
Shake their green heads.
"No, no — "
The naughty ones say
"All we have time to do
Now is to play.

If we want supper we'll
Nip at a fly
Or nibble a blueberry
As we go by;
If we feel sleepy we'll
Close our eyes tight
And snooze away in a Harebell
All night
But not now.
Now we must hop.
And nobody,
NOBODY,
Can make us stop."

— Dorothy Addis

Jump or Jiggle

Frogs jump
Caterpillars hump

Worms wiggle
Bugs jiggle

Rabbits hop
Horses clop

Snakes slide
Sea gulls glide

Mice creep
Deer leap

Puppies bounce
Kittens pounce

Lions stalk —
But
I walk!

Buttercup Cow

Buttercup cow has milk for me
I drink in my silver cup at tea.
Buttercup cow is speckled and white,
She lives in the meadow from morning
   Till night.

Buttercup cow hasn't got any bed,
But the moon and the stars look in her shed.
Buttercup cow, I'm glad to be me,
Drinking your pretty white milk for my
   Tea.

Bigger

The cow is big.
Her eyes are round.
She makes a very scary sound.

I'm rather glad the fence is tall —
I don't feel quite so weak and small.

And yet I'm not afraid. You see,
I'm six years old — and she's just three.

— Dorothy Brown Thompson

The Dragon Fly

A dragon fly upon my knee
Is sitting looking up at me.

He has a scarlet tail and six
Little legs like jointed sticks.

With two of them he rubs his head.
His eyes are brown, his mouth is red.

His wings are colored like the rain;
He lifts them, and flies off again.

My Pony

I have a little pony,
He is very nice and plump.
And he always nuzzles me,
For a sugar lump.

The smell of clover makes him stop
Much quicker than a Whoa:
That's why we named him Clover Top
He likes to eat it so.

Slow Pokes

Turtles are slow,
As we all know,
   But
To them

It is no worry,
    For
Wherever they roam,
They are always at home,
    So
  They do not
    Have
  To hurry.

        — Laura Arlon

Fuzzy Wuzzy

Fuzzy, wuzzy,
Creepy, crawly,
Caterpillar funny —

You will be a
Butterfly
When the days are sunny.

SEEDS AND PLANTS

Mister Carrot

Nice Mister Carrot
Makes curly hair,
His head grows underneath the ground —

And early in the morning
I find him in his bed
And give his feet a great big pull
And out comes his head!

The Apple

Within its polished universe,
The apple holds a star,
A secret constellation
To scatter near and far.

Let a knife discover
Where the five points hide.
Split the shining ruby
And find the star inside.

This Man Had Six Eyes

I met a man that had six eyes
And still he could not see.
He lay in bed and hid his head
And would not look at me.

I pulled him up and took him home
(I don't think I did wrong).
And I let him stay, and day by day
I saw his eyes grow long!

I saw them grow out of his head.
I saw them turn to me.
I saw them grow a foot or so.
And *still* he could not see.

"I think he could see the sun," I said,
So I put him on the sill,
And I gave him a drink. But, what do you
    think?
His eyes kept growing still.

They grew as long as I was tall.
They grew like a sleepy tree.
They grew to the floor and out the door,
And still they could not see.

Now what do you think has eyes that long?
You may tell me now — if you know.
Or, look in the pot: there, like as not,
You will find Mr. Pot 8 oh!

        — John Ciardi

Seed

In the heart of a seed,
Buried deep so deep,
A dear little plant lay fast asleep.
"Wake," said the sunshine
"And creep to light."

"Wake," said the voice of raindrops bright.
The little plant heard
And rose to see
What the wonderful world
Outside might be.

Spring

I like March, the soft wind blows,
The tree buds swell,
The white crocus grows.
I like March.

Dandelions

Oh dandelions as yellow as gold,
What do you do all day?
I wait and wait in the tall green grass
Til the children come out to play.

Oh dandelion as yellow as gold,
What do you do all night?
I wait and wait in the tall green grass
Till my yellow hair turns white.

And what do the little children do
When they come out to play?
They pick me up in their hands
And blow my white hair away.

BIRTHDAYS

Five Years Old

Please, everybody look at me.
Today I'm five years old, you see.
After this, I won't be four,
Not ever, ever, anymore;
I won't be three, or two, or one,
For that was when I'd first begun.
Now I'll be five awhile, and then
I'll soon be something else again!

The Birthday Child

Everything's been different
All the day long.
Lovely things have happened,
Nothing has gone wrong.

Nobody has scolded me,
Everyone has smiled.
Isn't it delicious
To be a birthday child.

When I Was One

When I was one,
I had just begun.
When I was two,
I was nearly new.
When I was three,
I was hardly me,
When I was four,
I was not much more.
When I was five,
I was just alive.
But now I am six,
I'm as clever as clever
So I think I'll be six now
For ever and ever.

My Birthday Candles

My mother made a birthday cake,
She says it is for me.
She put six candles on the top
For everyone to see.

When I have a party
This is what I'll do —
I'll make a wish and blow real hard
And hope my wish comes true!

ACTION POEMS

Riding

Rumble, rumble, ro
A-riding we will go.
Down the sunny street we ride
Out into the world so wide.
Rumble, rumble, ro
A-riding we will go.

A Swing Song

Up, down
Up and down,
Which is the way to London Town?
Where? Where?
Up in the air,
Close your eyes, and now you are
    There.

Swinging

Hold on tightly, up we go
Swinging high and swinging low.

See-Saw

See-saw Margery Daw,
Jack shall have a new master.
He shall have but a penny a day,
Because he won't work any faster.

Trains

Over the mountains,
Over the plains,
Over the rivers,
Here come the trains.

Carrying passengers,
Carrying mail,
Bringing their precious loads
In without fail.

Thousands of freight cars,
All rushing on,
Through day and darkness
Through dusk and dawn.

Over the mountains,
Over the plains,
Over the rivers,
Here come the trains.

Planes

Whenever I hear
Up in the sky,
Zzz zzz uuu mmm
I know an airplane
Is flying by,
Zzz uuu mmmmm mmmmm.

Marching

See, here comes the big procession
Marching, marching
Down the street.

Dennis and Charles are
    Marching, marching,
    Marching, marching
Down the street.

ABOUT YOU

Hiding

I'm hiding, I'm hiding
And no one knows where;
For all they can see is my
Toes and my hair.

And I just heard my father
Say to my mother —
"But, darling, he must be
Somewhere or other."

"Have you looked in the inkwell?"
And mother said, "Where?"
"In the inkwell," said father.
But I was not there.

Then "wait" cried my mother —
"I think that I see
Him under the carpet."
But it was not me.

"Inside the mirror's
A pretty good place,"
Said father and looked, but saw
Only his face.

"We've hunted," sighed mother
"As hard as we could.
And I am afraid that we've
Lost him for good."

Then I laughed out loud
And I wiggled my toes
And father said — "Look dear,
I wonder if those

Toes could be Benn's.
There are ten of them. See?"
And they were so surprised to find
Out it was me!

Choosing

It must be dull to be the street
And just see feet, feet and feet.
It must be dull to be the sky,
But of the two I think that I
Would rather be a slice of sky
Than a sidewalk or a street;
Stars when they go skipping by
Must be prettier than feet.

All Excited

I wondered and I wondered
When I could go to school.
They said I wasn't old enough
According to the rule.

I waited and I waited
I was patient as could be.
And now—I'm all excited
It's time for school for me!

Nose

It doesn't breathe;
It doesn't smell;
It doesn't feel so very well.

I am discouraged with my nose;
The only thing it does, is blows.

Daddy

When Daddy shaves and lets me stand and look
I like it better than a picture book.
He pulls such lovely faces all the time
Like funny people in a pantomime.

Lunch Time

I have my own table,
And my own little chair.
And my own little spoon,
And my own bib to wear.
There's always milk
In my own little cup
And I always, always
Drink it all up!

Mouths

I wish I had two little mouths
Like my two hands and feet,
A little mouth to talk with
And one that just could eat.

Because it seems to me mouths have
So many things to do,
All the time they want to talk
They are supposed to chew!

Hippity-Hop

Oh, it's hippity hop to bed,
I'd rather stay up instead.
But when father says *must,*
There's nothing but *just,*
Go hippity hop to bed.

Washing

With soap and water,
I rub my hands;
With the bubbly suds,
I scrub my hands,
Rubbity, scrubbity scrub!

Rub my hands
And scrub my hands,
Til no more dirt is seen!

Rub and scrub;
Rub and scrub;
And then my hands are clean!

Bumps

Hurrah, for Bobby Bumble
Whenever he gets a tumble
Up he jumps
And rubs his bumps
And doesn't even grumble.

Toys

See the toys on my shelf?
I can count them by myself.

One, two, three, four, five.
Here's an airplane, zoom, zoom,
And a drum, boom, boom,
A ball that bounces up and down.
A top that spins round and round.
A telephone, so I can say,
"Come and play with me today."

Raggedy Ann

Raggedy Ann is my best friend
She's so relaxed, just see her bend.
First at the waist, then at the knee
Her arms are swinging, oh so free.
Her head rolls around like a rubber ball,
She hasn't any bones at all.
Raggedy Ann is stuffed with rags,
That's why her body wigs and wags.

The Cupboard

I know a little cupboard
With a teeny tiny key.
And there's a jar of lollipops
For me, me, me.

It has a little shelf, my dears,
As dark as dark can be,
And there's a dish of Banbury Cakes
For me, me, me.

I have a small fat grandmomma
With a very slippery knee,
And she's the keeper of the cupboard
With the key, key, key.

And when I'm very good my dears,
As good as good can be,
There's Banbury Cakes, and lollipops
For me, me, me.

If I Were

If I were an owl,
At night, I'd prowl.
If I were a bear,
At night I'd growl.
If I were a sheep,
At night I'd bleat.

But since I'm a child,
At night I sleep.

PERSONAL HYGIENE

New Shoes

I have new shoes in the fall time.
And new shoes in the spring,
Whenever I wear my new shoes
I always have to sing.

Shoe Lacing

Across and across the shoe we go,
Across and across, begin at the toe.
Criss and cross us over and then,
Through the hole, and across again!

Loose Tooth

I had a little tooth that wiggled
It wiggled quite a lot;
I never could be sure if it
Was coming out or not.

I pushed it with my tongue
To see if it would drop;
But there it stayed and wiggled
Until I thought I'd pop;

My auntie tied it with a string
And slammed the kitchen door!
And now I haven't got a tooth
That wiggles anymore.

But Then

A tooth fell out
And left a space
So big my tongue
Can touch my face.

And every time
I smile, I show
A space where something
Used to grow.

I miss my tooth,
As you can guess.
But then, I have to
Brush one less!

A Good Thing

When I've finished with my tub
I always play about
With my little sponge and then
I pull the stopper out.

And every day I'm very glad
That I am big and tall;
To slip down through the stopper hole
Would not be funny at all!

Bed Time

This little boy is going to bed,
Down on the pillow he lays his head.
Wraps himself in the covers so tight,
This is the way he sleeps all night.

The Train

My train runs on a track
Chug-a-chug, chug-a-chug
Slow at first, then faster,
Chug-a-chug, chug-a-chug,
Chug-a-chug-chug!

Round and round the wheels go
Just listen to the whistle blow,
Toot-toot-toot!
Chug-a-chug, chug-a-chug,
Toot-toot-toot!!

Naughty Soap Song

Just when I'm ready to start
    On my ears,
That is the time that my
    Soap disappears,
It jumps from my fingers, and
    Slithers and slides,
Down to the end of the tub
    Where it hides,

And acts in a most disobedient
    Way,
And that's why my soap's
    Growing thinner each day.

Winking

It would be fun to wink, I think.
But when I try to shut one eye
The other closes too!
It won't stay open
No matter what I do.

When Daddy winks, it's easy—
Seems like there's nothing to it.
So I'll keep trying very hard
And one day I shall do it.

The Ball

Bounce the ball and catch the ball
One, and two!
Bounce the ball and catch the ball,
And I throw it back to you.

Bounce the ball and catch the ball,
One, two, three!
Bounce the ball and catch the ball,
And toss it back to me.

Blocks

Blocks will build a tower tall,
Blocks will make a long, long wall,
Blocks will build a house or plane,
A truck, a tunnel, or a train.
Get the blocks, so we can see
What they'll build for you and me.

Soap Bubbles

Fill the pipe!
Gently blow;
Now you'll see
The bubbles grow!
Strong at first,
Then they burst,
Then they go to
Nothing, oh!

ACKNOWLEDGMENTS

The authors gratefully acknowledge the contributions of the many people who helped make this book possible.

Karyl Gatteno, Christine Fraski, and Steve Knowlton - for the many excellent photos

Barb and Tom Yockey - for several special photos and drawings

Sister Rosarie, Marian College, Fond du Lac, Wisconsin

Helen Altman, Kindercare

Kindercare, Fond du Lac, Wisconsin

Bloomingdale Family Program: Operation Head Start

The Riverside Church Nursery School

The Dark Room, Milwaukee, Wisconsin

Iris M. Silverblatt - for permission to reprint materials used in unit 9

Houghton Mifflin Company - for permission to reprint materials used in units 9, 10, and 15

Charles E. Merrill Publishing Company - for permission to reprint materials used in unit 4

Margaret Belobradich, Director, Justin Day Care Center, Hazel Park, Michigan

John A. Murphy, Superintendent, Wake County Public Schools, Raleigh, North Carolina

John Cooper, Justin Day Care Center

The teachers at the Mary E. Phillips School, Raleigh, North Carolina

The parents and children at the Justin Day Care Center and the Mary E. Phillips School

Susan Skidmore, Joyce McDonald, and Orred Julien - for typing and editing assistance

Larry Hillman, Professor, College of Education, Wayne State University

Elizabeth Vaden, Sue Clark, Phillip Mayesky, and Paulette Hicks - for technical assistance

Julia Caldwell, Physical Education Director, Wake County Public Schools

Nancy E. Murphy, North Adams College, Massachusetts

David Keenan, Lake Shore Public Schools, St. Clair Shores, Michigan

Mark Smith, Assistant Dean, College of Education, Wayne State University

David Schwandt, College of Education, Wayne State

Claire Irwin, Professor, College of Education, Wayne State University

Finley Hooper, Professor, History Department, Wayne State University

John Vorheis, Principal, Oxford Junior High School, Oxford, Michigan

Anna B. Peele, Eastern Area Director, Wake County Public Schools

Rebecca Murray, Dean, College of Education, Meredith College, North Carolina

Prezell Robinson, President, St. Augustine College, Raleigh, North Carolina

Lawrence Thompson, Dean, College of Education, St. Augustine College, Raleigh, North Carolina

George Kahdy, Assistant State Superintendent of Instruction, State of North Carolina

Staff at Delmar Publishers:
Source Editor - Judith Barrow Thorpe
Sponsoring Editor - Barbara S. Mohan
Reviewer - Elizabeth Eames

The materials presented in *Creative Activities for Young Children* have been classroom tested with student teachers and the children themselves at:

- University of Wisconsin at Milwaukee under the direction of Donald Neuman
- Milwaukee Public Schools under the direction of Snowrene Saxton, Joan Nason, Martin Gutnik
- Junior Kindergarten, Whitefish Bay, Wisconsin, under the direction of Mary Mayesky
- Kindergarten, Milwaukee, Wisconsin
- Detroit Public Schools - Kindergarten and Preschool
- Hazel Park Adult Education: Child Development Class
- Justin Day Care Center, Hazel Park, Michigan
- Wake County Public Schools, Raleigh, North Carolina

INDEX

Musical instruments, rhythm band, 376-377
My birthday candles, poem, 398
My pony, poem, 396
My pumpkin, poem, 365
My rabbits, poem, 392
My tambourine, song, 380
My zippersuit, 262
Mystery box or bag, 350

N

Naming drawing, 34, 44
Naming objects, work with clay, 51, 52
Nature study trips, 172
Naughty soap song, poem, 402
New shoes, poem, 401
No-cook peanut butter fudge, 371
No drop of rain, poem, 315
Noisemakers, Halloween, 231
Nonverbal communication, 348
Nose, poem, 400
Not alike, 347
Nut cups, 243

O

Oatmeal drop cookies, 374
Object sculpture, 113
Objectives, arts and crafts program, 92-94
Observations, objects for, 164
Old McDonald, 253
Old witch and the cat, 235
On my way to school, 323
One, two, three, four, five, song, 377
One little leaf, finger play, 219
One pin bowling, 323
Opaque projectors, 191
Orange crush, 327
Orange nut bread, 250
Orange pops, 371
Orangeade, 369
Organized play, 126
Our house, poem, 248
Overhead projectors, 191

P

Package, A, Poem, 279
Painted pumpkins, 230
Painting, materials, 94
    techniques, 97, 98
    three-year-olds, 109, 114
    watercolor, 119
Painting with weeds, 215
Pancake people/animals, 328
Pancakes, 374
Pancakes, poem, 366
Pantomime activities, 343
Paper bag bunnies, 296
Paper bag puppets, 246
Paper bag turkeys, 244
Paper butterflies, 306-307
Paper lace, 284
Paper plate bunnies, 294
Paper plate clown face, 208
Paper plate puppet, 116
Paper pumpkin chains, 234
Paper snowmen, 257
Paper stencils, 120
Papier maché, 278-279
Papier maché harvest, 214
Papier maché materials, 96
    techniques, 99
Parade floats, 331
Partners, 355
Pasting, materials, 95
    techniques, 98-99
Patterns, Christmas, 276
Peach crisp, 328
Peanut butter, 282
Peanut butter fudge, 241, 371
Peanut butter song, 281
Peek-a-boo, art, 304
Peekers, 303
People, drawing, 245
Pepper the pumpkin, 236
Phonographs, media activities, 192
Photo albums, 64
Photographs, fall walk, 216
Physical-mental growth, 69-78
    activities, 78-87
    contribution of play to, 127
Picture recipes, 219-220
Pictures, role playing, 145
Pigs in a blanket, 369
Pilgrim mobile, 246, 247
Pilgrims and Indians, 244
Pine cone centerpieces, 271
Pine tree - Christmas song, 281

Pinwheels, 313
Pipe cleaner dancers, 310
Pipe cleaners, 113
Pizzas, 327
Planes, poem, 399
Planning activities, 195-198
Plaster of Paris molds, 123
Play, activities to encourage creativity, 133-139
    dramatics, 137
    group, 137
    play kits, 138, 144
    using large muscles, 133
    using small muscles, 135
Play, theories of, 125-131
    at different ages, 128-129
    characteristics, 125-126
    equipment, selection and care, 129-130
    importance, 126-128
Play clay creations, 278
Play dough, 99
    recipe, 100
    three-year-olds, 111
Play kits, 138, 144
Poems and songs
    autumn, 216-219
    cooking experiences, 365-366
    December, 279-281
    Easter, 297-298
    Halloween, 237-240
    spring and summer, 315-321
    Thanksgiving, 248-249
    Valentine's Day, 288-289
    winter, 259-263
Poetry, creative movement, 143
    resource unit, 392-403
    sources, 338-339
Polish paper cutting, 292
Polliwog, poem, 393
Pollution, environmental studies, 172, 173
Pom-poms, 311
Pop goes the weasel, 253
Popcorn, topless, 181
Popcorn balls, 240
Popcorn house, The, poem, 239
Popcorn vendor, 236
Posters, ecology, 330
Posture silhouette, 337
Potato candy, 372
Present for me, poem, 281
Presentation of activities, 198-201
Printed materials, media activities, 192
Printing, four-and five-year-olds, 120-121
    three-year-olds, 110, 115
Projectors, media activities, 191
Prose, creative movement, 143
Pudding, 181
Pudding cookies, 249
Pumpkin, poem, 239
Pumpkin accordion people, 231
Pumpkin seeds, roasting, 240
Pumpkins, Halloween art, 230-235
Pumpkins, poem, 365
Puppets, 246
    cut-up, 212
    dramatic experience, 146
    finger, 113
    food, 116
    hand, 113
    paper bag, 246
    styrofoam, 246
    techniques, 99
    three-year-olds, 112-113, 116
Pussy willow, poem, 318

Q

Quality of learning, 16-18
Questioning, creative, 9
Questioning strategies, 10

R

Radio, media activities, 190
Raggedy Ann, poem, 401
Rain song, poem, 319
Rainbow in your room, 308
Raindrop game, 224
Raindrops are falling, 321
Rains, poems, 315, 317
Raisin cornflake cookies, 374
Raking leaves, finger play, 217
Rattles, Halloween, 231
Reading readiness, 338-352
    activities, 338-340, 342-344
    art projects, 382

hand-eye coordination, 72
hearing and remembering, exercises, 344-352
listening exercises, 340-342, 344
Recipes, see Cooking experiences
Records, cooking experiences, 362
    for exercising, 254-255
    media activities, 190, 192
Rectangle and square, art, 31
Recycled paint, 310
Reinforcement, 12
Relationships, art program, 57-66
    activities, 65-66
    adult-to-child, 60-63
    child-to-child, 59
    group, 63
    self-acceptance, 57-59
Remembering exercises, 344-352
Reverse thinking, 75
Reverse trick or treat, 242
Rhyming game, 348
Rhythm, creative movement, 141-144
Rhythm band instruments, 376-377
Riding, poem, 398
Rigid-inhibited children, 206
Ring around the rosy, 323
Ring around the rosy - leader, 357
Rock candy, 182
Role playing, 145
Room and yard organization, 384-386
Rope skills, 354
Rope tag, 223
Rope tricks, 277

S

Safety, environmental studies, 172
    finger play, 216
Safety and health, 335-337
Saint Patrick's Day hat, 304-305
Salt ceramics, 121-122
Salt dough, recipe, 121
Sam Smith's suitcase, 343
Sand, mud and clay, building with, 135
Santa apples, 282
Santa on a stick, 271
Santa's visit, poem, 279
Sawdust, 386
Sawdust sculpture, 310
Schema, 33-34
    work with clay, 50
School grounds, environmental activities, 170-171
Schools, environmental activities, 168-170
Science, art projects, 381
Science, meaning, 148
Science activities, food in, 360
Sciencing, creative activities, 156-164
    developing the senses, 148-152
    materials, finding, 163
Scrambled eggs, 373
Scrap art, 123
    materials, 95
    techniques, 99
Scribble stage, 28-30, 35
    observation points for, 38-39
Sculpture, 113
Secret, The, poem, 317
See-ability, 339
See my pony, song, 378
See-saw, poem, 399
Seed, poem, 397
Seeds, collecting and using, 182
Seeds and plants, poems, 397-398
Seeing activities, 81
Self-acceptance, 57-59, 63
Self-awareness activity, 252
Senses, activities for, 81
    use, 9
Sensing and feeling, 22-23
Sensitivity, aesthetic, 18-19
Sensorimotor learning, 73
    smelling and tasting, 76
Set a healthy table, 337
Shapes, 345
Shapes, describing, 164
Shapes and sizes, comparing, 352
Sharing, 60
    activity, 65
Shoe lacing, poem, 401
Shuffling, poem, 217
Sight, concepts learned through, 74-76
Signs of winter, poem, 262
Silent snowfall, 263
Similarities, describing, 153